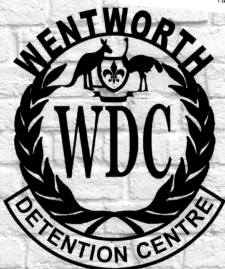

WENTWORTH
WDC
DETENTION CENTRE

BEHIND THE BARS

THE

UNOFFICIAL

PRISONER CELL BLOCK H COMPANION

Scott Anderson, Barry Campbell and Rob Cope

Tomahawk *Press*

First published in 2013 by
Tomahawk Press
PO Box 1236
Sheffield S11 7XU
England

www.tomahawkpress.com

ISBN 13: 978-0-9566834-4-1
Proofread by Kenneth Bishton
Edited by Bruce Sachs
Designed by Steve Kirkham – Tree Frog Communication 01245 445377
Printed in England

Photos for this book were kindly donated from the personal collections of:
John Allen, Janet Andrewartha, Elspeth Ballantyne, Paul Barnett, Jennifer Carmen, Lois Collinder, Mark Collins, Kenton Foxall, Caroline Garbett, Colin Gerrard, Jacqui Gordon, Peter Hind, Barry Humphries AO & CBE, Maggie Kirkpatrick, Maxine Klibingaitis, Glenda Linscott, Helen Martineau, Roslyn McCartney, Peter McTighe, Maggie Millar, Peter O'Connor, Viv Rushbrook, Paul Schnaars, Louise Siversen, Fiona Spence, Rob Summers, Graeme Sutcliffe, Leonie Treadwell, Rachael Wallis, Joy Westmore and the authors.

Additional photos were supplied by TV Week @ ACP Camera Press London, Newspix Ltd (Julie Kiriacoudis), Doug Lambert (ATV Network).

Maggie Kirkpatrick and Val Lehman appear on our front cover with full permission of both actors. All of the actors appearing in photographs and quoted in this book have given permission for the use of their images and quotations.

We apologise in advance for any unintentional omission with regard to any photograph copyright or credit and will be pleased to insert the appropriate acknowledgement to companies or individuals in any subsequent edition of this publication.

FremantleMedia does not authorise this book. It is a fan publication only.
All FremantleMedia rights are expressly reserved.
Prisoner™ produced by FremantleMedia Australia Pty Limited, a FremantleMedia Company. © Copyright FremantleMedia Australia Pty Ltd (Australia and New Zealand), FremantleMedia Ltd (Rest of the World).

Behind the Bars – The Unoffical Prisoner Cell Block H Companion is produced in association with 'On The Inside', The Prisoner Cell Block H Fan Club – www.prisonercellblockh.com

All numbers shown in square brackets after text throughout the book indicate the number of the episode being referred to.

The authors greatly appreciate the assistance of Lily Morrice on this special project.

The authors would like to thank the following people without whom this book would simply not have been possible:
Glen Allen, John Allen, Andy Anderson, Craig Anderson, Marylyn Anderson, Janet Andrewartha, Colin Baker, Elspeth Ballantyne, Joseph Banno, Paul Barnett, Zoe Bertram, Betty Bobbitt, Sally Bourne, Ian Bradley, Nigel Bradshaw, Jen Brown, Mark Caffrey, Declan Cardone, Jennifer Carmen, Allan Caswell, Anne Charleston, Kirsty Child, Jane Clifton, Lois Collinder, Mark Collins, Howard Cope, Lindy Davies, Maggie Dence, Coral Drouyn, Paula Duncan, Tommy Dysart, Roy Edmunds, Dame Edna Everage, FremantleMedia London & Sydney, Caroline Garbett, Ros Gentle, Colin Gerrard, Caroline Gillmer, Paul Glazebrook, Tottie Goldsmith, Jacqui Gordon, Sandy Gore, Dan Greensmith, Susan Guerin, Brett Hamilton, Lynne Hamilton, Virginia Hey, Peter Hind, Anna Hruby, Rosanne Hull-Brown, Barry Humphries AO & CBE, Glen Johnson, Peter Keogh, Maggie Kirkpatrick, Maxine Klibingaitis, Buffy-Jane Kyle, Debra Lawrance, Louise Le Nay, Glenda Linscott, Brenda Longman, Alan David Lee, Val Lehman, Genevieve Lemon, Anne Lucas, Brian MacDonald, Gerard Maguire, Helen Martineau, Vicki Mathios, Stephen McAllister, Roslyn McCartney, Ray Meagher, Maria Mercedes, Vicky Mathios, Babs McMillan, Janet Miller, Lily Morrice, Amanda Muggleton, Ken Mulholland, Peter O'Connor, Nikki Paull, Agnieszka Perepeczko, Anne Phelan OAM, Sean Nash, Lois Ramsay, Glenn Rhueland, Meron Roberts, Shirlie Roden, Ilona Rodgers, Viv Rushbrook, Paul Schnaars, Dave Shellard, Louise Siversen, Carole Skinner, Caroline Smillie, James Smillie, Jennifer Stanton, Mark Stubbs, Rob Summers, Graeme Sutcliffe, Sonja Tallis, Peta Toppano, Leonie Treadwell, Reg Watson OAM, Mary Ward, David Waters, Joy Westmore, Robert Williams, Mark Wilson, Michael Winchester, Greig Woods, Gav Worlledge

Special thanks from the authors to Bruce Sachs at Tomahawk Press and Steve Kirkham at Tree Frog Communication for helping to expertly transform our idyllic vision into the wonderful publication that you now hold in your hands.

FOREWORD

Hello possums! How wonderful that at last there is a book about my favourite television show of all time. It will not surprise you to learn that I have never been behind bars myself, though I have bailed out my dysfunctional daughter Valmai many times on charges of shoplifting, vagrancy and, I am ashamed to say, lewd behaviour. I tell you this because my therapist (who I see for my children) told me I was an 'enabler' and I must not protect my children from the consequences of their actions.

When I started doing shows with Mr Barry Humphries in the late 1950s, having won the Lovely Mother Contest, there were a lot of other young actresses around, mostly glamour pusses and their careers were short- lived whereas I seemed to go from strength to strength. I suppose I am lucky because I was not conventionally beautiful; just amazingly attractive. Many of the prettiest members of my contemporary theatrical circle never saw the light of day again but a few of them – the ones with talent – ended up in *Prisoner* and one of the great joys of watching that show is to realise how good I still look compared with them, poor darlings. You won't see such good acting in any other television show and you certainly won't see such an economical use of scenery. If only those poor prisoners knew there were only a few sheets of cardboard between them and freedom they would rattle their bars a bit more vigorously. Like me and *Neighbours*, *Prisoner* has an international fan base. Everyone adores the show – even Eskimos, and the only regret in my entire career is that I was never asked to be in it. This book is a precious souvenir of an Australian masterpiece.

Dame Edna X

Dame Edna Everage

CAPTIVE AUDIENCE

From the moment that a forced hand was held under the scalding steam press in the very first episode, *Prisoner* has held a grip on millions of fans around the world. Its contemporaries have by and large passed into the television wilderness, fondly remembered but largely ignored. That can never be true of *Prisoner*. Even now, some twenty seven years after the conclusion was aired on Channel 10, fan events are still taking place in its native Australia and the UK. But why? What is it that has fired our imaginations about this group of incarcerated women in a suburb of Melbourne?

Perhaps the answer lies in the sheer energy of the show. Never before or since has a soap or serial (define it as you wish) had so many physically aggressive confrontations between females of the species. The old adage of a 'hell hath no fury like a woman scorned' is multiplied a hundredfold, and you certainly wouldn't want to cross the vast majority of them if you encountered such characters in everyday life. The sheer voyeuristic joy of peeping into this largely unexplored world, the original bad girls, seems to be at the very heart of its appeal. The show is quite simply outrageous. The characters are outrageous. The sheer boldness of its plots is outrageous. It defies logic that such situations exist or have ever existed in penal institutions. But there it is, on our televisions screens – a microcosm of our society if ever there was one. We laugh and shed a tear at the plight of elderly recidivist Lizzie Birdsworth. She could be our elderly aunt or our grandmother. We recognise and revel in her mischievous antics. Then there is the anti-authority figurehead, Bea Smith. Proclaimed 'Top Dog', nobody dares to cross her and if they do, it's usually at the cost of some terrible retribution. But she battles for the underdog. That's why we like her. And oh, how we love an underdog! This series is packed to the gunnels with them. The fight for justice and to be heard above the constant efforts of the system to administer society's punishment is a constant theme throughout the 692 episode canon. There is often a fine line between the good and the bad. The keepers can be every bit as nasty or deadly as the cons. 'Vinegar Tits' Vera and her successor 'The Freak' establish that it is not only on one side of the bars do we find the bitter, angry and downright psychotic. Subconsciously, the sets and storylines echo everyday life for all of us. The excellent device of prison bars within the television context offers an insight into a parallel universe, where some of the officers are more socially isolated than the inmates, through lack of friendships and relationships. Feelings of being trapped, closet sexuality and loss of identity in a world that paradoxically takes no prisoners are conveyed through the officers and inmates alike.

Unlike most of the television programmes contemporary to *Prisoner*, there was no holding back when conflict arose. Sometimes a simple scrap but at others far more disturbing ways to settle scores were unveiled: hangings, electrocutions and even branding of the skin with a soldering iron. Yes, it could be gruesome. And this was again part of the appeal for the viewer. Without a doubt, it proved therapy for many. After a day of frustrations at work, college or any other enforced existence, what better way to unwind than to sit down and let these women in Wentworth Detention Centre give voice to all the unsaid expressions that we had held inward during the day. Instant catharsis!

The basic appeal of the show was without a doubt lifted to another level by the performances of many of the actors who were employed over that vast stretch of television airtime. Some have now left the profession; others have become iconic within the industry. Whatever their ultimate fate, they are immortalised in a brilliant fireball of high drama, heightened emotions and blistering battles. The sombre uniforms (grey for officers, blue denim for prisoners) caused the sheer

The famous scene featuring the steam press and Lynn Warner's hand.

FROM REG WATSON O.A.M

Reg Grundy and a man named Mike Firman had the idea for a serial on women in prison. Reg asked me to devise the serial and characters and I spent months doing research on women who were, or had been, in prison. I also decided to combine some policies of women's prisons in Victoria and New South Wales and that became the fictional Wentworth.

Many of the characters, like Franky Doyle, were based on women who had been in prison but some real life stories were too shocking for TV as it was in those days. New South Wales prisons suggested I talk to a woman who had been in prison for fifteen years. Her name was Hazel and her stories of the inside were amazing – and her own story was the most amazing of them all. I based the character of 'Mum' on Hazel.

The success of *Prisoner* is due to writers, producers, directors and actors, and my contribution as Head of Drama for Grundy Television was to ensure that my original concept was adhered to once I handed it over to the writers.

In Australia, Channel 10 demanded changes be made when they saw the first episode because they thought it was too strong for public viewing. But I refused and said 'What you see is what you get!' I had liaised with them on content, including the swearing, and they had approved it but got cold feet when they saw the impact it had on the screen. Fortunately for them they backed off because the serial was an immediate success.

I was thrilled when it was also successful in Britain and also in the United States. We were forced to add 'Cell Block H' when Lord Lew Grade objected to *Prisoner* as a title because ATV had *'The'* Prisoner and he threatened to sue. Unfortunately, pressure groups in America forced the cancellation of the serial because of the lesbian content. How times have changed!

Reg Watson

personality and charisma of the actors to shine like supernovas across our screens. For all the camp connotations aimed at the show over the years, there are some acting performances within the vaults that will continue to seer through our television screens whenever the show is watched in years to come. Never has there been such an amazing collection of strong, forthright, intelligent, resourceful, intuitive, resilient and downright dangerous women on our television screens, before or since.

Prisoner's audience is indeed diverse. It seems to cross all social barriers. The show has become perceived as having a predominantly gay following. This is not true, in that the show was clearly enjoyed by as many heterosexuals. Proof was often displayed by the mixed audiences at the stage shows and other public events related to *Prisoner*. But nobody celebrates it as loudly as the gay community. That it should appeal so equally to gay men and gay women is something of a feat. Gay men have always been attracted to strong, forceful personalities in women on the screen – think Bette Davis and Joan Crawford from Hollywood's golden age, or perhaps

Joan Collins in *Dynasty*, a show that was one of *Prisoner's* contemporaries on the airwaves, but was as far removed as you can get in tone and style. Lesbians might equally have enjoyed seeing their reflection acted out in the storylines. A section of society frequently pushed to the sides, ignored, mocked or the recipients of major prejudice was now represented with great sensitivity and understanding in the scripts of the programme. Indeed if *Prisoner* did anything for the gay movement, it was to de-sexualise, for the most part, its gay characters. Showing that whatever gender we may find ourselves attracted to, the emotions and problems are the same. The fears, paranoia, anger et al are universal; we are all the same. Our sexuality only divides us when romance beckons. In this respect the show was a perfect leveller and equaliser. Similarly, *Prisoner* gained a loyal following from older children despite it being broadcast after the Australian watershed. It has been said that the situation schoolchildren found themselves in during classroom sessions with teachers, and ultimately the Head of the School, and the disciplined school environment helped them to draw direct parallels

with the prison system. Ergo they could identify with Wentworth as an institution.

Whatever the attraction for a wide cross section of our society, *Prisoner* will not be confined to the television graveyard. It is too innovative, too ground breaking and simply too good for its followers to let it slip away. Fans far too youthful to have been around when the episodes first went to air are now proclaiming

its unique qualities. The series has been a hit West End show. The DVDs continue to be best sellers. *Prisoner* has found a longevity that many other drama shows simply have not been able to achieve. This is the story of the men and women who breathed life into this legendary piece of television both on screen and off. It's a celebration of the outrageous.

Welcome to Wentworth. Stand on the white line.

CHAPTER ONE
THE KING OF SOAP

> *A soap opera is a kind of drama that 20 million people love, and a few critics love to hate I suppose.*
> Reg Watson

Reg Watson can truly be called a legend in television. His influence in the field of soap opera spans the globe having laid claim to creating at least half a dozen classics of the genre and many more shows besides.

Hailing from Queensland, Reginald James Watson grew up on a sugar farm. An early interest in acting saw him performing in Brisbane theatres, moving on eventually to directing for the repertory company in the city. He drifted into radio acting and announcing, eventually moving to the UK in 1955. Reg worked briefly as a BBC Radio actor including a stint on the legendary long-running serial *The Archers,* but moved to the fledgling independent channel ATV soon afterwards. The arrival of commercial television was something new and exciting for broadcasters in the United Kingdom, and Reg was sent to America to soak up the culture of advert-funded broadcasting. He learned much from his time looking at the output and production techniques of the Americans. He particularly noticed how popular the daytime soap operas were. Upon his return to the UK, ATV London staff were seconded to the new Midlands operations base in Birmingham. In 1956 Reg was appointed 'Head Of Light Entertainment' for ATV's new centrally-based operations centre. His fellow executives included actress Noele Gordon ('Head of Lifestyle and Women's Programming') and a young Ned Sherrin ('Head of Factual Programming'). Reg undertook a vast amount of work, writing and producing all manner of shows which would include game shows and music programmes among the diverse mix. His blossoming working relationship with Noele Gordon produced an enormously successful chat show *Tea With Noele Gordon* in 1956 which led to the even more popular

Lunch Box the following year, a lunchtime chat and entertainment show, the format of which was to be copied many times over the years by rival channels. Lew Grade was keen to capitalise on Noele Gordon's enormous popularity with the growing television audience and asked Reg to come up with a vehicle for her. Reg, remembering the popularity of daytime soaps in America, suggested a daily soap opera format with Noele as the matriarchal figure. The format was devised by Peter Ling and Hazel Adair, but it was Watson who developed the initial outline and breathed life into the characters. It would go on to become one of ATV's most popular series ever, *Crossroads.* Detailing the comings and goings of a Midlands motel, it captured the imagination and hearts of viewers across the country and Noele's popularity was propelled to even greater heights with her character of motel owner Meg Richardson. Between 1964 and 1988 some 4,510 episodes were produced by ATV for the ITV network, gaining *Crossroads* one of the biggest devoted followings of any British television programme. This impressive episode tally includes twelve 'stand by' episodes which were produced in case real life events or a death caused the current episodes to be unsuitable for airing. These were stand-alone storylines that could be shown without impinging too much on any story lines going to air at the time. Although production paperwork is now by and large lost, it appears that at least eight of these stand-by programmes did make it to air for one reason

Top: Reg Watson strikes a deal at ATV circa 1973. Bottom: Reg in jovial mood.

or another. There were even episodes featuring Meg going to prison for dangerous driving, an early example of Watson getting his leading lady behind bars, although sadly these episodes no longer exist in the archive.

It was while writing and producing *Crossroads* that Reg met another famous Reg – Reg Grundy, the head of Grundy Productions. Watson was headhunted by Grundy, along with *Crossroads* director Alan Coleman, and he returned to Australia in 1974 to work for the flourishing Grundy Organisation. It was perhaps the most creative period of Reg's entire career. Watson again took a format, this time *The Young Doctors* devised by Alan Coleman, and helped develop it into the ratings hit which ran on the 9 Network from 1976 until 1983. He followed this with *The Restless Years*, a teenage angst drama following a group of school leavers as they entered the big world outside of education. It was again a popular hit and managed to run on the 10 Network between 1977 and 1981 for an impressive run of 780 episodes. The series was in many ways a template for later programmes such as *Neighbours* and its multitude of youth-orientated, frothy melodramas.

What Reg Grundy wanted though was a hard-hitting serial that could weigh in with material somewhat heavier than his organisation had thus far been able to provide. Having looked at the popularity of *Within These Walls* in the UK, it was decided Australia should have its own crack at a gritty drama set in a women's prison. They knew one man would be up to the job of devising the series: Reg Watson.

Depictions of women in prison had long been around on the big screen. The seminal *Caged* made in 1950 in now regarded as something of a cult classic in its own right. Set in an Illinois penitentiary it tells the story of a 19-year-old Marie Allen, played by Eleanor Parker, who is imprisoned for being an accomplice to an armed robbery. With wide-eyed fear she encounters the hardened brutality of both the keepers and her fellow felons. With the appearance more of the hospital matron than the uniformed warders of *Prisoner*, the character of Evelyn Harper (Hope Emerson) has become a landmark performance of an embittered corrupt and sadistic screw, a 'Freak' of her time. The whole screenplay comes over as a kind of public information film deterring women from breaking the law lest they find themselves in such an institution. The streetwise language is almost code-ish now from a modern day perspective. Just five years later Ida Lupino gives us another screen heavy in *Women's Prison*. Again, the theme is repeated with Lupino portraying a psychotic jail warder determined to stamp her authority on the women in her charge. (Lupino would further reprise a similar character in a 1974 television movie, *Women In Chains*). Even those most attractive of female detectives *Charlie's Angels* found themselves behind bars in a much-celebrated first season episode, 'Angels in Chains'.

Watson knew though that it was London Weekend Television's *Within This Walls* that he had to emulate. A British-made drama series starring a fellow Aussie and veteran screen star Googie Withers as Faye Boswell, the new Governor of Her Majesty's Prison Stone Park. This series was created by screenwriter David Butler, who would later have a recurring role as a vicar to Stone Park. The series was a big hit in Britain and followed the daily trials of the staff of the prison. The focus was very much on the people in charge, although a plethora of cons and keepers was brought into view featuring a Who's Who of British character actors. These included Liz Smith (*The Royle Family*), Kathy Staff (*Last of the Summer Wine*), Pam St. Clement (*EastEnders'* Pat Butcher), Joan Hickson (*Miss Marple*), another Aussie Pamela Stephenson, Stephanie Cole (*Tenko*) and future *Bird of a Feather*, Linda Robson. With an impressive run of episodes from 1974 until 1978, it had set the bar high in trying to depict incarcerated women on screen and the attendant problems for the staff.

When the Australian vision was launched, Reg Watson told *TV Week* that his series was being played for realism. 'We have relied strongly on the advice of prison officials in the creation of our elaborate sets, the development of characters and the scrutiny of our storylines. Our jail, the Wentworth Detention Centre, is a combination of Silverwater Women's Prison in NSW and Fairlea in Melbourne. We've come up with a prison which is a combination of the rules and regulations of both States. We studied the Royal Commission into prisons and some of the actresses visited the Detention Centres to talk with prisoners and warders.' This project was certainly not being taken lightly at any level by those involved – authenticity was a by-word from the off. The title of the new show underwent several incarnations – '*Women In Jail*', '*Jailbirds*' – before it was settled as simply *Prisoner* (not realising that ITC who owned the Patrick McGoohan fantasy series *The Prisoner* might have some objection.) It was an overnight sensation, with viewers lapping up the weekly drama on Channel 10.

Reg's creative genius did not stop with this ratings success. By 1982 he had devised yet another format based around warring families: *Sons And Daughters*, the premise being that twins born of an illicit affair had been separated and each had grown up into respective different backgrounds: the working class Palmer family and the somewhat wealthier Hamiltons. Just as *Prisoner* was introducing the less-than-attractive warder from hell, The Freak, Reg made sure we had a glamorous super-bitch fit for the image obsessed 1980s in Patricia Hamilton, played by Rowena Wallace. 'Pat the Rat' went on to become an icon of Australia's soap industry and when Wallace announced her intention to leave the show in 1984, it presented the producers with something of a problem. Their lead character was suddenly to be absent. In soap land, this was no problem. Cue the plastic surgeons table in Rio, and Pat the Rat comes back as Alison Carr (played by Belinda Giblin), who for a while nobody realises is really Pat. But it didn't stop there: in 1987 while serving a prison sentence Alison/Pat meets her own twin sister Pamela Hudson played by... Rowena Wallace! After such amazing events, it's perhaps little wonder that *Sons and Daughters* reached a dignified end that same year after some 972 episodes of classic Aussie soap.

Further creations from the prolific mind of Watson included *Starting Out* (1983), a short-lived series about a group of medical students, police drama *Waterloo Station* (1983) and a nod towards the shoulder-padded rich bitch American formula, *Possession* (1985). Watson was to hit the television jackpot again in grand style. His pitch for a series revolving around several generations of people living in the same street became the worldwide smash *Neighbours*. Best known for starting the careers of Kylie Minogue, Jason Donovan, Guy Pearce and Natalie Imbruglia

Noele Gordon as Meg Richardson behind bars in Crossroads (courtesy of ATV Network Ltd).

to name just a few, it is not without a chequered history. Originally commissioned for Channel 7, the programme was produced by Grundy and made its debut in March 1985. Centred around Ramsay Steet in the fictional Erinsborough, the initial focus was on three families – the Ramsays, the Robinsons and the Clarkes. However, while Melbourne audiences lapped it up, the all-important Sydney market gave *Neighbours* a very lukewarm reception and as figures started to nose-dive Channel 7 pulled out of the show and quietly let it drop. Watson and Grundy thought differently, they offered the show to the rival 10 Network, with whom they had successfully launched *Prisoner* and *Sons and Daughters*, who snapped it up. Furious Channel 7 burned the sets so as not to leave anything behind for their rivals, and from Episode 171 re-vamped *Neighbours* hit the airwaves of Channel 10 and never looked back. Within the year, it had started broadcasting on the BBC in the United Kingdom where it developed a seriously strong following particularly when scheduled before the early evening news. The feuding between the Ramsays and the Robinsons was given another dimension when the original Scott Robinson, Darius Perkins, was recast and Jason Donovan took on the role. Just a few episodes later, Kylie Minogue arrived as tomboy mechanic Charlene Mitchell and the world watched as the love affair unfolded on screen. Watson knew that the inter-generational hook of the programme was the key to its success and he was proved right. Teenagers throughout Australia and the United Kingdom came to identify with the plight of Scott, Charlene, Mike Young (Guy Pearce) and subsequently Craig McLachlan as Charlene's brother, Henry while the older family members also struck a chord with viewers: feisty Madge Mitchell (Anne Charleston), devout fuddy-duddy Harold Bishop (Ian Smith), harassed father Jim Robinson (Alan Dale) and lovelorn Des Clarke (Paul Keane), whose relationship with Daphne Lawrence (Elaine Smith) proved a ratings winner. These early characters were the springboard and template for thousands of episodes which are still going strong today, having transferred to 10's digital outlet, Channel 11 in 2011. In the UK, a high profile move from the BBC to the rival Channel 5 occurred in 2008. It remains perhaps Watson's most popular contribution to the international television market. Although often criticised for its frothy, family-orientated approach to subject matter, it is without doubt an iconic piece of popular culture around the world. Certainly, it's much re-arranged theme tune by Tony Hatch is infuriatingly catchy, and is as much a part of the brand as the Ramsay Street location and characters.

Even as *Neighbours* was reaching a crescendo of popularity Watson had already moved on to creating more serials in the same mould. His next project, again

Elspeth Ballantyne with Reg Watson toasting the success of Prisoner.

for the 10 Network, was *Richmond Hill*. A small-town drama whose set pieces would mostly revolve around the local pub and police station and with a wealth of experienced soap talent at the helm: *Prisoner* stars Maggie Kirkpatrick, Amanda Muggleton and Paula Duncan, *Young Doctors'* own Ada Simmonds alias actress Gwen Plumb and comic actor Ross Higgins. It also introduced Emily Symons who would become a favourite on both sides of the world as *Home and Away's* long running Marilyn Chambers and *Emmerdale's* barmaid Louise Appleton. Sadly, wavering ratings and politics at Channel 10 meant that the show was axed after barely a year and 92 episodes.

Naturally, Reg Watson was also part of the creative team behind the ill-fated 1991 prison drama made for the American market, *Dangerous Women*. Generally poor acting and low production values marked it as a blip on an otherwise exemplary roll call. Another soap aimed at the Dutch market *Goede Tijden Slechte Tijden (Good Times Bad Times)* was altogether more successful. It was inspired by Watson's *The Restless Years* and has been running since 1990, picking up a number of awards along the way.

Reg Watson's contribution to television drama cannot be underestimated. Although the form of drama serial he specialises in, the soap opera, is frequently damned by the critics as low brow, this

is at odds with the massive audiences worldwide that follow his shows. *Prisoner* is a glittering jewel in Watson's incredible 50-year-plus career in television. He was rightly awarded the prestigious Order of Australian Merit for his pioneering work in television drama in January 2010.

Wherever you are in the world, when you ask 'What's on?' the answer somewhere, at some time, will be 'Watson'. The enduring legacy he has given to Australian television, and worldwide broadcasting, is without equal. His rise as 'The King of Soap' fears no challenge to the throne.

CHAPTER TWO
BUILDING WENTWORTH

It is quite one thing conceiving an idea and getting it commissioned. However, this in itself leads to months of planning with huge amounts of creative and practical obstacles to overcome. Enter the components needed to make such a dream a reality: producers, writers, directors, script editors, production designers, lighting designers, costume designers – the list is endless. Realising Wentworth for the television viewers was going to take lots of ingenuity, skill and a fair amount of improvisation if the new drama was to come in on budget.

Australia's third commercial station Channel 10 started broadcasting in 1964 and was known as ATV-0. The licence to operate a third station, in the wake of Channel 7 and Channel 9, was given to Austrama Television, a consortium headed by airline magnate Sir Reginald Ansett. New studios were constructed in the outer eastern suburb of Melbourne, now known by its Aboriginal name of Nunawading, and thought to mean 'battlefield' or 'ceremonial ground'. The 10 Studios provided an excellent base for the new Grundy project, and attention centred on Studio B. This was a large space of 33 metres by 20 metres which could comfortably house the settings needed for the prison and additional dramatic areas such as Meg Jackson's unit. A $100,000 state of the art lighting rig needed installation before the start of production, as the producers knew that the prison had to be capable of various moods. The dark, shadowy interior of the corridors contrasted with more brightly lit areas such as the reception and Governor's office. Wentworth Detention Centre needed to look as real as possible on the small screen, or else the drama that was to unfold would not seem totally authentic. A lot was at stake with this new production; not just with Grundy Television but also Channel 10 which was seriously struggling behind its commercial rivals. Advertising revenue was starting to slip against the stronghold of the competition as Channel 10 searched for the 'next big thing'. 10 had played host to the massively successful *Number 96*, a night-time adult serial that readily acknowledged the sexual revolution. It had been a sensation from its 1972

The atmospheric bricked building of the Channel 10 studios was perfect to house the new television prison.

première and introduced the beautiful and beguiling Abigail to unsuspecting Australian viewers over a five year tenure on screen. However 10 was conceding a lot of ground to its rivals which had another Grundy/Watson collaboration at Channel 9 with *The Young Doctors* in addition to Crawford's wartime family epic *The Sullivans*, both fetching in very healthy ratings. Channel 7 boasted a police based drama *Cop Shop* while even the good old ABC had just waved

Top: Val Lehman (Bea Smith) in-between takes, filming the famous gun scene in episode 2.
Above: Peta Toppano stops for a continuity shot during the filming of her character's back-story.

But of course, the all important role of producer was yet to be found. The logistics of making a drama series are enormous, and the producer's role is to oversee all aspects of production including casting, finance, studio facilities – it all comes under the banner of producer to see it through to the end product. It is a thankless task as all problems lead to the producer's door. Thankfully, Grundy found an exceptional talent in Ian Bradley:

I was an Industrial Accountant when I left the UK aged 20. I sold my first script when I was 21. The next decade however was frustrating. When my scripts were produced they rarely resembled what I thought I'd written. So I started working on film crews to find out what was going wrong. Some years later Grundy sold The Young Doctors to the Nine Network. It was cancelled after three months, and then brought back by public demand. Actually they were selling so much advertising space in the slot, they couldn't afford to abandon it. The problem with The Young Doctors was it was costing a fortune to produce and crews were working long hours, sometimes into the small hours of the morning. Max Varnel, one of the directors who I'd worked with as a first director and producer in film, suggested I might be able to organise things a bit better.

I'd never worked on multi-camera television before but it was pretty easy to see the problem. The series was shot in a small studio, shot in sequence rather like the modern American daytime soaps. The main problem was that the same flats [pieces of scenery] were used for different sets. For example, the wards were redressed to be the operating theatre and so on. This meant that taping had to stop each time a scene moved from ward to theatre while the sets were redressed. All I did was give the Script Department a list of sets they should never use in consecutive scenes so that Staging could redress the sets while the crew moved on to another scene. The result was everybody went home on time. However, we still found ourselves re-writing a lot of the scripts on set during rehearsals. Things came to a head when the Head Storyliner tried to bring back a popular character who was the teenage son of one of the regulars. The problem was, he wanted to bring him back as a brain surgeon! The cast refused to shoot the story and as floor manager, I was nominated to explain the problem to Reg Watson. He must have agreed with me because the Head Storyliner was sacked and I was offered his job.

So, I just happened to be working alongside Reg when he wrote the first episode of Prisoner.

goodbye to the pioneering *Bellbird*, the story of country folk which had effectively kick-started the Australian soap industry. 10 was holding on to *The Restless Years*, a forerunner to the later teenage angst melodramas of *Neighbours* and *Home and Away*, but it readily needed a harder hitting drama ratings puller. Watson had run with the in-house feeling that a prison drama gave them the canvas they needed to up the ante.

By that time I had had enough of storylining The Young Doctors. I have never stayed in any job for long. Once I understand how something works I tend to get bored. When I resigned, Reg offered me the opportunity to produce Prisoner and take over the Script Department. In truth I think Reg was glad to hand it over. He found it rather depressing. I however, thought it was the opportunity I had been looking for. Since Prisoner was produced in Melbourne, some 600 miles away from the Grundy head office, we were allowed to operate virtually as an independent production company. This together with the fact that we used the fenced-in Channel 10 studios as the prison, and production facilities on site like the Green Room, Make-up, Wardrobe et

al. which were all located underground at the studios, helped give cast and crew a real sense of camaraderie that I think transferred to the screen. It was tough but we were all in it together, and in time many of the actors took on the characteristics of their characters. Val Lehman was Top Dog in any dispute. Elspeth Ballantyne was the quiet placator. Sheila Florance was always getting into mischief and for years later they were still finding her empty bottles of stout (which she had to take for 'medicinal purposes') hidden behind the flats in the studio. It made it very easy to write for the characters when we were all living so closely together.

Casting director Kerry Spence would prove an effective ally in scouring Melbourne and much

Filming the riot scene when Bill Jackson (left, Don Barker) is stabbed. Inset: Kerry Armstrong and Sheila Florance have fun while learning their lines.

Left: Colette Mann (Doreen Anderson) and Carol Burns (Franky Doyle) pose with the crew during the filming of their escape episodes.
Above: Day 3. Episode 36, scene 29.

wider afield for the women who would tread new ground in Australian television. Casting such a major drama can be both arduous and frustrating. Producers and writers both have a strong sense of how the character should look and sound based on the scripts, and finding the right actor to bring out these qualities is sometimes like searching for the Holy Grail.

Ian Bradley reveals the politics of territorial television making during the late 1970s:

To understand the casting process you have to understand the Australian Television drama industry in 1978. It was in its infancy but there was already tremendous rivalry between Sydney and Melbourne. I can't think of a British equivalent. It was far worse than England and Scotland. Crawford Productions who made The Sullivans, and later The Flying Doctors amongst many other successful series, ran Melbourne. So much so that when I first went to Melbourne to produce Prisoner, Hector Crawford put a block on me telephoning anybody at Crawfords and made it clear that anybody who worked on Prisoner would never work at Crawfords again. Ironic really because I later ran Crawfords and took over from Hector as Chief Executive Officer.

In Sydney, Grundy was one of several smaller production companies competing for local drama, and Prisoner was their first foray into Melbourne. So nobody really knew the Melbourne acting scene that well. I had worked

in theatre and television exclusively in Sydney, apart from a pantomime tour around Victoria which never made it to Melbourne. So, distanced from the Melbourne actresses who had worked in Sydney theatre, I was as ignorant of the scene as anybody else. As a consequence, we just did extensive screen tests in Melbourne to fill all the roles we hadn't filled from Sydney. It was in this way that we found actresses like Val Lehman, whose professional acting experience at the time was quite limited. The same was true for other actresses like Colette Mann, who had tremendous talent but didn't really fit into the pretty young thing mode then popular on Australian television. Reg Watson had already selected Peta Toppano and Kerry Armstrong when I took over. I auditioned actresses in Melbourne for all the other roles. And we did, wherever possible, cast in Melbourne because it was much easier than uprooting actresses from Sydney for a show that was at that time due to run just sixteen weeks.

All the Melbourne actresses we wanted accepted the roles. I had only two major problems – Vera, who we couldn't find for ages, and Bea. Val Lehman was the absolute stand-out in Melbourne for Bea but I worried about her inexperience in such a pivotal role. Consequently we initially offered the role to Carole Skinner whom I knew well from Sydney theatre and even better from the Sydney theatrical pub, the Gladstone Hotel. In fact, I cast Carole as the barmaid in the first show I ever wrote and produced. Her agent turned the offer of Bea Smith down. So we went with Val because she really was the stand-out. Finding a Vera was more difficult. We wanted an actress who could be tough, vulnerable, hateful and even attractive. Kate Winslet in The Reader comes to mind. We tried everybody. At one stage we were even thinking of Ann Sidney who was in Australia at the time. Eventually Kerry Spence rather tentatively said she had a sister-in-law named Fiona who was an actress and who had just returned from London. Would we audition her? Of course we did and everybody was sold. The only other casting story that sticks in my mind was casting Lizzie. Again this was a difficult job given that I didn't know the older Melbourne acting scene. This time Godfrey Philipp, who was Vice-President of Melbourne Operations and an old Melbourne hand, suggested Sheila Florance. She was perfect – but we had one problem. Denise Morgan had written an episode where Franky had stolen Lizzie's teeth. Eventually after staring at Sheila's mouth for ages, I had to ask her if she had her own teeth. 'Of course they're mine,' she said, and took them out to show me. When the show was a success, Elspeth Ballantyne later told me that Sheila used to terrorise the new young actresses by telling them I was the toughest producer she had ever worked for, so much so that I had made her have all her teeth taken out in order to get the role. Fortunately, Elspeth, who was the quiet strength of the cast, as was her character in the show, managed to placate the terrified young actresses in question.

A team of writers were gathered together to give voices to the characters who would inhabit the world of Wentworth. The earliest scripts were provided by Reg Watson, with series producer Ian Bradley, Denise Morgan and Ian Coughlan all providing early episodes as new characters sprang forth from each writers' meeting. They were aided in their researches by Sandra Willson, who had at that time been the longest serving woman prisoner in New South Wales. She had been incarcerated after she had shot dead a taxi driver following the emotional trauma of the end of her lesbian love affair. Declared insane by the authorities, it would take eleven years before her sanity was officially acknowledged. Sandra was finally released after eighteen years of imprisonment. On her release, a very highly educated Willson would be a leading light in the setting up of the first Halfway House for women in Australia, Guthrie House. She was the obvious candidate for the producers of Prisoner to approach in order to gain an insight from behind the bars. Willson was to remain an advisor to the series for many years.

Val Lehman models the latest fashions in night-wear.

Sandra died in 1999, aged 60. Ian Bradley remembers the input of Sandra when Prisoner was being devised:

It's always better I think for the writers to sit with someone who has lived through the experience. Sandra was one of a half dozen inmates we talked to when we were still doing the research, but she was released during the time of our pre-production. That whole story of being the longest serving, and the most feared prisoner in New South Wales and then being considered rehabilitated and going in a new direction, gave us a whole story arc. So she was very useful to us. Sandra was still quite 'damaged' when she came down to see us. We had to get special permission to fly her down because she was on parole and we agreed get her back the same evening. I remember at the end of the meeting I had to drive her out to the airport because we were running late, and traffic is atrocious in Melbourne at 5:00pm. I decided to take a short cut and as I turned away from the sign that said 'airport' I noticed she stiffened beside me and her knuckles went white. I realised that this was probably the first time she had been alone in a car in twenty years. I don't know who was the most nervous. She was physically strong, and I guess we were all a little wary. The big plus was we had worked out this concept very much inspired by Sandra. This was that everybody is a prisoner of their environment, the heroes overcome that environment and the villains succumb to it. That was something I think she understood, so she was quite open to talking to us.

Of course the biggest factor visually for the show was creating a workable but convincing prison interior in Studio B. Ian Costello would be instrumental in helping bring Wentworth alive from a visual point of view:

I had been employed at Channel 10 for about six years, starting as a Set Dresser and working my way up to Props Buyer with an ultimate goal of Set Designing. When the Prisoner *project came up, I was assigned as an Assistant Designer and Props Buyer. I worked closely with the main Set Designer Mal Nichols in researching, conceptualising and designing the entire Wentworth prison set from the ground up, inside and out. Mal left Channel 10 about the time* Prisoner *first went to air and I think I took over as Set Designer for the next three years or so. Mal and I pretty much created the complete Wentworth prison from designing the sets, to sourcing and purchasing the furniture and fittings – including the famous steam press – to organising the exterior prison grounds in the area behind the studio. We were also responsible for designing 'guest sets' and set-up of location shoots outside the prison. The brick walls were constructed on basic television 'flats', plywood sheeting on a timber frame. Thousands of individual bricks were cut from plywood and stapled to the flats. I think*

there was a little sawdust sprinkled over them for texture when they were painted. Varying sized sections were built plus columns so they could be reconfigured to create never-ending variations of the Prisoner *labyrinth.*

I do remember we toured the now defunct women's prison Fairlea in Melbourne with the producers to gain ideas. The final prison bears no resemblance to what we saw which was a collection of fairly ramshackle cottages surrounded by a barbed wire fence. Once it was decided to use the studio exterior as the prison, the style of the interior was more or less determined. On most levels I think the set worked reasonably well but I would have liked a little more 'character' to them. Unfortunately, we were limited in having to make the interiors match the studio exterior. I was lucky enough to visit ITV in 1975 where we saw the sets for Within These Walls, *the detailing was amazing. A lot of the cast were familiar faces from a variety of local television and stage productions and they quickly became a close-knit and professional ensemble. My wife and I became very good friends with Amanda Muggleton when our twin daughters were enlisted to alternate as Chrissie Latham's daughter Elizabeth for over a year. We kept in touch for many years whenever Amanda was in town with stage productions and took our daughters, Brooke and Tori, in their late teens to see Amanda give her final performance as Shirley Valentine.*

We decided to use the back of the studio as the exterior of Wentworth purely in the interests of economy and practicality. It made sense to be

EP. 20 – Sc 16.

**Left: Various crew members discussing the filming of Doreen and Franky's escape.
Above: Day 4. Episode 20, scene 16.**

Above Left: Sheila Florance (Lizzie Birdsworth) with Elspeth Ballantyne going through the scripts in the Rec Room set.
Above Right: Val Lehman takes a break in the Green Room. The sight of the many costumes in the background shows there was little privacy.

able to shoot the exterior locations within cable length of the studio where the interiors were shot. Also we had complete control over the site and were unhindered by the proximity of neighbours. The windows were simple metal boxes filled with bars and an opaque acrylic sheet. Inside each one was a weatherproof fluorescent light which all discreetly cabled off the wall for night shoots.

While thought had been given to the theme tune, the opening and closing titles were again the subject of much consideration. However, the style and content of the music would determine how the *Prisoner* titles would develop. Ian Bradley again:

Reg Watson commissioned the Prisoner *theme song in Sydney and sent it down to me as a fait accompli. I hated it! We were making a gritty hard-hitting show. It was a sentimental ballad, very much in the style of other Grundy serials. Initially I rejected the music but was advised that there was no money in the budget for a second theme tune. It was Graeme Arthur, the director of*

Episode 1, who suggested the theme would work as a closing theme. The problem then was: we needed an opening theme but we had no money. I decided to use sound effects. Gates clanging shut, camera shutters. This naturally led to the idea of mug shots. So necessity was the mother of invention once again. Incidentally, the green screen we used to superimpose the bars was cutting edge technology at the time and gave us enormous problems since 10's equipment was all pretty old. The bars would continually bleed, but eventually we got a usable effect and used the same master tape throughout the series.

Chief make-up artist for the first episodes was Vivienne Rushbrook who, like her colleagues striving to create Wentworth, was charged with supplying a wide array of cuts, bruises, scalds and scars. The make-up needs on *Prisoner* were generally more demanding than other dramas of the period due to the constant amount of physical altercations between characters. One of the big story devices occurred at the end of Episode 3, namely the stabbing of Bill Jackson.

Below Left: Fiona Spence has her makeup carefully applied. Below Right: The Solitary set.

Top Left: The Rec Room set featuring its own mini corridor. Top Right: The Visiting Room has very little set dressing necessary. Right: The familiar Wentworth Detention Centre loading bay, in reality leading through to the studios' huge storage area. Inset: View towards the Rec Room set from the corridor.

Perhaps a simple enough scenario for a drama, but the execution of such a moment required much planning. Vivienne recalls this landmark moment:

My memories of the day we stabbed Bill. It all seems so long ago, and it was one of the easier blood 'n' guts effects that we had done. We had completed the scene up to the real scissors being thrust downward. They then stopped the tape while we ran down into the make-up room to strip young Don's shirt off and attach the scissors. The props boys had cut the end off the scissors and welded them onto a steel plate with inserts on either side so that a very old seat belt could be threaded through in order to keep the scissors up high, and very secure. Jennifer Carmen then cut the wardrobe shirt in order for the scissors to protrude through. I threw a lot of fake blood around the site, and when the task was done and dusted, Don went back upstairs onto the set and lay down and acted his heart out – being dead. In those days we used to make our blood out of chocolate topping with a little blood-coloured water-based dye. Even food colouring from the local supermarket looked just fine and was not

too badly coloured. It was close to the real thing, though you had to be very careful with the amount of burgundy colouring used in bruises.

I found out early in the piece that red and burgundy were absorbed into the video system and the colour actually changed into a deep purple. Some very dramatic moments were had in other scenes when we checked the monitor and had to pull back the look of the bruises. The other thing that has disappointed me immensely over recent years is that Cadbury have changed their chocolate topping recipe. The topping, when poured on skin, now leaves welts. Not just

Below Left: The Channel 0 studios in Nunawading, Melbourne where the series was filmed. The big rectangular red-bricked building was the ideal choice to 'become' Wentworth. Right: Real life inmate and advisor to the series Sandra Willson with her TV counterpart Judy Bryant (played by Betty Bobbitt).

on sensitive skin, but on all skin. So we can no longer use our good old stand-by blood. It was also fabulous because you could put it in the mouth of an actor and it actually tasted fabulous. Quite often, in fact, an actor would call out just as the cameras were rolling to say 'Oops! I've swallowed the blood, may I have more please?'

In the late 70s and early 80s, special effects make-up was almost non-existent in Australia. You could only purchase basics such as latex and putty. We also used to use morticians' wax to create a lot of swelling wounds. We made our own blood as, at that time, all of the commercial bloods went either bright pink, or orange, and looked shocking. That's when we searched our kitchens for alternatives, hence the chocolate topping. I had so much fun trying to create wounds and injuries. I went to hospitals to see wounds, or to talk to doctors to find out the different types of burns. I did a St. Johns Ambulance course to find out how to bandage wounds and breaks.

The directing honours for Episode 1 were handed to Graeme Arthur who would direct five of the first ten episodes. However, the cast and production team would be rocked by Arthur's shock death shortly after completing work on Episode 10 following a massive heart attack. It rocked the whole team to the core that a leading player in getting *Prisoner* to the screen from the very beginning was suddenly gone. Many had come to regard Graeme very highly and he was never to witness the resounding success his work had achieved when the episodes went to air.

When Grundy and Channel 10 executives took a look at the early edits of the opening episodes, it became obvious that this was a show with a longer future than originally thought. The characters were strong, the scripting edgy but addictive and the whole show just burst through the screen with twice the energy of its rivals. The decision was taken to increase the workload from one to two episodes a week, effectively doubling the workload for everyone involved. Things were tight pulling in one episode but two would effectively send the production team and cast into overdrive. For many, although not too happy with their workload doubling, there came with it certain benefits, the increase in pay being one of them and the security to know the show was not ending after the contracted sixteen instalments, safe in the knowledge that a potentially longer term of employment was in the pipeline. The production had been recording from October 1978 and, as the New Year came and went, *Prisoner* prepared for its debut on television screens across the country. Nobody could have foreseen the massive impact it would eventually have, stretching across the globe. But back then, everybody at Grundy held their breath waiting for a verdict from the only source that really mattered, the Australian viewing public.

Costume Notes from the Tunnel

by Jennifer Carmen

The Prisoner epic started for me with an announcement from Deb Browning, Head of Wardrobe, that the channel was shooting a one–off over a few months – a new drama out of Studio B. As I had some experience with wardrobe continuity on a feature film, I would be working on it. We were sent some character notes from production house Grundy and met the cast for measurements very soon after.

It was an impressive line up which included grande dames of theatre Mary Ward and Sheila Florance and other seasoned actresses destined for the appellation. As is usual there had not been much television work around for older women and there were a lot in the cast, pleased to be working, and especially in a strong cast of respected performers. Some among the young and pretty 'actrines' made the transition to drama from a dancing and singing light entertainment background, but had considerable experience in the business. Deb knew many of them and, as we took notes and measurements, there were no muttered asides from her on this occasion about 'too much temperament, not enough talent'. Smiles all round, and we were off to a cordial and co-operative start. Grundy was well-known as a production house and everyone spoke highly of the warmth and intelligence of producer Ian Bradley, a confidence well placed.

No drama had been made at Channel 10 for years. Making relentless live talent and game shows meant that design, props, sets and wardrobe departments were used to fast turnaround. It was normal to just get stuck in, work quickly, improvise and adapt. Deb sent the warder characters off to be fitted for uniforms at a tailor we used so we didn't have to worry about that, at least not until later.

Denim was chosen for the prisoners' outfits as it was versatile. It would 'distress' well, was easily available and cheap – always a concern at Channel 10 – and easy enough on the eye in a mass on screen. We bought a big supply of pale blue and yellow shirts and had the blue ones dyed a nasty green so we had a bit of a palette to make a girl look reasonably good in the yellow, or not. It was not to be a glamour show.

Overalls and sleeved dresses with the option of shirts underneath gave enough variety for character. Pockets were needed of course for props, contraband and any striking of attitudes as required. We cut Lizzie's dress long loose and droopy and distressed it thoroughly, Marilyn's and Chrissie's short and tight. Franky was obviously and exclusively baggy overalls. Lynn and Karen got better fitting overalls and dresses and that was about the extent of the customisation.

Above: Jennifer Carmen, Prisoner *wardrobe.*

The best and fastest dressmaker I ever knew, Barbie Veitch, was permanently ensconced behind her industrial machine. A skilled cutter and maker of bias satin dresses, boned corsets, opera frocks, decorator of an endless stream of leotards and jazz pants for Young Talent Time to boot, she revved her machine at the top of a production line. All four of the wardrobe staff pitched in, as well as running the usual shows, to complete the stack of denim in a week.

'Daggy' was wardrobe's key word for our brief: Australian for ugly and unattractive. Some bolts of brown and blue paisley flannelette were found in a rundown haberdashery in an as yet un-gentrified Richmond. These would be pyjamas along with candlewick dressing gowns, dyed brown and dark green from the original pink and blue. In fact, the dressing gowns rarely appeared on screen but ended up as the unofficial wardrobe for cast and crew as the series went on rather longer than expected as it turned out, into years of cold Melbourne winters. Studio B was freezing and so were shoots in the prison garden at the back of the studios.

We had a chance to suggest character with the occasional jumper under the uniforms. These were raked out from the stock of garments on the bulging rows on the mezzanine above the vast shed-like hangar which housed the props and set departments. Lizzie was assigned an old brown cardigan big enough to swamp her slight frame; Sheila did pathos so very well. I did a blitz on the department stores of Melbourne for suits for prison Governor Erica. I scored a particular hit with Patsy with the green linen suit. It remained a favourite for years and she used it as a gauge to ruthlessly monitor any weight gain to her trim size 12. The handsome Dr. Greg was outfitted with a couple of tweedy jackets and co-ordinating trousers from the men's store which supplied most of the newsreaders' jackets.

I had a little skirmish with Deb about shoes. She maintained that they were never seen on telly, so it didn't matter much. From my theatre experience I knew how important they were to a character, for stance, gait and the sound on the floor. I was into artistry in those days. Warders got Mr. Plod shoes, prisoners were shod from the stock boxes. For prison Governor Erica, I bought ladylike cream T-bar medium heels. It was a good investment as it turned out: unseen maybe, but they clicked down the corridors for years.

The theme song was swiftly recorded, and pronounced lovely. The opening footage for the titles and credits was shot. With the first clang of the iron grille doors closing over the credits there was a tangible excitement in the air. Easy show, I thought – a few months perhaps, a bit intense. Uniforms, a few incidental frocks. What could be hard? Then the schedules came. Outside Broadcast [OB] on Monday, studio days Tuesday, Thursday and Friday. Wednesday was preparation for wardrobe and other crew, rehearsal for actors, two episodes shot simultaneously in studio and OB, and two in pre-production. Early starts for wardrobe studio days were 7:00am for 8:00am recording start till 8:00pm, earlier still for OBs.

The first scripts came, along with prisoners' background story notes which we and the actors needed to know, although the viewers probably never would. Nervous of my responsibility for wardrobe continuity, I made comprehensive notes on the chronology of action and was very careful about correctly marking screen days on a grid. Mistakes were embarrassing and expensive if you showed up on location far from the studio with the wrong day's frock. Strict and scary Bob Gillow ran the OBs as a military operation. It was to become a habit that saved panic more than once when the rate of production cranked up to double pace, and there were six episodes on my desk simultaneously. But that challenge was yet to come. There was one that brought me near to meltddown and we hadn't even started yet. On the initial scheduled set-up day, I lugged my laundry baskets of shoes and racks of clothes down to the tunnel, a long corridor which ran from the audience entrance above ground, down alongside both Studio A and Studio B, big arenas which took up the whole footprint of the building underground. I dumped armfuls on the benches fixed on both sides and looked down the whole length of the tunnel to the glimmer of daylight far away. There was nothing in the tunnel. Not a locker, nor a desk, no monitor, not even a screen to change behind. For make-up and hair there were no chairs, work bench or mirrors. The only piece of equipment was an intercom on the wall which soon began to buzz as Reception let me know another actor was upstairs waiting to be escorted through the labyrinth, into the bowels of the building for wardrobe and camera checks.

The first to arrive were seasoned pros, used to undressing in less than salubrious environments. I was thrown into a panic and deeply embarrassed at the lack of preparation evident, from the Channel I represented as first contact. There was a toilet block nearby for the modest. I screened off a section with racks, fought down my hysteria and we got on with it. There were notes on the floor, with actors gamely ducking behind the rows of garments. When I had a moment I ran upstairs to wail to Deb, who told me in no uncertain terms to pull myself together. Abandoning all requisitioning protocols, I ran to props and staging where I had a mate who grabbed an old desk and a chair or two and got it down there. Then, to Operations where I was together enough to screech to some effect.

Say what you will about wobbly *Prisoner* sets, the construction team, once galvanised, was fast. Within a few days we had a divider and a door in the middle of the tunnel, closing off for many years any sight of daylight. Walls of MDF pigeonholes appeared, which also served as a room divider and changing areas for each artist's shoes, hand props and personal effects. No lockers that actually locked mind you, but these were more innocent days. Make-up tables and chairs, a mirror and eventually an urn for the endless cups of instant coffee which fuelled us all appeared. There was a monitor to the studio, intercoms to the gallery, Reception and upstairs wardrobe and a phone line which was never silent. A notice board showed up and benches were wrenched from an area around make-up to create a seating area for actors. Many a plastic cup filled from the 'cardboard handbags' of wine-boxes secreted in the pigeonholes was to be raised here at the end of a long week. We created a dark and airless but cheerful little bunker which became more home than home was, until long after the pilot date ended. The show became a surprise success, and the

CAUTION
DO NOT ERASE

HOLD TILL...Ep.209...
REFER.....Sc.36...

Ep.112
Sc.25
D5

Above and opposite page: Wardrobe continuity polaroid shots.

sets created in a hurry with no expectation of longevity wore out with regular bashes and rioting.

From the start, enthusiasm among the actors was high. There was agreement that the scripts were much meatier than average, the characters strong and well-defined and casting was great. No one was 'starry'. Everyone settled into their roles, gave it full welly, and apparently relished the lack of glamour although some were suspected of secret trips with the mascara to the Ladies. Make-up was usually quick and minimal, that is, unless we got murders, wounds and burns.

The problem for wardrobe was logistics. With minimal time and budget for this 'one off', we had no duplicates of anything. A distinctive garment gone missing was a nightmare as was getting something cleaned or dirtied up again to maintain continuity when we shot out of sequence. Production management who did the scheduling apparently did not realise how ill equipped we were, not to mention understaffed. What the hell, it was only a few months. Initially, I did all OBs, preparation and three twelve-hour-plus studio days on my own. Washing, ironing, buying, borrowing on contra-deals and arranging returns were all thrown in. The one bolt of grey serge we had bought for warders' uniforms was soon used up, but then new officers appeared in the scripts. No internet in those days, just frantic phone calls around Australia until we located a match in Tasmania. After another Friday afternoon phone-around trying to get a blue shirt for a non-speaking police officer with an 18-inch neck who was out on OB first thing Monday, I enlisted the co-operation of Maura Fay – a young woman just starting as an assistant in what turned out to be a brilliant career in casting, who noted what we had on the racks and cast the non-speaking actors to fit the garments we had.

During the next weeks, with a few lurches and stumbles, the cast, crew and some members of the production team became a streamlined and tightly-knit group. Crew and cast were cooped up together in our underground factory for months, with the only change of scene on OBs on which we did everything out of beat-up caravans. Wardrobe, hair and make-up were the first to see the actors at the early morning starts. Sometimes unwell, exhausted or emotional, confidences were exchanged, stories were told and friendships formed, many of which were to endure long after *Prisoner*. As time went on, although enmities and resentments also arose, we became companions of the trenches. You won't find very many of us dishing the dirt for that reason.

Intense as filming was, it was also a lot of fun. I had never known such a hilarious, quick and bright group of women – ruthless in their black humour, sharp with one-liners, each with a wicked and uproarious story to top one another. At times we were reduced to howls of helpless laughter. A lexicon of a distinct theatrical origin prevailed. Costumes, for men and women, were always 'frocks'. An associate could 'turn like an ebony python'- or just 'turn'- betray you or get bitter. A furious or resentful mood was described as 'her lips were string'. There were more than a few days in which we were warned by someone of a string-lipped mood. Although dauntingly outnumbered, the male cast members gave as good as they got.

New entries to the cast could bring forth a wave of reminiscences from previous shows. Over the squeezing of the cardboard handbags on Friday evening, I awarded medals – the 'Sarah Bernhardt Award for Personal Drama of the Week' was one of them. 'Snake of the Week' (the ebony python award) was muttered about, but rarely presented. The 'Wardrobe Award For Costume Care' almost always went to Patsy.

One afternoon we were in need of a bit of light relief. Officer Meg took to the floor armed with a dustbin lid 'shield' and a mop to rehearse a scrap with prisoner Noeline Bourke. In answer, wild card actress Jude Kuring went on the attack, brandishing an item of feminine hygiene. The floor manager did not know where to look. Casting clearly had moments of genius, or perhaps some artists became possessed by their characters.

A well remembered highlight was an afternoon with Betty Bobbitt. Not only a wonderful actress but also a singer and writer, Betty regaled a full tunnel with a comic song written for a charity event about the characters of *Prisoner*. Perfectly rhymed, scanned and witty as Victoria Wood's best. The staging was to include a mute chorus line of non-speaking extras nodding in unison. This was hilarious to us as Equity or production costs would not allow the morph of a regular non-speaker to a speaking part and back to non-speaker again. It resulted in ridiculous situations

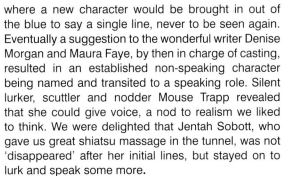
where a new character would be brought in out of the blue to say a single line, never to be seen again. Eventually a suggestion to the wonderful writer Denise Morgan and Maura Faye, by then in charge of casting, resulted in an established non-speaking character being named and transited to a speaking role. Silent lurker, scuttler and nodder Mouse Trapp revealed that she could give voice, a nod to realism we liked to think. We were delighted that Jentah Sobott, who gave us great shiatsu massage in the tunnel, was not 'disappeared' after her initial lines, but stayed on to lurk and speak some more.

In the tunnel we were very supportive of the actors' preparations for more emotional or demanding scenes. From the early episodes I particularly remember Franky's one-take rampage. No chance, of course, to do it again. Vera's poignant attempt at femininity, Sheila Florance's suffering-for-her-art in the episode of Lizzie's nicked false teeth and Patsy's feats of memorising. One Tuesday, Patsy recorded fourteen Governor's Office scenes in a row – four different screen days, with solid slabs of script that did not differ very much from each other. Her only respite was a quick sprint downstairs for a wardrobe change and a dab of powder. No time for the hair to change, however. She got a cardboard medal for that feat of memory.

An 'Absurdity of the Week' medal should also have been awarded. To me, the nun episode with Doreen and Franky on the run started to feel as if a grab bag of joke ideas had been ransacked. However it was a fun day out in the light. We felt for Colette and Carol after the OB shoot of Franky's death. They were worked up to act their socks off and Carol and Colette's intense association on the show made Franky's final scene a personally emotional one for them both. But it was all diluted in long shot as it turned out.

The OB of Lynn's wedding was a welcome day in sunshine as well. I had a chance to do a romantic look for Kerry in an old crepe nightie and a floral garland as a wedding outfit. I was put out when director Gary took one look at the beautifully made and completely realistic pregnancy bump made by Barb and had me stuff what I could find, a rolled up jumper, under it so it would 'read' on screen. He was right. Fancy that! TV reality is not the same as real reality. I enjoyed contributing to the little details which might add a grace-note to the factory production. Writer Denise Morgan responded to my suggestion that the perfume which reminded Doreen of her mother should be *Je Reviens*. Props guy Steve kindly went to the trouble of locating a bottle but I wonder if anyone noticed it?

Somewhat surprised by the show's steadily rising ratings, the Execs on 'Skid Row' informed us that the 'few months one-off' was to be extended without a pause and the output was to be doubled. Never mind killing a golden goose, just stuff it. There was a rapid crunching of gears and a change of pace.

I was to get an assistant. The first appointment did not turn out well. After a few weeks running in of the new team member, I had to take a trip out of town, and left comprehensive notes in my absence. For one scene, I wanted Doreen draped with an antique Spanish shawl, obviously a treasure from the past belonging to the old lady who had innocently given shelter to the runaway Doreen and Franky. This was to suggest the dressing up box of childhood and a sense that Doreen had been, at least temporarily, taken under a motherly wing. When the scene aired I was aghast to see that a second shawl had been supplied as well for the older woman, losing the point entirely. The characters looked ridiculous, twin spectres wafting around the room. I was proprietorial regarding what little touches of art we could add under soap opera conditions. This incident, and other silly choices and too many piles of neglected laundry, meant that action was needed. I marched again to Operations to deliver an ultimatum. Harmony and efficiency were restored with the appointment of cheerful, unflappable and hardworking Jan Peterson.

There was a fast turnover of directors, each with his own style, some keen on action and car shots with arty reflections. Some were experienced telly storytellers who knew what worked and did it fast and efficiently. Others, like the beloved Leigh Spence, were sensitive and actor centred. As episode followed episode into triple figures, maintaining internal continuity became more of a problem. Some writers were aware of the characters' back-stories and allowed something of an input regarding what they had done, would or would not do. But the story lines became more subject to contingency. The imperturbable floor managers and the lovely props guy Steve maintained awareness of the mysterious inner geography of the cells and corridors and would have a quiet word with a new director if the action threatened to warp into strange territory. Mostly, the long serving actors kept things on track as months turned into years. We heard stories of a far off land called the BBC where dramas had three weeks of rehearsal for thirty minutes' screen time. It was incredible that the actors got their lines learned as well as they did in the time they had. It was tough on those of us confined to the tunnel. For make-up, hair and wardrobe it was usually dark when we arrived and dark when we left.

The show gobbled up actors from the conveyor belt. It was interesting to see who turned up for a stint in the denim or serge: Jane Clifton, who I knew for her music; Sigrid Thornton, never before seen out of pin-tucked cambric. The actors were mostly friendly and down to earth; there was rarely any starry behaviour. I was never star-struck except by gorgeous George

Mallaby whose voice on the phone on his first call-in to wardrobe rendered me speechless. He strode in to the tunnel on a wave of effortless charisma and I had to control my stutters as I measured his inside leg.

As we doubled the episodes per week, some casting of new characters passing through created challenges as there simply were fewer available actors to cast. I don't remember anyone who was not good in their role. Wardrobe often did a double take when confronted with the look of the actor who showed up on the day compared to the notes appended to the script regarding their character and appearance. There were scrambles to rummage in the mezzanine on those occasions.

Ah, the treasure trove of the mezzanine. There I found a perfect dress in hound's-tooth wool for one of Lizzie's out-of-prison adventures. However, it was black and white and would 'strobe' badly so I sent it off to be over-dyed dark green. I was more than crestfallen to receive outright rejection of my find from Sheila. This was late on a Friday before the early start of Monday's OB. Slightly 'tired and emotional', the cardboard handbags were sometimes squeezed after the last scene on Friday evenings. Sheila declared her revulsion for green. It had sad associations for her, which she then explained. We both ended up in tears. I had not clocked this as a problem as she had worn green shirts without mutiny. We were very fond of each other, and it may have been the colour draining from my face that caused her equally dramatic capitulation. Perhaps because she was a trouper whose professionalism overruled her tragic memories? The dress looked great with her droopy black hat and she wore it many times thereafter without a murmur.

My emotionalism over the green dress was followed by a deepening exhaustion. My marriage had not survived the long hours and immersion in my episodes. I was falling asleep wherever I was on Saturday. One day, as I faced recycling with some slight change yet another set of St Kilda prostitute outfits for an OB, I knew it was time to break out of Wentworth. I had made friends, in particular with Patsy, Peta, Barry, Fiona, Maura and Denise. The tunnel crew were like sisters and it felt like leaving the family. My dear Sheila sulked.

I was away on leave of absence for many months abroad and although I resigned during that time, when I came back I was met at the airport by Jan who told me that I was to take over from her while she had a break, like it or not. I returned as Jennifer Kay before reverting to Carmen later. I never did catch up on all the story lines which played out in my absence, but by now it didn't matter. A soap opera within the soap opera had developed over the months I had been away. Liaisons had formed, had stuck or broken up. The atmosphere had changed. Cast members new to

me had long been installed, the show had a life of its own and it was clear *Prisoner* would run and run.

There were new make-up people and permanently appointed hair dressers, not just on loan from their studio. They were all lovely people, and we grew close in a tunnel now feeling grim and dusty. It was bereft of actors hanging out as they now had a Green Room upstairs, the old Operations room, once the scene of many a desk-thump and charm-offensive.

Vivienne of make-up had added pyrotechnics and special effects to her repertoire. Ribbing about her shaking hands notwithstanding, she engineered gore-explosive murders. The tunnel often smelled of chocolate syrup fake blood, an improvement on stale air and shoes. Wound and mess continuity had become more significant and there was even the luxury of a Polaroid camera that belonged exclusively to the tunnel. A gallery of 'Murder Frocks' had accumulated which hung from a wall in the tunnel until the array resembled the tattered sails of the wreck of the Hesperus – too scrappy to be amusing any more.

I rarely, if ever, went on OBs as I was wrestling with the logistics of six episodes, even though we now had the luxury of duplicate costumes. Wednesday was shopping day. A later start and a chance to see daylight as I swiftly cased my usual haunts in town for armfuls of garments piled up around me in the taxi back to the studio at Nunawading. The taxi ride was as 'glamorous' as it got for wardrobe. As *Prisoner* was now well established and the budget increased a bit from starvation rations, shopping became a bit more fun. Designers lent us garments for the occasional out-of-prison character. After proving myself with the endless itemisation of receipts to fierce Gwen in accounts, I started to buy instead of doing contra deals. Selling them on to recoup costs to actors who liked the clothes. Most did not have time to shop.

The occasional foray into the boutiques of Toorak and South Yarra was not adequate amusement for long. The days were long, laughs were fewer, and I was planning to go abroad again to follow the beat of a more exotic drum. The house I shared with a friend from promos and actor Wayne Jarratt was packed up. My books went to Amanda Muggleton. Seventeen tea chests of stuff were kindly stored by 'Pocket Mouse' Wendy Hughes of make-up in her cellar. Stashed inside one of them were a handful of old polaroids I had grabbed at random as a memento. A precious item was left with Fiona on what turned out to be a very long loan. Lovely Monica Maughan presented me with an award to commemorate the times I could have had the vapours and didn't, as cardboard handbags were wrung out and we said our goodbyes. This time there was to be no return to the tunnel.

Years later, now immersed in a very different world with rather more sequins than *Prisoner*, I was

astounded to hear that as well as the fact that it had continued to run for years, *Prisoner*, now dubbed *Cell Block H* and other titles in other countries, was an enduring cult hit. A stage show was to come to the UK. At a theatre in Richmond, I went to meet Patsy backstage. She was still perfectly immaculate as Erica, looking small and delicate but bravely composed as she prepared to face her public, an enthusiastic crowd of mostly women. Black and studded leather was much in evidence at that event.

Recently, thirty years after I escaped from Wentworth, I had the pleasure of meeting for a coffee with Peta Toppano. Peta is still beautiful, still telling a funny story at her own expense, and in the Midlands for an 'Audience With' event. Among my photographs I found her picture, her lips temporarily like string, as she swotted her lines on a Sunday walk in the Dandenongs with Barry, me and my ex. Husbands had come and gone for both of us, but *Prisoner* had endured beyond all. If only we had known, we said. Foreknowledge could have meant proper residuals for the actors, and I would definitely have kept Karen's overalls!

Definitely Denise

There is an agreement among both *Prisoner* fans and those involved with the production that a Denise Morgan script was always a benchmark against which other writers were judged. Such was Denise's skill with character and dialogue that each of her 42 credited episodes of *Prisoner* are examples of the show at its very finest.

Denise went on to become one of the most respected screen writers in Australia. Coming into the world in Oakley, Queensland on 22nd June 1947, Denise was the daughter of a bank manager John Morgan and his wife Hazel. She claimed that it wasn't until her mid-teens that she discovered television. Her peripatetic existence because of her father's job meant that as she was growing up, the family would be based in small country towns with poor or no television reception. However as soon as the small screen phenomenon was unleashed upon the bright and eager young Denise, she was fascinated by the medium. Leaving school with qualifications in typing and short-hand resulted in a number of secretarial jobs. However it was when her sisters moved to Melbourne that Denise followed and found herself working as secretary to Ian Crawford of Crawford Productions, firmly established as the leading independent television production company in Melbourne. They were responsible for the massively successful *Matlock Police*, a drama serial set in the fictional small country town of Matlock and was Channel 10's answer to the rival *Homicide* on the Seven Network. Out of the blue, Morgan was asked to re-write a scene in one of the scripts. She found that despite her reservations as to her ability, she could write for characters easily. On the 8th January 1976 Denise was credited with her first full episode of the show, 'Judgement Day', and it was the start of a career in writing, script editing, producing and adaptation which would see her become a writer of huge respect from her peers. She continued scripting episodes of popular screen shows such as *Solo, Bluey, Chopper Squad* and *Young Ramsay* before landing at the door of Ian Bradley and Reg Watson who were looking for talented writers to script and storyline their new women's prison drama for Channel 10.

Denise's first full script for *Prisoner* was Episode 6, and clearly displayed her ability to get to the very core of the characters. None more exemplified this than the tender scenes between Franky Doyle and her brother Gary. It was almost as if Denise had found her perfect television format as she excelled in displaying the inner workings of the hard bitten

characters which would parade across the screen. Her scripts found a way of connecting with the deepest fears and thoughts of the character, a psychological truth which was illuminated in moments of lesser action that delved in the very core of their being. A small example of her talent is exemplified with this short exchange between Lizzie and Officer Bennett:

EPISODE 75

LIZZIE: Have you got a family, Miss Bennett? Not even a brother or a sister?

VERA: I was an only child.

LIZZIE: I bet you were spoiled then. We used to spoil our kids. Even when we were that skint. We always had a tree. Yeah, a real family time. I reckon everyone's the same, hey, Miss Bennett?

VERA: I wouldn't know.

LIZZIE: Didn't you have a tree?

VERA: My mother had asthma, didn't like plants in the house.

LIZZIE: You could always get a plastic one.

VERA: The whole thing's a waste of time. It always gets out of hand. Everyone trying to out do everyone else with presents.

LIZZIE: Didn't you even like opening your presents, Miss Bennett?

VERA: Oh, I don't know Lizzie and I don't particularly care. Now come on.

LIZZIE: Oh, please Miss Bennett, I've still got me palpatations.

VERA: Then you should be lying down.

LIZZIE: I can remember one present. I was 8 years old. It was a little pup. It was the ugliest looking little mongrel you ever saw, but I loved that little fella. Did you ever have a dog, Miss Bennett?

VERA: My mother wouldn't let me have pets.

LIZZIE: Gawd, was she mean or something?

VERA: No. Just old.

LIZZIE: Well, I am going to have plenty of fun this Christmas, no-one is too old for that. I reckon the concert is going to be real good if we get enough time to practice by ourselves.

VERA: I know exactly what you mean, Birdsworth. Come on.

LIZZIE: Oh, PLEASE Miss Bennett, just a little while longer.

In 2009 Denise shared some of her memories of *Prisoner* with Brian McDonald:

The wonderful Reg Watson had written two scripts. He gave me both to read. Which one did I think should open Prisoner*? I chose the second one because the first one took far too long in setting up the drama. So we went with the second script. Reg had developed some of the characters for the opening episode. Then Ian Bradley, myself and another writer continued fleshing out the characters and story arc. We were originally only going to do 16 or 18 episodes and then finish the show. No-one, especially myself, thought it would be a success. But with a quirk of luck and fate, the programme manager of the network (he was also suss about the show) showed it to his family. They loved it and so (without audience testing per se) the network said we were to go to two hours a week. We then had to revamp the initial episodes to extend the series because we had already rounded off their character arcs. And that's when Carol Burns said she didn't want to do two hours of television per week which is when we decided to kill her off in Episode 20.*

My favourite episodes are Lizzie and Doreen getting high; Franky stealing Lizzie's teeth; and a scared straight episode I did for Bea when she wanted to terrify a young girl out of being a recidivist. A funny thing – I could hear ALL the characters in my head when I wrote. So, in some respect they were my muses and the characters could write themselves. So many favourites but Vera, Lizzie, Doreen, Franky, Chrissie, Mum, Bea were all stunning. All diverse, but full blooded. I loved creating some of the guest characters too and we had such wonderful actresses in the roles.

With an amazing body of work behind her on *Prisoner*, Denise's career flourished in screen writing. She became an increasingly in demand writer of series and serials which saw her penning episodes of *A Country Practice*, *Home And Away*, *The Flying Doctors* and *McLeod's Daughters* amongst others. Denise guided the long success of *Blue Heelers* as a script editor and storyliner. She subsequently played

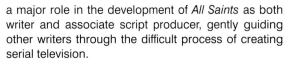

a major role in the development of *All Saints* as both writer and associate script producer, gently guiding other writers through the difficult process of creating serial television.

Denise passed away on 26th June 2011, robbing the Australian television industry of a supreme talent, a writer whose body of work will be remembered as achieveing the very highest standards of Australian drama television. In terms of *Prisoner*'s enduring success, Denise Morgan will always be the Godmother of the series, having firmly put it on the path to greatness.

Unchained Melody

As the great English variety comedian Ken Dodd was once heard to observe wittily, 'Husbands all over the land trembled when they heard *Prisoner: Cell Block H* finishing downstairs!' The finish he referred to is, of course, the now iconic theme tune. Television theme tunes have become bedrocks of pop culture. From the marching beat of oil baron soap *Dallas* to the eerie radiophonic sounds of the BBC's *Doctor Who*, the specially written and performed snatches of music accompanying the opening and closing moments of our television favourites are ingrained into our psyche. They have become a catalyst for recollections not only of the shows themselves, but our lives when we first discovered the programmes. Music is a powerful memory stimulator.

In the case of *Prisoner*, there was no opening titles theme. This was jettisoned in favour of the stark click of mug shots. The closing titles however were to be adorned with one of the most recognisable tunes in television drama history – a beautiful ballad which would top the charts on both sides of the world.

Enter country singer and songwriter Allan Caswell. Born in Chester, Allan moved to Australia in 1966 where he started to write, record and perform his own songs. By 1978, Allan's career was decidedly on the up, and he signed a deal with the music publisher ATV-Northern Songs, who at that time held the publishing rights to the Lennon and McCartney back catalogue. The boss of the new Sydney office of ATV-Northern songs, Chris Gilbey, was having lunch the same week with a member of the Grundy Organisation. Gilbey was informed about a new show going into production for which they intended to use the classic 1955 pop song 'Unchained Melody' as its theme (immortalised in the 1965 version by The Righteous Brothers and produced by Phil Spector). Ever the opportunist, Gilbey convinced the executive it would be cheaper for Grundy to have their own specially composed piece to use for the show. For Allan it meant a chance to pen a song which would be heard throughout the land, as he recalls:

> *Chris picked up a script for the pilot episode and passed it on to me without opening it, and by this time it was Friday. I had a 'Boots' gig on the Saturday so I couldn't get to it until the Sunday. The deadline for getting the song to them was Monday. Once I got the idea, which came from a*

Opposite page: Allan Caswell, writer of 'On The Inside'. Above: Allan Caswell remembers this scene featuring Mum which inspired his writing of the theme tune.

shot where one of the characters called Mum was clipping off a rose in the prison garden, I wrote the whole thing in the most lucrative 45 minutes of my life. I wrote it as a love song because I figured if we missed out on the deal, I could still use it somewhere else and because, after watching women in prison for an hour, the closing song didn't need to labour on the point.

Allan quickly recorded a demo version of the song 'On the Inside' using a $100 string guitar and a mono portable cassette recorder. Caswell delivered it post haste to Gilbey at the publishing offices.

Being in the middle of setting up the office, Chris didn't even have a cassette player so he handed it to Grundy without even listening to it. When they asked him what he thought of the song, Chris apparently said, 'I think this is the best thing that Allan has ever written.'

Grundy advised Allan that a better demo was needed as the production office in Melbourne would need to judge it for the final approval. Gilbert was very canny in persuading Grundy that they should release a vinyl single of the theme to maximise publicity for the forthcoming show. The ballad was about to get a voice in the form of Lynne Hamilton.

Born in the UK county of Lancashire, Hamilton had been a teenage backing singer with The Desperadoes. Lynne later joined The Caravelles where she toured with all the famous groups of the Sixties including The Who, Freddie and the Dreamers and an up and coming group from Liverpool called The Beatles! After emigrating to Australia in 1971, a period spent running a car hire company took her out of the music business before a return to music saw Lynne singing the song that would give her a worldwide hit. Lynne remembers her career springboard:

The producers of the television show approached the RCA recording label to see if they had an artist for the theme song. The criteria were that a) the artist had to be female as it was a woman's song and b) the artist had to be completely unknown in Australia. It was Christmas 1978 and I was RCA's newest signing, scheduled to be marketed early in 1979. No one had heard of me yet. They gave me a rough demo cassette to learn overnight. When I got home and listened to it for the first time, I broke down and cried. It was Allan Caswell singing his song with just him playing the guitar. I cried because it told my own story. Not because I'd ever been in a literal prison but I was going through a divorce and all the grief that goes with that. My view is that there are many kinds of prison, emotional and psychological, that people can find themselves serving time in, either by their own design or someone else's cruelty. I knew that many broken hearted people would relate to the song for these reasons. I hadn't

been told anything about the series itself except that it would probably be huge.

And so it came to pass that Lynne joined Allan in a recording studio for a second demo version of the song, again with Allan on guitar. Allan remembers Lynne bursting into tears during the recording. Lynne remembers running it through a couple of times before recording it in one take. At this stage, it was far from certain a single release would ensue but the signs were becoming good that something special was being created.

Originally it was conceived that every second episode would have an instrumental version performed by a group of session musicians going by the name of The William Motzing Orchestra, named after the respected arranger and producer who had been given the task of seeing the completed recording through. An orchestral backing track was recorded and mixed in with Hamilton's vocal to create the completed version of the theme. Lynne and Allan were also guaranteed a credit on the end titles of all episodes. Lynne again:

When Grundy and RCA heard the finished theme, they immediately decided it ought to be released as a single so we went back into the studio and recorded a full-on version. My only input, apart from the vocal itself, was to insist on singing it slower to make more space for an emotional feel. This recording session was a very

Top Left: Reverse cover of the UK single release featuring a later cast photo. Left: "In Your Arms", the love song from Neighbours which Lynne also put her voice to. It received only a fraction of the success that the Prisoner theme tune had. Below Left: Allan Caswell's 2012 album "It's a Country Song". Below Right: Cover of the UK single release for the song, featuring a small cast photo.

emotional and healing experience for me. When the series went to air in Canada I was asked to film a clip dressed as a prisoner with me walking through the actual set of the show. This was then played in Canada during the credits to end each episode. I also ended up making a proper video for the pop charts. We filmed this in Australia, in the Blue Mountains, complete with a rainbow!

For Allan Caswell the success of the song and the effect it had on his career was immense:

The record went to number one in all Australian territories and was only prevented from going to number one nationally by the fact it didn't chart in Western Australia until a few months later when they started showing Prisoner *there. The record stayed in the National Top 100 charts for some 52 weeks.*

Lynne and Allan were both award Gold record status and an ARIA – Australia Recording Industry Award. Lynne was recognised as the highest selling female artist of 1979 in Australia. Lynne recalls meeting with the lags for the very first time:

Network Ten brought all the cast together onto a popular evening talk show and they presented me with these awards in front of the whole nation. That's when I met the entire cast for the first time. I did watch the show in the early stages but then was busy touring so didn't track with it overall. It was interesting in that most of the song's fans presumed I would know what was happening in the series, and would ask me about it. The show was recorded in Melbourne, and I lived and worked mostly in Sydney. I was amazed to discover that many of the actors on the show were Shakespearian actors, and very highly qualified. I have the greatest respect for their ability to play the kind of characters featured in the show. Soap operas have never appealed to me personally but I have obviously been emotionally connected to Prisoner. 'Lizzie Birdsworth' was one of my greatest fans actually, and would regularly remind me of that. She was a great lady and quite posh in real life!

The single was released both in Australia in 1979 and then again ten years later when *Prisoner* achieved

Below: The 2012 re-release of Lynne Hamilton's original version of "On The Inside" was welcomed by fans

its almost overnight success in the UK. Both times the 'On the Inside' was backed with 'Love Theme from *Prisoner*', a minor key instrumental arrangement of the song by William Motzing, used for emotional moments during the show. When the single climbed the charts in the UK, a search went out for Lynne Hamilton who had long since left the music industry. The record company wanted to fly her 10,000 miles to promote the surprise hit. It resulted in Lynne appearing on the legendary BBC music show *Top Of The Pops* when the song eventually climbed to number three in the officially BBC recognised pop charts.

Lynne went on to record a wedding theme entitled 'In Your Arms' for *Neighbours* although Lynne admits: 'It didn't get much promotion.' Lynne now spends her time spreading the word of the gospel with Christian ministries in Australia. Allan has continued his career as a country flavoured singer and songwriter to great effect, with a loyal following for his recordings and live performances. Occasionally they are called upon to get back together and deliver their spine-tingling version of 'On the Inside'. Most recently they reunited for Channel 7's *Where Are They Now* series in 2007. The continuing success of the song is something that Allan is particularly proud of:

> *Chris Gilbey's theory was that it was great having a hit but then you had to turn it into a standard. He worked to get Lynne's version on as many compilation albums as possible. All kinds of covers started coming out of the song, some*

were good and some were hysterically bad, but they were all out there. The first time I heard a Musak version in a lift, I knew I had arrived as a songwriter.

The highly publicised repeat showings on the Australian Foxtel channel 111 HITS in 2011 were trumpeted by a newly commissioned version of 'On The Inside' featuring singer Ella Hooper. Heavily re-imagined, it drew lots of criticism from staunch fans of the original. Lynne comments:

> *I have heard Ella Hooper's version. She's a great singer in my opinion. It's always a risk doing a cover of something that has been so massive for someone else. There is a saying about being 'the original and best'. It may just be that the original genre of 'On the Inside' should have been preserved. It's nice for the fans to pay me the compliment.*

There can be no denying that the compelling beauty of the melody and lyrics, given voice by Lynne Hamilton's lilting vocal, has been a major factor in helping the *Prisoner* brand get full recognition. Wherever you may hear it, be it on your television, late night in a bar or simply over the radio, the song still resonates with millions of viewers around the world.

On the inside the roses grow, they don't mind the stony ground, but the roses here are prisoners too, when morning comes around...

CHAPTER THREE

1979
Episodes 1 to 79

While the world wondered what changes the Ayatollah Khomeini would bring to the stabilisation of Iran following the revolution to overthrow the Shah, an event at the end of the month would bring significant uproar to cities in Australia. The first episode of Prisoner was actually a double episode and went to air at 8:30pm on Monday 26th February in Sydney and thereafter Tuesday 27th February for Melbourne.

Following months of press stories touting this major new drama series, Reg Watson's baby was finally given a birthing before the Australian public on Channel 10. And what a dramatic impact it had. Viewers were hardly prepared for the significance to Australian television history of the characters on screen: The ferocity of Franky Doyle, the bitterness of Vera, the emotional minefield of Lynn Warner – outrageous and bold characters, the like of which had not been seen on prime time television. And they lapped it up. Reg Watson's decision to stand firm about the content of

Sally Lee, played by Lisa Aldenhoven, Wentworth's first suicide victim.

the show, and not back down to Channel 10 bosses, who feared an audience backlash at the controversial subjects, was vindicated. The Australian public decided that *Prisoner* was a weekly date they wanted to keep. Watson and Bradley had tapped into the voyeurism that exists in us all for a glimpse into a world that is by and large, alien to the largest percentage of viewers. The thorough research by the writers and production team was now seen to maximum effect. The plight of the women in Wentworth struck a chord with Australians and tapped into their emotions. Love them or loathe them, the inmates of Wentworth were addictive viewing.

The first character to be seen on screen is Karen Travers, alias Peta Toppano. Travers is sent to prison for stabbing her husband to death after she arrives home following an abortion to find him in bed with another woman. The role is hugely central to the early episodes, as for much of the time Karen is our eyes and ears in Wentworth as we tune into the emotions and fears of a newbie to the prison system. Peta Toppano recalls her feelings on getting the role of Karen:

The first thing I thought when I got the role in Prisoner was 'Great'. Barry Quin (my then husband) and I get to work together and do not have to be in different cities! Reg Watson had written the part of Karen Travers with me in mind for the role from the word go. I was very honoured and humbled to be included in such a great cast; Sheila Florance being one of the most respected actresses in Australia. I was also approached by

Left: The first Recroom.

Below: Marilyn Mason played by Margaret Laurence

Reg to sing the theme tune for the show, which a lot of people don't know about. I had come from a musical background performing from an early age with my family, but I never really took that too seriously, as back then I was far more concerned about becoming a serious actress. How silly of me. I was also extremely proud that the entire cast was made up of strong women. We were all actors with a strong theatre background and, of course, I was very lucky to be cast alongside Carol Burns, a beautiful and brilliant actress who played the fabulous Franky Doyle, with whom I shared some of my personal favourite Prisoner scenes. Of course, the 'no make-up' policy was a little daunting for a girl like me!

The character of Sally Lee, seen being chased down the corridor by Meg and Vera, directly after the opening mugshots, was played by Lisa Aldenhoven. Unable to take the horrors of the prison system Sally is found hanged in her cell in the first episode. Lisa now has her own recruitment business, but is happy to recall her times at Wentworth:

I was actually invited to audition for the role of Lynn Warner, the role Kerry Armstrong eventually got. It was only the second speaking part I had ever auditioned for, the first being the opening episode of Cop Shop. I got down to the final two for Lynn, and when Kerry was cast they then offered me the role of Sally. I was working as a cadet reporter on The Herald, Melbourne's afternoon broadsheet newspaper at the time, so had to take a few 'sickies'

and sneak off to the set to film my part. I was incredibly nervous, not only out of fear of being caught sneaking out of work, but it was only the second speaking role I had played. I was terrified of making mistakes, forgetting my lines or missing my marks. Everyone was very excited at being part of a new show, particularly a show for women. The opening chase was very funny. I was very young and incredibly keen and clearly a lot fitter than the rest of the cast and crew. No one could keep up with me and they kept asking me to slow it down. The climax, running into Franky's elbow and collapsing onto the cement floor, was particularly painful. Unfortunately I had not at that stage learned how to fake things. I'm not sure how convincing it all looked when it

Above Left: Marilyn's friend Yvonne, played by Jane Clifton.
Left: Continuity shot of Lynn Warner (Kerry Armstrong).
Above Right: Peta Toppano, Kerry Armstrong, Barry Quin.

was cut together. Fiona Spence particularly was very kind and supportive. For the suicide, they suspended me in a harness from the lighting grid. Unfortunately, it took a long time to get the lighting and positioning right. I remember just hanging there, turning slowly, wondering if this really was the career for me.

Eight weeks after I finished filming Prisoner, Grundy offered me a six-week role in The Young Doctors playing Julie Holland. I moved to Sydney and spent the next two and a half years with the show. There wasn't a lot of time to watch Prisoner but of course I watched the first few episodes

and managed to catch a few more over the years. I returned to Prisoner in 1983 playing a character called Cheryl Armstrong [387 – 388]. By the time I returned, the sets were a lot stronger. Many parts were unfinished when we were doing the first episode including the cell door window. In that first episode I had to thrust my hand through the cell door and ripped my arm open. I came away very battered and bruised.

I still see Kerry Armstrong around the traps. We went to State School together. I was in the show for such a short time I did not make any lasting friendships from it. Prisoner is unique. It was well acted, well scripted and well directed. I think the idea of women being locked up together appeals to people on all sorts of levels and I am surprised no one has managed to replicate its success so far.

Two very prominent ladies featuring in the early episodes were both very much the eye candy for the series. While it must be noted that *Prisoner* is remarkable for presenting woman in stark reality, devoid of social trappings, occasionally some genuinely glamorous women made their mark. Lynn Warner [Kerry Armstrong] was imprisoned for supposedly burying alive the baby boy she was looking after as a nursemaid. It was something of a harrowing subject and, of course, Warner protested her innocence – although sympathy with the character was hard to gain when her constant crying seemed to get on everyone's nerves. Lynn was also the first victim of the judgement of Queen Bea which resulted in the iconic scene where the Top Dog trapped Lynn's hand in the steam press as a punishment for her perceived crime. Marilyn Mason [Margaret Laurence] was somewhat less troubled, having gotten herself in Wentworth for soliciting. Marilyn is an archetypal dizzy blonde who winds up having a relationship with the prison electrician Eddie Cook [Richard Moir]. After some ups and downs, Marilyn and Eddie head off into the sunset and run a milk bar together. Lynn, in between enormous amounts of sobbing, manages to get her case re-opened and eventually it is revealed the child's mother was responsible for burying the baby boy. Lynn is released but not all goes well. Her ex-con boyfriend Doug gets involved in an armed robbery and she is persuaded to drive the getaway car. Cue more crying and another induction into Wentworth. Eventually Lynn is released again and, after being kidnapped having been mistaken for Bea's friend Monica Ferguson [Lesley Baker], presumably leads a crime-free life and one where smiles instead of sobbing dominate.

A focal point of the first six months was the plight of Mum Brooks, played superbly with gentle dignity by Mary Ward, whose act of euthanasia upon her husband had seen her serve a lengthy sentence. Upon release she heads to her daughter, a first *Prisoner* outing for future *Neighbours'* legend Anne Charleston, who is less than pleased to see her mother and unwilling to let her young family into the secret of their grandmother, whom she has passed off as dead. While Lizzie Birdsworth would be the razor-sharp scalpel in the comedy arsenal of the show, Mum Brooks is the epitome of isolation and loneliness as she tried to make her way on the outside in a largely unsympathetic and uncaring world. A few words from Mum herself, Mary Ward:

> My agent rang me to say they wanted to interview me, and that was it. I got the part of Mum. I remember going into the Green Room on the very first day and they were all smoking. I had just given up cigarettes so it was very difficult for me. And of course, except for Lizzie, I was the oldest person there. But I thought it was a very interesting idea for a TV show. I remember the scene when I told my granddaughter why I was in prison – it was euthanasia. I had helped my husband to die. And at that time it was an offence in Victoria – at least fifteen years inside. Of the cast, Elspeth Ballantyne as a warden was always

Left: Peta Toppano catches up with her script for the day. Above: Very much still in character, Colette Mann and Carol Burns break between scenes.

very pleasant. And of course my granddaughter was in prison also. I didn't have any input into the character of Mum from a writing perspective. But I think it was brilliant to make her a keen gardener. It made her a little apart from the other prisoners, in age and background. Mum was very popular. I did get quite a lot of fan mail from the USA and UK. My career has been very long. Two visits to the UK in 1938 and 1940. Then after the war I returned in 1948 and stayed until 1956 when I returned to Australia for family reasons. During those last years I played Peter Pan with Margaret Lockwood. I did lots of BBC work and two plays at the Liverpool Playhouse as well. I was amazed and still am, at the popularity of Prisoner. Keep watching everyone!

Nuns on the run – Carol and Colette try to disguise Franky and Doreen.

Anne Charleston made just two appearances in Prisoner as Mum's daughter Lorraine but still receives mail about them to this day:

    I started my soap career in Bellbird, which became an Australian TV institution. Elspeth Ballantyne played one of the leads for most of it. It was basically a soap set in the countryside and went out for a quarter of an hour each evening on the ABC. I played Wendy Robinson, a district nurse, for about 18 months. In that show I worked with some actors who would go on to have prominent roles in Prisoner *later on: Gerda Nicolson, Annie Phelan, Alan Hopgood was wonderful as always, Beverley Dunn was in it too.*

    Funnily enough I was never asked to audition for Prisoner. I was just cast in the role. I know a lot of people had to audition for their jobs but it just came to me on a plate. I can't quite remember why now. It was a new show so you didn't know how long it would last or even if it would be successful. I'd seen Googie Withers in Within These Walls *and just assumed it was going to be something similar. For me it was just a job for a few weeks. Mary Ward had played my mother several times before in one-off plays for the ABC. She was one of the most beautiful women I had ever seen, funny and charming. I didn't watch* Prisoner *when I was in it or afterwards because I just don't like gratuitous violence and felt the whole programme was full of it. I don't recall why I didn't re-appear as Lorraine, who was a really selfish stuck up cow. I assume I probably wasn't available as I was working a lot for the Melbourne Theatre Company around that time.*

Eldest granddaughter Judith-Anne has discovered the truth about the 'Aunt' who has come to stay and bursts in during a major row between Lorraine and Mum. The mystery surrounding the 'Aunt' who has been staying is discovered. Thinking that the revelation means she has no family on the outside now, Mum shoplifts and deliberately returns herself to Wentworth. However, all is not lost because Judith-Anne turns up wanting to know more about her grandmother. Mum explains the terrible decision she had to make to end her husband's suffering. As is the way in soap land, this begs instant forgiveness. However, Judith-Anne has her own secret – she is pregnant. Mum knows that if she can get out again she will be able to help. New social worker Jean Vernon helps her get parole once again [16] and sets Mum and Judith-Anne up in a flat, both ready to start a new life.

The earliest episodes provided sensational television. Wentworth is represented as a dark depressing environment, with forbidding corridors and shadows, immediately planting a feeling of unease into the armchair addict. It's harsh television, the complete antithesis of its contemporary serials such as Crawford Productions' *The Sullivans* and Grundy bedfellow *The Young Doctors*. The brightly lit environment of the Albert Memorial Hospital was positive paradise compared to the confines of Wentworth Detention Centre, and certainly the serials of the time could not hold a candle to the powerhouse characters housed within Cell Block H.

As early as Episode 3, the viewers get to experience the first on screen riot. The battle for supremacy between the factions led by Franky and Bea was a short-lived physical encounter, but one of the most dramatic. The major casualty being prison psychologist Bill Jackson who ends his brief stint on the show with a pair of scissors sticking out of his chest. It's high octane stuff with the tensions reaching fever pitch as the denim dogs of war are unleashed on

Top: Happy times – filming Lynn and Doug's wedding.
Above Left: The wedding of Lynn and Doug is under way.
Above Right: Kerry Armstrong looking stunning while filming Lynn's wedding scenes.

each other. The casualty on this occasion was actor Don Barker who played Bill Jackson [2-4]:

After about ten years of acting in amateur theatre here in Adelaide, I took the plunge and decided to take up acting as a profession in 1967. TV was in its infancy in this country at that time so I did mainly theatre work for a few years but then started to get some work in Melbourne with Crawford Productions which at that time was the major, if not the only, company making TV shows. These were mainly cop shows: Homicide, Division 4 (a suburban police station) and Matlock (country police). I was always cast as a baddie and every time I went to Melbourne I was either killed or arrested. Then in 1973, out of the blue, Crawfords offered me a continuing role in Homicide, that of Det. Sgt. Harry White. This role kept me busy until the series ended in November 1975. As a consequence I was able to get many other television roles, all of them of a varied nature, and then came an offer from Grundy Productions to take a role in their new show Prisoner. Whether I was considered for any other part I don't know. I knew that I would only be involved in the first three episodes and on the first day, when I was called, I was thankful that was the case.

Because the show was new and I don't think anyone expected it to last, there were very limited facilities at Channel 10 allocated to the show – one room for make-up and wardrobe, and no Green Room for the actors. The cast and extras, all women except for yours truly, had to sit in a corridor when not on set. So, as you can imagine, 50 to 60 women spending hours in a crowded corridor was not conducive to a peaceful atmosphere. I remember spending the first week wondering what the hell I had let myself in for – it was chaotic. Of course, things improved after the show proved to be a hit but by that time I was long gone. I don't remember much about the family scenes. I knew Elspeth Ballantyne quite well. She was also from Adelaide so working with her was a joy and all the domestic scenes went smoothly but not so the big riot scene. As is usually the case with really dramatic sequences, the atmosphere on set prior to filming was relaxed and jovial but once filming began it became too jovial. On the call of 'Action' Meg and Bill would look at each other in anguish and then begin to giggle. We just could not stop cracking up. There was no reason for it; it was just one of those strange things that sometimes happen. It got so bad that the director Rod Hardy eventually lost patience and gave us both a good talking to after

which we managed to get our act together. Very embarrassing! As to why the cast seemed to have a firm grasp on their characters from the word go, it's probably because at that time, actors were used to working fast with very little rehearsal so it was not all that unusual.

I don't see much of the cast these days although I did have the pleasure of working with Amanda Muggleton in a production of Twelfth Night a few years back so we had a few laughs about the experience. She's still not sorry about stabbing me.

Why the show was so amazingly successful is a mystery to me. I think it just struck a chord with the general public although it was very different from the usual cop shows and happy family series that were on air at the time. Mind you, if you can predict what will make a show work you would make a fortune. So to conclude; it is very satisfying to have been part of such a popular show and although it was chaotic and at times frustrating, I wouldn't have missed it for quids.

After a lot of finger pointing by the police, the murderer is revealed thanks to being witnessed during the riot by Marilyn's electrician boyfriend Eddie, and thus Chrissie Latham is unmasked as the first screen murderer within Wentworth! The producers were quick to see the potential in Amanda Muggleton's feisty Chrissie who would become a staple of the series on and off for the next four years. Chrissie is, by and large, an unsympathetic character during her early appearances, all hard-faced aggression and selfishness. It is only later when she returns for a second term that we start to warm to her as she prepares for the arrival of baby Elizabeth. For actress Amanda Muggleton, Latham proved to be a landmark role which would catapult her into a career of constant success on stage and screen.

Following the loss of Bill Jackson, the flag for male staff within the prison is kept flying by Dr. Greg Miller [Barry Quin], former fiancé of Karen Travers. This, of course, gives him *carte blanche* to become personally involved in Karen's case and to rekindle their love once more. Hardly the stuff of Mills and Boon but viewers were willing the pair to be reunited on screen. Karen had been the victim of physical abuse during her unhappy marriage to the husband she eventually murders, and it is obvious that the two of them are well suited. But as ever in soap land, it takes time. In reality Peta Toppano and Barry Quin were in fact, an item off screen. Within the first few weeks of *Prisoner's* transmission, they would tie the knot in Melbourne. Quin had met Toppano when he toured Australia with a visiting English theatre company. Toppano encouraged her future husband to send tapes of his

UK television appearances to the casting department at Grundy. Clearly they liked what they saw and Greg Miller would become physician to the ladies in the slammer for some twelve months. Barry was more than happy to remember his time on the series:

Having toured Australia with the Chichester Festival Theatre Company in 1978, during which I met and fell in love with Peta Toppano, I wanted to return there. Peta had already been cast in Prisoner *so I sent the producers a video of some of my work on UK television and was offered the role of Greg Miller, which I happily accepted. Everything was new and exciting in Australia, as was the cast of* Prisoner*. They made me feel very welcome and life on the set was not very different from a set in the UK. I've always preferred the non-competitive company of women so I was very happy. I didn't do much research into the character, I have to admit. It was all a bit of a whirlwind as I arrived late after numerous problems with Australian Immigration. The character, like most characters that one plays, was based on observations of numerous people and the way they behave in life – no-one specific. Mostly, it was putting myself in the situation and being informed by the text.*

Carol was great to watch and to work with. She became a close friend and was Matron of Honour at my wedding to Peta. Kerry Armstrong also became a close friend. I played tennis with her father once a week – he usually won. It was obvious that she had the makings of a great actress, which she now is. I always felt she was under-used in the series. As she said herself, 'All I get to do is cry!' I guess the producers were able to get a lot of publicity out of the relationship between Peta and I off the set and our subsequent marriage, so it was inevitable that they would create a story line that required our being romantically involved. Fine by us. We always enjoyed working together and subsequently appeared in several stage productions together in the 80s: They're Playing Our Song, My Fair Lady, Danny and the Deep Blue Sea. Initially the atmosphere on set was very exciting with a strong feeling of unity and the sense that we were making something new and different. After the series proved to be enormously popular, it went from one to two hours per week output and became much more in the 'soap opera' mode. It gradually became less exciting to work on, especially after Carol Burns' exit from the show. Peta and I were being made some very nice offers and much as we enjoyed and appreciated all that Prisoner had

Top: A fun continuity shot featuring Lizzie, Clara and Erica.
Centre: Fiona Spence as Vera Bennett, dressed to impress!
Bottom: Patsy and Elspeth go over their lines before filming the next scene.

done for us, we decided to move on to other things. I remember a funny direction in one of the scripts which ran 'Dr Greg crosses the surgery, tossing off as he goes.' This created some amusement, especially among the crew. God knows why.

Carol Burns' decision not to continue beyond her initial contract period was a huge blow to the show but the producers had to respect Burns' judgement. So with Franky and Doreen on the run, a police shoot-out would see the final moments of a blistering character which would go down in Australian television history as one of the finest portrayals of a character in a serial. Franky's final utterance in Episode 20 – 'Bloody bastards' – summed up Franky's fight against the system that had failed her to the very last. Once again make-up artist extraordinaire Vivienne Rushbrook was called to administer her skills to Franky's final moments:

Another first was my first 'bullet hit' on an actor – Carol Burns as Franky, the first explosive device that I had ever strapped on. I was so nervous and excited at the same time. When you create a bullet hit, the 'squib' is held in a metal washer that has been welded onto a steel plate. That is then strapped tight around the actor; there is padding also between the actor's body and the plate to absorb the shock when the hit is detonated. The washer also helps with the direction of the mini explosion – it blows straight out, away from the body once the squib is in place. A condom with fake blood in it is then taped using gaffer tape – great holding power – onto the metal plate. It also held the wires in place. I was fairly anxious about the condom slipping out of place as I had put quite a large amount of blood into it, so I put extra tape around it to ensure no accidents occurred. I ran the wires back to my little hiding area, set it all up, when the director called action and I pressed the button, it went off like the real McCoy. However, the half a pound of gaffer tape also blew out, along with the condom, and the wires. It just looked so funny, and to this day I still chuckle about the paraphernalia that came flying out of this simple 'hit'. I did learn to be very meagre with the amount of tape I used.

The beefcake quota was further enhanced on the show with the arrival of solicitor Steve Wilson, played by James Smillie. Wilson is suave, handsome with a great deal of charm. Naturally he has the women swooning inside and outside the prison very quickly. James Smillie explains his entry into the realms of Wentworth:

Sheila rests in the Channel 10 grounds before filming her next scene as Lizzie.

In regards to Prisoner, *really good memories! I had a great time on the show working with all the 'girls'. They had strong roles which to that date had bypassed lady actors in Australia. I managed to catch a couple of episodes in the re-screening and it was a fun experience recalling happy times. I certainly had no problem fitting into the environment as it was all shot at Channel 10 at Nunawading. This was a place where I had started my career in 1965 when I was a finalist in Showcase and then spent a further year reading the news and working in light entertainment, so it was great to get back there some fifteen years later. During this time I had worked with Godfrey Philipp, a gentle man, who was there as the producer and director of Magic Circle Club. I subsequently worked with him again on* Adventure Island *at the ABC in Ripponlea a couple of years later.* Prisoner *was, of course, Godfrey's baby. I had gone to England to work as an actor in 1972 and got a call from him saying this part was available, would I be interested? As I needed to return to Australia to pick up my Australian Citizenship, the opportunity was timely. I don't think Godfrey had written the part specifically for me, but clearly he felt I must have suited the role.*

It was a great pleasure to work directly with the very glamorous Peta Toppano and Kerry

Armstrong. There were certainly never any 'leading lady attitudes' during those early days of shooting. My time in the show was limited as I had to return to London to be in a musical. Consequently the phasing out of my character was necessary, though at this moment I can't quite recall what happened. I subsequently toured the UK in several shows including Kiss Me Kate, 42nd Street and Annie. I toured venues as diverse as Hull and Glasgow and all points in between and always had fans at Stage Door with fan cards of Steve Wilson in Prisoner. *They never seemed to be there to see the show I was currently in, simply as devotees of this remarkable programme,* Prisoner, *which seems to have stood the test of time. Perhaps programmers today would be advised to reintroduce the concept once more.*

The series internal logic is fairly consistent during the eight years that Channel 10 broadcast it. The early episodes feature the debuts of recurring characters such as Joyce Barry, Inspector Jack Grace and Colleen Powell as well as a glimpse of actresses who would go on to be seen later in the series in more prominent roles: Kirsty Child, Billie Hammerberg, Anne Phelan and Jane Clifton. Clifton particularly would weave her way through the legacy of Wentworth combining her alternative career as singer and sometimes pop star with life as a jailbird. Having had a small role as Marilyn's prostitute friend Yvonne [9] she would find lasting fame as Wentworth bookie and troublemaker *par excellence*, Margo Gaffney.

Kirsty Child notched up three different characters during *Prisoner's* tenure on our screens, the first of which was corrupt screw Anne Yates. She gets caught bringing in contraband for the prisoners in return for cash [5]. Later she turns drug dealer [26] and tries to involve Vera Bennett in her activities. After being caught and taken to Wentworth as an inmate, she dies hiding in the dryers. It was Kirsty who was seen strolling down the corridor on the end credits for a number of early episodes. Kirsty Child recalls her first brush with the ladies of Wentworth:

I auditioned for the role of Vera Bennett, which of course went to Fiona Spence, who was terrific in the role. And this is how I came to be cast as Anne Yates as a sort of consolation prize, I think. The closing sequence of the character locking up was filmed quickly with very little direction. Just moving through and along corridors in a warden-like way doing what she had to do. I don't think I realised at the time that it was to be used for each episode (initially) and I don't think the producers knew either. We just did it to see how it looked and if it fitted. My lasting impression of the show is what a great opportunity it was to be involved in a series that was completely different and employed more women than any other Australian show at the time, and still to this day. Not only that, but it had such talented actresses. It was very well and carefully cast. I truly don't remember my first day but the excitement around that time was high – lots of energy, lots of laughs. It was hilarious, especially jumping in that dryer.

The writers were very creative. Sheila Florance was a great pro. So many years of

Left: Patsy, Jude and Fiona break during their outside broadcast scenes. Right: Doreen's poor teddy bear gets attacked by Jude Kuring (Noeline Bourke).

Left: A large gathering of the 1979 cast wait outside for their next scene to begin shooting Right: Bea, Martha and Monica.

theatrical – and life – experience which she brought each day to the set. She was a generous performer, a kind woman. If she liked you! Woe betide you if she did not. And she was absolutely hilarious. I didn't know Sheila at all well before Prisoner. I had worked with her only once before and got on well with her. So it was a delight to be up close and personal and our friendship lasted until her death. I miss her.

The holy trinity of Bea, Doreen and Lizzie is one that defines the show for many fans. Colette Mann proved to be a fine leading player in 1979. Doreen is not a confident person, she is easily influenced by others and when we encounter her she is sharing a cell – and an implied lesbian relationship – with Franky Doyle. Doreen Anderson is serving three years for fraud and theft and it is quite clear that she idolises the strength of Franky. She ends up on the run with her cellmate and sees Franky shot dead before her eyes. For a woman who clutches her teddy bear for comfort frequently, this is a devastating personal blow. She had been drawn to Franky's strength and dominance within the prison gang wars and following the sudden loss of her idol and protector, Doreen goes into a decline as she recklessly tries to replicate Franky's bullying tactics, but with little hope of making any real impression. Doreen's story arc within the 1979 season is far more advanced than either of her two constant cell mates, Bea and Lizzie. With Franky gone, Doreen finds a substitute mother in Lizzie and when the friends are paroled they to make their way in a world that has no sympathy for ex-cons, Doreen's real life mother (recognisable to soap fans as *Neighbours'* Helen Daniels, alias actress Anne Haddy) makes an appearance and is initially rejected for abandoning Doreen to a life of care homes. However, just as Doreen comes to accept her birth mother's reasons for rejecting her, her mother is found dead after a terminal illness. Another huge blow for Doreen,

but this time coming with it a healthy inheritance which provides a financial basis for the marriage to her new boyfriend Kevin Burns. Make-up supremo Vivienne Rushbrook recalls a memorable moment with one scene featuring Doreen:

One really hysterical moment was with Colette Mann. In one scene she had stuck a pitch fork through her foot [55]. This scene was shot on location. The following week we had to reproduce the swollen, very sore foot with the pitch fork injury inside studio. We came in to work a little earlier to create this masterpiece as it was going to take about an hour to finish. Colette was comfortably seated with her foot on my knees as I worked away. Many jokes and coffees ensued while we worked. Then, just as I finished the foot, Colette got up and, as she hobbled away, she said 'Wouldn't it be hysterical if this is on the wrong foot?' You guessed it; it was on the wrong foot! I have never worked so fast in my life as trying to reproduce the hugely swollen foot and, of course, I hated the rushed end result.

A (by now) twice weekly serial needs fresh characters on a regular basis to give the storylines new impetus, and there were some terrific additions to the cast. One such was Noeline Bourke, played with great jaw thrusting relish by Jude Kuring. A brave performance in its execution, as such a brash interpretation of a clearly low intelligence character might have been OTT, but Kuring just manages to keep Noeline on the side of believability during her stay with the show. The script writers opened up her background and family by having brother Col and daughter Leanne wheeled out. Col decides to hold hostage the lady for whom Noeline used to clean, when he is caught red handed stealing the silver during a break in. During a police shoot-out, the armed Col

Left: Mrs Davidson always had a soft spot for old Lizzie. Below Left: Sheila poses with one of the extras in the kitchen set for a continuity shot. Below Right: Sigrid Thornton (Ros Coulson) and Deirdre Rubenstein (Janet Dominguez).

is shot dead and Noeline's anger management takes another regressive step. Social worker Jean Vernon is another prominent arrival [14]. Initially angering Meg Jackson for clearing out Bill's things from the office, they establish a firm friendship and eventually Meg offers Jean her spare room. Jean goes on to try and help the poor unfortunates but disappears all too suddenly [56] as characters frequently do in soaps with little explanation.

The sale to overseas channels cemented the rising popularity, with Val Lehman often citing its American audience as being in excess of 39 million although this is likely to be based on the number of States that were showing the series and its potential audience rather than any documented ratings information. Carol Burns was invited to a lesbian wake for Franky Doyle in Los Angeles where the show was being aired on KTLA. Although Burns had long since left the series, she was nonetheless happy to join in with the good-natured farewell to an icon of Aussie TV. It was reported that in the Los Angeles area *Prisoner* had come a ratings second only to another female led, but rather more glamorous, American series *Charlie's Angels*. The Australian import held more than a quarter of Los Angeles viewers on its highly publicised 8th August 1979 premiere, quite a feat in the influential LA market.

There was something of a family reunion on the set when Bea escapes from a hospital and goes on the run [31]. After calling on Mum Brooks, she ends up at the home of her friend Valerie [Billie Hammerberg] where her neighbour's daughter Yvonne is played by none other than Val Lehman's own daughter, Joanne. Ironic then that Miss Lehman Junior shops Bea Smith and has her returned to Wentworth. Val's other daughter Cassandra had appeared as Debbie Smith in a flashback during Episode 2 of the series.

Irene Zervos, an illegal immigrant forced into prostitution, winds up for a stint at Wentworth. She is played by Maria Mercedes, now a well-known musical theatre performer in shows such as The Phantom of the Opera and Sunset Boulevard. This was the first of two stints with *Prisoner*, and here Maria describes what it was like being thrust into the world of the wild women of Wentworth for the very first time:

Left and Above: Val Lehman with her real life daughter Cassandra, playing Bea Smith's troubled youngster Debbie

My role as Irene came about directly after finishing a guest role in the ABC series Patrol Boat. I went to the Grundy offices and did a casual read through of a few scenes. It wasn't a formal audition as such. In my career I have steered clear of stereotypical 'ethnic' roles. What attracted me to the role of Irene was that she was sent to Australia from Greece to be married off and unfortunately ended up in prostitution, unknowingly. The wonderful director Nadia Tass played my sister-in-law and I also got to speak in Greek, my heritage language. My parents loved it. Joining an established show is daunting at the best of times quite honestly. But arriving at 7:00am, sitting in the make-up chair and having Val Lehman swan in, look at the make-up artist and say, 'What role is she playing?' without even acknowledging me! This made me even more nervous. Was Val method acting or what? Or had Bea completely taken over her persona? Needless to say I didn't really have much to do with Val. Years later she was cast in a show I was in, Nine the Musical, and I found her to be a fabulous woman. One thing I will never forget was Sheila Florance opening her locker in the dressing rooms and asking me if I'd like a drink – of alcohol, at 8:00am! Peta Toppano took me under her wing. She was from an Italian background and I was from a Greek background. We had, I guess, a lot in common. She treated me like a sister, and I looked up to her. I thought she was the most beautiful woman, inside and out. As fate happens we ended up starring in Nine the Musical together in 1987,

and we became even closer. Her nickname for me was 'M'.

We have to wait until Episode 40 for our first glimpse of the much loved new Deputy Governor Jim Fletcher, played with testosterone glee by Gerard Maguire. Here was a man's man in a woman's prison. A Vietnam veteran with lots of military experience, he is given the nickname of 'Fletch the Letch' as he has a tendency to take a personal interest in the prettier of his charges. Jim is firm but generally fair, and for the most part supports Erica Davidson's decisions. But there are times when he finds himself piggy in the middle of Erica and Vera's differences. Fletcher would, though, be a staple of the series storylines for the next three years.

Towards the end of the year another unsavoury character surfaced in the shape of ex-Vietnam army colleague of Jim Fletcher, the odious Geoff Butler [78], played with every inch of passion by the one and only Ray Meagher. Ray has been a stalwart of the Australian acting industry for five decades and is now principally known for his twenty-year-plus portrayal of *Summer Bay's* Alf Stewart. Although arriving at the tail end of *Prisoner's* first year on screen, Meagher had plenty of villainy lined up after the post-Christmas break which would result in heartbreaking loss for his former Vietnam colleague.

A major change at the top of the tree saw Ian Bradley step up to oversee the overall production output as Executive Producer from Episode 87; it was this same episode that welcomed a new producer in Philip East. East had already directed a number of episodes of *Prisoner*, and found himself in the

Early set design for the prison reception

Ted Douglas over a three-year period also added to Smith's massive workload. It is clear that Smith must have lived and breathed *Prisoner* for much of the series production at Channel 10. The pressure on all departments to ensure that two hours of television are produced each week is tremendous and Smith would ascend to the lofty position of Associate Producer from 1983 until the show's conclusion.

As the first screen Christmas approaches for the prisoners – in fact, it would be the only screen Christmas during the entire eight years of the series – we get a self written play by the inmates [75] in which they lampoon their captors. Bea slicks back her hair back to become Vera, Lizzie dons a moustache in tribute to Fletch the Letch and Chrissie dolls up as Governor Erica. The scriptwriters would often try to come up with some light relief for viewers in the wake of the substantial drama that was at the core of the show. It was this balance that helped keep *Prisoner* at the top for so long. Without some laughter moments the show would have been pretty grim viewing over the long period it remained on Australia's screens.

driving seat ultimately responsible for the day-to-day production of the series. The final episode of the year also sported a new name on the credits as incoming Script Editor. Ian Smith had already been seen on screen as Departmental Head, Ted Douglas [61 and 66], but now Ian Smith's deft skill of editing and commissioning scripts was felt heavily behind the scenes. Smith can only be described as a key player in *Prisoner's* long-term success. From adopting script-editing duties on this high-pressure show, he went on to write over fifty episodes. Regular appearances as

The end of 1979 saw Karen Travers taking a bullet from a sniper in Dr. Greg's surgery. She is rushed to hospital with fragments of the pellet moving closer to her heart and hovering on the brink of death. A montage of stills and an acoustic rendering of the theme song leave viewers on tenterhooks as to the outcome [79].

HELEN MASTERS

Played by Louise Pajo

First episode: 8
Last episode: 10
Total featured: 3 episodes

Wentworth's first celebrity inmate is initially seen being interviewed on television in her role as an 'International Beauty Consultant' which the women take an interest in. She meets ex-inmate Marilyn Mason on the outside at the hotel where she is working but reports her to management for poor service when Marilyn has problems in opening a bottle of champagne that Helen has ordered to her room.

Helen is arrested following the hit and run killing of a twelve-year-old boy but when she is released on bail she attempts to catch a plane to New Zealand which results in a stretch in prison. Her attitude towards the inmates on her arrival meets with a frosty reception.

She makes an attempt to mix with the women and agrees to share some of her beauty secrets with them and persuades Doreen to forge her business associate's signature on a legal document then is later cleared on the manslaughter charge. Having made numerous promises to the women, they are all made to look like fools when Helen tells the media what she really thinks of them during a TV interview.

Viewers, fearing that the happy ending for Dr. Greg and Karen that they had longed for would be robbed from them, were kept on the edge of their seats over the Christmas festivities. It was a suitable cliff hanger for *Prisoner* to end its first year. The show had proved that Australian audiences were ready for something completely different. Reg Watson and Ian Bradley's faith in their show had been justified as *Prisoner* became a firm fixture in the Channel 10 schedules. A pay dispute with cast members over the length of their break had been settled, with a ten-week suspension of production being cut down to six weeks. Getting through the first year had seen production skills and organisation go from trial-and-error to become a well-oiled machine rolling out two hours of television a week. As plans were laid for a new decade, the show was about to become bigger and bolder with an abundance of exciting characters and storylines to make sure Channel 10 audiences kept their 8:30pm twice weekly date with the staff and inmates of Wentworth.

MONICA FERGUSON

Played by Lesley Baker

First episode: 15
Last episode: 60
Total featured: 35 episodes

Loud and bolshie Monnie arrives in Episode 15 and turns out to be an old friend of Bea's who shared a cell with her before Wentworth was constructed. Much to the dismay of Vera who hoped that Monnie would challenge the Top Dog position, she and Bea appear to be a force to be reckoned with when put together. When Bea finds out that Monnie owns a shop, she suggests it would be a great idea if she let Marilyn and Eddie run it. While Monnie isn't interested at first it turns out to be just what Marilyn needs to put her on the right path, to stop her from getting into trouble again.

Monnie is framed for drug smuggling [18] when she gets involved with Erica's niece Barbara, but later takes over as Top Dog when Bea is in hospital following a stabbing by ex-Officer Anne Yates. Monica's popularity suffers with the other women as the power begins to go to her head [33]. When the women decide they need a new leader, Clara Goddard takes over with Monnie backing her up as the 'muscle'.

With her release to look forward to and a shortage of cash due to her husband's gambling problem, Monnie agrees to help Joyce Martin to hide the proceeds from a payroll robbery to a safe place until she gets out – in return for a cut of the money. Unfortunately for Monnie, Fred's gambling has escalated out of control and he's in more trouble than she originally thought, in addition to seeing another woman, Blossom Crabtree, behind Monnie's back. Blossom steals the money that Monnie has arranged for Fred to pay off his debts and when Monnie finds out she bashes him so a return to Wentworth is on the cards [45].

Monnie becomes the prime suspect for a bashing when child killer Bella Albrecht is found murdered in the shower block [53], following a previous fight in the prison garden. When Martha Eaves is tricked into confessing that she is the guilty party, Monnie is in the clear. She gets herself into hot water, literally, when Martha pours boiling soup onto her in the kitchen [60]. Luckily, she is not too seriously injured and is later released in the same episode.

The Formation of Franky

" I jumped at the offer when I was approached to do Franky. She's a wonderfully interesting character. You can hate her and pity her at the same time. She is a kind of lost soul in a society where the bikie and the lesbian are misfits. "

Carol Burns, TV Week, February 1979

The original actors in *Prisoner* displayed a firm grasp on their characters in a very short period of time, but one actress in particular was about to show the world what *Prisoner* was capable of, and is one of the reasons that the series was catapulted to success from such an early stage.

Carol Burns was perfect as Franky Doyle, a deliciously enriched piece of casting that has since entered realms of television history as one of the best TV characters that Australia has ever produced. Staying with the show for only twenty episodes, Burns' masterful portrayal of Franky heralded more than just another token inmate added to the mix; there was a psychological truth to her performance that would take viewers to a new dimension in terms of enticing them from their sofas to enter this imaginary world 'on the inside'.

Burns' study of the character was so effective that it proved to be a catalyst in bringing the other ensemble to the fore. Each of the fellow actors clearly had abilities and strengths of their own, not to mention a sense of direction for their character, but it was in direct response to Burns' Franky that the fellow crims developed their personalities and behaviour – something that stayed with the series from that moment on. Franky was also the nucleus of Prisoner, one single character that was the beating heart of the show from the moment she arrived. The other characters were peripheral to Franky in her lonely world, and also largely to the viewers who began to realise that the other characters were being established in response to their fear of Franky, not just in the episodes that followed but even after the character's demise.

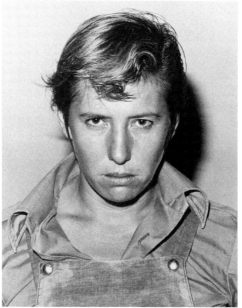

The series opens with chaos, a foot chase with Officers Meg Jackson and Vera Bennett running through the corridors of Wentworth in pursuit of troubled inmate Sally Lee. The powerful first scene is filled with energy, pulses racing and with the viewer unsure of what exactly is going on. They suspect that the officers are chasing an inmate who is potentially about to wreak havoc, and already they are faced with the fight between 'good and bad', officer versus inmate. The chase throughout the prison is our first real introduction to *Prisoner*, but the second and even more powerful introduction that followed is the appearance of Franky who elbows Sally in the ribs and she falls to the stone ground, symbolic of the sheer impact this one character was set to have on the entire series. In many ways, the first scene could be seen to be reflecting the high emotions and physical despair of an intense pregnancy and birth, and unsurprisingly whether it was meant in this fashion or not, the drama of the chase is over in a split second as the sudden impact of Franky's arrival was felt. A television legend had been born.

With the words 'She bumped into me', Franky Doyle launched *Prisoner* onto an unsuspecting public. Frieda Joan Doyle was indeed a figure who was at the very centre of conflict within Wentworth. Doyle was trouble with a capital T. Illiterate and with anger management issues to an extreme, Franky thirsted on getting to the Top Dog position held by her rival Bea Smith. The first indication viewers have of Franky's vile temper is when her reluctant girlfriend Doreen Anderson is removed from sharing a cell. Unable to cope with the decision Franky trashes the Rec Room and winds up in solitary to the great delight of Vera Bennett. However, Franky is not slow to bait Vera right back, coining the phrase 'Vinegar Tits' which would become a legend both in and out of Wentworth for the duration of the programme's popularity. Franky is very much a bully and a predatory lesbian. Karen Travers' arrival is particularly significant for Franky not least because she finds Karen supremely attractive. Initially, Karen is scared of Doyle but as she adjusts to life in Wentworth she stands up to Franky more and more, and this only fuels Franky's fascination with the teacher. Bea Smith's parole is seen as a new beginning. When Bea leaves Wentworth seemingly to start life on the outside after ten long years, Franky knows none of the other women inside are capable of standing up to her; it is the chance that Doyle has been looking for. In every way, the character of Franky Doyle is probably the most important to the formation of those early days in *Prisoner's* history.

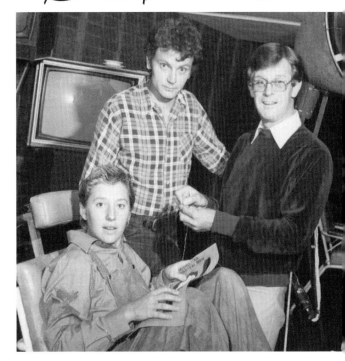

The entire prison is wary of Franky Doyle. The officers know her temper and her ability to cause trouble will always be a problem for the smooth running of Wentworth while those locked in with Doyle are scared of the punishment they might receive if they come into contact with Franky. When it comes to getting her own way, even the older prisoners are not safe from Franky's spitefulness as Lizzie witnesses when her teeth go missing and she is forced to go without food in the dining room until she gives into Franky's demands for a slice of her cigarette rations. Franky's dominance of the prison is short-lived for Bea Smith's parole lasts all of one day before she is brought back into Wentworth for the murder of her wayward husband. The showdown for support within the confines of Wentworth results in the series first riot. It's a brief moment of madness with Franky toppled once again and Meg's husband Bill Jackson stabbed to death. Unusual for a television series to have such a gripping and powerful riot played out so early in its conception, but once again Franky was the nucleus of the action and the riot unfolded as the other inmates responded to their fear of her. Val Lehman's Bea was quickly established as the character that would compete with and challenge Franky, a characterisation that would remain with Bea until her departure almost 400 episodes later.

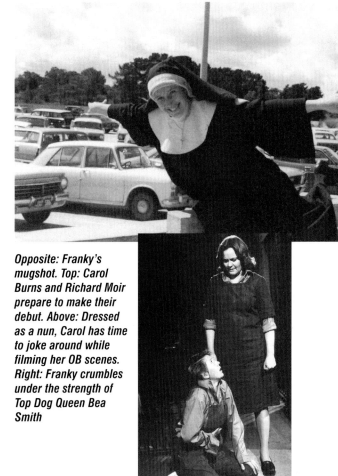

Opposite: Franky's mugshot. Top: Carol Burns and Richard Moir prepare to make their debut. Above: Dressed as a nun, Carol has time to joke around while filming her OB scenes. Right: Franky crumbles under the strength of Top Dog Queen Bea Smith

Lizzie and the other inmates are naturally frightened of Franky and the potential violence that could unfold. Another fine example of how the formation of Franky helped launch the direction of the other characters was evident in Doreen. Doreen idolised Franky's strength and ability to control the women; she was essentially a person with no ambition or drive, but had metamorphic ability inspired by others around her. She would imitate and copy others as she was so uncertain of her own identity. This would be a personality trait of Doreen's that would emerge once again in the wake of Franky's demise when she adopts the same physical style of Franky in an attempt to intimidate the women, but she fails miserably. Much later in the series, Doreen is seen being successful and living in Sydney, but even here she once again becomes an extension of the people and the situations around her.

Franky does however have a weak spot. Out of the blue, her 16-year-old brother Gary turns up, having moved out of the orphanage and started a life for himself with a job and a room of his own. Their life together has not been easy. Franky left school at 11 and she had to deal with a drunken and abusive father who would often take his temper out on her Mum and younger brother. She was forced into getting a job to try and provide for her closest family, and eventually drifted into a life of crime to try and stay afloat. Gary offers Franky the hope of a new life. He plans to run a farm out in the country and slowly persuades his sister

that they can make a go of it together – if only she could stay out of trouble, as she might be free in three years. Staying out of trouble won't be easy, but Franky realises that this might possibly be a chance of a new beginning for her, away from the power struggles of the penal system. Gary is Franky's Achilles heel – a brother she loves and would do anything for. Fate, however, is not going to be kind to the Doyles. Gary is involved in a farm accident and it is only Franky's inability to read a note that is passed to her that stops her getting to the hospital before Gary passes away. It is one blow too many. The hard faced and tough jailbird ends up on the very roof of Wentworth ready to throw herself off. It is Karen Travers who manages to talk Franky down, thus in Franky's eyes creating a further bond with the beautiful and intelligent newcomer to the prison. It is when Karen tries to teach Doyle to read that we see the true nature of the affection being displayed towards Karen by her pupil. It backfires and the rejection fuels Franky into an escape attempt

BEHIND THE CAMERA: Ken Mullholland's Memories:

1979 – FRANKY'S FAREWELL

I'm not sure whether Carol Burns had any more location scenes to do, but I can recall her last moments in Studio B. At that time the cast and crew didn't have a Green Room, (that was specially built later when the show had proved its worth) and instead had their very rough facilities: toilets, wardrobe and possibly make-up down in what was known as The Tunnel. This was literally a below ground tunnel built in the original design of the Channel. It was entered through a cutting from the car park and was used to bring audiences into both Studios A and B via staircases. In its heyday it boasted seating, public toilets and a snack bar. By the time of *Prisoner* the area just past the first stairway was walled off and used by the cast alone.

I'm fairly sure they had tea and coffee and a hot water urn and a fridge where they kept the Cardboard Handbag. If you don't know, ask Ellie Ballantyne what that is and I bet you'll get a smile in return.

In any event, I'm quite sure the remaining cast had marked Carol's final studio night with some bubbly before they all went home.

All except for Carol.

Upstairs in Studio B there were only two crew members left still winding up cables and fiddling about with equipment. One was a very good audio boom operator Paul Covington and the other was me.

The Studio was lit only by the house lights and the sets were all in semi-darkness when Carol emerged through the audience doors; now of course dressed in street attire, small and quiet and so un-Franky, to find two guys still there, yakking about the day's work or whatever. I can't remember the exact conversation, but I'm pretty sure she thanked us and asked us to pass on her fond regards to all the crew.

I got the distinct feeling that she just didn't want to let go of the studio and its atmosphere; after all she had been a dominating force there for quite some time and it was a defining point in her career – one that brought her face and presence sharply before the television viewing public. On the other hand I guess that she didn't want to be typecast in the Franky-mould because, of course, she was a much more proficient actor commanding a range of stage and screen roles before and after *Prisoner*.

I do recall her asking if Paul and I would like a drink down at the hotel while she waited for her cab.

Sadly we both declined, because it was probably a Thursday, and we would both be fronting up to the studio ten or eleven hours later for another long day. We worked seven in the morning to nine or ten at night back then.

We said our goodbyes.

I can't say for sure what happened then, but I should like to think that both of us made our exit, leaving Carol alone with the studio.

with Doreen and Lizzie. After several days on the run, Franky dies after being shot by a policeman. Her final words on the planet: 'Bloody bastards'.

Franky's life was tragic and one which viewers could easily sympathise with. That is squarely down to the fine playing by Carol Burns. An experienced 31-year-old theatre actress when *Prisoner* started recording, Burns took the nucleus of the character off the page and turned it into a dazzling performance of quiet brooding, with frequent flashes of violence and not a little sarcastic wit. Her Franky laugh is now legendary, sounding like a psychotic hyena. Her performance readily set the standard for all the no-gooders that were to follow in Wentworth. Burns' Franky operated on so many levels. Her look of brooding hatred conveyed more emotion than other actresses might be able to establish in a whole speech. It is little wonder that Franky Doyle rose above the other characters to become a cult in her own

right. It took twenty episodes for the story of Franky Doyle to be played out before the eager audience on Channel 10. No other character has left such a lasting impression with *Prisoner's* devoted worldwide fan base with so few episodes to their name. Carol about her brief time working on *Prisoner*:

I was known as a theatre actress and had ten year plus career already behind me. I'd done television, but never for a commercial channel or a producer like Grundy. My television work had been for the national broadcaster, the ABC, and drama or mini-series on the ABC were only watched by aficionados in those days. So I came to the audition as a relative unknown. I returned to the theatre for Marsupials soon after my short stint on Prisoner and then went back to the ABC for another couple of contracts. Later I

Carol Burns

worked for Crawford Productions, another high profile commercial producer. There were a lot of actresses I knew auditioning for all sorts of parts in Prisoner. I know that another Queensland actress, Carole (with an 'e' unlike me) Skinner was auditioning for Franky as well. The actual process is a blur, as are most auditions. They are stressful things and best forgotten as soon as you've done them so that if you get the job it's a nice surprise. If you don't get the job you never hear from the producers anyway, such are the manners of the industry. Actors always wish each other well, as I did Carole, who was going to test after me. I think it was Ian Bradley who asked me when I was offered the job if I was prepared to be the most hated woman on television. Of course I said yes, so long as I was allowed in the scripts to show why she was so belligerent. When you do that everyone learns to understand and you aren't hated but loved. Franky became one of the most loved characters in the series. I've never known whether Franky should be spelt with a 'y' or an 'ie'. The fans will know. They always know more about a series than the people in it because they follow it each episode. I never did. As a working actress it's always more fun to be in it than watch it. The fun comes from the people you work with. I always prepare well and pay attention when I'm working because I want to be proud of whatever I do. Just as well; when you're asked to look back over thirty years you don't want to be ashamed of anything. The crew were the crème de la crème. They were kindness itself and some of them stayed with the show for years. The poor directors are always

frantically busy up in the biobox so it's the people on the floor that you get to relate to more and they help you a lot with a nod or a wink to let you know if you're where you should be and if they liked your performance. No one person stands out in my mind as more impressive than another. It was an ensemble show and we all played into the scene as it were rather than for self-aggrandisement. In the storylines, the writers would highlight one characters plight over another so that one episode would have more to do with them than another. But even if you only had a little to do, or were in the background of a shot, you still had to be focused and true. If I did have to pick someone as most impressive, I suppose it would be Sheila Florance for her sheer stamina. No matter what was asked of her she would have a go – a true professional. When you've worked with an actress like Sheila and then with youngsters who complain about being tired at the end of the second ten hour day of the week when you're not even half way through the week, that attitude is annoying. The abiding joy of the Prisoner series for me was the camaraderie. I was only in it for a short time, nineteen episodes, before they increased the workload even further. The pleasure was in how every department worked together in those early days. Wardrobe and make-up were stuck in a tunnel, the shifts for the crew were long and arduous, the actors called for hours on end either waiting or on the floor, the writers trying to keep up with characters and events. It was hard graft but very satisfying. The series was and is great entertainment. Long may its memory be green!

BEHIND THE CAMERA: Ken Mullholland's Memories:

'What's going on here? Clean up that mess or you'll be on a charge!' Want to know what went on behind the scenes when Franky Doyle went bananas in the prison canteen? Well, I'll tell you. I know, because I was there. It was decided by the director, Graeme Arthur, that we could only shoot the scene once because of the time factor. We worked a very tight schedule. So, being a multi-cam set-up, three video-tape machines were booked, each linked to one of our cameras so the scene could be taped from three different viewpoints. We talked it through as to what would happen leading up to the violence and what would happen in the aftermath. Having rehearsed the beginning and end with the principal cast, the non-speaking extras were brought onto the set and we began the one and only take of that scene.

All went fine up to the point where Carol Burns, as Franky, erupted into her rampage. Then it was everybody for themselves. The smashing plates and cups were real; the thrown chairs and overturned tables were real. Carol Burns wasn't real, but Franky Doyle sure was. My camera, a fairly large one mounted on a pedestal, was my protection from the shattering debris. And when all the flying crockery and furniture came to a halt, we heard the 'real' crying of a non-speaking extra that had not gotten out of the set and was in fact sheltering behind a table on its side. She was obviously shell-shocked by Carol's so realistic and prolonged outburst and was led out of the studio sobbing. Carol herself was pretty exhausted and I doubt that she could have done justice to another take. The scene was later edited together from sections of all three videos.

But What About My Baby, Bea?

The Life And Times Of Chrissie Latham

Joan: You're not going anywhere, Latham, until you tell me what's going on around here… answer me, you bitch!
Chrissie: Ain't you worked it out yet? As far as we're concerned you're dead, and we can't take orders from a dead screw, now can we?
Joan: You'll never get away with it, the other officers will…
Chrissie: The other officers will think we're darling little angels. We do everything that we're told. But you… you're history, lady!

Chrissie Latham, a prostitute first seen in Episode 3, is swiftly transferred out to Fairlea after being found guilty of murdering prison social worker Bill Jackson with a pair of scissors during a riot.

For obvious reasons she makes an instant enemy of Meg Jackson and the other prisoners, who are shocked and upset at one of the prison's most popular staff members having his life cut short because he didn't reciprocate Chrissie's sexual advances. At first, the murderer's identity isn't known but when electrician Eddie Cook admits that he saw who killed Bill, the women take things into their own hands and force Chrissie to admit the truth after a very radical forced hair cut…

She isn't seen again until an unexpected return from Barnhurst [65] where she is inducted as Christine Margaret Latham by Meg, who is horrified to see her back at Wentworth. Chrissie wastes no time in bragging to the other women about her sexual conquests while at Barnhurst and claims to have had affairs with both male prisoners and the prison Governor during her time away. She taunts Meg about Bill and tells her that she should have killed *her* instead [67]. The women decide to ignore Chrissie and so 'send her to Coventry' along with getting her in trouble with the officers.

When a bottle of medicine goes missing from the prison hospital, it is revealed that Chrissie is the robber and has been trying to make herself sick to disguise the fact that she thinks she is pregnant. When her fears are confirmed

by the doctor, she instantly decides that she would like to have an abortion, but has her mind changed after spending some time working in the maternity wing. She's in trouble after a fight [72] resulting in a punch to the stomach and it is feared that Chrissie could lose her baby, but surprisingly Meg comforts her while she is being checked out and luckily the baby is fine. Chrissie's pregnancy initiates a huge turning point in the relationship between the two of them and although the prospect of becoming a mother would eventually result in Chrissie becoming more mature, her behaviour at the prison continues to be erratic.

Inmate Ros Coulson escapes from the prison [83] and the authorities ask the women if they know anything about it. Chrissie decides to come forward and spill the beans in return for some remission to her sentence for sharing the information, but Ros is quickly

Portrait of Chrissie Latham, played by Amanda Muggleton

found and returned. After further squabbling between Chrissie and the other women something has to give and during another scuffle Chrissie is shoved out of the way resulting in premature contractions. She is rushed to hospital [93] to slow down the process but nothing can be done and she gives birth early. She wakes from heavy sedation to find that she now has a baby girl whom she names Elizabeth, after Lizzie Birdsworth. Unfortunately, her happiness is short lived as she has to return to Wentworth alone while Elizabeth stays at hospital for the foreseeable future as she requires constant medical attention due to being born so early.

Newly inducted Sharon Gilmour appears to seduce Chrissie and the two team up to bring drugs into the prison [95] but when Sharon's girlfriend Judy Bryant finds out what's going on she conspires to be an inmate herself. Any brief fling between Sharon and Chrissie is over before it has begun. When the prison authorities get to learn of the new drugs trade, Erica puts pressure on Chrissie to tell all in return for more visits to Elizabeth. She agrees to stay away from Sharon and confides in Judy that she prefers men anyway [100].

During a visit to the hospital, Chrissie gets the news that she has been waiting for so long. Elizabeth has made excellent progress and will soon be strong enough to stay with her. However, a full psychological assessment and Governor's report shows that good behaviour is the only way that this will be allowed to happen. Chrissie vows to stay out of trouble, but this promise doesn't last for long. Judy and Sharon

have an argument and Chrissie tries to stop Judy from attacking Sharon by breaking a chair over her head. Unfortunately for Chrissie, Erica tells her that the Department had granted permission to move Elizabeth to Chrissie but, in the light of this latest attack, she is now having second thoughts [102]. It is a tense wait for Chrissie as Erica decides to wait until Judy has recovered before a decision is made. Judy tells Erica everything and manages to get her to reconsider telling the Department about the incident so finally Elizabeth arrives at the prison and Chrissie proudly shows her off to the women [103] before getting transferred to the Maternity wing.

We catch up with Chrissie some time later in the Maternity wing itself where Doreen has been transferred to help out [151]. Although Doreen's help is appreciated, she is beginning to get on the mothers' nerves and there is a bit of friction between them all. However, when the women allow a stray cat into the prison, Doreen saves Elizabeth's life when the cat is found to be sitting on top of the baby in her cot. She performs mouth-to-mouth resuscitation on the little girl and her presence in the Maternity wing is then appreciated by everyone. Doreen is later allowed to work at the local hospital's children's ward when granted parole, following the care and attention she has demonstrated whilst at Wentworth.

With Elizabeth's first birthday approaching, Chrissie is worried that when she turns one year old the authorities will take the child away from her. This

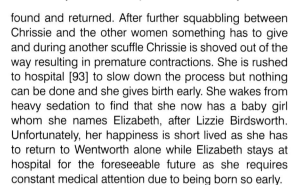

BELLA ALBRECHT

Played by Liddy Clarke
First episode: 51
Last episode: 52
Total featured: 2 episodes

Mystery surrounds this new prisoner who arrives at Wentworth in secrecy [50]. The women's daily schedule is interrupted and the television is taken away. However, when Bella demands to be let out of solitary she is transferred to the women but her crime is kept a secret. Inevitably, such secrets cannot be kept. Prison visitor Peter Clements is tricked into confirming that Bella killed her own child [51] in a particularly horrific case which sparks war.

Bella fears for her life and is befriended by Martha Eaves [52] who decides to become her 'protector'. Unfortunately, Martha can't be around her all of the time and Bella is attacked in the garden by Monnie. When Martha overhears Bella making fun of her to Karen, she decides to leave her unprotected and her ex-friend is attacked in the shower block, murdered by drowning. With Monnie being the prime suspect it is later revealed that Martha is in fact the murderer when she is tricked into admitting what she has done.

worries Doreen too and when Elizabeth is sent to hospital for tests on her breathing, Doreen decides that the risk of Chrissie losing her is too great and kidnaps her out of the hospital. Taking refuge in her late mother's home, Elizabeth's condition begins to deteriorate; she is in need of urgent care. Doreen uses a false name at the hospital and brings Elizabeth in to see a nurse but detectives have already arrived and luckily the child gets the attention she needs. Doreen is sent back to Wentworth to face a distraught Chrissie [157]. Initially threatening to kill Doreen for what she has done, Chrissie realises that Doreen thought she was doing the right thing by stopping Elizabeth from going into a home, so forgives her.

Sadly, Elizabeth is taken away from Chrissie [167] after her first birthday party which is held at the prison. She has a couple of photographs taken with her before it is time to hand her over to Child Welfare. Crazy inmate Anne Griffin steals the photos and Chrissie attacks her, resulting in Chrissie being transferred to a different block of the prison.

Chrissie is released on parole and sets up home with Elizabeth's father, Mick O'Brien [191]. However, she doesn't stick to the rules on when she can visit her daughter so the police are called when she doesn't return

Elizabeth back on time after a day-visit. Unfortunately for Chrissie, this leads to Mick being recognised as escapee Mark Brendan and he is sent back to prison himself. This leaves Chrissie alone but she later moves in with her brother Derek and his wife Brenda [197]. Before this, we learn that Chrissie was sexually abused by her father when she was a child. She hasn't had a great deal of contact with Derek because her father was living with him and Brenda until his recent death.

Almost a hundred episodes later, Chrissie returns and is spotted by Meg as she is signing on the dole at the local employment office [285]. Chrissie's main focus is Elizabeth and she's trying all that she can to get enough money saved up so she can start a new life with her away from Derek and Brenda. She steals money from the boss of the local pub after sleeping with him and flees. Taking Elizabeth with her, she packs her bags and heads to the airport but Brenda tells the police and they catch her at the airport and arrest her for breaking the terms of her parole agreement and for Social Security fraud. She's back in the slammer once more and has to explain to Bea and the others what has gone wrong this time [287].

Still with Elizabeth being at the front of her mind, she is determined to do all that she can to stop Brenda

Left: Playing the pregnant Chrissie, Amanda looks like a convincing mother to be.
Inset: Chrissie with Meg Jackson in the Rec Room

gaining custody of her. She attempts to blackmail male prison officer Steve Fawkner into helping, but when he isn't able to, she accuses him of rape. The allegation is swiftly revoked and she even tries her luck with Joan Ferguson. However, Joan prefers to see Chrissie lose everything and so tells Brenda that she'll act as a character witness against Chrissie. After an escape attempt goes wrong with Hannah Simpson, Chrissie returns to Wentworth and is severely beaten by Joan [298], resulting in serious injuries and a stay in hospital. This time Joan blackmails Chrissie into not lagging – with Elizabeth as the bait.

The arrival of prison nurse Neil Murray [305] sees Chrissie fall in love once more. It appears that he feels the same and takes a special interest in her, even arranging a day on the outside for her while she's meant to be undergoing tests at the hospital [315]. However, Neil has an ulterior motive after finding out about Chrissie's past as a prostitute. He kidnaps Chrissie and tells her he's going to kill her. Luckily, Steve makes the connection between Neil and a number of recent prostitute murders and Chrissie's life is saved when Neil is shot by the police in his country hideout where he has held her captive. He is sent to Woodridge prison [316] but Chrissie bumps into him once more when rehearsing for the charity concert to be held there with the Wentworth women [320]. Her life is saved again, this time by Andy Hudson, when Neil is set up to kill her.

Neil: You're a whore! Whore! You came here to sell your body, you slut! The Lord will sell your soul for it!
Chrissie: It's not true, it's not true… You stupid bastard, you poor stupid bastard! They were using you. Do you hear me? They were using you! Duncan Campbell wanted me dead; Benny set me up so you did their dirty work!'

Chrissie meets with Neil one last time and almost loses her life again [320]

Following the events of the Wentworth fire, Joan Ferguson continues to make life difficult for Chrissie until finally, behind the Governor's back, she arranges to have Chrissie shipped off to Barnhurst [338]. The last we see of Chrissie Latham is her kicking and screaming as she is dragged away to the waiting police car to transport her to the country prison where doubtless the incumbent Governor Vera Bennett will have a special welcome for her.

Amanda Muggleton talks to MeetThePlayer.com. au (February 2011)

I'm always terrified, and I think if you're not always terrified there's something wrong. I suppose I'm an adrenaline junkie because what happens to you is unbelievable, before an opening. You're so keyed up, you've worked so many weeks to get this thing right – and your biggest fear is that you're going to get it wrong…

British-born actress Amanda Muggleton moved to Australia in the 1970s following her training in London at the Guildhall School of Music and Drama and the prestigious Royal Academy of Dance.

While *Prisoner* is undoubtedly her most famous role, Amanda's career as an actress has been non-stop. Playing the recurring role of Chrissie Latham for over 100 episodes paved the way for Amanda to demonstrate her versatility both on stage and on screen. She was able to return to her prison role in between other jobs, thanks to a considerate and flexible production team on the Grundy TV show. She made guest appearances in *Holiday Island*, *Women of the Sun* and *A Country Practice* through the early 1980s and literally jumped out of one character straight into another one during that time. She also returned to a very Chrissie-like role for Grundy Television and a screen reunion with Maggie Kirkpatrick as part of the cast of *Richmond Hill* in 1988.

Amanda has become a much loved and sought-after theatre actress, having played the lead role in a number of productions including Shirley Valentine as well as major parts in shows such as Steaming, Annie and more recently the 2010 Australian tour of Calendar Girls where she played the part of Chris. She has won significant awards for her stage work including two Helpmann Awards for Best Actress (Master Class) and Best Female Actor in a Supporting Role (Eureka!). She has starred alongside other critically acclaimed stars such as Magda Szubanski and Natalie Bassingthwaighte in the 2011 production of Love, Loss and What I Wore at the Sydney Opera House where she played multiple roles and closed the year playing the part of Mrs Johnstone in Blood Brothers, written by Willy Russell, which was a long-term ambition of Amanda's.

Amanda became so busy in 2011 that she had to resign from her additional role as Director of the Scene and Heard Acting School. Her professional commitments and demand for theatre and television jobs meant that she was unable to dedicate enough time to this important cause. Amanda has continued to support the school as Patron and Creative Director, helping shape aspiring actors of the future.

Muggleton Memories

Amanda Remembers

Make Love Not War – the two Governors collide...

On my first day at the studios, it was quite competitive in the Green Room. People were still sorting out who was going to be number one, who was going to be the most popular, who was going to have the funniest stories... You could smoke back then so it was full of smoke, which was horrible because I had never smoked so I hated that side of it. It was very cramped. We were all in a room full of dirty posters and chairs. It just wasn't glamorous at all. They had no idea of how popular this show was going to be. At one end of the room was the wardrobe department run by the

fantastic Jennifer Carmen who, in actual fact, was a belly dancer. We used to go to the club where she performed, a Lebanese restaurant, to see her strut her stuff and she so wanted to be a performer, but she was the wardrobe mistress on *Prisoner*. The other person who started out in the Wardrobe Department was Maura Fay who is no longer with us, but she ended up having her own casting agency. It definitely felt special. For once, it was a television show for women about women. That had never happened in Australia. Before that, they were all cop shows with these butch men in them. We were just handbags, prostitutes or wives. You had very little to do. I remember years ago in *Cop Shop*, I was a bashed up wife. It was always those types of roles.

When *Prisoner* came to the fore, every woman in Australia wanted to be in it. You knew you had to be special to have been picked. To get the job in the first place I pushed my way in to the auditions on the coattails of Nano Nagle who was up for the role of Val Lehman's sister. She had the same colouring, fair skin and red hair. I couldn't get an audition. My agent at the time said to me, 'Oh no, you are a theatre actress.' And I couldn't understand that. I am an actress. I don't claim to specialise in anything. My agent said they had been told not to send anyone who had no experience with camera work. So, anyway, I forced my way in to the auditions which was really nerve-racking. It was a cattle call and you had to queue. Your bottoms went to the next seat, then the next seat. Eventually, they got through

The perfect family? Chrissie with Baby Elizabeth and Mick O'Brien (Michael Long).

the list, found out I wasn't on it and were going to throw me out. So I flipped out a bit and said, 'How dare you! I have queued here for an hour all keyed up to do an audition...' So I was taken in to see Ian Bradley who looked at me for the part of Marilyn. He eventually told me I wasn't right for Marilyn but there was another character called Chrissie Latham who would be in the show for two episodes, principally to kill Bill Jackson. I don't even think they knew at that stage how he was going to be killed, using the scissors. So, when I got into the Green Room, I felt a bit naughty knowing I had got the part through stealth really and cunning. Thank goodness I had the chutzpah to do it. When you are young you are fearless. There is a line in Shirley Valentine which says: 'When I was a girl I used to jump off our roof just for fun. Now I get vertigo just standing up in me high heeled shoes.' And I think that is what happens. As you get older, you are fearful of being out there. But at the same time you have more confidence. I am

much more aware of my talent now than I was then. Grundy phoned my agent after it went to air, and I was off doing lots of other things like working for the Melbourne Theatre Company, saying they would like to offer Amanda Muggleton a regular role.

I really resented giving my agent the commission because she was the one who wouldn't let me go. I went to another agent and told them what happened and asked if they would represent me. I really resented paying the commission for work that hadn't been earned. Not that there was a lot. In those days we were paid NOTHING. I think I was paid $350 a week or something. If you were in all four hours of television, you would get double. That was the same with all of the original cast. You would get a week when you were constantly on screen then you'd get three weeks when you were in it, but not really. Then they could be really cunning about it so you weren't in more than two episodes unless it was your storyline but you might just be in the background. So

ROSLYN LOUISE COULSON

Played by Sigrid Thornton

First episode: 63
Last episode: 92
Total featured: 30 episodes

An idealistic young woman, Ros first appears at Wentworth demanding to see Toni McNally – the woman who killed her mother – but when she shoots Toni outside the courthouse she arrives back at the prison as a criminal [64]. She faces life imprisonment when she finds out that Toni has died because of her injuries and thus begins a very depressing time for Ros, even contemplating ending her life.

She escapes from prison in the back of a typewriter van [72] during a fire alarm which she has purposely arranged, ending up at the Halfway House and is told in no uncertain terms by Karen Travers that she isn't welcome. She stays the night and ends up working at a massage parlour but steals some money from the boss in the hope that she will be able to buy a bus ticket so she can travel further away. As bad luck would have it, just as she is about to board the bus, a man collapses in front of her with chest pains and as she helps him she is spotted by a member of the public who alerts the police. Ros returns to the prison and is sent straight to solitary [74].

As Ros continues to battle with the other inmates and officers, the thoughts of escape are always in her mind. She becomes friendly with new arrival Janet Dominguez who is arranging an escape of her own, so Ros decides she wants to be involved. With the plan in motion, Governor Erica Davidson gets in the way and is shot in the arm when the two women are making their getaway [82]. Janet is also shot but Ros manages to make it to freedom although it is very short lived as she is captured and returned to the prison after a short spell on the outside.

Education becomes Ros's saving grace. Realising that she can't battle against the system forever, she decides to study and finally calms down, transferred out of H Block [92] to concentrate on her future.

EP 197   SC 23 D2
CHRISSIE LATHAM,

Above: Continuity photograph from Episode 197 shows Amanda in high spirits.

you wouldn't be paid, even though you were working your arse off!

I always loved Val Lehman's performance. She was so natural and right for that role. She would throw lines away and so many actors don't know how to do that. Most actors hang onto every word they are given so that they give too much value to everything, but Val had the ability to throw stuff away. She was always on the ball thinking about props and actions she was doing, really reading between the lines. Watching Val was a real lesson for me.

I didn't base Chrissie on anyone in particular. Difficulties came when they took on new writers with fantasies about your character and you'd get the script and say, hey, no way! That's why soap opera is brilliant for you as an actor. Back then, all the drama schools were telling people not to go into a soap as you'd never work again. But now they can't wait to get into them.

A typical day on *Prisoner* would start at 5:30am. If you were on the first scene which was about 7:00am, if it was an outside scene with light you could be filming by 6.00am. If it was your full storyline you'd be up at 5:30am. You needed to get yourself out to the studio, take your jewellery off, and the wardrobe people would control exactly what you had to wear. We'd be filming out of sequence so you had to have many changes every day. It was very hard work on everyone, the crew, props department, wardrobe, make-up; in the

make-up chair you'd be in there for two minutes then off! For me, they allowed me to have a bit of 'eyes on' and that was it. It didn't matter what you did. Vivienne Popplewell was tough. We were all in the toilets with eyelash curlers and with vaseline, trying to get a bit of blusher happening by pinching our cheeks.

But that was the gift of *Prisoner*. The majority of women just don't go around with a full face of make-up on. I used to lose my patience early in the morning when you'd have runny eyes, and you'd have to be glammed up when you went out for OB work so early in the morning. The make-up artists are as sleepy as you then and, if make-up got in your eyes, you'd spend the whole day with a weepy eye. It was hideous. Peta Toppano did have blusher and any tricks we could get away with we tried, but they were constantly wiping it off.

I loved scenes in the canteen. It wasn't hot but I loved acting with food. I loved the shower scenes, with us all in boob tubes. The fight scenes really got our adrenaline running. I loved scenes going mad and throwing things. I loved the scene with Michael Long (Mick) in our flat when Chrissie starts throwing things.

Chrissie was a fabulous role. I think the writers saw I could be very dramatic but also do comedy. That's something Val Lehman also does very well. Poor old Kerry Armstrong – 'I'm innocent!' – what a horrible part. And Colette with her teddy bear – there wasn't an awful lot for her to do, aside from when she got into the Halfway House there was some good stuff. I felt blessed with the good scripts I had. Denise Morgan and Dave Worthington were brilliant. I really sensed they cared for Chrissie and they would write things for me that they knew I'd like doing and get good at carrying it off. I loved doing 'outside broadcast' and I never got enough of it. I was always a show off and I loved doing outside scenes where the public would stop and stare. They always kept me in the prison. Good value I suppose. It was a funny, pathetic, bitchy, fabulous role.

Who would I have wanted to play other than Chrissie? Well, I loved Franky Doyle. Carol absolutely went for that role and was perfect. I loved to watch her. And Sheila Florance, who had been around so long. Val, Sheila and Carol were my favourites in terms of what I could glean from them. I think Franky was a fabulous role. I don't think I could have done Val's role. You get what you are given and it's meant to be. I was glad I didn't get Marilyn in a way, as there wasn't an awful lot for you to do after that.

I loved the way they let me come in and out of the show. I never got stale as Chrissie. To leave and come back meant I added another dimension to Chrissie and was fresher. I didn't ever watch the show as I just never had time, so it's lovely for me to watch it now. When you're in it, you say to yourself I need to watch myself, but after a few weeks you don't have time as you're learning lines and you don't stop.

Listings magazine ads from the USA to promote the series in 1979.

So many have since passed away. Arkie Whiteley [Donna Mason] was lovely. Gerda Nicolson was simply marvellous. Fiona Spence had hardly done any acting before Prisoner, and she just went straight into 'Vinegar Tits'. I think she was actually better than 'The Freak'.

When they realised they were onto a winner they kept pouring money into it. The crew were fantastic. They never made you feel that they had seen it all before. The ones who they really trusted and knew could do the acting and that you wouldn't fluff your lines, they would leave your scenes to near the end, perhaps 6:45pm, as the plugs on the cameras would have to be pulled and be taken to do the news. So you had to finish at a strict time. There were some who wouldn't get their lines right. Julieanne Newbould was always very good at lines, as was Val. We'd be called in to do one scene in the morning and all our stuff was in the afternoon. It was too far to go home and back to Nunawading again so you would basically stay there all day. One day they explained why. It would be because they didn't trust particular actors to get a scene right as the sequence of the day was mapped out, and you didn't get many shots at it. If it wasn't right first time you'd be lucky to get a second and a third time. On the one occasion when I did a scene with Julieanne it took seventeen takes! Kendal Flanagan was directing and the scene was like a Monty Python sketch. They had to change the dialogue in the end as we simply couldn't do it for laughing.

ANTONIA MCNALLY

Played by Pat Bishop

First episode: 57
Last episode: 64
Total featured: 8 episodes

Wife of gangster Sean McNally, Toni kills her husband's lover Jackie Coulson in a bar with a single gunshot [57]. She is brought straight to Wentworth and shows the women just how powerful she is by taking over the press from Monnie immediately, then paying Kathleen Leach to operate it for her. Money buys everything in Toni's eyes and she is quite happy to buy the women's co-operation without giving it a second thought. She appears to receive special treatment from the Department because of her connections on the outside, much to the dismay of Vera. She becomes more popular with the women when she makes Vera look silly when drugs are suspected to be in the prison and they can't be found [59].

Erica resigns as Governor due to all of the special favours that Toni is being treated to [61] but is persuaded to take three weeks leave instead. Meanwhile the witness to Toni's crime is being pursued in the hope that she can be silenced before the court trial. A surprise visit by Jackie Coulson's daughter Roslyn gives Toni the brief glimpse of a face she will see again very soon. When Toni's trial concludes in her favour, her release is to be very short lived. While she is celebrating, minutes after the 'not guilty' verdicts have been read, she is shot at point blank range by Roslyn [63]. She later dies in hospital and Roslyn takes her place at Wentworth.

DOCTOR ERIC WEISSMAN

Played by Byron Williams

First episode: 28
Last episode: 589
Total featured: 30 episodes

Aside from Meg Morris, Dr Weissman is probably Wentworth's longest serving character and stayed with the series for a number of years while only appearing in a relatively short number of episodes.

He mainly specialises in psychoanalysis of the inmates to check on their mental state, sometimes arranging for them to be transferred to a mental institution but in some cases manages to cure their problems for good. In the early days, Dr Weissman assists with Susan Rice, Ros Coulson, Rosie Hudson, Doreen Burns and even the great Bea Smith during her famous amnesia phase [201].

Eric, also called Carl at one point [203], has a particular success with hypnotherapy. He manages to cure Paddy Lawson of her fear of claustrophobia and more impressively treats Laura Gardiner for her many split personalities in a particularly memorable storyline. This culminates with Laura being free of her demons and apparently ready to live a normal life in a short space of time [382]. He is last seen with Reb Kean [589] who is about to face life on the outside after finally getting released.

Incidentally, actor Byron Williams is also responsible for writing almost thirty episodes of the series.

CHAPTER FOUR
1980
Episodes 80 to 165

The first year of *Prisoner* had been a rollercoaster ride of violence, emotions and frustrations. The viewers had been treated to a nail biting cliff-hanger over the Christmas holiday season as Karen lies unconscious in her hospital bed with fragments of the bullet which shot her nearing her heart.

But she survives and is sent to recuperate in Queensland, and it is the end of Karen's journey and Peta Toppano's admirable contribution to the show. Viewers had identified with Karen's plight and her attempts to get a life back after the traumas of the stabbing and the subsequent trial. 1979 had been the year of *Prisoner* finding its feet before the television audience, toying with concepts and characters, relationships and high drama. Lessons had perhaps been learned along the way in both areas of production and scripting. With the arrival of a new decade, the production team on *Prisoner* now had feedback on what the audience liked and, perhaps more importantly, what they didn't. The trio of Bea, Lizzie and Doreen had particularly risen in popularity and future storylines were set to reflect this. But three characters a series does not make, and new producer Philip East had plenty of ideas for keeping the audience on the edge of its seat for the twice weekly Channel 10 visits to Wentworth. The prison gained a new social worker in the guise of rugged George Mallaby as pipe smoking Paul Reid. Mallaby would go on to write twelve episodes of the series in his other role as a sought-after television scriptwriter.

For the first time *Prisoner* found itself represented at the prestigious Logie Awards, presented by Bert Newton from the Hilton Hotel in Sydney. In a swish ceremony on Friday 14th March 1980, the show picked up the 'Best New Drama Series' gong and Carol Burns was rewarded for her exquisite portrayal of Franky by being bestowed with the 'Best Lead Actress in a Series' honour. It was indeed the boost that all involved needed. It had been a risk getting *Prisoner* to the air but the audience reaction more than justified the initial reservations some Channel 10 top brass had voiced

Top: Gerard Maguire smiles during takes of a corridor scene. Bottom: Sigrid Thornton as Ros Coulson.

on the eve of transmission. With viewing figures very healthy and awards under its belt, *Prisoner* was very much now running in the top league.

The arrival of Sharon Gilmour [Margot Knight, 90] and Judy Bryant [Betty Bobbitt, 91] would prove a real watershed for *Prisoner*. Gilmour has been peddling drugs and gets busted and subsequently transferred to Wentworth. Her loyal taxi-driving girlfriend Judy Bryant gets caught up in Gilmour's mind games and in order to be near her young lover deliberately gets herself caught smuggling drugs into the prison during a visit, ensuring her own incarceration. Once again, lesbian relationships were tackled head on, for the first time since Franky's unrequited crush on Karen Travers. Gilmour was a heap of spoilt, manipulative trouble. Judy and Sharon are polar opposites, the former caring and loyal while Gilmour would seize any opportunity that came her way, lying and stealing in order to satisfy whatever need she has.

An influx of new characters paraded across screens and, in a perhaps unexpected move, there was a love interest for Bea Smith. Ken Pearce, played by *Number 96* star Tom Oliver, is a reformed prisoner turned teacher. Ken's wayward daughter Debbie [Dina Mann] gets sent to prison to experience what life is like inside in order to deter her from following in her father's footsteps. Ian Bradley explained the inspiration behind the storyline to TV Week:

> *We have based this storyline on Scared Straight, the documentary that followed a group of delinquent children into prison. When the kids were exposed to the harsh reality of prison life they received such a shock that any romantic notions they may have had were quickly swept away.*

The decision by Reg Grundy Productions to re-edit the material and present *The Franky Doyle Story* as a two-hour tele-movie destined for the overseas market sparked a very vocal reaction from those involved. Having received no consultation or indeed fee for work being included in the new feature length compilation, the entire cast went on strike and stayed away from rehearsals and recording for a full two days as the argument raged between the actors' union Equity and Grundy. An Arbitration Commission was applied for with Colette Mann and George Mallaby nominated on behalf of the cast to fly to the hearing in Sydney. The following day Grundy had to accept most

KERRY VINCENT

Played by Penny Downie

First episode: 112
Last episode: 124
Total featured: 12 episodes

Talented artist Kerry is transferred from Barnhurst prison and special arrangements are made for her including a cell of her own and access to all of her artistic materials. She reveals to the women that while she was working as a prostitute she hit a man with an ashtray which killed him. Kerry's agent David Austin puts pressure on the Department to allow her to attend an exhibition on the outside and gets Vera into trouble when she accepts a painting from Kerry.

When Kerry is suspected of lagging on the other women, she returns to her cell to find her masterpiece painting ruined [114], so spends the night repainting it in time for the exhibition which she attends in her prison uniform. David is apparently only keen on Kerry so that he can make as much money out of her as possible and the media are keen to write about her.

While released on parole [117], she is told that she is not allowed to contact David without whom she cannot cope. She turns to alcohol and to Helen Smart to look after her while in such a state. She becomes jealous of David, when she finds out that he is spending time with a pretty young female artist, she attacks him – again with an ashtray. Kerry's life spirals further out of control and she almost loses it when mixing drugs with alcohol, only for Helen to find her in time to save her. Realising that she has a major problem, she accepts psychiatric help [124] rather than have her parole revoked for breaking it.

Above: Betty Bobbitt (Judy Bryant) filming in the Governor's office. Below: Margot Knight as Sharon Gilmour.

of the demands for payment regarding the new movie version, and as such further plans for movie length re-edits of characters stories were quickly abandoned.

Geoff Butler returns much to the chagrin of Leila Fletcher. However, Meg Jackson is more than happy to have his attentions at dinner dates until it is discovered that Butler has beaten up a gay man at a local pub. Butler then attacks Meg and is rescued by Jim Fletcher. With Butler now on the run he devises the ultimate payback for his former army mate. He constructs a bomb hidden inside a cigar box which unwittingly Leila and the boys take up to Jim's hotel room where he is staying during his marital estrangement [109]. In a shocking turn of events the blast kills the boys outright and Leila dies a few hours later. Butler eventually gets what is coming to him when he once again calls on Jim Fletcher but reckons against a police sniper on protection duty. A bullet finally finishes off this most disagreeable of men. [112] Ray Meagher remembers the first of his memorable turns in *Prisoner*:

> *I used to drink in a pub in Sydney called The Strand, which was a hang-out for a lot of people in our business. One of them was Ian Bradley, years before he became producer of Prisoner. He knew of me and my work from those days, so when it came to casting the show he must*

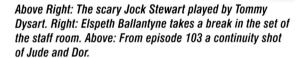

Above Right: The scary Jock Stewart played by Tommy Dysart. Right: Elspeth Ballantyne takes a break in the set of the staff room. Above: From episode 103 a continuity shot of Jude and Dor.

have remembered me and thought I'd be good for Geoff Butler. Prisoner was a different job in as much as it was mainly women dominating the screen. There had, of course, up to that point been a lot of cop shows on the box which featured women, but this made them the focus and was very different from the other shows around at the time. It was a very welcome addition to the television landscape in Australia. I can't remember there being a massive audience reaction to Geoff Butler's activities. Occasionally I used to cop the odd insult in the street. I was asked back a second time to play Butler and I said to Ian Bradley, 'This can't go on, you can't have an evil bugger like him keep coming back.' So Ian asked me how I would like to go out, life imprisonment or to be bumped off. I chose to be bumped off so the audience could see him truly getting his just desserts for what he had done.

Jim Fletcher certainly knows sadness during his early months in the series, but that does not stop him keeping an eye on the good-looking ladies who flit in and out of his life. Gerard Maguire is remembered very fondly by fans and cast members alike, and here Gerard explains his arrival as Jim Fletcher:

I got the part in Prisoner by asking for it. If I have any advice to actors, it is knock on doors.

Ian Bradley was a pal of mine, he was married to Anne Lucas. Annie and I had been in the play Juggler's Three for the Melbourne Theatre Company and were friends. Sandy Gore was also in the play. I had been doing lots of theatre and although I had starred in one TV series – Luke's Kingdom – I had also done many guest roles in just about every Aussie TV series of that time. I was not very well-known outside the theatre though. My bank manager thought I should do something about that. I had seen the first couple of episodes of Prisoner when they were doing just one hour a week. I thought it looked rough but interesting. I heard that Ian was the producer and called in to see him. No appointment. I just walked in. I think it was Ian who had thought about bringing in some male hunk for eye candy. I was not considered pretty, not by TV standards at least, but I had a sort of gruff appeal for the ladies. So, as it is in most things in life, it's all about the timing. There I was, a good actor in the right place, at the right time. I was hired.

Looking back it was a wonderful couple of years. Jim Smillie, a very handsome actor, was another male in the series at the time. He and I tried to get a glimpse of Kerry Armstrong or Peta Toppano getting changed. Although we were all in the tunnel together, we never did. I knew most of the women from the stage with the exception of Fiona and Val. Sheila Florance was a fan of mine as I was of her. I think our respect and liking for each other showed in our performances. The writers noticed it and Jim and Lizzie's relationship was one of the softer, sweeter stories of the time I was there. She has a special place in my heart.

Even by the standards of the time, the Prisoner cast were poorly treated and even more poorly paid. Other contemporary series which were more glamorous but not as popular, got far more publicity. The actors were also much better paid than 'us girls' which is how the Executives saw us, not Ian Bradley though, I hasten to add. When it came time to re-negotiate our contracts, most of the cast were afraid to ask for more money. Grundy had fired a whole cast from another of their shows and the feeling was that they would do the same with us. I was confident they wouldn't. It was at that point I began to appreciate Val. She was a force to be reckoned with. Although we didn't achieve much of a raise, we did get something thanks to the strength of Val. The suits quickly learned that Val was a pistol. And later it was Val's forceful personality that resulted in better pay and conditions for all of us. I like to think that I was her main back up and supporter.

I seldom watched the show myself if I am honest. I never have enjoyed watching myself on television. It's different now. I have seen a few episodes of Prisoner and enjoyed both the episode and my performance. I suppose that's because I was in my prime, and I have more respect for what we achieved with so little. I think because we had so little production value, it was the scripts and the performances that carried the series. And what a cast! Not full of the pretty young things that carried other shows. These women were real, women in tough circumstances making the most of their situation. Creating friendships, bonding and fighting with each other, the stories not backing off. The violence, when it was there, was not gratuitous and had consequences. Made all the more memorable because it was the women who were not just the victims but also the perpetrators. These women were not just someone's wife, lover, daughter, mother. They were there at the very heart of the series as their own fully-fledged characters. And

that was rare for the time, maybe even still now.

The story I tell Vera in the bar about Vietnam, the child he shot thinking he had a hand-grenade, was a true story. It was told to me by Bill Nagle from his time in Vietnam. It was very powerful probably because it was true. The shocking killing of my family was beautifully written and sensitively directed by Rod Hardy. I saw it again the other night. It still creeps me out. They might have written that in to free Jim up for relationships with the guest prisoners, but I don't honestly know.

I used to joke I left the show because I started knitting and got over-emotional every month. But the truth is I wanted to cash in on my new found fame. Prisoner didn't pay much and there was an offer of a movie, Kitty and the Bagman. They originally wanted me for the Bag Man but I liked the rascally Cyril better. Plus there was another series on the horizon, Starting Out. I also had a run in with the new producer, a pompous Kiwi. I wasn't the only one to have problems with him. I had become close to Fiona, good pals nothing more, and her friend Denise Morgan. I was starting to write and had an idea for a kids' TV series which Denise would later write. Anyway, I had ambitions that were not compatible with Prisoner. Looking back I probably should have stayed. But life takes you where it will.

While a good screw is always welcome, a bad screw is even better and few come with a pedigree of evil as Jock Stewart. His arrival in Wentworth from Pentridge [114] brings a whole heap of trouble for Judy Bryant. While Anne Yates had been a bent screw, Stewart was a psychotic killer and in many ways was the male prototype for The Freak. Glasgow-born actor Tommy Dysart brought a chilling presence to the new officer; he recalls his time as the menacing keeper and Judy Bryant's nemesis:

'The evil that men do lives after them!' wrote The Bard [Marc Antony in Julius Caesar] and that sure is true of Mr. Jock Stewart. My strongest recall of that period when Prisoner was at its zenith is not of our performing but rather the tsunami that followed our roles going to air. When it was first shown on TV, our son Kole (then still at school) encountered a truckload of trouble, firstly for being the son of 'Jock' and then later for his mother playing a social worker in the show. Neither of our characters was very popular with the hero-worshipped inmates of Wentworth. Kole did himself proud in his retaliation – not so his parents whom were verbally abused on

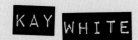

KAY WHITE

Played by Sandy Gore

First episode: 127
Last episode: 145
Total featured: 18 episodes

First seen working in Andrew Reynolds' factory while the prisoners are on work release, Kay appears to be a very competent and professional member of staff but she is hiding a major problem: her gambling addiction. When she finds out that Margo is running a book, Kay decides to place some bets and it isn't long before she has accumulated quite a debt. She also strikes up a deal with Judy who is planning an escape. However, she is caught out when she steals the employees' pay packets to help fuel her addiction. Sent to Wentworth on remand, she is shunned by all of the women she used to be in charge of before the work release scheme was cancelled. The women pay her back by further getting her into more gambling trouble and she is sentenced to five years at her trial.

With Bea later out of the way in solitary, Kay decides to set up a book of her own at the prison and starts taking bets. The women realise that this is a chance they can use to trick her so an elaborate plan is hatched to break the bank. Kay falls for it and goes bust. However, she attacks Lizzie when she finds out she has been fooled. She loses her temper with the old jailbird, almost throttling her to death until another inmate, Linda Jones, walks in on the commotion and smashes a china jug off Kay's head to stop her from killing Lizzie.

Kay is sent to Wentworth General Hospital for emergency attention but dies of a blood clot on her brain shortly after.

several occasions, then physically attacked – in particular, hit by umbrella-and-handbag-wielding matronly blue-rinse ladies right in the middle of Melbourne city centre. We did manage to escape their full venom by seeking refuge in a nearby shop. It sounds comical but it ain't with ten or twelve humans looking for blood (even 'tartan' blood), added to which one dare not retaliate for the old theatrical adage dictates 'treat your audience with respect.'

Jock bullies and threatens those around him, with a brooding malevolent presence that easily sent shivers up the spines of the viewing audience. Sharon Gilmour as usual thinks she can exploit the situation when she overhears Jock threatening Doreen into forcing her to sell her late mother's house. But this wild animal cannot be tamed, and Gilmour's body is discovered at the bottom of a flight of stairs with Judy kneeling beside the limp figure [116]. Erica has enough evidence of Stewart's corruption to ask for his resignation [119] and he leaves Wentworth quietly admitting to Bryant that he was the guilty party in Gilmour's murder. Naturally, Judy is incensed that although Stewart has lost his job he is effectively walking free from murdering Sharon. She even ropes Bea into taking Erica and Meg hostage to protest at the injustice. Judy is determined not to rest until Jock Stewart is behind bars, but she is powerless in Wentworth for the time being. Fate however decrees that the Bryant vs. Stewart feud is not forgotten and will be resurrected in the months to come...

One arrival in Episode 118 would have, at first glance, a fairly short stay in Wentworth, but was in fact the building blocks for a character who would be the most regular re-offender to turn up at Wentworth over the next four years. She is upbeat prostitute Helen Smart, played by the highly respected actress Caroline Gillmer. Gillmer has since gone on to have an impressive array of credits in movies, theatre and television which would include a return to the Channel 10 studios in Nunawading as Cheryl Stark in *Neighbours*. Indeed, there were plans for her own sit-com based on her *Neighbours* character to be called *In Cheryl's Arms* which subsequently failed to get the green light. However, Caroline here remembers her time as Helen:

I got the role of Helen in the usual process via my agent. The establishing episode for Helen

Top Left: Filming in the Recreation Room. Above Left: Helen Smart, played by Caroline Gillmer. Top Right: The famous Wentworth laundry set. Above Right: Episode 104: Bea and Lizzie.

Smart was being directed by Bill Hughes. I had worked with Bill on another series, The Sullivans, playing Maryanna De Jong, a World War 2 Dutch resistance fighter. It was a period drama and a long way from this character of Helen Smart. I didn't have to audition but I had always hoped that if something special came up in the series I would be available to do it. I would describe Helen as a tart that beats with a different heart. The cast at that time were fabulous. It was refreshing to see such strong roles in capable hands. I knew and loved and had worked with almost all the actors for many years prior to being cast in the show, so our bond was strong, trusted and reliant from the get-go. I enjoyed acting with the entire ensemble on Prisoner. The regulars, the guests, the experienced, the new-to-television. It was easy to rehearse and improvise because of the enormous respect and outstanding female work ethic. The Helen Smart who came into the show had a fake French accent. Whatever your interpretation is of her first appearances, they are the ones that propelled the character from a small guest appearance to what followed. I am grateful for being cast as Helen and grateful for the room the network and producers gave me as an actor to contribute to shaping her as a less than predictable tart with a heart. I was not aware that Helen would grow and return so many times. I was booked for the original maybe eight weeks from memory. I was as surprised as the next person when the producers rang to discuss more episodes for Helen. At that point, I was previously committed to several plays at the Melbourne Theatre Company and a musical season interstate, but there were slots of time in between the three commitments. So thereby began the idea of Helen becoming a

KEV & LIZ

EP. 95
D·2
Sc 80

EP. 91 - Sc 35 - N3

JIM

EP. 117
D3
Sc 4

LIZZIE

EP. 100
D·3
Sc 31.

GEOFF

EP. 111 - Sc 37 - D3

Top Left: Episode 95: Kevin and Lizzie. Top Right: Episode 91: Colette Mann checks over her script. Above: Episode 100: Lizzie looks ready to face the outside. Right Centre: Episode 112: Gerard Maguire as Jim Fletcher strikes a pose. Right: Episode 111: Ray Meagher as Geoff Butler, one of his many roles in the series.

recurring character who would re-appear given these pockets of availability. It was a clever resolution by the network as it gave the storyliners an 'inmate trusted contact' on the outside who could come 'inside' for the women to plot and plan a plethora of revenges, escapes, contact with loved ones and news from the outside on a variety of issues. Thus, Helen could be referred to in the scripts as present and active on the outside without the audience necessarily needing to see her.

This arrangement was a rare gem as anyone in a regular television series can attest as it allowed one to perform in the theatre and also have meaningful storylines on the screen. Betty Bobbitt and I shared a musical background in Melbourne prior to the series. Given that live theatre is all about 'responding to the audience on the night' and in cabaret ad-libbing, building on the script, handling slip ups, etc. We had the perfect recipe for an on screen 'double act'. Judy and Helen's affection for each other mirrored Betty's and my personal affection off camera. I adored all the girls in the series and Betty and I still stay in touch, though not nearly often enough. The most challenging thing about playing Helen was to find a way to play her not as a cliché of her type. In the initial planning she was quite one dimensional, and breathing and imagining something less typical, less predictable for the audience's intellect is always where I try to pitch choices and a character's energy. The work was fun but disciplined when it was time for a take. We were all guilty of corpsing and fluffing I am sure. I am recognised daily for the series.

Some years ago I was in New York and had booked and paid for my theatre tickets by credit card via the phone booking system. The facility requires you to produce the same credit card at the box office on the night of the performance you are attending to collect your tickets, as a security measure. I had used my credit card in my married name and, at the box office counter, I requested my ticket in that name. The American booth operator gathered the tickets, asked for identification and the credit card. I handed it to him and he said, 'Sorry, these tickets are not for you.' For I moment I thought darn, I must have used the credit card in my maiden name. So I foraged through my hand bag, found the other credit card and put that on the counter. He took it and said. ''Hmmmm... No, I am sorry, this is also not a match either.' Flummoxed and feeling the glare of hundreds of eyes in the queue behind me staring at the back of my head, impatiently wanting to get their tickets and move on to imbibe drinks and conversations with their friends, I asked the operator did he have the right tickets? Did he misunderstand me with my Australian accent? Could he look again for the tickets? And he stared me right in the eye and said, 'None of these are in your name. I know you are Helen Smart and none of these credit cards are yours!' Oblivious of the queue behind me he then started on a huge rave and revealed what a compelling viewing the show was for him and all his friends. How he watched the show he described was the same type of group viewing sessions in bars and living rooms that I later witnessed when Sex in the City first came on the scene. With every re-run the next audience can smell the integrity the women brought to their time on screen. We knew we were being given a challenge with such a low budget show, but the chance to do more than wash and wipe the dishes in the scene background was why we had learned our craft and we were eager and skilled to flex our acting muscles.

A focal storyline for 1980 sees the women leaving the confines at Wentworth for work release at a clothes factory owned by Andrew Reynolds. Naturally, the selection process of trusted women to go on the trips is heated among the women. The supervisor at the factory is Kay White, who is hiding her own secret. She is a gambling addict and has been embezzling funds from the firm for some time to support her habit. Kay was played with great fervour by Sandy Gore. Sandy recalls how she came to get the well-remembered role:

At Elspeth Ballantyne's fortieth birthday party a woman introduced herself to me as Maura Fay, the casting agent for Prisoner. We made small talk and pleasantries and then she said, 'What size shoe do you take?' And I answered, 'Nine and a half B.' Her response was 'Do I have a role for you!' And so began my attachment to Kay White. Over the years, Maura and I developed a long and abiding friendship. Indeed such was my love for her that eight years on I asked Maura to be my daughter's godmother. And what a mighty godmother she was. I was an avid viewer of Prisoner from the outset, the extraordinary acting and the no-frills glamour. This was a show to be reckoned with but, above all, it was the quality of the scriptwriting that made the show so successful. It was very unusual at that time to have such unsentimental and brutal dialogue to deliver, and with writers like Denise Morgan, it was always about the pursuit of excellence. As an actor I always try to find the misunderstood

*Above Left: The two ugly sisters – the pantomime begins.
Above Right: As the pantomime is in full swing, nobody is
ready for what is yet to happen. Inset: Who is under the
bride's veil?*

*side of a woman to give her full reign. Kay White,
I quickly came to realise, had no redeeming
features whatsoever. Indeed her misguided sense
of entitlement was a joy to portray. Kay was just a
mad, bad girl.*

There was never a bad day on Prisoner. *We
were all locked into revelling in what it was to be
bad. I loved my scenes with Fiona Spence who
is a lifelong friend courtesy of* Prisoner. *Recently
friends threw up on YouTube the fight with Val
and myself. I have to say I roared with laughter
at my young self battling it away with Bea Smith
and holding my own in the process. When you
are young and in your twenties, loving what you
do, two hours a week of taping is not hard to do.
However, as a guest artist I was often called upon
to be first up of a morning. I don't ever recall a
time when I was there before Sheila Florance
and that worried me. Sheila was not a young
woman and although she did not ever begrudge
her working hours I felt that there perhaps might
have been a little more consideration given to
her. I signed on for fourteen weeks and at the end
of that time Grundy asked me if I would like to
continue and I said no. I am a theatre beast and
wished to return to what I love best, so the door*

*was left open after my hit on the head for Kay to
lie in a coma until any such time when she might
be resurrected.*

*Sheila Florance was my Melbourne mum. I
left Sydney in my teens and it was into Sheila's
arms that I flew. She guided and advised me and
we remained friends for the rest of her life and I
still sorely miss her. Having watched* Prisoner *as a
viewer for over a year, I felt quite privileged when
asked to join the team and loved every minute
of the experience. I think the show's success
and ongoing popularity over the decades is
due to all the components already mentioned
– the abundant talents of all the women, the
high standard of the storylines and the fabulous
dialogue. The gritty 'no make-up' look of the show
and the fact that it was a gutsy show starring a
bunch of women and that was a first as it was the
popular conception that only male actors could
guarantee a viewing audience.*

Kay White inevitably finds herself behind bars
after an attempt to rob the factory again goes awry.
Naturally, her continued baiting of the women and her
desire to further her gambling needs meet with an
unhappy end. White comes a cropper when attacking

Lizzie, as Gore remembers above. Kay is bashed over the head with an electric kettle by inmate Linda [Elaine Cusick, 145] although Lizzie takes the blame in order to enable Linda to secure her parole.

Another fan favourite makes her first appearance in 1980, none other than Lois Ramsey. Lois would later find greater *Prisoner* immortality as the permanently befuddled Ettie Parslow. Here she plays a fractionally less confused social worker Agnes Forster [135]. In fact Agnes, on the point of retirement, is really only good at making the tea and fussing over her cat Butchie. Managing to rile many of the staff with her vagueness in the process, she lasts all of six episodes before being forced to resign but it is an encouraging first visit from one of Australia's finest character actors.

The end of the year saw another classic *Prisoner* cliffhanger. This time the inmates have discovered the sewer plans of the Wentworth area and a convenient access point in the prison grounds. Creating the set for this memorable moment was certainly memorable for the designer Ian Costello:

> *One of the most challenging sets I had to design was a sewerage tunnel for Bea, Doreen, Lizzie and Judy to escape through. It was built in sections so it could be shot lengthways and also had removable panels to allow cameras to get side on perspectives. It all seemed to be coming together well until the afternoon before the shoot when the director did a walk through and was not happy that is didn't 'sound' like a concrete tunnel. Well, it wouldn't. It was made out of plywood. That night we had a cement mixer backed into the studio pumping quick drying cement into the base of the tunnel so it could be ready for an early morning shoot.*

A daring escape plan is worked out which uses the cover of a pantomime being performed by the inmates for some visiting children. Security is, of course, very tight but everything is going to plan when Judy, Doreen, Mouse and a clearly expendable, uncredited character named Irene escape in the tunnel. However, Lizzie finds Doreen's beloved teddy bear and goes down the tunnel after them in order to return it. Bea, having discovered what Lizzie is up to, follows too, in order to bring Lizzie back safely. The disturbed Anne Griffin [*Sons and Daughters* legend Rowena Wallace] offers to replace the cover to the sewer system which is hidden at the back of the marquee that the pantomime is being performed in. However, Griffin then fetches a wheelbarrow full of soil and tips it over the entrance to the tunnel thus hiding from

Sheila takes a break, still dressed as the fairy godmother.

anyone evidence of the escape and blocking Bea and Lizzie's return to Wentworth. Worse is to come when Irene grabs a beam in the tunnel bringing the roof in. Irene is killed and the women are separated by a huge mound of debris which has fallen in. There is no way forward or back for Bea, Lizzie and Doreen. Trapped, with nobody knowing where they are or able to get back the way they have come, things look bleak.

This classic end-of-season cliff-hanger [165] closed the second full year of *Prisoner* on Australian screens. Now a major attraction on Channel 10, the festive season meant that the devoted audience – it was far too early to call them Blockies – had to try to enjoy their Christmas and New Year knowing that their anti-heroines were trapped and possibly dead below the grounds of the prison. But Philip East knew exactly what he was doing. Viewers couldn't wait to get back in front of their screens to see who would survive, if anybody, from this latest catastrophic event as 1981 beckoned. If 1979 had been a learning curve, 1980 cemented the format and storytelling style of *Prisoner*. It had seen a host of memorable characters introduced which were to remain favourites for fans many years later, chief among these being Judy Bryant, whose influence inside and outside Wentworth would prove to be one of the brand's greatest assets.

The Legacy of Lizzie

> *I play my part with love. I am a warm and honest actress and I think that comes through on the screen... Lizzie is very popular and deeply loved. People actually come up to me in the street, throw their arms around me and tell me they love me.*
> Sheila Florance – TV Week interview (12/07/1980)

At the age of 62, actress Sheila Florance was approached about a possible role in a forthcoming television drama series about women in prison. Channel 10 had long been in need of an injection of quality drama, which would hit the headlines and improve their flagging ratings and asked Sheila if she would be interested in playing the part of an alcoholic 'old lag', who would later become Lizzie Birdsworth. There was no audition necessary and Sheila agreed straight away.

Elizabeth Josephine Birdsworth is an alcoholic chain-smoker and completely institutionalised within the prison system. Lizzie has spent over twenty years behind bars for murdering four sheep shearers by poisoning them during her time working as a cook. Initially a 'filler' character, Sheila played Lizzie so well that she became an instant hit amongst viewers and critics, with Brian Courtis of The Age commenting that Sheila was 'the most captivating actress in a drama series right now'. It inspired the production team to make Lizzie a much more focal character than had originally been envisaged. The winning formula of comedy duo Lizzie and Doreen was subsequently used more frequently and to the programme's advantage to help break up the scenes of stark drama with a bit of humour.

Lizzie is mostly treated sympathetically by the prison inmates and officers. Due to her poor heart condition, which she often plays on ('Oooooh, it's me old ticker!'), Lizzie is not allowed to be sent to solitary confinement and it is generally agreed and accepted that she should have another inmate for company at all times. This doesn't stop her from getting into trouble and even from the early days she is involved in all kinds of misdemeanours, notably the prison riot during Episodes 3 and 4 which sees the murder of prison social worker Bill Jackson. Lizzie sides with Franky Doyle's crew, but it doesn't take her long to realise that she's on the losing side and swiftly moves over to Bea Smith's camp where she stays.

Following the confession of her old boss Ralph Campbell whilst on his deathbed, Lizzie is surprised to learn that the original case against her is being re-

Below: Promotional shot of Sheila Florance as the much loved old lag Lizzie Birdsworth. Opposite Page: Top Left: Sheila catches up with the latest news in the set of the Recreation Room while waiting for her next scene. Top Right: Another break between scenes with Elspeth Ballantyne. Bottom: A stunning shot of Sheila looking in deep thought, the cigarette is never far away!

investigated. She finds out that although she did put a small amount of poison in the cooking pot to make the workers poorly, this wasn't enough to kill them. In fact, it was Campbell who had increased the dose which had caused their deaths in an attempt to keep their wages so he could pay off his own debts [87]. When she is released with substantial compensation,

Lizzie is sent to the care of the Halfway House where she is looked after by Karen Travers but has ex-inmate Doreen for company as well.

For Lizzie however, Wentworth is never too far away. She and Doreen decide to steal some booze from a local liquor store and they are both caught and arrested. Initially, Lizzie is let off with only Doreen having to return to prison. Without her partner in crime, Lizzie can't cope so she upsets the court judge by flushing his memoirs down the toilet. She ends up with a much stiffer sentence than she would have received originally [105].

Salvation Army Officer, Captain Barton, starts looking for Lizzie's family and gets in touch with a woman claiming to be her daughter, Marcia. Lizzie is overjoyed to find out that she also has a long lost granddaughter Josie. Soon the two of them are living in Doreen's house. Marcia tells Lizzie that Josie is in need of an operation following a break in her leg when she was younger, but the process costs too much. When Lizzie reports the news to Bea, she smells a rat and it is later discovered that both Marcia and Josie are not Lizzie's family after all: they are both imposters who genuinely need the money to help with Josie's operation and have pretended to be relations. They know about Lizzie because Marcia, whose real name is Ellen, was in the same orphanage as Lizzie's daughter who died in a car crash when she was young. Lovable

Lizzie decides that they will become her new family and agrees to part with the cash that they need for Josie [124] and the two of them swiftly leave and fly to Chicago for the treatment.

> Lizzie: I'll tell you what I think of you. I don't care who you are, you're my daughter now and Josie's my granddaughter and that's all that matters to me. I knew all along you weren't Marcia, but it was nice to have a new family.
> Ellen: Oh Lizzie, you're wonderful!
> Lizzie: No, I'm not! I'm just a silly old goat who can't keep out of trouble, but I will from now on... now that I've got you two!
> From Episode 124

Trouble is never far away from Lizzie and she finds herself being charged for manslaughter in [146]. She takes the blame for fellow prisoner Linda Jones who comes to Lizzie's rescue from the vicious Kay White, who is about to throttle her after a betting sting which Lizzie was involved in. Linda smashes a china kettle over Kay's head to save Lizzie which does the job but Kay later dies from her injuries. Lizzie convinces Linda to lie; otherwise her forthcoming parole release will be in jeopardy. Lizzie realises that someone like Linda, who has a family to look after on the outside, is more deserving of release over herself.

ANNE GRIFFIN

Played by Rowena Wallace

First episode: 160
Last episode: 167
Total featured: 8 episodes

Troubled Anne arrives at Wentworth after threatening a shopkeeper with a knife and being found with a large sum of stolen money on her which she claims is a loan from her friend Megan.

When unexplained problems start happening at the prison, including lagging to the screws, Anne is suspected of being behind them, so Bea puts a stop to it and instructs the women not to tell Anne any of their secrets. Unfortunately, it is too late for their major secret: an escape plan. No matter how much they try to convince Anne that there is no escape taking place, she doesn't believe them. When the said escape actually does happen and the women scarper off in some underground tunnels [165], Anne decides to seal their fate by covering the tunnel entrance with earth so they can't get out again from the same side. When disaster strikes and the tunnel collapses, the women inside it are trapped.

Doctor Weissman diagnoses Anne as being mentally unbalanced and so a transfer to a psychiatric hospital is the only resolution for this confused young women in need of a great deal of help.

Even as a pensioner, Lizzie proves that you're never too old to have a bit of romance in your life. When Sid Humphrey arrives at Wentworth to fix the television set [169], he and Lizzie strike up a beautiful friendship. Helped somewhat by Bea, who arranges for various things to go wrong in the prison, Sid becomes a regular visitor. He asks Lizzie to come and live with him when she's eventually released. When Sid has a stroke [174], Lizzie is allowed to visit him in hospital. Later she casually walks out of Wentworth disguised as a visitor and makes her way to Sid at the nursing home [187]. Unfortunately, Sid isn't there so Lizzie takes the opportunity to get drunk before she comes back home to Wentworth.

After Sid has made a recovery, he is allowed to return to his own home and Lizzie is granted some visits to check up on him. She finds that Sid is partially paralysed following the stroke and arranges for him to accept 'meals on wheels' [212]. She starts knitting clothes for him and also manages to use the prison kitchen to provide him with some culinary treats until the officers find out. On another visit to Sid, he proposes to Lizzie. After giving it some thought, a wedding is being planned for the two. Sid's son, Gordon, disputes the wedding and makes the suggestion that Lizzie is only doing it for the money, and the wedding is called off. When Bea gets involved, Gordon quickly changes his mind, and Bea Smith is the last person you would want to have as an enemy, so the wedding plans are quickly put back into motion again. Sadly, Sid passes away suddenly [222] and Lizzie handles the whole thing with dignity before finding out that she has been left Sid's house in his will. Unfortunately, Gordon is less than happy with this and makes it clear that Lizzie will have a fight on her hands if she ever wants to live there.

Lizzie finds out that she's to be released and is overjoyed before remembering that she'll be all alone. The only reason she was looking forward to it was to spend her last days with Sid. She finally comes to terms with his death: 'Dor, I just realised... Sid's dead. My lovely old Sid's dead and I'm never going to see him anymore' [225]. With the support from Bea and Doreen, Lizzie pulls herself together and is released to live at the house that she was going to be sharing with Sid. Unfortunately, a campaign by Gordon to frighten her succeeds. She is scared witless and the only way that she can see of stopping him is by taking away what he loves the most. She burns down Sid's house [239] and is again returned back to Wentworth [241], charged with arson. She is acquitted [250] and now homeless, checks herself into a hotel.

As ever, Lizzie can't cope on the outside. She is soon tricked by a young lad in a bar who makes off with her money when she gets drunk. Her parole is revoked when she ends up with a huge taxi bill that she is unable to pay. Again, Wentworth is home again for the old lady who doesn't know any different [253].

The arrival of corrupt officer Joan Ferguson changes the direction at Wentworth forever, with Lizzie always being caught up in the action one way or another. She's quickly fooled into spilling the beans about an illicit alcohol still which the women have been using, having been easily bribed with a bottle of whisky [295]. With Lizzie drunk, Joan is on the warpath to earn some recognition for finding something which originally went unnoticed by the other prison staff. Luckily, the women manage to sabotage things before she catches up and this begins a long and drawn-out fight between the prisoners and 'The Freak', which will continue until the very last episode.

When Joan stops an escape attempt by Margo [321], she pushes Lizzie out of the way, injuring her. This results in the old lady becoming seriously ill. She has a long stay in hospital to recover and is luckily outside of Wentworth during the 'Great Fire'. She later returns when the women are at their temporary home in Woodridge Prison, where she soon gets herself involved in more rackets and the acquisition of booze is naturally high on Lizzie's agenda. There is so much alcohol available that the women fill their hot water bottles up with it and smuggle them back into Wentworth without anyone noticing [332].

Lizzie is heartbroken at the departure of her closest prison pal Bea Smith in Episode 400. She breaks her wrist from banging on the security gate after Joan purposely leads Bea away in front of Lizzie. Her mood is lifted when her real son, Arthur Charlton, makes a surprise arrival at the prison [404]. After over 40 years of separation, the two are reunited and Lizzie is given the chance to meet her new family and is offered a place to live with them.

A final drama is ahead for Lizzie as she finds a severed hand in the prison garden. Officer David Bridges has been murdering the inmates while promising that he's going to help them escape. When he sees Lizzie's reaction outside, he pulls a penknife out on her [416] and she collapses with the shock. She ends up seriously ill in hospital following inmate Cass Parker's decapitation of David using a garden spade. Lizzie gets some welcome visitors at her hospital bed in the form of Minnie, Judy and Pixie. Her final appearance during Episode 418 is finally a happy ending for the loveable scamp – she will leave hospital and live with her son and his family.

The character of Lizzie Birdsworth, superbly played by Sheila Florance, created a template for the series which was repeated numerous times again after Sheila had left. Future characters such as Dot Farrah and Ettie Parslow tried to fill the void left by Lizzie, but nobody was quite able to step into those well-worn shoes as successfully as Sheila had done. She was

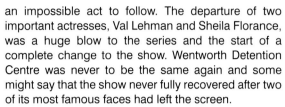

an impossible act to follow. The departure of two important actresses, Val Lehman and Sheila Florance, was a huge blow to the series and the start of a complete change to the show. Wentworth Detention Centre was never to be the same again and some might say that the show never fully recovered after two of its most famous faces had left the screen.

For actress Sheila Florance, *Prisoner* was a tiny part of a packed professional and personal life. She was born on 24 July 1916 and learned from an early age that comedy would give her the attention that she liked to receive. At school, she would often take part in some of the jokes that the other pupils played and regularly got into trouble for disrupting the rest of her class. She imagined herself growing up to become a doctor, like her grandfather, and pictured herself being in charge of a whole hospital. When she left school in 1931 at the age of fifteen, her ideas of studying medicine at University went out of the window as she discovered boys and spent a lot of time on the beach with her friends.

After watching a play at her brother's school in 1932, Sheila became stage-struck and a new passion for the theatre quickly developed. She enrolled for classes at the Little Theatre School of Dramatic Art and a large part of her spare time would be spent at the theatre. Her first post-school performance was at the age of seventeen, as the lead female role in a play called *A Pair of Sixes* at the Caulfield Town Hall with the Old Caulfield Grammarians.

Sheila's former daughter-in-law, Helen Martineau, picks up the story during an interview in 2005 with the *Prisoner* website *On the Inside*:

> *She started acting in Melbourne in 1934 when she was seventeen – a beautiful blonde, with a wide sensual mouth. People who know her as Lizzie find it hard to imagine how stunning she was. Over the following years Sheila was a lively part of the development of professional theatre, television and film in this country, apart from the thirteen years she spent in England, including the awful war years (and what she got up to there is quite a story). The stage was her first love and she played some major roles over the years, but better paid work came through film and TV, even though she did mostly small roles until* Prisoner.

Sheila moved back to Australia with her second husband in 1948 making the family's new home in St Kilda, where she continued to work in theatre as she renovated their house in Raleigh Place. Sheila's place became renowned for the many parties that she and her family would hold regularly after an evening of acting. It was very much an 'open house' and Sheila was always the centre of attention, continuing to act

for the enjoyment of friends and family. She acted with a number of regular thespians including Peter Batey, Fenella Maguire, George Fairfax, Sylvia Reid and a then relatively unknown student called Barry Humphries. Barry became a familiar face at Sheila's parties at Raleigh Place and even tested out new characters on an unsuspecting audience at Sheila's house, with mixed reactions. His 'Les Patterson' character was one of many which were premiered at Sheila's home.

Throughout the 1960s and 70s, Sheila continued to work and was also successful in films. However she wasn't yet managing to find an actual career in the business. Sheila's son Peter Oyston had dreams of being a filmmaker and when Sheila told him about her own visions, the two worked together in an hour-long feature *The Kings,* which was Peter's latest project. Sheila, and some friends of hers whom she had persuaded to get involved too, worked every weekend for free during the summer of 1962-63. Sheila was proud and supportive of Peter and this was to be the start of her film career, although her all-time love would be the theatre as Sheila enjoyed the immediate response from an audience in the same room as her.

Sheila first got to know actress Elspeth Ballantyne in late 1963 during a Patrick White play, *A Cheery Soul*, although Elspeth already had experience of Sheila's now famous parties at her home. Sheila's father had recently died and this was her first production after his death and the two women got to know each other well during their time together. They became good friends and in the late 1970s their paths would cross again in *Prisoner*.

The family moved to Robe Street in St Kilda in July of 1969. Sheila was a proud home keeper and their new place was no exception. Back then, the town was nothing compared with how it is known today. It had a reputation for being full of criminals, prostitutes and squatters but Sheila worked hard to bring the house up to her own expectations. She loved her garden but couldn't enjoy it because, as the years passed, things in the town got worse with the introduction of hard drugs which were linked to the large numbers of prostitutes who were working in the area. Sheila believed that enough was enough and took action, although she also felt sorry for these poor young women who had to work as they did and take drugs to make ends meet. She was a strong supporter of the local residents' protest meetings and was very vocal in making her opinions heard. She was known by just about everyone in the town and even took to the streets to knock on neighbours' doors to gain their support.

When Sheila got her big break in television in 1978, she arrived at the Channel 10 studios in Nunawading for the first production meeting for *Prisoner.* She had

Above: At the height of Prisoner's fame, Sheila loved the attention from her fans. Inset: At the Logie Awards with Val Lehman and UK TV star Dennis Waterman.

met some of the other cast already, but Val Lehman's first personal experience of her was when Sheila turned up and quite happily told the rest of the cast and crew that she'd just been 'hosing the prostitutes' who had been rehearsing on her lawn! With this unusual way of breaking the ice, Sheila was to grace the series for an impressive 402 episodes.

Working on *Prisoner* was a gruelling schedule with many early starts necessary, simply to get all of the day's scenes shot. A typical day for Sheila and the others would begin as early as 7.00am at the Nunawading studios which could often last until recording finished at 10.00pm. The days were long and even if the actors weren't needed for major scenes, they still had to be on set.

Sheila would often dispute the way that her scenes were to be played out and regularly had heated debates with the crew about how the camera would shoot her and the other cast. It was inevitable that there would be some conflict and sniping among the cast, given the long hours they were required to work. However, there was also an awful lot of professional

respect for each other and Sheila formed many close friendships during that time. Sheila thought that some of the scripts were particularly poor. *'Who writes this rubbish?'* she would exclaim when stumbling over her lines. When Sheila got a storyline to get her teeth, however, it became clear as to just how much talent she had.

Helen Martineau:

Sheila did come to appreciate Lizzie. One night she was sitting with her husband John watching an early episode. 'Ooh, what a sweet old dear that Lizzie is,' she said, forgetting who was actually on screen. John chortled, 'Sheila. That's you!'

Following the ill health of her husband, Sheila decided that her time on *Prisoner* was up so she could look after him. She was persuaded to stay on for a few more weeks after Val had gone because a double-whammy of two major characters leaving at the same time was seen as too much for the viewers to handle,

Above: Sheila celebrates her 75th birthday with some familiar faces: Jentah Sobott, Belinda Davey, Sandy Gore, Fiona Spence and Kirsty Child. Inset: More fan appreciation.

so after 402 episodes credited to her name, the gates of Wentworth slammed shut for the final time for Sheila. During her time on *Prisoner*, Sheila had won two Logie awards in 1981 and 1983, both for Most Popular Actress.

Now approaching her seventies, Sheila's career began to slow down. Her health wasn't at its best and Sheila was forced to take things easier. This didn't stop her from working however. She continued to act and appeared in TV guest roles on series including *Winners* and a memorable episode of the children's favourite *Round the Twist* in 1989 as Madame Fortune in 'Lucky Lips'.

Sheila's final remarkable piece of acting came in 1991. *A Woman's Tale* was written by Paul Cox especially for her. Sheila played the lead role of Martha, an old lady who was dying of cancer, facing her final days. An uplifting but haunting story, art imitated life because Sheila was, in fact, going through exactly the same experience as the character she was playing. Just like Sheila, Martha faced death on her own terms but never lost her sense of humour or sense of living until the very end. 'Some of my best friends have cancer. I'm not afraid,' Martha confided to her devoted nurse while she continued to puff on her cigarettes. Sheila was painfully ill during the recording. She knew she was dying but managed to convey a message to everyone who watched the film – *Life is so beautiful, keep love alive.*

This dignified swansong was well received by the critics and saw Sheila win the prestigious AFI Award for 'Best Actress In A Lead Role', with nominations for her supporting artist Gosia Dobrowolska along with Paul Grabowsky being nominated for Best Original Music Score and the film itself receiving a Best Screenplay nomination. In 1992 writer Paul Cox won the *Grand Prix* Award at the Ghent International Film Festival.

Sheila only managed a few more months after completing the film before she passed away. Close friend and *Prisoner* actress Fiona Spence recalls Sheila's death during a special feature on the 2009 release of *Prisoner* on DVD – Australian volume 14:

I had a nice friendship with Sheila Florance. It developed towards the end of my time there and really continued outside the show. She was a wicked woman but we had a lot of fun. She was an extraordinary human being. She could be very very funny and she shared her life with us and she also shared her death with us which was a privilege. It meant that we all 'completed' with her. I was going to Sydney to be in a play and she wasn't at all well. I can remember it was a rainy day as I was driving out of Melbourne. I was actually crying as I was driving on my way to Sydney because I didn't think I'd see her again. I was away for six weeks but when I got back she was still alive but she died on 12th October 1991. It was too soon. She was 75 but we would have loved to have more time with her. She was an extraordinary actress and a very generous, lovely friend.

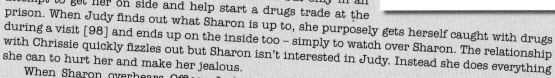

SHARON GILMOUR

Played by Margot Knight

First episode: 90
Last episode: 116
Total featured: 27 episodes

Drug pusher and girlfriend of Judy Bryant, Sharon doesn't make a great deal of friends when she first arrives at Wentworth following a drug raid. Her manipulative nature even sees her try to blackmail social worker Paul Reid whose son Tony was also involved in the raid. She is sentenced to two years at her trial [94].

She becomes friendly with Chrissie Latham but only in an attempt to get her on side and help start a drugs trade at the prison. When Judy finds out what Sharon is up to, she purposely gets herself caught with drugs during a visit [98] and ends up on the inside too – simply to watch over Sharon. The relationship with Chrissie quickly fizzles out but Sharon isn't interested in Judy. Instead she does everything she can to hurt her and make her jealous.

When Sharon overhears Officer Jock Stewart trying to blackmail Doreen over the sale of her mother's house, Sharon uses it to try to blackmail Jock into offering her protection against the other women who are often out to get her. Soon after the conversation, Sharon is found at the bottom of a flight of stairs: motionless with a broken neck and with Judy standing over her [116]. And so begins a long drawn out campaign to prove that it was Jock who murdered Sharon and not her loving girlfriend Judy.

The Governor Will See You Now...

"Erica was a rebel when she was young. Her father was a judge and told her that, to change society, one must work from the inside.
Patsy King, GMT Magazine, 1989

Early promotional shot of Patsy King as Erica Davidson.

Although Bea Smith might have been a competent force in dealing with internal power struggles at the prison on a ground-floor level, there was only ever really one Top Dog at Wentworth, The Governor. And for much of the series' tenure this meant one woman, Erica Davidson. The year 1979 was significant many thousands of miles away from Wentworth as the people of Britain welcomed in Margaret Thatcher as their first ever woman Prime Minister, and Erica did indeed have shades of Thatcher both in look, manner and a steely determination to see that order was maintained within her jurisdiction. And let's not forget that fabulous bouffant and power suits that were such a feature of Erica's administration.

Coming as she does from a privileged background, her father was a Chief Justice and her brother James a prominent MP and barrister. It is clear, however, that Erica's relationship with her mother is difficult. Florence Marne, Erica's mother, is not at all sympathetic to her

daughter's chosen profession. 'With your background you could have had a distinguished career at law,' she barks at her daughter in Episode 208. 'I notice there are a number of lady judges these days. But, on the other hand, I will never know why you didn't settle down to your marriage and have children. At least James has had the decency to procreate!' Hardly the stuff of undying affection. Florence sums up her feelings best when she says, 'If you showed as much concern for your own mother as you do for social misfits, perhaps I would feel better.' Erica, perhaps, carries the guilt of indifferent feelings for her mother and admits sadly to James, 'You know, I often think of Nanny as being more of a mother to me, especially when I was little.' The wound wedged between the two is shown at its most raw when Erica erupts, 'All my life I wanted a mother I could talk to, be with. But you were never there; you were never available. When I was a little girl you hardly ever talked to me and, as soon as possible, you sent me off to boarding school. You didn't want me, you didn't care about me!'

Florence collapses [209] and is rushed to hospital where a family secret is revealed. James was not the first-born child to Erica's parents. Florence had had a boy who had died of a brain haemorrhage following a fall. Blaming herself for this tragedy, when James and Erica came along she was terrified of another accident. Hiring a nanny, she set about alienating herself from her children, preferring instead a life as a socialite and charity worker. Upon Florence's death, Erica remarks, 'I've never really known her. My own mother.' This perhaps affected Erica's ability to have stable relationships herself. Certainly, when Erica's niece Barbara is brought to Wentworth on drugs charges, a meeting with her ex-husband Michael is cold and impersonal. Any love and caring all but forgotten.

It would have been easy for Erica to be detached and completely at odds with an ability to relate to the problems that society brings before Wentworth. However, Mrs. Davidson is a remarkable woman. Her compassion is married with a sense of knowing when the wool is being pulled over her eyes, making her a tough cookie to crack for the women in her charge. She demands standards of the prisoners and the same is true of her staff. Vera Bennett particularly questions the Governor's decisions on matters of

Above Left: New year, new hair. Later promotional shot of Erica. Above Right: Looking good Erica! Patsy plays up to the camera in her green Governor's outfit.

discipline and security but, like those inmates hauled before her on numerous charges, Vera gets short shrift when questioning a decision made with great thought and deliberation. This makes them an uneasy alliance. Erica knows that trying to rehabilitate the women is the way forward, however Vera's *modus operandi* is to ensure they endure the daily punishment that society demands having sentenced them to imprisonment. From the earliest episodes Vera and Erica are frequently at loggerheads over prison discipline. Erica tries her best to ignore Vera's digs, criticisms and sharp put-downs but certainly knows when insubordination rears its head. Following Vera's latest acid quip after Erica is sympathetic to Marilyn and Eddie's burgeoning relationship in Episode 13, the Governor makes her stand. 'You had a great deal to say yesterday and I let you say it, only because I do not wish to humiliate an officer in front of her colleagues, but I will speak my mind now, Miss Bennett, and you will listen very carefully. I am well aware that you exceed your authority in some areas and that your overall attitude to the women is quite at odds with the way in which I would have this prison run.' She is on a roll and not even Vera can intercept her verbal missile. After a dressing down Vera is dismissed. 'Let me remind you that I am in charge here and you are not. Return to your duties.' The Department clearly has not chosen Erica for the job based on her exquisite dress sense.

Erica's relationship with Meg is much easier. Having the trust and the support of her senior officer makes the two of them suited bedfellows and more often than not it is Meg who stands by Erica when the dreaded Department Head, Ted Douglas makes an appearance

demanding higher standards and compromising the running of the prison with his ill thought-out decisions that would frequently stall Erica's attempts to run a fair and educational incarceration for the women. Very early in the series run, we meet Barbara Davidson, Erica's niece, which places Erica in a very difficult position. Barbara has been arrested for possession of drugs and this means that 'Aunty Erica' has to walk a fine line between fair treatment and the desire to be rid of her niece as soon as possible lest she fall foul of the firmly anti-drugs policy of Queen Bea.

Life for Erica is never easy at Wentworth. Her hands are tied by the Department and more than that, she is often frustrated when dealing with the women as they betray her trust and try to manipulate the Governor into thinking and doing what they want. Erica is quite intuitive and knows that there is often more to what the women are telling her, but the 'no lagging' rule prevents any real trust between the Governor and her charges. A little nod to romance was briefly introduced when suave factory boss Andrew Reynolds enters Erica's life, providing work release for the Wentworth girls. It is short lived, of course. In soap land there can be no such thing as happy endings. The fight for ratings mean bigger and bolder drama scenarios and certainly the writers of *Prisoner* had no shortage of storylines to test the firmness of that perfect hairdo. The arrival of Joan Ferguson into Wentworth brings a whole new level of trouble for Erica. As Governor, Erica has deep suspicions about the motives behind Officer Ferguson's daily actions. She struggles though to prove that the imposing newcomer is anything other than a competent officer of the old school.

Above Left: Patsy King. Above Right: Maggie Kirkpatrick, Patsy King, Val Lehman, Sheila Florance. Right: Patsy King circa 1989.

Erica disappears quickly after a run in with Ted Douglas [360] and it is some time before we see her again. Erica makes a somewhat surprise appearance as a representative of the Department who is sent to investigate conditions in Wentworth [424] and then turns up again [451] acting as negotiator with the striking women. Commanding and forthright to the last, Mrs. Davidson is never seen again in Wentworth. Her reign as leading light in the Department of Correctional Services is over – at least on screen.

When Patsy King first stepped onto the *Prisoner* set she had a wealth of experience at her call on television and stage. Born in 1929 in Melbourne, Patsy trained at The National Theatre as well as becoming a permanent member of the Melbourne Theatre Company. Her earliest role was actually in a school play as Richard II, she told the *TV Times* many years later: 'I wasn't a very butch Richard II but as I was at St. Mark's, an all girl school, the role had to be played by a girl and I won the role!' Having spent some time in England, Patsy returned to Melbourne and by 1964 she had won an Erik Award as Best Actress in a play called *The Fourposter*, thereby showing great potential for this striking lady. Patsy was seen at the very dawn of ABC Television in Australia with a role in an early production of Sheridan's *The Rivals* in 1961 and continued to appear in guest roles for the ABC and Crawford's in such well remembered shows as *Bellbird*, *Dynasty* (the Australian series of the 1960s), *Homicide* and *The Sullivans*. It was a guest role in *Chopper Squad* which went to air in 1978 that brought Patsy to the attention of Reg Watson as he was casting his new drama serial, a show that would make Patsy a recognisable face around the world. 'I am enjoying playing Erica Davidson because she is different and the character is really developing now. I can see a lot more aspects of her.' Patsy told the *TV Times* in July 1979, 'When the series began she was a stranger, austere and completely without feelings, but now she has changed, become more complex, a woman who has feelings but controls them. It's quite a challenge these days.'

Patsy's theatre career has flourished since saying goodbye to Erica. Patsy cites her favourite stage roles as being Helen Walsingham in *Half a Sixpence*, Margaret in *Absurd Person Singular*, Elvira in *Blithe Spirit*, Angelica in *Love for Love* and Helena in Tennessee Williams' *A Lovely Sunday for Creve Coeur*. She did, of course, return to the role of Erica for the 1989 UK tour of the *Prisoner* play.

Patsy King provided a firm presence at the very peak of Wentworth's internal chain of command, her performance adding to the tension and taut nature of many of the scenes as events take their course. She is, in short, a Wentworth legend.

You may go!

PAT O'CONNELL

Played by Monica Maughan

    First episode: 065
    Last episode: 110
    Total featured: 40 episodes

Transferred from Barnhurst prison with Chrissie Latham, mother of three Pat is surrounded by a criminal family. Her husband, Eric, and one of her sons, David, are both being held at Pentridge prison for their part in an armed robbery. This leaves her two younger children in the care of her frail mother. When the kids get too much for her mother to handle, she tells Pat that she must be released by Christmas because she has to go to hospital for an operation and won't be able to manage for much longer.

When Pat is released on parole, in time for Christmas, David manages to escape and turns up at the family home armed with handfuls of presents for the kids. The police find out and an armed siege takes place. Pat is arrested and is forced to return to Wentworth for another year when she is charged with aiding David's escape [77].

Pat's sentence is reduced to six months on appeal and she is finally set free to rebuild her life with her family [110].

Hey Jude, Don't Be Afraid,
(Take A Sad Song And Make It Better...)

Although some people might think of long serving top dog Bea Smith as a matriarchal figure, in fact the true 'earth mother' of Wentworth has to be Judy Bryant. Judy arrives at Wentworth concerned for the welfare of her girlfriend of three years, Sharon Gilmour [Margot Knight], who has been busted for pushing drugs. Initially something of a prickly persona, and not averse to brawling with the Top Dog, it becomes apparent that Judy's life thus far has been far from a bed of roses. In her native America, she and her teacher girlfriend Barbara were the targets of small town scandal when their relationship was revealed. The ensuing bigotry and intolerance of a lesbian relationship eventually caused Barbara to commit suicide. Unable to face the fall out of events in her hometown, Judy emigrates to Australia where she earns a living driving a taxi and falls for Sharon's charms. Judy though, is well aware of Sharon's shortcomings, her selfishness and often behaving like a spoiled brat when she wants her own way. It is Sharon's attempts at making Judy jealous by insinuating that she is having affairs with other prisoners that causes Judy deliberately to get caught smuggling in drugs during a prison visit. This is the start of a prolonged stay both inside and outside the confines of Wentworth which would mark Judy out as being among its most recognisable inhabitants to *Prisoner*'s loyal fan base.

Almost as soon as she arrives, Judy is unwell, and a heart condition is diagnosed by Greg Miller. After a pacemaker is fitted, Judy's health improves but the pacemaker proves to be her Achilles' heel on more than one occasion when physical violence is centre stage of Wentworth internal politics. Judy's greatest characteristic is that she cares. She champions the under-dog and protects the weak. Bea Smith and the other inmates are quickly judgemental of new arrivals but Judy always sees beyond the crime, to the events that led to the incarceration. That often means she is taken advantage of – Noeline Bourke being a prime example of knowing how to spin Judy a yarn to get her onside – and Judy is not afraid of going against the Top Dog if she considers that the 'Wentworth law' is at fault and a fellow inmate is not being given a fair hearing.

Playing Judy in a powerful piece of casting, is Betty Bobbitt, herself an immigrant from the US and rising to the challenge of playing a 'bull dyke' figure. Whilst Franky Doyle has been full of angst, self-loathing and violence, Judy's compassion proved to be Bobbitt's focal trait. Through Betty's intense ability to convey the deeply felt need to look after those less fortunate, it became obvious that Judy should leave the confines of the prison and set up the Halfway House that became a mainstay of many of her episodes. Bobbitt's natural ability to play accurately a vast array of traumatised emotions in close-up made it easy for the scriptwriters to target her with some heavy story lines. None more so than the bitter war between disgraced officer Jock Stewart, played with great relish by Tommy Dysart, who murdered Sharon by pushing her down the stairs of the jail. Although forced

 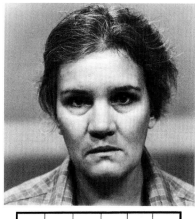

Above Left: Judy Bryant promotional image. Above Right: Mugshot complete with her prisoner ID number.

to leave the prison service for misconduct, Stewart's brutal despatch of Gilmour cannot be proved. From that moment on, Judy is determined Sharon's death should be avenged. Feigning a heart attack, she later escapes from a hospital and finds refuge with Helen Smart. Judy ends up working at Doris' Massage Parlour in her effort to track down Jock Stewart (we kid you not). But, when the two finally meet, Judy's attempt at killing him backfires. She is overpowered and Jock makes more threats. He demands $300 from Judy every time he visits the massage parlour otherwise he'll bash her and turn her and Helen over to the police. Judy decides the only option is to call the police and tell them to follow Jock Stewart if they want to find her. This they do and burst in just as Stewart is bashing Judy [172].

Life for a *Prisoner* regular never runs smoothly and Judy has the joy of having a long lost daughter Lori turn up looking for her birth mother (don't you just love soap land?) and finding she has a grandson into the bargain – all this despite claiming to Jock Stewart, in an earlier episode, that she was a virgin, thereby turning *Prisoner* into something of a tale of Biblical proportions. It is during a visit from daughter Lori and her husband that Judy encounters Jock for the third and final time, spying on him during a day at the races. Thinking she has not been seen by the dangerous Scotsman, she makes her exit. But Stewart has spotted Bryant and revenge is on his mind. He finds out where Judy lives, and follows her to work in her taxi. This time Stewart is demanding $5,000 in order to keep quiet to Lori about Judy's stint as a prostitute. When this doesn't work he threatens to harm Lori. Worse is to come when Jock forces his way into Judy's flat and rapes her. By now desperate, Judy manages to enlist the help of Meg Morris. Meg hides

in a bedroom when Jock next calls, and overhears him demanding the money. As she enters the room, she finds Jock holding a broken bottle to Judy's face, and demands that he leaves immediately; otherwise she will testify against him. This he does. But he is just lying in wait until Meg leaves. He forces himself into Judy's flat again and tries to kill her. Judy sprays aerosol in his face and rushes out. Stewart sets off in pursuit but he has been blinded by the aerosol spray and takes a bad fall down the steps leading up to the flat. Lying on the floor paralysed, he begs Judy for help. She calmly walks away leaving Jock to his fate. It is the end of the war between the two. Although it will never bring Sharon back or make up for what he has put her through, Judy feels some revenge against Jock in the outcome.

Although many more traumas and heartbreak were to come for Judy during her 427 episode stay in the series, Judy does at least have a happy ending. After meeting up with singer Sheila Brady [Colleen Hewitt] in Wentworth, Judy is paroled and hired as a songwriter. 'Pixie's Song', written by Judy about Pixie Mason, is heard over the closing credits of Episode 534, as Judy leaves Wentworth for the last time. It is the only time the familiar theme tune is absent from an episode of *Prisoner*.

Betty Bobbitt brought an exceptional depth of quality to Judy Bryant. Born in February 1939 in Philadelphia, Betty started her career as a theatre actress in Los Angeles before moving Down Under in the early Sixties after an Australian television producer had seen her comedy performance in the play *Auntie Mame* on the stage, and thought she would be great for a night time variety show. Betty never looked back. She was working regularly for the Melbourne Theatre Company when the audition for *Prisoner* came about.

Above Left: From one of her early episodes, Betty poses for one of many continuity shots. Above Right: Judy's worst nightmare – Jock Stewart. Right: Betty Bobbitt portrait. Far Right: Unused promotional shot of Betty as Judy.

I was asked to audition for the role of Bea Smith and, of course, lost it to Val. At the time I was mainly working in theatre but the series interested me a lot as it had a predominately female cast and good roles for women were pretty rare in those days,' says Betty. 'I had already worked with many of the cast when I joined Prisoner – Patsy, Elspeth, Colette, Anne Phelan and Sheila Florance to name a few – but knew many others through various functions. In a way, it was like being a kid again and going on a play date every day! I was made very welcome.

Did Betty feel that Judy was well catered for in the scripts generally?

I pretty much accepted and liked what the writers created for Judy. Denise Morgan, one of the main writers on the show, became a friend over the years and I trusted her judgement completely.' What about the rooftop protest scenes that saw Leanne Bourke fall so tragically to her death? 'The rooftop scenes were stressful for a lot of us but being extra nervous of heights and ledges, I found them pretty scary. The director and crew were very

careful and reassuring but accidents do happen and all I can say is that I was extremely glad when it was all over. The riot scenes were always difficult in that again accidents do happen – a misplaced fist, an unseen elbow – that sort of thing. We eventually had stunt co-ordinators to guide us through the tough stuff but the fire scenes were the worst. Smoke, and potential out of control flames. It made us all quite thoughtful but was always carefully handled by the crew.

And what of that demon Jock Stewart?

Tommy Dysart is a terrific bloke. I loved working with him, scary as those scenes were. Usually after a full-on scene, we'd hug each other while recovering from the violence and anger. Then we'd laugh. After the rape scene I cried a little. Tommy did too I think. He's a sensitive guy.

Betty was lucky enough to work with two Governors. What are her memories of those ladies?

I loved both women governors. As you know, Gerda Nicolson tragically died and it was a

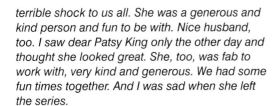
terrible shock to us all. She was a generous and kind person and fun to be with. Nice husband, too. I saw dear Patsy King only the other day and thought she looked great. She, too, was fab to work with, very kind and generous. We had some fun times together. And I was sad when she left the series.

One of the biggest problems an actor always has is keeping the character true and fresh. This is an obstacle for every actor in a long running soap faces.

There are definitely challenges when playing the same role for a long time and for me the main one was keeping Judy separate from Betty. 'What would Judy feel?' I used to ask myself, but toward the end of my time I either responded instinctively or went with what Betty was feeling! Complex. But actors like working on a new character and I began to long to play someone different.

Like many of the actors in the show Betty is amazed by the continuing popularity of the series:

It always amazes me how popular the show still is. I can't go anywhere without being recognised. Recently I've been watching a re-run of the early episodes on television and have begun to understand why it's still so popular. Prisoner gets you in, as they say. Great characters, interesting storylines. If only we received residuals, I could have been rich and famous!

Betty's greatest enduring memory of working on the show is Judy's rape by Jock Stewart:

That's the hardest, most upsetting acting I've ever had to do. Tommy, who is a gentle man, was upset too, as were the crew. We all felt the horror of the crime and when it was over Tommy and I held each other for the longest time.'

Betty released her memoirs of her time on *Prisoner*, *From the Outside*, in 2011.

Prisoner fans took Judy Bryant and Betty Bobbitt to their hearts. To this day, Judy lives on in their minds as the one inmate who fought their fears; Bobbitt was able to portray fear meticulously but in a way that captivated the viewer in a way that proved to be a testament to the very title of the series. From the fantastically written feud with Jock Stewart, through to the more sensitive portrayal of her love for Pixie, Bobbitt always managed to put in a faultless performance.

The sexuality of the character was an important part of Judy, but helped the world to see that it certainly wasn't a defining one. Judy's battles and traumas, her family and what's important in life made her the person she was. However, in true fashion, just as she proved with every other character trait the writer devised for her, Bobbitt would embrace Judy's sexuality by offering a portrayal of a multi-coloured personality and radiant woman who could be funny as well as serious, light as well as dark. The luminosity she achieved in the role as Judy Bryant was never equalled.

BEHIND THE CAMERA: Ken Mullholland's Memories:

1980: LIGHTING THE SET

When we began the series, Les Swift was the, or one of the, Lighting Directors. Following him (I think) Keith Ferguson was the next I can remember.

Some years into *Prisoner*, a Lighting Director, Harry Myers, came over from ABC Channel 2. Now Harry had some new and different ideas re: lighting and wanted to leave his imprint on the show. I can't say for sure that he brought in the 'Blown Out' or 'Bloom' lighting where you see windows in the set that are so intensely lit that nothing can be seen through them, but if he didn't he certainly was an advocate. Before that, windows would have painted backdrops and maybe the odd real tree branch, shaken gently by a stage-hand, or a scrim of material or blinds.

Another device Harry decided to use was known as a lighting 'Go-Bo.' It was nothing more than a large cardboard sheet with cut out apertures through which a light could be played that would cast the pattern across a wall or down a corridor, a bit like making finger-shapes with a lamp against a wall, but in reverse.

So, if you study the later corridor scenes of the show you will see shadows along the floor or against walls that are apse-shaped or oval or round. These are the legacy of Harry. Whether he asked for permission to turn Wentworth Prison into a Mission, a Church or a Cathedral I don't know. At least I sounded it out with the 'Powers That Were' before my suggestions about doors in the walls that weren't originally there.

Harry Myers eventually moved on and I think Stuart DeYoung took over as Lighting Director, along with Rod Harbour.

CHAPTER FIVE

1981
Episodes 166 to 246

I was absolutely ecstatic when I learnt the sort of character I'd be playing in Prisoner. It doesn't bother me in the least that Vera is sometimes a hard case. Fortunately, the script-writers also give her softer moments so viewers realise she is not always a bitch.

Fiona Spence, Australian Women's Weekly, 1980

Prisoner fans had a nail-biting wait throughout January to get more insider knowledge on events in Wentworth. Channel 10 recommenced the show on Tuesday 3rd February 1981 in an earlier 7:30pm slot with a recap of Episode 165, to remind people of the dangers that the celebrated crims had gotten themselves into. The TV listings page of Melbourne's popular daily newspaper The Age described it as a 'generally well-acted Australian drama serial'. One wonders who they thought the offenders were that were not up to scratch.

Prisoner would occupy the 7:00pm slots on Tuesdays and Thursdays up until July when it reverted to its traditional 8:30pm air time. Perhaps ratings were being unduly affected by the toning down of the language and violence. This extra vigilance was necessary for the show to go out before the 8:30pm television watershed, after which traditionally adult programming could begin in earnest.

Regardless of scheduling politics, *Prisoner* hit the ground running with the continuation of the plight of Bea, Lizzie and Doreen trapped in the sewers below the prison. Judy, meanwhile, being on the other side of the fallen debris, legged it to safety with Mouse Trapp, whom she quickly shook off. Seeking refuge with a new semi-regular Wally Wallace [Alan Hopgood], she very nearly comes a cropper when a videotape she makes, exposing the prison system, is traced back to her hideout with Wally. While Judy makes off to stay with Helen Smart, they come up with a plan to get even with Jock Stewart who has frequented the local massage parlour. With Judy enrolled as a prostitute, she attacks Stewart. He easily overpowers

her and blackmails Bryant into working for him at the parlour, demanding big payments from her. Judy turns the tables and tells the cops everything, resulting in a return to Wentworth for her, but with the feeling of managing to do some good out of escaping by getting Jock arrested [172]. This isn't the last we'll see of Jock Stewart though – the best is yet to come!

Sheila Florance (TV Week, 1981):

Like Lizzie, I'm gregarious. I also like a drop of booze now and then on the occasion. At Prisoner we all get on so well. It is like a wonderful family. The cast gave me a magnificent surprise for my birthday a few weeks ago. Betty Bobbitt baked a gorgeous cake for me. They're wonderful. I had a few days off recently and they were so glad to see me and I was so happy to see them. Prisoner could go on for years. I don't see why it should change.

One new face to *Prisoner* would turn out to be a lady who, under a later guise, would become another

Above: The comedy duo of Doreen and Lizzie proved extremely popular with viewers. Right: Judy and Lizzie in the dining room. "Like Lizzie, I'm gregarious" says Sheila Florance who played the old lag for over 400 episodes. Below: Jim Fletcher (Gerard Maguire) comforts Erica Davidson (Patsy King) following her kidnap ordeal.

Left: Two Top Dogs meet at Barnurst: Marie Winter (Maggie Millar) and Bea Smith (Val Lehman)… Below: …but they both lock horns fairly quickly and a return back to Wentworth is on the cards for Bea. Right: Episode 215, scene 4. Terry Harrison (Brian Hannan) with Inspector Grace (Terry Gill) and an un-named Gate Guard.

popular inmate in the series' final years. Julia Blake turned up as self-righteous herbalist Evelyn Randall, intent of proving herself innocent of the poisoning charge levelled against her by the authorities. As is the way with soaps, logic never gets in the way of a good storyline and Evelyn secretly poisons the inmates and staff, in an attempt to prove she can cure them of their 'illness' with her herbal remedies. Her wonder cures are inevitably short-lived when Bea suspects foul play and forces a confession. It is then that Randall feels the full force of the Queen Bea wrath, when a booby trap of methylated spirits and a candle causes an explosion resulting in nasty facial burns [179]. End of storyline and a quick trip to Barnhurst for the wayward medicine meddler. Julia would return later in a second smaller role before making her presence felt in a major way in 1986 as battered wife Nancy McCormack, one of Rita Connors' infamous Wentworth Warriors.

Two years in from its 'on air' debut, Prisoner was still pretty much flying high with viewers. Bea, Lizzie, Judy and Doreen had become familiar faces across Australia's television landscape and much loved by those tuning in. Even Wentworth's bit of sour cream, Vera Bennett, was enjoying enormous popularity with the viewing audiences. The storyliners were working overtime to come up with new and tantalising scenarios for the avid follower. One of these involved the kidnap of the bouffant extraordinaire herself, Erica Davidson. Some rather daring students decided that their pal in Wentworth would benefit from an early release and who better to lobby than Mrs Davidson via the persuasive argument of a loaded shotgun? But our Erica is made of stern stuff. With impeccable vowels intact and her hairspray holding body and soul together, Erica sees off the threat with typical efficiency although some police marksman have to take some credit for getting her out of the scrape too [232].

Although the series continued to rate well with viewers and the media, the Sydney Morning Herald believed that the show was doing nothing to promote healthy eating with Wentworth's own dining room meals being brought into question. The newspaper declared that there were far too many close-ups of the meals being served and that the cast's waistlines were being affected: 'Doreen, particularly, has eaten herself into a prime podge and the other two (Bea and Judy) aren't far behind, or rather they are far behind and broad to boot,' they wrote. Another attempt in 1982 to bring to everyone's attention to the dining room scenes fizzled out as quickly as their first did, while only further demonstrating the media's fascination and obsession with the female body, even in the early 80s. The real truth with *Prisoner*, however, was that it portrayed women of all ages in all shapes and sizes, just like the real world.

Speaking of prison food, it was no secret at that at the best of times the food used during the dining room recordings was just about edible after the first few scenes. Due to the series being filmed out of sequence, it made sense and cut down on time if all of the scenes in the same sets were filmed at the same time for that particular week, thus saving money on what was an expensive production to record. Therefore, a selection of different dining room scenes was always filmed within the space of a couple of hours, to save having to continually re-dress the sets and arrange camera angles. If you watch closely enough you'll notice that only the brave few managed to actually eat something and there was a lot of 'food acting' taking place. Quite often, food was simply just moved around the plate because after half an hour it would be cold. Generally though, there wasn't a great deal of waste because the days were long during filming and so the cast and crew needed to eat. So good old Wentworth slop became the meal of the day for around eight years.

The Logie Awards for 1981, hosted by Michael Parkinson in Sydney, once again confirmed *Prisoner's* popularity. The show was named 'Most Popular Drama

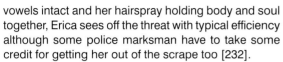

TERRY HARRISON

Played by Brian Hannan

First episode: 199
Last episode: 223
Total featured: 25 episodes

A welcome new male officer, Terry quickly becomes friends with Jim Fletcher who challenges him to go on a date with Vera. He accepts but gets more than he expected when the two officers' meetings turn into something more serious and so an affair with Vera quickly develops. The two move in together and appear to be very happy.

Terry, however, is persuaded to start putting bets on the outside for the women. Margo Gaffney shows Vera the money that she has won and tells her that Terry brought it in for her. Vera naturally doesn't believe her [205]. He continues to exchange bets and alcohol with Margo in exchange for useful information about the prison. However, Margo has taped their conversations and attempts to blackmail him. Cue a long drawn out search for the said tapes.

As Terry and Vera's relationship reaches breaking point, it isn't helped by the arrival of Terry's ex-wife Kathy Hall [213]. He suggests that Kathy keep their marriage a secret but inevitably it becomes public knowledge.

When Kathy is killed in a hit and run when she's released, Terry thinks that all of his troubles are over but in true Prisoner style they're not. He has managed to get himself involved with the notorious John Fitzwater, who admits to killing Kathy [223]. When Terry is seen talking to the police, he is shot down in front of Vera's eyes when they're walking outside of the prison. He dies instantly and Vera is left alone once again.

BEHIND THE CAMERA: Ken Mullholland's Memories:

1981: THE SCENE WE JUST COULDN'T GET IN THE CAN

I can't recall the Director, yet I think this took place one night in the studio cell-corridor junction. I recall it to have been a two-hander, the culprits Fiona and Elspeth. Possibly, the 'cardboard handbag' may have contributed, but of course I had come back from a liquid 'meal' break and was a willing part of what followed. And what followed were many takes, up to somewhere around twelve/sixteen.

Much face slapping, big breaths, stomping of feet, coughing and throat clearing, and still the lines dissolved into tears of laughter. The two of them couldn't even look at each other in the finish without bursting into gales of mirth.

Eventually, the Director suggested the abandonment of the scene and we moved on. I don't recall us re-shooting it another day, but possibly it happened when I was absent, or was re-written.

Left: "The Frustrations of Vera" was one of the novels based on the series which caused huge uproar with the cast.

Series' and the mighty Sheila Florance was crowned 'Best Lead Actress in a Series'. Both Colette Mann and Gerard Maguire found themselves among the nominations too. It was further evidence that *Prisoner* was among the prize stallions of television.

An attempt at novelising the series for the American following backfired in a big way for Grundy Productions. Pinnacle Books obtained the rights to the storylines and characters and issued a series of novels written by Murray Sinclair, Michael Kerr, Henry Clement and Maggie O'Shell. These started off as being based on the television series but quickly descended into free-for-all plotting and characterisation.

Titles such as The Frustrations of Vera referred to the 33-year-old Officer Bennett as being hated by the inmates and ruling with an iron fist. Quite accurate until it started delving into Vera's private life and apparent craving for a man – 'She stood there in his embrace, naked except for her shoes and stockings'. A surprise change in direction from the old Vinegar Tits that viewers knew and by now, had loved to hate, it appeared that the whole series of books had been written simply to sensationalise the series and bring in some inappropriate profit from the familiar *Prisoner* brand.

It came to the notice of the cast, and in particular union rep Val Lehman, that the depictions of the characters were bordering on the pornographic, a far cry from the carefully crafted personas and behaviour on the small screen. Val was certainly not amused:

> Our American fans alerted us to the grubby tone of these books. Due to the actions of the cast, led by me, they were withdrawn from sale. Only to appear again suddenly when the show was airing in the UK, and disappear just as suddenly when I got involved!

1981 also brought to television screens the long awaited male counterpart of *Prisoner* in the form of *Punishment*, written by Reg Watson and Alan Coleman. Hot on the heels of the phenomenal success of all things Wentworth, the Reg Grundy Organisation was keen to replicate a similar story with a television drama series set in a penal institute for men. The pilot episode was filmed in Sydney and directed by familiar faces Rod Hardy and Bruce Best. The action took place in the fictional Longridge Prison and a great deal of research went on to ensure that life on the outside would also be featured in addition to

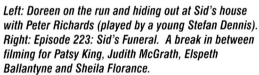

*Left: Doreen on the run and hiding out at Sid's house
with Peter Richards (played by a young Stefan Dennis).
Right: Episode 223: Sid's Funeral. A break in between
filming for Patsy King, Judith McGrath, Elspeth
Ballantyne and Sheila Florance.*

behind the iron bars. The opening scenes introduce the series' main characters including the Governor played by Barry Crocker, the man responsible for the original voice of the *Neighbours* theme tune. A number of flashbacks attempted to tell the backstory of why the prisoners had been sent to Longridge and were cut in between the various arguments taking place between the Governor and his chief officer in scenes which could easily be compared to those with *Prisoner*'s Erica Davidson and Vera Bennett. However, the difference between *Punishment* and *Prisoner* was the integrity factor – while Erica and Vera were quite believable and realistic characters, Alan and Jack from Longridge were seen as very poor imitations.

The expectations of *Punishment* were perhaps too high and even a young Mel Gibson in the cast couldn't give it the start that it needed to become as big a success. He had left after the first few episodes and new characters were quickly introduced. Storylines became inconsistent and attempts to bring in some light comedy to the show failed. Even though production on the series was completed by late 1980 it took some time for the first episodes to air, and with the decision to screen it in Melbourne on a Saturday evening at 8:30pm the chance of its picking up the thousands of viewers it needed was slim. After only three episodes, the series was taken off the air and didn't return until November when the whole series was shown from the start, but with changes in timeslots and schedules, before disappearing completely.

Punishment was seen as an absolute disaster for the production company. A great deal of time and money had been spent developing the series which they thought would be a huge success. However, no amount of money could make up for the poor characterisation, boring plots and ill-chosen time-slots by the TV network. It appeared to be doomed from the start and it goes without saying that a second series was not even considered.

Back to Wentworth and, in an attempt to shake up the series, a major storyline saw Bea transferred to Barnhurst by Ted Douglas [196]. The often referred to country prison rewarded us with our first glimpses of a couple of Wentworth greats. Gerda Nicolson, later to replace Patsy King as the Governor of Wentworth, makes her *Prisoner* debut as stern faced Officer Roberts. On the other side of the metaphorical fence, the Barnhurst Top Dog turns out to be none other than that greatest of nasty lags, Marie Winter, played so superbly by Maggie Millar. Her gutsy swagger and throaty laugh marked her out as a *Prisoner* great from the off and the writers must have known Millar's performance was one of those special melds of an actor and character that marks a truly memorable television performance. Another returning face saw Bob Morris' daughter Tracey being forced to collect 'magic mushrooms' to enhance Barnhurst life. Inevitably, after a few skirmishes with Marie, Bea is recalled to Wentworth. However, a minibus crash sees Bea escape unknowingly, and on the outside suffering from amnesia. Cue a long drawn-out storyline that would involve the return of Wentworth favourite from the early days, Mum Brooks [Mary Ward], who harbours the vague redhead until events take their rightful course and Bea finds her way back to her friends, with little memory of life before the crash [200]. A bash on the head from Margo eventually restores Bea's memory and the Top Dog resumes her command of the steam press [202].

The normally stony-faced Vera Bennett manages to find love for a short time with the arrival of new male officer Terry Harrison who is hiding a secret in the form of his ex-wife Kathy Hall, who turns up in Wentworth as an inmate. The path of true love never goes according to plan and, not long after Kathy is run down by a car on her release, Terry himself is shot dead by gangsters when he leaves the prison [223]. Vera finally reaches the coveted position of Governor when she is asked to take on the task of running Barnhurst prison [224]. She slips away from Wentworth unnoticed, not even attending her own leaving party to say goodbye to her colleagues.

Fiona Spence (Prisoner Cell Block H Volume 14, Shock DVD, 2007):

She wasn't as old as she looked or behaved, but I liked playing a complex character like that. I was a lot more fun than her! I did enjoy playing her very much and enjoyed all of the interaction with all the other characters working on the show. I had the opportunity to work with so many people which was a great pleasure and great working experience for me. Where would we have all been without shows like Prisoner *– even for just*

Top Right: One of the Wentworth corridor sets, with Gerard Maguire and Judith McGrath exchanging words. Bottom Right: Patsy and Elspeth receive some directions while filming the scenes for Vera's leaving party. Above: Meg, Steve, Colleen and Erica discuss the day's events in the office.

Above: Sid and Lizzie fall in love. Bottom Left: "The Frustrations of Vera" was one of the novels based on the series which caused huge uproar with the cast. Right: The arrival of officer Steve Fawkner (Wayne Jarratt) saw some younger male eye-candy for all at Wentworth.

a consistency of work for women, which was another of its absolute plusses.

Episode 224 also saw long-serving producer Philip East step down to be replaced by another of the shows longstanding contributors, John McRae. McRae had directed a number of *Prisoner* episodes so was perhaps once again ideally placed for dealing with the production difficulties of making two hours of television per week. McRae had the difficult task of ensuring that the loss of Spence, one of the real lynchpins of *Prisoner*, was felt as little as possible on screen. He planned that viewers would welcome an influx of new characters while continuing to enjoy the further escapades of the loyal regular cast, all of whom had developed such a devoted twice-weekly following.

With Vera now out of the way, a battle between the officers takes place for the much sought after Chief Prison Officer job. While Meg has tried her hand at working on the outside as a parole officer, her marriage breaks down and she returns to Wentworth as a screw again. It seems that she and Colleen Powell, now nicknamed Po-Face by the women, are both keen to get the role. Colleen is victorious after some behind-the-scenes dealings with the prisoners and dirty tricks, to make her application for the position look more appealing than her loyal and probably better qualified colleague.

Someone who is luckier in love than Vera was Lizzie. After becoming close to prison handyman Sid

Humphrey, the two love birds begin making wedding plans. Sadly, Sid's health deteriorates after suffering a stroke shortly after they meet. He dies in his home with Lizzie by his side. When she is released on parole, she lives in Sid's old house and has been given everything by him in his will, much to the disapproval of Sid's son Gordon. He starts a campaign against Lizzie by scaring her witless in the hope that she'll move out. When Lizzie finds out the truth, she takes matters into her own hands and burns down Sid's house, only managing to hold on to a bagful of prized possessions [239]. A swift return to Wentworth is, of course, on the horizon for the old jailbird.

Towards the end of 1981, Val Lehman extended her annual break from the show to stretch to five weeks in order that she could film the part of 'Big Lil Delaney' in the movie *Kitty and the Bagman*. Thus, Bea was destined for a kidney transplant, enabling Val to record a batch of scenes from Bea's hospital bed and Val's hefty presence on set could be explained away as recuperation. And while Val reaped the rewards of a $5,000 a week movie role alongside fellow *Priz* stalwarts Colette Mann and Gerard Maguire, the series was about to get if not a 'breath of fresh air', at least a waft of summer breeze to fill the gap. Wentworth is soon to be under the rule of new inmates, psychotic Doctor Kate Peterson (Olivia Hamnett) and a new welcome toughie in the form of Sandy Edwards (Louise Le Nay).

With Bea out of action in hospital, the Top Dog position is up for grabs. Sandy wastes no time in

taking over and there is the usual power struggle on for who works the famous steam press in the laundry. But with Judy's weak heart and nobody strong enough to back her up, she sides with Sandy and so a new era begins. Sandy isn't all good, however, and when she's approached by mobster John Fitzwater to recruit young women to work in his massage parlours on their release, she is happy to go along with the plans.

Kate, meanwhile, is a force of her own to be reckoned with. She is two-faced but very clever as we'll find out later. To settle into the prison, she stays on the winning side with Sandy but finally she reveals her true colours. Olivia Hamnett proved a tour de force during her stint in *Prisoner*. Her multi-layered portrayal of Doctor Kate Peterson drives the show for much of the time she is behind bars. British-born Olivia explained her character to TV Week in November 1981:

> *Kate is more sophisticated than the usual criminal. Although she commits a crime, she's still very intelligent and remains a class above the rest of the women. I was hoping to play someone of a lower status in Prisoner, but I can't seem to get away from my image. My brother in England says I sound very Australian but, obviously, Australian producers think otherwise.*

Olivia went on to reveal her apprehension during one scene when she arrived at Wentworth in a paddy wagon:

> *It was an horrendous feeling getting inside that thing. It's just galvanised iron with bars on the windows. When the doors shut on you, it's like being in a metal box. I've always had a fear of ambulances and the same applies to prisons.*

As the storylines geared up for a Christmas break cliff-hanger, the prisoners were given an early festive present. A redesign of the famous Wentworth uniforms arrived complete with denim jacket emblazoned with the WDC logo in yellow. They were definitely the must-have fashion accessory amid the designer chic of the Correctional Services year. The real reason for a surprise change in uniforms was due to the originals almost dropping to pieces, having been worn since the very first episode was filmed. Nobody had expected them to be used for more than the original 16 episodes and, over 200 showings later, they had faded and were wearing very thin. It was quite some time before the officers were treated to a new look though. Jennifer Carmen remembers having to re-style the uniforms:

> *There was a change of prisoners' uniforms: a heavier weight, more durable denim, built to last beyond a few months, and a wider range of garments. Rather more attractive checked shirts too. A flash of colour came even to Wentworth as the 1980s rolled on.*

Just in time for an end-of-year classic cliffhanger, Wayne Jarratt joined the regular cast [245] as rather dishy officer Steve Fawkner. A favourite with cast and viewers alike with his Tipp-Ex smile and knee-trembling suave manner, he was to become the only regular male cast member of the series when Gerard Maguire left early the following year. Talking to TV Week about his appointment to Wentworth, Jarratt explained:

> *He's nothing like Gerard's character. Obviously Steve is much younger. But, apart from the age difference, my character has no ambition of becoming Deputy Governor like Fletcher. He doesn't want to get involved with the Wentworth power plays. My character does develop and change, but not in the same direction as Fletcher. All Steve wants to do is get enough money together so he can build a boat and go sailing around the world. I've learnt a great deal in my short stay on the set and I consider myself very lucky to get such a solid role. It's a great experience and I would like to continue on Prisoner as long as possible.*

By Episode 246, the cauldron of emotions had reached bursting point with a newly transferred Marie Winter happy to guide Sandy in heading an all-out riot, rampaging through the prison armed with cobbled-together weapons and petrol bombs. Viewers love a riot and this one is a humdinger! Steve and new officer Janet Conway [Kate Sheil] are trapped inside the prison with the women in control while Meg and Jim narrowly avoid a nasty confrontation at reception and manage to flee the building unharmed. The final moments of 1981 were explosive in every way as Grundy Productions sought to make the traditional Christmas cliff-hanger one that the loyal viewers would remember throughout the festive period.

SLAM. 'He used to give me roses...' For Australian viewers, there was an agonising gap of several weeks. For the rest of the world catching up years later, there was a slightly annoying nail biting wait until the next scheduled episode.

Vinegar And Vulnerability

> "She struggled in the outside world. She couldn't dance. She didn't know how to dress. Didn't know how to do her hair or make-up. But when she put on that uniform and signed in at Wentworth Detention Centre, that is where she ruled!
> Fiona Spence, Prisoner DVD interview

Left: Early shot of Fiona Spence as Vera 'Vinegar Tits' Bennett. Above: Fiona takes a break in between scenes, in the staff room set. Below: Poor Vera was often the butt of jokes played by the inmates.

If any resident of Wentworth is a true contradiction it is Vera Bennett, senior officer and sometime Deputy Governor. Within the walls of the prison she does not allow even the slightest hint of a chink in her armour. While constantly barking orders and ensuring that the women know they are in Wentworth to be punished, outside the prison she is lonely, insecure and lacking any real friends or the social abilities that allow her to find a social circle.

Franky Doyle gave her the nickname that became legend, 'Vinegar Tits'. It is a phrase that would find its way outside of the programme and into popular slang to describe someone who is sour and a killjoy. Vera makes up for her ineptitude outside the prison with an obsessive ambition within it. She envies Erica Davidson and her position as Governor, and frequently clashes with her superior on all matters of prison security and discipline. Vera has the ability to be deliberately spiteful, and this is mostly saved for the prisoners although on occasion fellow officers can feel her acidic presence too.

Vera's home life is not easy. She looks after her increasingly frail mother to the best of her ability and gets only criticism and put-downs in return. For someone with so little personal confidence this mental

abuse is wearing and damaging. Each time Vera's mother lays into her it is like a knife into Vera's own heart. 'You are old and tired before your years, Vera,' barks her mother, perhaps conveniently forgetting that she herself has played a large part in making that happen. When Vera's mother passes away, what little outside company Vera gets away from the prison is all but gone, and she turns to drink to drown her sorrows. Her loneliness eats away at her. She longs to be loved but her own emotional wall prevents friends from entering her world. Inside, Vera is a scared and emotionally scarred girl, but she masks this with a singular desire to take out her aggression on the prisoners in her charge. It makes for an uneasy combination. The one prisoner who Vera particularly takes a dislike to is Bea Smith. Bea is one of the few who directly refers to her as 'Vera' rather than 'Miss Bennett' which immediately demonstrates a total disregard for Vera's authority. Perhaps she senses that Vera is as much a prisoner as they are. Certainly, Vera's decision not to allow Bea to attend her own daughter's funeral is a wedge between them that can never be removed, and because of this Bea likes to make things as difficult as possible for Bennett whenever the opportunity presents itself. While the inmates are trapped within brick walls, it's a mental barrier that suffocates Vera. As a result, she resents the bonding between the prisoners when she in fact has no abilities socially at all.

Perhaps because of Vera's reliance on drink to give her courage in rare social situations, she is very bad at choosing potential friends. A prime example is

George Lucas [acting legend Bill Hunter], a gangster boss whom she meets in a bar with her former colleague Anne Yates [played by *Prisoner* stalwart Kirsty Child]. She is forced into protecting Yates when she is imprisoned in her desire to please Lucas but, as with any romance in Vera's, life it ends in disaster as Lucas is forced to go on the run. He does, though, have enough feelings for her to spare her the career she lives for, feigning overpowering Vera for effect when the police inevitably call round to her apartment.

Once again, any social failures are readily taken out on the women. Vera's spite comes to the fore during Doreen Anderson's parole, taking great personal delight in causing trouble for the ex-inmate. However, the combined might of the women is a powerful force within the walls, and Bea makes sure that retribution is dealt out by snatching Vera's keys and forcing the Governor's whisky down her, so that she is found drunk and passed out. It's only Meg's intervention that stops Vera from being sacked on the spot. The only prisoner Vera shows any sympathy for is Lizzie. And for her part Lizzie is inclined to be less critical of Miss Bennett, and even on one occasion gives her a

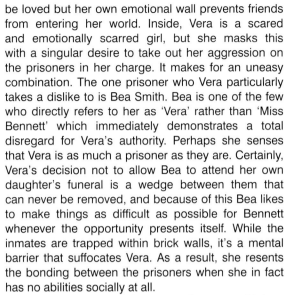

ANDREA HENNESSEY

Played by Bethany Lee

First episode: 228
Last episode: 236
Total featured: 9 episodes

During a protest outside of the Detention Centre in aid of prisoner rights, Colleen Powell is attacked by Andrea Hennessey, which leads to the protestor becoming an inmate of the very prison she was protesting against.

She isn't popular with the other women, so her mates on the outside arrange to get her out of the prison one way or another. After their first attempt fails, they decide to kidnap Erica Davidson and hold her hostage demanding that Andrea is released.

With Erica being held captive out of the city, the women at Wentworth decide that they don't take kindly to having their Governor taken away, so arrange a sit-in protest and hold Andrea hostage in return for Erica being released!

Andrea's friend Linda Golman is caught and sent to Wentworth. Luckily, Erica is found safe and well. The friendship between Andrea and Linda becomes strained as the two become enemies and blame each other for what has happened. They fight and both end up in hospital after an accident in the kitchen. Linda manages to knock out the officer who is watching over them at the hospital and steals a gun. Andrea and Linda end up on the fire escape of the hospital as they continue to fight and Jim manages to bring the situation under control, even after being shot in the arm [234].

Linda hangs herself over Andrea's bed [236]. After Andrea is bashed by Sandy Edwards she is moved to E Block for her own protection until her release date.

Top Left: Her favourite place of all in the prison – the Governor's chair, although she didn't get to sit in it very often. Above: Elspeth Ballantyne with Fiona during filming. Top Right: Vera finds love with fellow officer Terry Harrison (Brian Hannan). Right: Their love affair is over when Terry is shot dead in front of her.

birthday present of a bar of soap. Obviously, years of looking after an elderly disabled mother makes Lizzie's plight in Wentworth resonate to some degree.

An engagement to fellow officer Terry Harrison looks as though it may bring some lasting happiness to an otherwise blighted life but, as is the way in the world of soap, happiness is not to last. Terry is being pursued by gangsters, and not only is Vera attacked but Terry is shot dead before her eyes.

The viewers bid goodbye to Vera Bennett in Episode 224. She had applied for and been granted the Governorship of the country prison Barnhurst. Finally, she had made it. She has reached where she wants to be – the top of the pile. Vera shows no emotion on her last day and, looking every inch a Governor in the mould of Erica, she walks out of Wentworth with barely a look back. It's a new start for her professionally, but personally who knows?

30-year-old Fiona Spence was among the last of the regular players of *Prisoner* to be cast. Producer Ian Bradley and creator Reg Watson were looking for an actress who might be right to play a hard-bitten warder but with the ability to play vulnerability during the course of the show. It proved a bigger task than had been imagined. Scores of actresses were auditioned in Melbourne and Sydney, before casting director Kerry Spence suggested her sister-in-law Fiona at the eleventh hour. Fiona, born to an Irish mother and an Australian father in Kent, had only recently graduated from studying drama with a fleeting appearance in *Glenview High* and a few commercials to her name as a professional actress.

Fiona revealed to *TV Times* in July 1979:

Up until a few years ago I was only interested in having a good time. I worked for a firm of architects but decided that wasn't for me. I have lived in Canada for a year and studied drama for three years at the University of New South Wales. Last year I visited my mother in England for eight weeks and saw a lot of theatre. I never looked for a job because I wanted to see how well I do in Australia.

Prisoner is my first major role in a television series. I am very happy with Vera Bennett. She's very dramatic and in some ways like myself. She is very unpopular with the public and the more they hate her, the better it is for me. Then I know my character is working.

Similarities between Vera and her *alter ego* Fiona are few and far between. Fiona is very much a social delight, great fun with a wonderful sense of humour, miles away from Vera's inner turmoil.

I remember a particular night when I was at the movies with Elspeth Ballantyne. An avid viewer congratulated Elspeth on her performance and asked me whether I watched the series!

Post-*Prisoner*, television roles have included *I Can Jump Puddles* and *Law of the Land* while Fiona was to make a big impact with viewers at Channel 7 as Celia Stewart, puritanical sister to Ray Meagher's gruff no-nonsense Alf in *Home and Away*, a role she played as a regular between 1988 and 1990. Fiona achieved her ambition of acting on the British stage in the *Prisoner* stage show along with the play Lipstick Dreams at the Shaw Theatre, London. Fiona drew great reviews for her pantomime debut playing the Wicked Queen in Snow White and the Seven Dwarfs, and then subsequently The Empress of China in Aladdin, both in Stoke-on-Trent. While in the UK, Fiona appeared in the ITV game show *Cluedo,* among many other promotional television appearances. Back home, Spence was also one of the *Prisoner* team competing for the *Sale of The Century* with fellow cast members Val Lehman, Colette Mann and Maggie Kirkpatrick in a 1995 special. Fiona returned to acting in 2012 as Eleanor in Channel 7's *Packed to the Rafters* and reprised the role of Celia Stewart in *Home and Away*.

Left: In pantomime playing The Wicked Queen in Snow White and the Seven Dawrfs at the Theatre Royal, Hanley in 1990. Co-starring Jessica Muschamp as Snow White and Mark Thrippleton as Prince Charming. Bottom Left: The menacing glare of Vera which could curdle milk. Bottom Centre: Vera's final scene, she didn't even attend her own leaving party. Bottom Right: Fiona Spence's fan card from her time on Home and Away as Celia Stewart, circa 1988.

Fiona Spence

Best wishes
Fiona Spence

⑦ *Home and Away*

Prisoner in Concert

"
*I remember being involved in a 'Village People'
sequence. Betty Bobbitt was the Indian,
Sheila Florance was the motorcycle guy, Val
was the construction worker, but I was
in a gold kind of foil suit. I kept thinking that I just look like a
'Crunchie' bar jumping up and down on the spot!*
"
Jane Clifton, Prisoner documentary (unscreened)

The continuing popularity of *Prisoner* on Channel 10 was cemented when a variety special featuring the talents of the series' cast was commissioned. The plan was to record the special in front of an audience of real life criminals and their families at Pentridge Prison (which closed its gates as a working penal facility in 1997). Betty Bobbitt was tasked with writing the dialogue and sketches, with Jane Clifton taking on many of the lead vocal duties. Prisoners had been invited to be in the audience, including some from the new high-security division Jika Jika, later renamed K Division, which housed some of the most dangerous and longest-serving inmates.

Inset Right: Prisoner in Concert was broadcast on 7th May 1981 and hasn't been screened again since.
Below Left: Lead singer Jane Clifton as Margo Gaffney, with Betty Bobbitt as Judy Bryant on guitar and Val Lehman as Bea Smith on the trombone. Below Right: The cast perform Jailhouse Rock.

The television company set up a large marquee in the grounds of the jail with a stage and rostra to seat the audience. Following a fraught rehearsal period, the musically talented ensemble from Wentworth went through a series of sketches and songs, all in character. The spectacular opened with our heroines Colette Mann, Betty Bobbitt, Val Lehman, Sheila Florance and Jane Clifton dressed as The Village People and belting out that pop classic 'Y.M.C.A.' which had been a hit in the Australian charts as

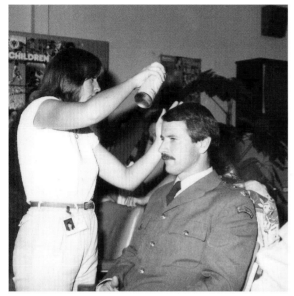

Top Left: Gerard Maguire gets his hair and makeup completed before turning back into Jim Fletcher on stage. Bottom Left: Bea, Jim and Judy mid performance. Top Right: The finale of the show. Bottom Right: The girls pose whilst in their Wild West outfits.

indeed it had around the globe just a couple of years earlier. This pop onslaught is broken up with the arrival of Gerard Maguire in the guise of Jim Fletcher, who advises that they need some 'style, flair and *je ne sais quoi*' (a song from the 1974 musical *The Magic Show* written by Stephen Schwartz, composer of the hit shows *Godspell* and *Wicked*). Next it is the turn of Sheila Florance to shine in a laundry room set piece in which she performs 'Steam Heat' (from the musical *The Pyjama Game*), making up with enthusiasm what she lacks in real musical skill. Colette Mann proves what a fine vocal talent she is with a version of the 1934 ballad 'I'll String Along With You', sung to Doreen's ever-present teddy bear. Jane Clifton is perhaps the most experienced of all the performers

when it comes to singing and she certainly delivers the goods, as she takes the lead on the Elvis Presley hit 'Jailhouse Rock', with each of her fellow inmates pretending to play an instrument in the background as Jane rips through the number in fine form.

The trio of Bea, Doreen and Judy offer some advice on men with 'Find Out What They Like' from the musical *Ain't Misbehavin'*. Bea is concerned that she is a player short for the next sketch and so Mrs Davidson offers to step up into the breach as we head to the Wild West with cowboys in Coburg City. Thus, a parade of cowboys, bartenders and a beautiful Southern belle is completed by Val Lehman's turn as Mae West singing 'That's All Brother, That's All'. Finally, our Wentworth ladies accept their lot in life with a medley involving re-worked lyrics to 'We're a Couple of Swells' and 'There's Gotta be Something Better than This' (from *Sweet Charity*).

The real inmates had been auditioned for a role in the special finale and 25-year-old Jimmy Doyle had won the talent search and performed the song 'Going Home' at the end of the special, particularly appropriate as he was being released the following day! Recording was not as smooth as everyone had hoped, with frequent recording breaks for costume changes, lighting and set adjustments. The live audience thankfully didn't get too restless and riot, although this might have upped the entertainment value a notch.

Speaking in 1981, one of 10's producers Paul Stone described the production as a 'variety romp – pure entertainment' but also admitted that there was a lot of planning and preparation needed, with plenty of tension in the air when it was time to put on the show.

He explained further during an interview with *TV Week* in 1981:

> There was an incident in a Sydney jail some time ago, when the Salvation Army gave a concert and a prisoner tried to rape one of the girls and stabbed her. So we had to be careful nothing like that could happen. There were armed guards sitting in the audience and all around the area. There was no trouble.

The programme went to air in the Channel 10, 7.30pm slot on Sunday 3rd May 1981 in Sydney, while the good people of Victoria had to wait a few more days until Thursday 7th May to catch up with the larks at Pentridge. Val Lehman recalls:

> I remember hardly any rehearsals. Less for me than anyone as we had to fit them in when

GEORGIE BAXTER

Played by Tracey Mann
First episode: 175
Last episode: 186
Total featured: 12 episodes

One of the first new arrivals of the 1981 season, Georgie arrives at Wentworth with a bang having attacked another prisoner in the paddy wagon during the journey and soon causes a kerfuffle in reception while she is being inducted and smears fingerprint ink all over Jim Fletcher's face. She's sent straight to solitary and wastes no time in ripping up the uniform which she has been told to wear. Similarities between Georgie and Franky Doyle are immediately noticed.

Georgie's main problem is her temper. Teacher David Andrews stands up for her and suggests that she comes to his classes, but she refuses and ends up in the laundry instead. This doesn't go too well as she can't accept instructions from anyone else, resulting in her attacking Bea and ending up back in solitary. When she has calmed down, she is moved in with Judy to whom she admits that she can't read or write very well.

When Judy misreads Georgie's friendship with her and a fight breaks out between the two, it isn't long before David realises what might be the cause of her problems – her hearing. A quick test confirms that she has 'glue ear' and this can be corrected with a small operation, which is swiftly arranged and completed without any problems.

She gets involved in further brawls with the other women and causes a lot of issues between them. When a fight in the dining room gets out of control after Mouse stubs a cigarette out on Georgie's plate, Bea gets caught in the crossfire and is left unconscious on the floor with an injury to her head [182].

When she is released, Georgie appears to go back to her old ways and returns to her old boyfriend who only uses her for sex. Georgie, though, has a new job at the local supermarket and a huge improvement in her health and reading, and she realises that she's doing herself no favours. She resolves to start anew, leaving the past very much behind her.

not on set shooting. The audience in the real prison were not told it was a concert. They were expecting it to be a special contact visit with family and loved ones. They were then forced to sit and be a rather unresponsive audience. The power games the real screws played!

Looking at the broadcast now, with the benefit of hindsight and tongue firmly in cheek, it is probably a fair crack at showing off unknown talents of the cast. The television audience were, by and large, unfamiliar with the actors outside their *Prisoner* characters. However,

by today's standards, it lacks polish. Think of a keen group of amateur theatricals putting on a show, and it is more of a curiosity than a highlight of the *Prisoner* brand. It can generally be found unofficially on popular internet video sites, and fans have campaigned to have it released on DVD but various copyright and screening issues have prevented this from happening. Frankly, you are better waiting for it to escape as then there is always the hope of recapture! Some of the stars involved might not be too impressed at reliving their experience either: 'If you plan to show an excerpt of this, I'm leaving town,' says Jane Clifton.

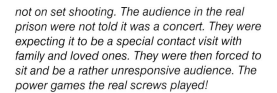

DAVID ANDREWS

Played by Serge Lazareff

First episode: 171
Last episode: 194
Total featured: 24 episodes

Teacher David Andrews arrives at Wentworth during Episode 171 and quickly has his idealistic intentions brought back down to earth again when Vera welcomes him to the prison. Initially, the women are not that impressed either.

Unfortunately, only Doreen attends David's classes but she is not interested in learning as she has, in fact, developed a crush on the handsome young chap who is trying to teach her the brilliantness of Shakespeare and kisses him when he's in mid-flow. Unfortunately, Jim walks in right at that moment to catch them in the act [172]. David is reprimanded by Erica and is told that they can't be left alone together.

Surprisingly, he and Vera strike up an unlikely friendship and they even go on a shopping trip together to buy David some new clothes. Vera is disappointed after inviting David to dinner only to find out that he has a girlfriend, so any feelings she might have had for him are quickly extinguished.

David is responsible for changing Georgie Baxter's life around after taking an interest in her and finding out that she is deaf and that this has been the source of all of her childhood problems. When she is released and seems to make a go for herself on the right track, this is David's one and only success story.

When his relationship with the prison staff begins to deteriorate, he realises that he doesn't have their support and can't continue teaching the women. The education centre has been a failure and has only resulted in problems for both the officers and the prisoners, who are now on strike. He resigns and the prison is forced to search for another teacher.

In Hind-Sight
by Peter Hind

Studio and Location Cameraman – Episode 3 to 618
Audio and Floor Manager – Episodes 619-692

Left: Filming on location with Maggie Kirkpatrick.

Leftt: In the shadows of the studio the cameras are set up for filming the next scene. Right: Ken Mulholland.

Working on *Prisoner* was a bit of a learning curve for most crew. For a start, not many programmes anywhere, and most assuredly in Australia, had a cast like it. Predominately female and comprised of such strong characters and personalities, it was an extremely interesting Green Room. It was one of the few TV drama productions on which I have worked where the cast and crew were really quite tight and worked to a common purpose. Many lasting friendships were forged between cast and crew. In many ways it was a case of us, cast and crew, against them, production house and network management.

Workwise, it was both fun and demanding. It is not on many programmes that a camera operator can drag or push a pedestal at full pelt around a corridor complex through doorways and into a cell and then cover a scene encompassing anything from a chat to a murder or a full-blown riot. Long, long days and an ever-increasing work load. Managements always want more for less. Somehow, we managed to get it done. This could not have happened if the cast and crew did not have a good rapport. Mayhap it was more through necessity than friendship but the fact remains IT WAS.

Pressed For Time
By Mark Collins

Cameraman and Props between Episodes 233 and 636

Left: Mark Collins with the Prisoner *girls. Right: Val Lehman on the famous steam press.*

I finished my final year at school, 18 years of age, and had applied for a job at ATV 10. During my last month at school, I was lucky enough to spend one week on 'work experience' at Channel 10. I had made good contacts and was told about a new show called *Holiday Island* that was waiting for 'sign off' and to begin production very soon.

Straight after the Christmas break I called the Production Manager on a regular basis, reminding him that I have finished school and was ready to begin working at Channel 10 doing anything. Finally I received the call. *Holiday Island* got the green light to begin production, meaning most of the crew working on *Prisoner* would transfer to the new show and *Prisoner* would need more people to 'top up'

that crew. So, my first job in television production was 'props' on *Prisoner*. How good is that! My job was to supply all props for the actors and extras, plus 'dress' the set ready for recording. The most nervous but exciting part of being in the props department on the set of *Prisoner* was operating the steam for 'The Laundry Press'. Just off to the side of the laundry set was a small boiler with a gauge and control valve. About twenty minutes before we started shooting scenes in the laundry set, I would top up the water tank and turn on the boiler so it was ready to produce 'steam' for the press. The actual surface of the press was not heated, so when someone's hand was put under there, it was actually a little cold being solid stainless steel. There was, however, piping running along the outside where steam originally came out of, which is where my job came in. As Val (Bea) lowered the press down, I would turn the valve at the right time to release the steam. Then when the press was lifted up, I would close the valve to stop the steam from coming out. I had to watch closely so my timing was right. We had rehearsals of course, so it all went well -most of time. I must say, we didn't have to do a 'take two', thank goodness. Another part of my role in 'props' on *Prisoner* was supplying the food for the Dining Room scenes. I would pre-order the pots of prison food from the Channel 10 kitchen well in advance. One day, we shot thirteen dining room scenes in one afternoon. I have never washed so many dishes (in an industrial machine) in all of my life. Funny thing is, the women would get right into eating during the first couple of scenes. However, by the time we got to shooting the 5th, then 6th and so on up to the 13th scene, the girls were finding it very challenging to act like they were starving prisoners craving a meal!

Cast assemble for a group photo in 1981.

CHAPTER SIX

1982
Episodes 247 to 326

The usual Christmas time cheeriness obviously blotted out the plight of the Wentworth ladies until it was time for Channel 10 to put our future Blockies out of their misery as the riot is reaching its dramatic peak [247]. Steve and Janet are trapped inside the building, hiding as best they can from the women baying for blood. Sandy alerts the media to the action by the women, and gives a list of demands to the Department. Erica is called back from home and is rather shocked not only by the action of the women but also by the fact that a rather hefty breeze is playing havoc with her hair. Ted Douglas arrives with his usual sensible advice: call out the troops and liberate the prison from the rule of the rebels. While trying to phone the police from the Governor's office, Steve is captured by the women and stripped to his underwear as the tension reaches fever pitch. Jim, the Vietnam veteran, launches an offensive into the prison and quells the riot with tear gas. In the confusion, snow-haired tough nut Marie, dressed in Janet's prison uniform, attempts to leave the prison in disguise but is foiled. So the status quo is restored for the time being. However, 1982 is about to witness some prison politics at its most corrupt.

The on-going story threads continued with Sandy and Kate leading the action. Bea is given a clean bill of health, and the power triangle suddenly becomes a four-way tussle. Naturally, Bea and Marie are at loggerheads once more, with the ginger one putting a stop to Marie's drug dealing in the block with her usual 'hands off my steam press' stance. Judy is given her parole but promptly runs into Jock Stewart during a day at the races. This third clash with the deep throated Scotsman has much wider-ranging ramifications for Judy. In a harrowing scene which demonstrates what fine actors the series had in Tommy Dysart and Betty Bobbitt, Jock brutally rapes Judy but, as in the settling of all villains, is shortly to get his just desserts when he falls down some stairs in pursuance of Bryant, thus leaving himself permanently disabled. It is perhaps fitting that our nastiest screw to date should bow out in troubled style to make way just a few short months later for the leather-gloved force of the series' greatest villain.

Louise Le Nay, a young actress who had little experience on television, was making her presence felt on screen as Sandy. Here Louise shares her time as one of the famous Top Dogs:

The audition wasn't a lengthy process at all. I flew down to Melbourne from Sydney and read a few scenes for the casting person at Grundy. What I really remember was the producer at the time was Godfrey Philipp, and my nervousness at auditioning for Prisoner *was overshadowed by my excitement at meeting him. He was a well-known producer of some famous Aussie children's TV shows in the sixties and seventies. One in particular,* Adventure Island*, I had enjoyed for years and I continued to watch long after I was too old to really fit the target age group. I don't know if many people auditioned for the role of Sandy. Certainly there was no one else there on the day I was called in. I was cast and*

Top Left: Louise Le Nay as Sandy Edwards. Top Right: The madness of Dr. Kate Peterson. Left: Sandy knifes Fitzwater [256]. Above: Val Lehman accepts a Logie whilst Olivia Newton-John looks on.

at work in a fortnight. I remember it being a low-key business. Part of me was philosophical. It's a tough industry and I was new to it and didn't want to break my heart over missing out. So I tried to be relaxed, but deep down I was excited at the prospect. I loved the idea of working with such a well-known group of women, and getting to play an interesting character. At the time, there weren't a lot of stimulating roles for women. Sandy was described to me as 'tough but fair', which isn't a complex description. Sandy was supposed to be someone who grew up tough through a lot of childhood difficulty and deprivation. Not educated but street smart. But I think, as with all the characters on the show, we were expected to bring something special about the character to life ourselves. I wasn't sure about Sandy. It's easy to play simple emotions, so I just went for 'tough' in the first episode, because it takes time to feel those more complex and real emotions. Vulnerability on the other hand is more difficult because it requires some amount of emotional honesty. I think because I was young, and therefore nervous about showing my own emotions, it took a few weeks before I began to connect with Sandy's vulnerability. And it was her vulnerability that brought her to life for me.

On the set, it was relaxed usually and focused. We had a number of scenes to do every day, and no way of catching up if we fell behind. So we all worked at a cracking pace from the 6:30am call until we were finished for the day. Occasionally – very occasionally – someone would get the giggles about something and it would go through the cast like measles. It probably drove the director mad, especially if it happened to be a scene in the dining room for something and we were all struggling to be serious. In the Green Room, where we all waited to be called on set, it was more chatty. People knitted or read books. I did a bit of both. I am a terrible knitter and turned out a couple of garments full of holes or knots. I am a big reader though. Sheila Florance was a talker and had lots of stories. Judith McGrath was always very funny, and there was often some singing because Betty and Colette had great voices. They had a singing act with Jane Clifton. When the three of them were in the Green Room together they'd occasionally sing a number or play around with a song. It was delightful.

I learned a lot about television from Peter Hind, one of the chief camera operators. He was always gentle and funny – and patient. I learned about the importance of hitting my mark and I learned what the crew expected from the actors. Up until then I had not really had much experience on a set. Ray Lindsay – 'Uncle Ray' – who was the First Assistant Director, I think, was totally calm always. Good natured and friendly. I learned how important those traits are in a working environment. In fact, I think the crew on Prisoner were some of the nicest crew guys I've ever worked with. I wish I could name them all, they were all brilliant. I doubt I ever thanked them enough or showed them enough gratitude for being patient with me.

It was a great cast – the leads; the extras. Nearly everyone was someone that you wanted to spend time with. I really loved Elspeth Ballantyne whose pragmatic approach to work and warmth and wonderful sense of humour I really admired. Sheila was a legend, of course. Olivia was always elegant, always professional. Maggie Millar, my great enemy on camera, was, of course, a real, sincere, decent human being whom I care a great deal for. Jentah Sobott, who played Mouse, was a terrific person and utterly committed to the craft of acting – smart and sincere. There were many others.

No one had put together a show that was almost completely female before. Not many have done it since. So the show had an immediate appeal because it felt different. There was no emphasis on beauty. There was no glamorous make-up. The women were meant to look real. The show also appealed to the love we all have of seeing through keyholes into a world that we might not normally experience. Ronnie Barker had given us a humorous and semi-serious look into gaol in Porridge. I'm sure the success of Porridge and, in particular, its brilliant cast of characters must have influenced some of the creative planning for Prisoner. Prisoner had a core collection of characters that were immensely appealing: Lizzie Birdsworth, Doreen – certainly a new representation on TV at the time. I also think there was something likeable about the characters who were not high achievers – people who were struggling with poverty and hard times; people who were making mistakes, either willingly or unwillingly. The actors who created those characters were all skilled. So it was a compelling combination. Characters to care about; characters to hate; characters that we hadn't seen on TV before. It was a world that fascinated us because we didn't know much about it. In the end, it comes down to a mysterious chemistry that worked at that magic moment in TV history.

There were lots of storylines I enjoyed, although it's funny to think about it now. I had a

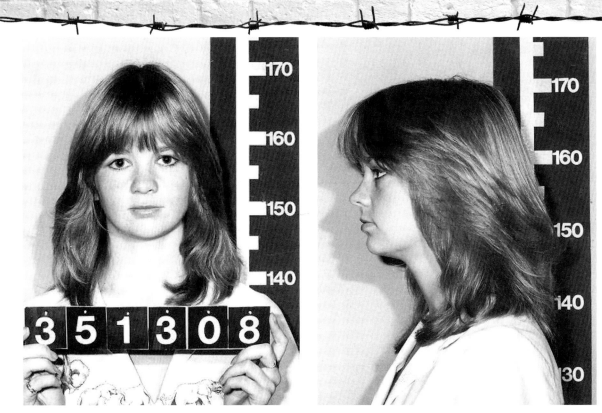

Unused mug shots of Jacqui Gordon as Susie Driscoll.

story line where my enemies tried to hang me in the bathroom. It gave me a chance to yell a lot. And I had an affair with a male prison guard, the lovely Wayne Jarratt. That gave me a chance to get my clothes off. Well, not really, I wore a body stocking, but it was fun pretending.

There are periods of time when people do still recognise me. Usually, it's when Prisoner *is being repeated sometime. When I have had a haircut, someone will stop me in the street. It always takes me by surprise. It's both disconcerting and flattering. I'm really glad I entertained people, even if only for a short time.*

Judy's story arc takes another turn when she opens up a Halfway House with the backing of the Department. Judy's caring side is given official status as she welcomes women as a stopgap between prison and returning to everyday life. Betty Bobbitt's masterful portrayal of loveable mother hen Judy makes her the perfect character to front the Halfway House storylines. It would never have worked had, say, the much more power-hungry Bea Smith been granted release to do so or indeed the other paroled Musketeer, Doreen. These characters were too essentially flawed to make the situation tenable. Naturally, being proprietor is no walk in the park for her. To a certain extent, Judy now has to enforce the rules and regulations of this official

safe haven and is a warder in all but name, albeit one in kid gloves.

The reign of Janet Conway is brought to a close, ending Kate Sheil's year-long contract with the show, in Episode 274. Having started a relationship with printing press guru Ian Mahoney [Peter Curtin] and finding herself pregnant, she disappears into the metaphorical sunset for one of *Prisoner's* happy endings, we would like to think. The character of Janet Conway has divided fans who constantly discuss the merits of Janet's time in Wentworth. Certainly Kate has seemingly has put Wentworth firmly behind her.

Doctor Kate Peterson, meanwhile, moves into the main focus of the storyline. She has been feeding the police information on the inmates for months. Peterson has been showing signs of more mental instability as she realises Sandy and Bea know about the lagging. With just about everyone after her, including Marie Winter who has been charged with drug trafficking in the prison, Kate and Sandy head to the rubbish skips for a showdown [264].

And that is the last we see of Sandy Edwards. It is never established what went on during that clash. Did she escape? Was she murdered by Kate and hidden in the skip? Actress Louise Le Nay was seven months pregnant by this stage and hiding the bump was becoming harder for the directors. Le Nay finally had to break her six-month contract in order to be released from the series. Sadly, hopes of a return for Sandy were not forthcoming and she remains a bright beacon that shone through a time of upheaval within the *Prisoner* legacy.

Kate Peterson survives longer at the epicentre of prison action, with Olivia Hamnett's characterisation highlighting clearly displayed psychotic tendencies. Inevitably, after trying to strangle Judy, she is transferred to a secure mental hospital for the criminally insane

KATE PETERSON

Played by Olivia Hamnett
First Episode: 235
Last Episode: 273
Total featured: 39

SANDY EDWARDS

Played by Louise Le Nay
First Episode: 235
Last Episode: 264
Total featured: 30

Sandy's arrival at Wentworth [235] leads to a shift of a balance of power between the ladies of Wentworth. Sandy has been in jail before – a stint in Barnhurst, but here she is facing a murder charge and life imprisonment. Immediately gunning for the Top Dog position which Bea cannot defend due to her frail state of health, she tries her best to be good steam press material but hasn't quite got the staying power of Bea. Her arrival coincides with that of Kate Peterson. It is Peterson who would prove to be the worst ally that Edwards could wish to choose. Dr. Kate has all the guile and cunning of a jackal. Using her medical condition she diagnoses Bea's kidney complaint which endears her to the women at first. But it soon becomes clear that Peterson's sole motive is to look after number one. Putting herself forward as an informant to both Inspector Grace and Colleen Powell, she is playing dangerous games. Meanwhile Sandy Edwards has come up against the sneering might of Marie Winter who has been transferred from Barnhurst. Marie is instrumental in goading the women into a riot [247]. It is Sandy who is blamed squarely as ringleader for the riot and ends up in solitary. This is great news for Marie Winter having Sandy out of the way whilst she lays claim to the steam press for herself. However, Bea and Sandy team up to topple Marie, with Hazel hiding some dope in Marie's cell when a cell search is due. Kate tries to ingratiate herself with Marie, Bea and Sandy but all the time she is handing information to the authorities. Treachery comes easily to Dr. Kate Peterson. A lagger is at work in the prison and everyone is under suspicion, but Bea has worked out where all the strands of deception lead – to Kate Peterson's door. Marie and Sandy, now united against Kate, draw cards to see who will dispose of her. Sandy gets the job. During an exercise period, Marie causes a diversion so that Sandy can get Kate alone. But in a shock twist of fate, Kate rejoins the exercise period with Sandy nowhere in sight. As the garbage truck empties the hopper, Kate is consumed with the noise of the crusher [264]. She is now quite unstable and psychotic. When a transfer to Barnhurst is ordered she refuses to go after seeing Marie Winter also in the transfer van [269]. With all the women now against her, Kate tries to kill Judy but Kate is now so far over the edge she loses grip with reality and whilst in solitary starts holding an imaginary surgery for her patients. There is no other choice but to transfer Kate Peterson to a hospital for the criminally insane [273].

[273]. Hamnett's multi-layered performance had been driving the show for months, as her web of deceit builds. Olivia's untimely death in 2001 from a brain tumour robbed the industry of a fine actress. Her Dr. Kate Peterson is a stand-out performance which has endured among the fans' own list of favourite inmates.

The Logie Awards of 1982 once again paid tribute to Australia's finest in all departments and *Prisoner* came away with the 'Most Popular Drama Series' award for the second successive year, having beaten *Cop Shop*, *The Sullivans* and wartime epic *A Town Like Alice*. Val Lehman scored an impressive double and was reduced to tears as she collected both the 'Most Popular Actress' and 'Best Lead Actress in a Series' honours. Sheila Florance and Betty Bobbitt were also among the nominees for 1982 but, sadly, both were beaten to the post. Ironically, Florance was beaten by Val Lehman when they found themselves pitted against each other in the 'Best Lead Actress' category.

One character that was to find favour with viewers was the young Susie Driscoll, who is placed into Wentworth at the age of sixteen [260]. She is deemed a big risk since she keeps running away from the institutions she has been placed in from an early age. She continues her attempts at escaping. During one of these involving crawling through the prison air conditioning ducts, she becomes stuck in the confined space. Not knowing what is causing the blockage, maintenance men pump some powerful chemicals into the system to clear it. As a result, Susie is hospitalised. Seeing another opportunity, she absconds from the hospital and goes on the run only to be returned several episodes later. Jacqui Gordon remembers her time in Wentworth:

I started modelling at the age of five. This also helped bring money in for Mum who was a widow.

Kids were not able to go on TV in those days until the age of seven years old. As I was one of a few kids in the industry I got a lot of work on Homicide, Division 4 and Matlock – a police show my soon-to-be father was in. My dad, Vic Gordon, was also an actor and comedian. Mum married Vic in 1975. So Prisoner happened after I had left school. From memory, Jan Russ helped me with getting the part – I was about twenty years old. I do not remember being auditioned as I was on quite a few shows at the time. The role was only to go for six weeks and the writers kept me there for six months!

When I first arrived in the Green Room, I was shitting myself. At the time, Colette Mann and Betty Bobbitt were friends of the family, so it was great to have them there. Sheila Florance was also lovely. You see, I may have been twenty but only looked sixteen. My memories of the set were fun, although very long days as you had to be in most of the scenes even if you had no lines. The day after my first episode went to air, I went to the local shopping centre and some of the tough kids yelled out, 'There is that slut from Prisoner'. *In my first episode I did not even open my mouth. To this day, I remember the scene on the show and the kids at the shops as though it were yesterday. It's funny how some people perceive you as being different. I guess you are in their home on the TV and they think they know you. This is the part I do not miss. The 'escaping' storylines made it very exciting. My favourite would have to be the air conditioning ducts. Everyone was so worried for me as I had to get in to a real duct that they had put on the studio floor. Trust me, I was in there for quite a while. And loving it.*

Despite some of the strongest episodes to date, viewing figures were starting to waver and original

New arrival Joan Ferguson wouldn't have much to smile about for long.

producer Ian Bradley was summoned to assume his chair again. He figured the series needed a bad screw, a character that would be able to match Bea Smith in the power struggle stakes, a deadly and vicious woman who could be every bit as nasty as the worst of the crims but hiding behind the safety net of the officer's uniform. Initially conceived as a lesbian character nicknamed 'The Bear', this later changed to 'The Freak' and in came the biggest impact on the show since the original cast had wowed audiences back in February 1979: Maggie Kirkpatrick as Joan Ferguson. Ian Bradley explains her arrival:

> Some years after I'd left the show, and when the show's ratings were wavering, I was persuaded to return to produce for six months and boost the ratings. While I was away, Vera had left the show. Franky had already gone and there was a complete absence of a regular hate figure, either prisoner or warder. I decided to fill both requirements with a crooked screw. I actually created the role of The Freak for Maggie and discussed it with her before the character was even written. Again, I knew Maggie from Sydney fringe theatre and the Gladstone Hotel and knew she would be perfect. She is totally fearless as an actor and a person. I recall that when I went to meet her at the Gladstone Hotel, Carole Skinner was there. She and Maggie were great mates and they worked a lot together, and for the first time we discussed the fact that Carole had turned down the role of Bea. She told me her agent had told her we weren't paying actors to relocate in Melbourne, which was bollocks, so she couldn't afford to take the role. Had she called me directly, things would have been different.

While Wentworth was still reeling from the sheer brazenness of Ferguson's run for power, only a few short episodes later, viewers were having to say goodbye to another of the original jailbirds. Colette Mann had decided that after more than 300 episodes, it was time to seek pastures new. She told Jill Fraser of TV Week:

> Since June last year I have been considering a move, but it's not easy to turn your back on a secure job that helps you make a lot of money. It's a big decision and I never make decisions quickly. Working on Kitty and the Bagman was a happy experience for me. It forced me to think more seriously about my future and gave me a chance to play comedy for the first time since I did stage work. Prisoner was, and still is, a happy experience too, but I've felt over the last year I haven't been contributing as much as I

Margo Gaffney is tarred and feathered for the bashing of Meg Morris [310]

can... I leave on very good terms with the Grundy Organisation and I am welcome back at a later stage, if that is what I want.

Doreen is finally released to see what the big wide world has to offer her [303] and for viewers it was a sad moment to see one of the original Wentworth Musketeers walking through the gates for the final time. However, it wasn't quite the last we were to see of Doreen but it was certainly a wrench for viewers to see such an important character in the development of the show sail off into the sunset figuratively speaking. Mann's own bubbly presence on set would be greatly missed too by all who worked on *Prisoner*. For many, Bea, Lizzie and Doreen were the very backbone of *Prisoner*'s early success.

Behind the scenes, there were ructions in the scripting department. George Mallaby – social worker Paul Reid – had passed behind the camera and was a regular, penning scripts for the show along with Crawford's high rating *Cop Shop*. However, a clash with *Prisoner* producer Philip East over a rewritten script

MAXINE DANIELS

Played by Lisa Crittenden

First Episode: 297
Last Episode: 392
Total featured: 91

Maxine Daniels is a spritely new arrival at Wentworth, full of bravado and mischief. Maxine knows Ferguson from Queensland and uses secrets from The Freak's past to blackmail her. Upon release from Wentworth she heads to the Halfway House being run by Judy Bryant where she wastes little time in making a nuisance of herself. Whilst Judy is absent, she throws a party for her boyfriend Spud and his biker friends much to Judy's horror when she returns home. Maxine finds work as a babysitter for Peter and Sally Dempster but finds that their daughter Anne is being subject to child abuse [316]. After another short stint in Wentworth, Maxine finds herself working for Judy at Driscoll House. She feels she has to return home after her father dies of a heart attack. But Daniels relationship with her mother is not good and when Spud turns up and goads Maxine into stealing from her brother-in-law Roger, it is inevitable Wentworth beckons once more. A daring escape results in Maxine injuring her ankle. But on the outside, she meets Belle 'Tinkerbell' Peters [Lesley Baker]. Together they both plan to rob a factory but the plan goes tragically wrong when Maxine is shot and killed by the security guard [392].

effectively ended his association with the show. TV Week reported East as saying, 'The effects of his story had serious ramifications at that stage and affected a lot of the following scripts. George didn't agree with us over a story and we had to end the arrangement.' However, East's claim that the parting was 'mutual' was quickly refuted by Mallaby who said, 'I was not planning to quit at all. Philip East may be saying it was mutual but that is not so. I have a letter from Philip East which contradicts that.' It seemed there could be no resolution, certainly on the part of producer East, who effectively dismissed Mallaby from the pool of scriptwriters working on the show. Despite having to part ways with the ladies of Wentworth, George Mallaby continued to provide scripts for television. His death in 2004 robbed Australian television of one of its most respected writers and performers.

Things start to look up for Judy Bryant in 1982 despite her almost deadly final encounter with Jock Stewart. By Episode 291, she is paroled to work for the Department running the Halfway House project which is named Driscoll House after Susie. Judy has purchased the house out of an inheritance from her father's will, and rents it to the Department for the new project. It is to be a mixed blessing for Judy, whose good intentioned idea of making sure women are helped as much as possible when they are set free is

beset by problems. New inmate Barbara Fields [Susan Guerin, 300 – 326] is sent to Wentworth after stealing money from the shoe factory where she worked. She is a canny operator within the prison, and soon starts to get romantically involved with Officer Fawkner. More significantly for Barbara, her plotting and blackmailing, result in her getting possession of Joan Ferguson's diaries. Quite conveniently for this particular soap, Joan has been keeping a record of her every wicked deed in the prison system and Barbara hides the nest egg in the prison as a weapon against Joan's bullying. But the diaries are to be the centre point of a storyline that would result in the most dramatic, and popular, episodes of *Prisoner* ever.

Wayne Jarratt worked out the end of his contract. Steve Fawkner was an early casualty of Ferguson's machinations. Joan was wasting little time in baiting both colleagues and the ladies of the Wentworth charm school to maximum effect. Steve leaves Wentworth in Episode 316 by offering his resignation in order to save Meg from being fired. Actor Wayne Jarratt continued to appear on screen and in theatre until his death on 14th May 1988, aged just 31. His talent had burned brightly before being brought to a devastating end by a brain tumour.

Among the newer faces during this period was Lisa Crittenden. Already a veteran of *The Restless Years*

Above: Lisa Crittenden as Maxine Daniels. Top Right: Faye Quin (Anne Lucas) tries to do a deal with Paddy Lawson (Anna Hruby). Right: Anna Hruby as Paddy Lawson.

and *The Sullivans*, she was to be seen in Wentworth as Maxine Daniels [297]. It turns out that Maxi has done time before at the same jail in Queensland as Joan Ferguson, and knows of Joan's history. Before she is paroled, she shares the knowledge of Joan's relationship with prisoner Audrey Forbes, and her subsequent murder at the hands of the fellow lags who had found out about the romantic liaison. It ignites, of course, much discontent within the ranks as the fairly new arrival is revealing herself to be murkier as each day passes, as far as the Cell Block H ladies are concerned.

Episode 304 featured the arrival of an apparently untamed wild child in the form of Paddy Lawson who immediately has to be sedated by the sister on duty. It turns out Paddy suffers very badly from claustrophobia, and she has been imprisoned for attacking a man at an office party after they were shut together in a darkened storeroom. Paddy's journey in *Prisoner* is one of self-discovery, of finding love and then finally of finding pure evil in a prison uniform.

Actress Anna Hruby had just gotten the key to the door, as the adage goes, when she was cast as Paddy Lawson. It would be a role for which she is remembered to this day. Anna explains:

I originally auditioned for the role of Maxine. I was then told I'd been cast in the role of Paddy Lawson and knew very little about the role until I actually arrived in Melbourne. I remember reading a line another character said about Paddy – 'She's got more muscles than The Freak' – and thinking 'Oh dear! How am I going to act that?' as I was an extremely thin young woman at that point in time! Auditions were held in Sydney at Reg Grundy House in the northern suburb of Artarmon. This would have been 1982 and actors were flying up and down between the two major cities of Sydney and Melbourne to work a lot in those days. Ian Bradley, the producer, was there for the auditions too, which was unusual. I think it was all a bit more hands on back in the eighties.

Originally, I was contracted for thirteen weeks. This suited me fine as I had just met the love of my life in Sydney and was anxious to get back to him. However, the role was extended and I had to spend a little longer in the chilly southern city and make do with long phone calls from the phone box in St Kilda Road. You'll be happy to know we recently celebrated our 25th wedding anniversary, so I guess I had good reason to be keen to get home. I did do some personal research into claustrophobia. Of course, we didn't have the internet in those days so I recall ringing some medically connected friends and getting in contact with a psychologist who had had some experience with the condition. And I think the writers slightly softened the character of Paddy when they saw such a physically slight actress had been cast in the role. I was terrified of all the regulars, familiar household faces by that stage – and with good reason. They were a scary bunch. I was quite a lot younger than most of the cast, only 21, so that was fairly intimidating, too. I remember my first day vividly. I arrived at Channel 10 and was shown into the Green Room. All the main cast were on set filming at the time so I found a chair in the corner and sat down to study my upcoming scenes. The cast finished their scene and wandered into the Green Room. As I recall, there was Val Lehman, Judith McGrath, Elspeth Ballantyne and Sheila Florance. Sheila walked straight up to me and just stood there, saying nothing. 'I'm Anna Hruby,' I said. 'I'm playing the role of Paddy Lawson'. Sheila continued to stand there silently. I looked around nervously wondering what was going on until Elspeth finally said, 'You're sitting in Sheila's chair'. I hurriedly got up and found a chair that wasn't taken, sat down and buried my head back in my script. I'm pretty sure those girls enjoyed playing with us young ones and scaring the crap out of us. It certainly worked. I have to admit I don't have any specific memories of that time, except that there was a lot of laughing going on as I recall, mostly because most of the cast was involved, and a big crowd of actresses always know how to have a good time. In fact, I'm sure other cast members must have told you stories about cast getting sent off set to contain their laughter. There was an awful lot of going up – especially by Judith, Elspeth and Sheila who were notorious!

Another young cast member using *Prisoner* as a training ground was Alan David Lee. Alan arrived in Episode 306 as social worker Tony Berman who becomes a target for Maxine Daniels' amorous advances. Today, Alan is a veteran of many high profile movies and television series but, like many others, he has fond memories of his work experience in this seminal show. He is credited on *Prisoner* as simply Alan Lee. Here Alan sheds some light on

HANNAH DALE SIMPSON

Played by Julieanne Newbould

First Episode: 288
Last Episode: 303
Total featured: 16

On remand in Wentworth for armed robbery, Simpson finds she becomes the object of Joan Ferguson's unwanted affections. During her court appearance, Hannah is the subject of an armed snatch but this is foiled by Ferguson who holds Hannah hostage bargaining for the release of Meg Morris [289]. The gunmen are forced to back down when Joan uses Hannah as a hostage to bargain for the release of Meg. Hannah finds herself sharing a cell with Chrissie Latham and Simpson offers Latham money to help her escape. Bea decides to use The Freak's obsession with Hannah to her advantage, and sets up 'gifts' supposedly given to her by Ferguson for the other officers to find. Ferguson finds out about this and has Hannah sent to solitary. Even there, Hannah tries to compromise Joan when she rips her blouse and accuses Joan of attacking her in front of Colleen [294]. Hannah is eventually transferred to Barnhurst [303].

the change of billing and his experiences in Judy's Halfway House:

I was born in Kenya, East Africa, and the only white child in our area. The Africans I lived with called my father Mister Lee. I thought 'Misterly' was our surname. I became Alan David Misterly until I reached Australia and realised my mistake. But I still thought of myself as having three names, as the family joke of calling me the African name of Alan David Misterly had stuck. At NIDA, having three names was seen as a bit pretentious. Australia loathes any sort of class snobbery. I argued Alan Lee was too short and soft. I cited other actors such as Jan Michael Vincent, Mary Louise Parker and so on, but to no avail. So I was Alan Lee for my first few jobs until my Equity membership came through and they informed me they already had a member called Alan Lee. I reverted immediately to Alan David Lee – it seems a much more natural fit.

I had watched Prisoner *before I was in it. The show was rating well and as a student at NIDA in Sydney there was lots of discussion on its merits and whether we would work on the show if offered a part. Like a lot of the top drama schools, the emphasis was on theatre as a good basis for work – Stanislavski, Chekhov, Shakespeare and all that. But, as always, the debate was over the value of television exposure, the better money*

and the experience of fast-paced studio work. I was swayed by the encouragement of previous graduates working on the show, well-respected theatre actors, and the advice that working with multi-cameras would be invaluable to a young actor. The advice was 'not to stay too long' so I only stayed for three months, despite being offered much longer contracts. I spent a year in England in the late 1970s doing amateur theatre in Stourbridge. Some of the actors from the BBC drama Poldark, *a very popular show at the time, did some theatre there too. They drilled me with the benefits of being versatile and working in as many mediums as possible.*

I was asked to screen test for Tony Berman. I came up with the earring, beard and shoulder bag look, and agreed to do three months only. I thought of Tony as a caring person, not soppy, but really wanting to rehabilitate people. He was not afraid of feelings, outside the traditional male role, but still straight and honest. I remember very clearly my first impressions of meeting the other actors. Wayne Jarratt was on the show and also a NIDA graduate. He did Death of a Salesman with Mel Gibson and Warren Mitchell in Sydney. Wayne was so friendly and supportive. He was cheerful, full of life. Forever fixing his van, doing up a boat and handling all the publicity with ease. He was just a lovely, energetic, positive bloke. Tragically he died so young. It was a great shock for us all.

DONNA MASON

Played by Arkie Whiteley

First Episode: 290
Last Episode: 303
Total featured: 13

Donna Mason is a prostitute who lures Susie Driscoll into her world of sex for cash. Together with her pimp Des, they set up a double date for Susie with a guy called Len. Susie wakes up in bed the next morning and finds payment under her pillow [293]. Donna is beaten up by Des and uses this to coerce Susie into going on the game. Donna is doing drugs and gets herself arrested by the police and sent to Wentworth [296]. Bea realises Donna is an addict; she also finds out that Donna was responsible for putting Susie on the game and is furious. Donna's withdrawal symptoms are getting so bad; she is desperate and raids the medicine cabinet in the infirmary [298]. When Donna is released on remand she goes to stay at Judy's Halfway House and immediately starts shooting up with heroin again. When she is returned to Wentworth, Donna takes a lethal dose of spiked heroin and dies in Bea's arms [303].

Left: Alan David Lee as Tony Berman. Right: Judy and Tony in the Governor's office.

The ladies were a little different. On my first day in the Green Room, Sheila Florance and Val Lehman told the rudest girl jokes they could think of while the other eight or nine actresses watched to see my reaction. I gather I did OK because Betty Bobbitt and Lisa Crittenden, whom I mostly worked with, became great friends. The rest of us soon formed a pretty good working relationship too. When we worked together again over the years, there was always a Prisoner bond I think, because of losing Wayne, too.

Betty was warm and natural, a great introduction to Americans. No airs and graces, relaxed, generous, great fun. Lisa was terrific. We had a mutual admiration, a bit of chemistry (no gossip) and worked well together. It's a shame we didn't do more work together. We had a good rapport. We were always good friends and kept in touch until she moved to New Zealand.

I have always enjoyed working with women actors. Prisoner was different as they were mostly tough, mean characters, as dominant and ruthless as any men. I realised I had to stand firm, not to rise to the bait on that first day or they would peck me to death. I think being in the Halfway House was an advantage as I wasn't directly exposed to the older toughies. They were very experienced and enjoyed being the Top Dogs instead of the usual victims and girlfriends they played. To work with experienced actors was priceless. The multi-camera studio experience likewise. Wayne Jarratt's advice on fame and finance was invaluable. But the most dramatic lesson was the danger of loose and free talk in the studio in between takes. It's easy enough to forget when you are miked up on a film set, even

with the bulge of the battery pack in your back, but in a television studio it is so easy to forget there are powerful people in the control room able to see and hear ALL. Nothing of the nature of Alec Baldwin and Kim Bassinger, but I made some, what I thought were, witty and perceptive remarks – perhaps 'unmeasured' is a kind description – about a particular director. I was given a right bollocking as a result. Others may have been amused but he definitely was not. I have a pattern of injudicious remarks, which have had consequences in my career and life, but I'm sure that incident saved me from a premature death.

I was asked to stay on in Prisoner but I stuck to my 'only three months' stand. I have been offered many long-running contracts on many TV shows and have declined them all. Perhaps theatre snobbery, fear of boredom, but I think really it is fear of publicity and the effect it has on your life. I am personally shy and private, and these shows seem to have a requirement for personal publicity that I struggle with. I live in a remote place, away from all, where I happily seclude myself. Happy to go anywhere to work, and to cause a great stir about the show and character, but then I am off to my corner to observe again.

Perhaps Prisoner has been so popular because there was an opportunity for women to be the protagonists, to be active and assertive, to stand up and confront. This still seems to be an issue in so many women's lives. I have three daughters, and in some ways I think it's even more difficult to be a healthy strong woman now. So the issues still seem to be relevant. Imagine

if the Prisoner *girls had access to social media. The bullying would be extraordinary!*

It doesn't bother me at all when I meet people and they are excited about Prisoner. *As I said, I am personally a private person, and so this reflects in my work. I am inevitably approached as the character – people rarely know my actual name – so it's easy to enjoy their connection to the show or character as if it were a shared experience, an old friend. The oddest people connect with different characters, so I am fascinated to find out why, enjoy it immensely and see it as completely separate from me.*

Now thirty years have gone by. I imagine Tony Berman would be living in an Earthship-style house, possibly as a life coach and living a gentle alternative life. He may well have written books on rehabilitating prisoners, and be against private

'jails for profit'. He would most likely encourage prisoners to write poetry, do drama and paint and would be into yoga and sailing. He would probably be happily married. Perhaps even to Maxi!

The tension between Bea and The Freak was ratings gold, and over the weeks their tolerance of each other was fast running out and the production team knew that inevitably their end-of-year cliffhanger would have to centre on a clash between these two mighty forces. The Wentworth Fire episodes would become not only fan favourites but scenes by which the public at large would affectionately remember the characters and the programme way beyond *Prisoner's* natural television lifespan. It had to happen. Ending 1982 was the one showdown that no telly soap fan could afford to miss. Finally, with nobody to stop them, it was Bea Smith versus The Freak...

BARBARA FIELDS

Played by Susan Guerin

First Episode: 300
Last Episode: 326
Total featured: 26

Barbara Fields is a secretary in a shoe factory where Doreen and Susie Driscoll have applied for jobs. But Barbara is embroiled in a deal with conman Phillip Langdon who convinces her to steal $7,000 from the safe in the factory after which Langdon torches the building and burns it down killing the night-watchman. But her schemes are busted by boss George Logan who plants another $3,000 in her flat and gets her arrested. When in Wentworth, Fields proves herself to be a canny operator among the women. She strikes up a romantic entanglement with Officer Steve Fawkner who offers to try and help with her case. Fields blackmails Logan and Langdon, and a contract is drawn up to make her a partner in Logan's new hotel business. However she is busted by Joan Ferguson and uses the contract to keep Fields doing her bidding. More blackmailing ensues and Langdon arranges for someone to break into Joan's house to get the contract back. In the process, Joan's dog is poisoned and her diaries are discovered, packed from cover to cover with her illegal deeds at Wentworth. Barbara knows the diaries will be her protection from Joan and the women and she hides them in the Governor's office for safety. The women find out that Fields has something over Joan and ransack her cell to discover the secret. Finally, Bea forces Fields to co-operate in luring Ferguson to the isolation block where Bea is waiting... A fire started as a diversion gets out of control and during the pandemonium that follows. Fields tries to retrieve the diaries from the Governor's office. Her charred body is later recovered from the gutted building [327].

Blaze of Glory: The Icon Ignites

Two episodes bridging 1982/83 seal Prisoner's place in TV history

When the women of Wentworth got a Bea in their bonnet, it normally meant that the viewers were in for a spectacular treat. Tension, confrontation, betrayal, mixed with a Molotov cocktail. The first four years of *Prisoner* were about to culminate in a jaw-dropping stand-off between two of the show's best loved characters. The journey arc for Bea Smith had taken her on a whirlwind adventure in only a few short years. While the Top Dog and overseer of the women, Queen Bea's meticulous reign over the women was about to be challenged as she locked horns with Joan 'The Freak' Ferguson in Episode 326, in a deadly encounter which fans still claim to be one of *Prisoner's* defining moments.

Ever since The Freak's arrival, the tension between her and Wentworth's original Top Dog had been simmering away, keeping the viewer on tenterhooks as to when Ferguson would push Bea too far. Ferguson deliberately tries to exploit Bea's weaknesses; she is able to see that there is a chink in her armour. Apart from the memories of her late daughter Debbie, Bea's life revolves around her friends in the prison. She has largely forgotten about a life that could exist on the outside. As Bea's parole gets closer, Ferguson could tell that underneath her hard exterior lay a woman who was frightened of the outside world which by now was completely alien to her.

'Got nothing to say, Smith? That's unusual for you. I ought to book you for dumb insolence right now. But there's no hurry, is there? Got at least another six months yet.'

Episode 326 opens with a shattered Bea Smith being returned to her cell by one of the background officers. Nothing is said as she is put back in her cell, having been told her parole was denied and she would remain in Wentworth for at least another six months. In stark contrast to the non-speaking officer, Ferguson arrives in the background and still manages to tower over the Top Dog from the doorway. Such was the expert work of the directors who would often place one opponent at close range of the camera and audience and their nemesis in the shadows, standing well in the background but with their strength and presence still dominating, overpowering and menacing. Our attention now fixed to the back of the cell door – Ferguson moves closer to the weakened Top Dog. She sneers and mocks Bea who, by now, is at breaking point. Able to realise that she may never be released from Wentworth if Ferguson remains an employee of the prison, one of the series' most talked about and hailed episodes was about to unfold as the entire cast move their performances up a scale and tensions reach fever pitch.

Testament to two extraordinary performers breathing life into the two titans, Kirkpatrick and Lehman played the parts of two nemeses to perfection, each displaying a firm grasp on their own characters as well as a masterful understudy of their opponent. The result was dynamite.

By now, Ferguson's role in the series had been cemented. An unremitting evil genius who would go much further than Vera Bennett in ensuring the women were punished and kept in line, Ferguson used muscle and violence to keep the inmates in check. This provided contrast to Vera, who would seldom be seen in a violent confrontation. Yet Ferguson's main

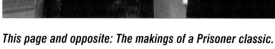

This page and opposite: The makings of a Prisoner classic.

strength was that she was unpredictable. It would call for a punctiliously concocted chain of events to fool the mighty warder and give Bea the chance to deal with Ferguson. The writers of *Prisoner* excelled themselves in delivering a brilliant plot which would make all of the assembled cast shine in their own right. Each of the characters playing a key role in the ensuing madness, testing their character's endurance and in many ways, bringing the series to a point where it would no longer have to prove its worth. The entire team of producers, directors, writers and actors were about to put *Prisoner* on the map by delivering one of the finest and masterfully produced episodes of any Australian television drama.

The stage was set. A supporting cast featuring some characters that had come and gone in the first few years but had returned at the right time to showcase one of the finest pieces of television *Prisoner* would produce in its eight-year run. Chrissie Latham and Margo Gaffney were present to ensure the mayhem would commence with a capital M. Sue Guerin was drafted in to portray the socially aloof Barbara Fields, a character whose cunning intelligence on the outside would prove fatal when she becomes embroiled in

the revenge attack on Ferguson. Paddy Lawson, who suffered from claustrophobia, would have her fears put to the test as she would find herself in a live-or-die situation.

Barbara Fields has become the owner of Ferguson's diaries, detailing stories about the corrupt officer that would ultimately lead to exposing her and losing her job. Ferguson knows that Fields has the diaries and is determined to get them back. She allows Fields to blackmail her into giving her a good report at the next classification meeting. Intent on getting them back, Ferguson is drawn into a web of deceit, unaware that Bea is controlling Barbara and luring the officer to her downfall. Actress Susan Guerin won the role of Barbara Fields as she explains here:

It was the first time I had been involved in an ongoing TV series. In fact, it was the first time I had actually ever auditioned for a part in a TV series. I remember that Colette Mann and Amanda Muggleton really helped me settle in. As you can imagine, I was rather nervous at the prospect of joining this series that had already been playing for a long time, feeling that the cast

Left: Barbara Fields (Sue Guerin) tries to retrieve Ferguson's diaries from the Governor's office. Right: Writer Anne Lucas in her better known role as prison bookie Faye Quinn.

members would probably be a ' tight knit ' little group and, in the main, they were. But Colette and Amanda were both very kind, and really took me under their wing. I also liked Maggie Kirkpatrick very much – a wonderful actress with a great sense of humour. She was a very warm person, completely opposite to The Freak. I thoroughly enjoyed my time on the show.

Ferguson has no idea that the diaries are being used to bait her as the stories contained therein would be enough to have the authorities remove her from Wentworth. She vows to get them back or she will make Fields' life hell until the inmate tells her where they are hidden.

A relatively normal day starts at Wentworth with Officers Powell and Morris on duty in H-Block. A large quantity of turpentine arrives at the prison by mistake, having been intended for Woodridge Prison. Colleen instructs for the boxes to be taken to a storeroom until they are collected. Meg is in the staff room along with a jubilant Ferguson, still rejoicing from the termination of Bea's parole. She overhears a conversation between Meg about how Lizzie Birdsworth is progressing in hospital.

Take off your rose coloured glasses. How long have you been in this job? You know you can't treat whores, murderers and thieves like a bunch of girls at a finishing school.

Ferguson lays down the law to Morris, reinforcing her position in the prison as someone who will be unremitting in making the women pay for their crimes. Kirkpatrick plays Ferguson with devilish charm, enticing the viewer into a love-hate relationship with the character as she demolishes the saintly officer's words of protest. 'You'll have your nervous breakdown long before I have mine' is her reply to

Meg who, by this point, is furious with Ferguson's contempt for the women. As Meg storms off, Joan shakes her head and laughs. Subconsciously, the audience laughs with her.

In the laundry, Bea informs the women that the time has come to launch her attack on Ferguson. The assembled inmates are informed of the role they will play in the proceedings.

With The Freak being lured to her demise, a diversion is required to keep the officers occupied. Chrissie starts a fire in the library by throwing some books onto a table and settling light to them. Unbeknown to Bea or the others, Margo Gaffney decides to light a second fire which would prove to have devastating consequences.

'You're bloody piss weak, Bea. As soon as she comes back you're as good as dead.' Margo nonchalantly delivers the words to the bloodthirsty Top Dog, sceptical over her leader's abilities. In true Gaffney style, she chooses to do her own thing and puts the lives of all her fellow inmates in jeopardy by lighting a Molotov cocktail and throwing it into the very storeroom where Powell had instructed a delivery of turpentine to be kept.

In isolation, Bea lies in wait for her nemesis. Ferguson has been fooled. She searches all the dorms in the block and still no sign of her diaries. It's not until she hears Bea sneak up behind her that she realises that the Top Dog has concocted the plan from the start.

'Congratulations. You really fooled me this time, Smith. How did you get Fields to set me up?'

The mighty warder turns to face her opponent but is quickly brought down by Bea. She overpowers the officer and begins strangling her. Ferguson lies helpless, apparently unable to fend off her attacker. When Joan falls unconscious, Bea staggers out of the room. As the fire spreads through the prison, we return to Isolation where The Freak opens her eyes....

Bea and Joan escape from the inferno.

Maggie Kirkpatrick was one of the two combatants fighting it out in front of the cameras, as she remembers here:

As I recall, the whole physical battle between The Freak and Bea was down to the fact that I had stopped Bea getting her parole and she had managed to get hold of The Freak's diaries. So up we went to solitary to sort it all out while a fire was brewing down below as a distraction for the other screws. The whole fight scene didn't take that many takes as I recall, and the entire thing was down to the extremely talented stunt co-ordinators we had on the show. They choreographed the fight sequences beautifully. It was very professionally handled at all levels. We had little pockets of fire set around the studio, again with the effects team and fire safety people in attendance. We, the actors, were only a small cog in that whole set up. The director, Chris Adshead, was liaising constantly with the stunt people to achieve the best possible result on screen the whole time. We actors were merely put into place and told to get on with what we had been taught.

After Bea's attack on The Freak, Bea stops for a rest at the security gates outside isolation. Having faked being strangled, Joan opens her eyes and makes her way to find Bea. Battered and bruised, she confronts Bea and pulls her to the ground, banging her head repeatedly on the concrete floor.

As the fire spreads and causes all the security gates to automatically close, the two of them are separated by the gate to Isolation. Ferguson looks on in horror as she realises Bea has taken her set of keys, and is lying unconscious out of reach as the smoke begins to fill the corridors.

As Episode 326 gives way into 327, Paddy makes her way through the prison's air conditioning duct in a hope to get to safety. She eventually reaches Bea, with Joan pleading for help from the opposite side of the gates. Joan eventually persuades Paddy to use the keys and open the gates so all three can make their way to the prison roof.

The writer of Episode 327 which resolved the cliffhanger was Anne Lucas, wife of producer Ian Bradley and known on screen as bookie Faye Quinn. Anne gives us the 'good oil', as they say:

The riot and fire which ended the 1982 season here was one of mine. They tell me it's one of the 'iconic' episodes now. I remember it mainly because the director Julianna Focht did such a good job. It's rare for a writer to see their own vision exactly translated to the screen. I was so pleased – and then she rang me and said what a great script it was to work on – another rare

thing, for a director to bother thanking a writer. She was just leaving for a holiday in Bali, but she took time out to ring me. About a week later, her partner rang in great distress to tell us Julianna had died in a motorbike accident in Bali.

The Freak's rescue by emergency services from the Wentworth inferno proved to be something of an ordeal for Maggie Kirkpatrick:

When Bea and The Freak tried to get to the roof we both had safety harnesses that were attached to the ladder. If I recall correctly, Bea kicked back at me and I fell. I, somehow in the middle of it all, managed to swing my right leg which banged into the side of the steel ladder. This resulted in a large bruise and a nasty blood clot. So I suffered for my art with that one. I cannot stress enough though that, throughout the whole of these two episodes, every care was taken to make sure the actors were both OK. Our safety was their prime concern at all times.

I was lowered from the roof on the stretcher. My goodness, it was the best adrenaline rush a girl can ever have. I was terrified and exhilarated at the same time. You just don't get jobs to do like that today, or perhaps I am just too old to do them now. Again, safety was always paramount, but great fun to be in such an overly dramatic rescue scene.

I think we were nominated for awards for those fire episodes. I was immensely proud of the scenes during the fire with Val Lehman. As the antagonist in the piece, I felt we created quite the best conflict between two characters in all 600 plus episodes. Some of the clashes with Glenda Linscott were pretty damn good in later episodes, but truthfully I don't think the dramatic conflict was ever bettered than those taut scenes with Val Lehman. I think they stand as the best work by both of us in the show. The end of that particular season was highly dramatised and because of this, I think, the audience remembers the fire episodes with great affection. Certainly whenever the media talk about the conflict between The Freak and Bea it always seems to be those episodes that are shown as an example. I am enormously proud of them.

Black Gloves and Dirty Deeds:
The Wrath of the Freak

Tuesday 29th June 1982 was a watershed for *Prisoner*. At 8:30pm Channel 10 were about to unleash their special weapon in the nightly soap ratings war. Joan Ferguson stepped into Wentworth [287]. From that moment onwards, the series was never going to be quite the same again. Joan was transferred from Queensland where she had reportedly been involved in a love affair with a prisoner named Audrey Forbes. This resulted in Audrey's death at the hands of fellow lags when their affair was discovered. Joan is completely devastated by these events and sets out to make sure that from now on, any prisoners would pay for the hurt she has locked inside her. Joan wastes little time in showing herself to be manipulative, corrupt, intimidating and psychologically scarred.

From the moment they set eyes on each other, it is hate at first sight between Joan and Bea Smith. Joan recognises that Bea is never going to be onside and will always be a major obstacle in her own quest for complete domination of the women. It is the start of a feud which would come to define the series for millions of viewers around the world. They appeared in just over one hundred episodes together and the sheer intensity of the clash seemed to reverberate through the television screen like no other feud the series had seen before. Ferguson's trademark quickly became her leather gloves. From her very first episode, it was established that when she pulled them out of her pocket there was going to be big trouble: an over-enthusiastic body search, a bashing... or worse. Ferguson was physically taller and more imposing than most of her charges, and this made it quite easy to get her own way through physical intimidation whenever she could. The stark face with no make-up and hair pulled back only heightened Ferguson's look of brooding malevolence to such an extent that the population of Wentworth would come to fear the worst of her at all times.

In many ways Ferguson is as trapped in Wentworth as the women she presides over. During one revealing moment with Hannah Simpson [294] Ferguson lets her guard down just a little, and we see the reality of her life. 'I've been inside most of my life,' she tells Simpson. 'Not as a prisoner maybe, but it amounts to

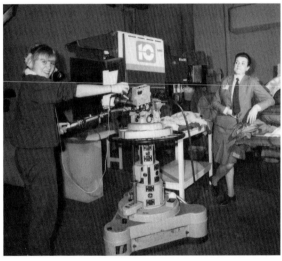

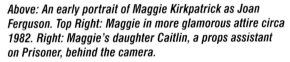
Above: An early portrait of Maggie Kirkpatrick as Joan Ferguson. Top Right: Maggie in more glamorous attire circa 1982. Right: Maggie's daughter Caitlin, a props assistant on Prisoner, behind the camera.

the same thing. People on the outside hate the screws as much as they hate the inmates – maybe more. We do their dirty work for them and that's all they know about. I've learned to take what I can from this rotten lousy job...' The arrival of Maxine Daniels, a young offender who had known Ferguson from her former posting in Queensland, informs the women that she was known as 'The Bear' but by then the Wentworth girls have already decided on a suitable nickname for Ferguson. Lizzie and Doreen are the first prisoners heard to refer to 'The Freak' [296] and subsequently the very mention of the name would instil fear and distrust with anyone having to deal with Joan.

The feud with Bea Smith sees sniping and point-scoring on both sides, but it is evident that both women are itching for a more physical dual. When Ferguson's machinations finally rob Bea of her parole, there is nothing that is going to stop the Queen of the Steam Press from locking horns with the black gloved tyrant. This happens when Ferguson – trying to retrieve her damning diaries – is lured to solitary by Smith just as a fire that has been started as a distraction becomes an inferno thanks to Margo Gaffney [326]. It is the moment *Prisoner* fans had waited months for. The mighty she-devils slug it out on the top floor as the alarms sound and Wentworth is evacuated. In a plot twist, it is Ferguson who is helped to safety by Smith with a roof top rescue consigning them both to hospital. However, it is just a blip in the ongoing

hate-fuelled campaign by Ferguson to rid Wentworth of the red-haired leader of the pack. Spotting the weakest chink in Smith's amour, The Freak uses self-proclaimed psychic Zara Moonbeam [Ilona Rodgers] to deliver bogus messages from Bea's dead daughter Debbie. Ferguson forces Moonbeam to push further and further, hoping to send Bea into such a frenzied distressed state that she commits suicide [366]. However, in the nick of time, Lizzie discovers the plot and reveals the devastating truth to her old friend. There is no Debbie, only the very sickest instalment of Ferguson's ongoing vendetta. Ferguson plays her final ace when she convinces new Governor Ann Reynolds that Smith is cooking up trouble for the prison. Having witnessed Queen Bea assaulting another prisoner, Ferguson escorts the embittered Smith to solitary. 'I'm so close to having you where I want you, I can smell it!' she sneers. It is there Ferguson goads Bea into attacking her by declaring that Sonia Stevens will be bringing in drugs to the prison and making reference to Bea's dead daughter yet again [400]. 'Thank you, Smith... You are very dangerous...,' snipes Joan after the attack, and with this trump card she demands Ann Reynolds transfer Bea Smith to Barnhurst, for the safety of the Wentworth officers, although why Bea should be transferred to a lower rated security jail is anybody's guess. The immoveable object has finally defeated the unstoppable force. It is with an undisguised glee that Ferguson escorts Smith from H Block. 'Sooner or later I had to win,' is her parting shot to a tearful Smith as Lizzie wails at the prison security gate at seeing her oldest mate shanghaied. Thus, arguably, the most memorable of all *Prisoner* feuds is brought to a close.

Ferguson's bombastic behaviour and thirst for power in Wentworth belies the lonely, insecure existence she seems to lead outside it. A visit from Joan's father, a retired Army Major, reveals a lot about their relationship. Joan is desperate to impress and, on a tour of the prison with her father, the women guess the Major's identity and deliberately flout Joan's authority [363]. Later, when she walks out of a meal the Major has thrown for her, it is clear that Ferguson has spent her life trying to impress her regimental father. Her deep-rooted insecurity is that she has been ignored, the Major seemingly favouring Joan's brother Brian and his former Army colleagues. However, all is not lost in the relationship. When Ferguson accompanies her father to medical tests in Sydney, she visits the grave of Audrey and when she returns Major Ferguson reveals he knew all along about Joan's affair and subsequent loss. It is a revealing and healing moment for both of them. Joan discovers a young boy called Shane Munroe

[Robert Summers] breaking into her house. It is the start of a friendship with the young waif that develops into something deeper for them both. Shane has no mother and an alcoholic abusive father and Joan knows she can give him a good home and the love that he has been denied. So she becomes 'Aunty Joan' to Shane, and also becomes an unofficial guardian. However, when the matter comes before the Courts, it is decided Shane should be fostered out. The Major realises that Joan needs him now more than ever and is there to support her as both Shane and Joan have their hearts ripped out, knowing that whatever they themselves want is not going to be. Back at work, Joan manipulates everyone around her, officers and inmates combined. She sides against future Top Dogs Myra Desmond and Nora Flynn until suffering from complete burn out, and wanting to be rid of Wentworth for good she makes the mistake of trusting one of her greatest enemies.

BEHIND THE CAMERA: Ken Mullholland's Memories:

1982: CORRIDOR CAMERAS

Peter Hind was probably the most adept at handling a pedestal camera in the cells and corridors; although Noel Penn was pretty good too. Both were tall and Peter had a strong build. Noel was nick-named 'The Show Pony' because he operated with style and flare.

When we first began the series, our cameras were mounted on a pedestal which could elevate up to about two and a half meters or say nine feet. De-elevated, the lens height was around five foot approx. The barrel of the pedestal was hinged and could be opened to add or subtract the lead weights that were used to counter-balance the weight and to stabilize the whole thing. The base was triangular and housed the three wheels, which were steered by the use of a steering ring at waist height that could spin them 360 degrees. We later changed to gas pedestals which were lighter and handled better.

The camera had a zoom control on the left side which was operated by the turn of the thumb as the hand gripped the cylinder-shaped control and on the right was the focus control which was a circular object with winged projections so that your fingers wouldn't slide around it. There was also a gizmo called a shot-box which could be set up so as to zoom the lens to exactly the same place every time. This also had a timer control which could be set to zoom really fast or extremely slow.

I rarely used it, except on commercials where the camera didn't move and you wanted an exact same length zoom and timing.

Over the course of nearly 500 episodes, Kirkpatrick's performance never falters, always delivering a complete study of Joan Ferguson. She manages to discover ways of playing evil which give Ferguson a surprising depth away from the pantomime villain the character could easily have become in lesser hands. It is a testament to Kirkpatrick's commitment as an actress that her creation is perhaps the most recognised from the series to the general public at large, and has become a recognisable symbol of the show's massive worldwide success.

Maggie Kirkpatrick was a vastly experienced theatre actress of twenty years standing when Ian Bradley cast her as Joan Ferguson. Born in Albury, New South Wales, on 29th January 1941, Maggie's father was killed in action while fighting in Tobruk, North Africa during World War II that same year. A talent for showing-off led Maggie's mother to enrol her into drama training. This in turn led to Maggie's first professional engagement with John Alden's Shakespeare Company playing one of the witches in *Macbeth*. Influenced by her husband Norman, Maggie took an interest in the New Theatre, a left wing theatre group in Newtown. It was here she experienced playing classics and the work of new writers and this really cemented Maggie's love of live theatre in all its forms. A highlight from this time was a chance to work with one of her heroes, Sir Michael Redgrave, on a tour of *A Voyage around My Father*. Maggie here reveals why she prefers a live audience:

I always feel in control when on the stage. I have dallied in television and film but it is on the stage where I am really at home. It is for theatre work that I have won my awards and I am aware that it is, perhaps, the medium in which I am most comfortable. Therefore, I think it is where my best work has been found in this working life we call a career.

Despite a firm preference for the stage, Maggie added some small roles in television series such as *Chopper Squad*, *Cop Shop* and the Australian version of the British television comedy *Father Dear Father* to her blossoming CV before the phone call came inviting her to play a new sensational character. Immediately prior to this Maggie had been working with director Ken Annakin on the musical parody of Gilbert and Sullivan, *The Pirate Movie*.

I had auditioned, along with most of the Australian female acting fraternity, for the original cast of Prisoner. I went up for Vera Bennett. Obviously that didn't come my way. But then a couple of years or so later I got a phone call saying that Ian Bradley – who had been an old mate in Sydney – wanted to talk to me about playing a new character. It was described to me as 'a sadistic bull-dyke screw'. Well, who wouldn't rise to the challenge and the fun of playing such a sensational role on prime time television? Having only had limited experience in television, I found going in as a fairly major character quite daunting. I had watched the show on and off, when my working life permitted, during the previous years and had seen a lot of mates going in and out of the show. I never thought then that I would find a place in the regular cast. I have said many times that the stillness of Ferguson in those early episodes came from sheer terror in front of the camera. It took me quite a while to feel comfortable with the technique of making television, but it would seem that that tense quality worked in my

MAGGIE KIRKPATRICK as IVY HACKETT

RICHMOND HILL

TEN

Opposite page: Joan finding comfort from her father, Major Ferguson [Carl Bleazby]. Left: The black gloves still in evidence in 1985. Centre: A signed fan card from Maggie's role as Ivy Hackett in Richmond Hill. Above: Appearing as Madame Morrible in the musical Wicked.

favour because subsequently many people have commented how scary they thought Ferguson was when she arrived. The down side of this was that as I became more confident I started doing 'tough acting' where my head would wobble and, when I became conscious of this, I always asked incoming directors to stamp on it if they saw me doing it. So often I would hear on the tannoy from the production gallery, 'The head is wobbling, Maggie!'

Even before the episodes had aired, the senior figures at Grundy Productions had decided that they wanted Joan Ferguson in the series for an extended period as they realised that here, finally, was a truly worthy opponent for Bea Smith. Maggie was initially put on a 12-week contract. Viewers confirmed this decision as ratings steadily climbed. It grew increasingly clear that there was not enough room in the prison to house both these bombastic women. Maggie again:

A portrait from Maggie's trip to the UK in 2010.

> The work that I did with Val Lehman was among the best I did during my four and a half years on the show. We quickly came to work very well together. Val had been there a long time and had come to know the technicalities of the show. I was feeling my way with the work at first but then, when I had a few episodes under my belt and there wasn't as much fear of the camera, it was then I really could concentrate on developing Joan's relationship with the characters. Bea, of course, was the person she hated most in the prison because she recognised an equally strong force opposing her. In many ways, she saw Bea Smith as a challenge worthy of her. She was going to see the feud through to the end. So that was wonderful work, with each of us helping to bring out the best of each other as actors. I did some terrific work as well with subsequent Top Dogs. Annie Phelan and I had been mates for years so working with her was always good fun and she is a solid actress to play against, a fine talent. The final few episodes with me and Glenda Linscott seemingly teaming up together are something I am very proud of, too. We had some great guest stars in the show. Maurie Fields [Len Murphy] is one that springs to mind – a great pro, Maurie – and the fight scene we did was hysterical. Both of us didn't want to hurt the other. I always used to turn into a really girly girl after those scenes. 'Oooh, darling, I didn't hurt you, did I?' Carole Skinner [Nola McKenzie] I had known since the 1960s so it was great having her around, one of the few times we have worked together even though we have been close friends all that time. Although I

hadn't known Elspeth Ballantyne before Prisoner, she has become among my closest friends since we finished making the show. So yes, lots of very happy memories of the cast and the crew, who were all fantastic.

Like all actors in a long-running role, Maggie became quite protective of the character when writers and directors would try to put her in a position she didn't feel was in keeping with the character.

> There was one occasion when they wanted Joan to take up ballroom dancing. I said, 'I don't think so'. They wanted Joan to meet a man at the ballroom and then to have a romance with him. It made me really angry. We had established Joan as a lesbian loner. She definitely wouldn't have turned straight just for the sake of a convenient storyline! I remember saying to my agent at the time, 'If this storyline goes ahead I am handing in my resignation.' I meant it too. A compromise of sorts was reached when Joan took up golf and the man tried to woo her, but to no avail. The earlier relationship with Margot Knight's character [Terri Malone] was handled better. I said to the writers that the pain Joan goes through when Terri leaves her must mirror the same emotions as a straight relationship. The pain is the same, whether it is a man and a woman or between two women. I think we handled it with some sensitivity and remained true to Joan's nature

as had been established in the years previously. Another example was having Joan learn to drive. How stupid was that? Here was an independent woman who could in all probability have stripped down an engine and rebuilt it from scratch.

It is an actor's job to make the unbelievable believable but occasionally one had to speak up when the character was compromised too much. I know all the actors on the show suffered as an array of writers delivered scripts which would often contradict what had been done and said the week before. If it hadn't been for us caring so much about the show and our performances, some of it might have been sloppy. But we picked up on inconsistencies in the script and characterisation and for the most part fought for the truth of the character as we saw it.

In the years following *Prisoner*, Maggie again asserted her talent on the stage. She has been seen in productions as diverse as *Anything Goes*, *Absurd Person Singular*, *The Beauty Queen Of Leenane* and the musical phenomenon *Wicked* in which Maggie was Australia's Madam Morrible. Maggie's own favourite, a moving tale of two women thrown together as prisoners of the Japanese during World War II, *The Shoe-Horn Sonata,* was performed in Sydney and London. Television and film have been sporadic but a regular role came Maggie's way playing socialite Ivy Hackett in short-lived Grundy's soap *Richmond Hill.* A highlight for Maggie was playing opposite Rod Taylor on the big screen in the cult movie *Welcome to Woop Woop.* She has also been seen in high profile television series such as *All Saints*, *Blue Heelers* and *G.P.* All of which have helped keep Maggie's face in front of Australian television audiences. Maggie returned to play Joan again in the West End romp *Prisoner Cell Block H the Musical.* She continues to be held in awe by the younger generation of actors and remains an iconic figure within the industry. Away from work, Maggie is a mother and grandmother and for the most part shuns the celebrity lifestyle, preferring to live in rural New South Wales. 'My family, my mates, my books and my movies are what are important,' she sums up.

The Third Musketeer

 Excuse me lady, could you get out of my way..?
...not too close to the baby, you could give it germs!

Doreen gives Vera a taste of her own medicine
on the outside [155]

Doreen May Anderson – one of the first characters featured when the series began. She's a young girl in her early 20s who has experienced a poor childhood, abused by her father and institutionalised for most of her life. She became pregnant at the age of 16 and was forced to give her child away, later turning to crime which resulted in her being sentenced to imprisonment for forgery among other things and since then her life has been spent stuck at Wentworth.

Initially a supporting character regularly teaming up with Lizzie Birdsworth, Doreen is seen often clutching her teddy bear and sucking her thumb. Her childlike qualities make her gullible and easily led by others, especially by Franky Doyle who becomes her partner in crime as well as a love interest. Doreen and Franky share a cell together but the prison sees just how much Doreen appears to mean to the bad-tempered Franky when a cell change is arranged which results in a one-woman riot in the Recreation Room [1]. Franky needs Doreen more than the other way around – 'She scares me at times does the old Franky', Doreen admits. She is relieved when Franky turns her attention to Karen Travers instead.

When life inside the prison gets too much for Franky, she arranges with Doreen and Lizzie that they'll go over the wall and escape. Lizzie of course can't keep up with the two young ones so has to turn back, but Franky and Doreen manage to make it to freedom [12]. Unfortunately, they haven't thought out their escape very well and have no money and no plans, even stealing a bag of chips from a young boy so they don't go hungry. They live rough, tired and dirty until they come up with the crazy idea of dressing up as nuns so they can trick the public into giving them cash donations. They keep up their disguise and make friends with a Miss McBride, an old lady who lives by herself, and are invited to stay with her – the perfect result.

The time with Miss McBride is short-lived when her son makes a surprise appearance and recognises the two escapees, so they bundle him into a cupboard and make a quick getaway [17].

Doreen gets friendly with a guy called Toddy while she and Franky are formulating their next plans but, when he turns rough and starts bashing her, this results in a reprisal beating from Franky. They decide that the only way they're going to get somewhere while on the run is to commit an armed robbery so they can get some money. A hardware store is to be the unlikely location but, when a policeman spots them and recognises them from Wentworth, the girls have to make a run for it. Franky pulls out a gun and wounds the cop, but he manages to recover and returns fire at her – the bullet wounds her in the stomach and she falls to the ground. Knowing she's about to meet her maker, she demands that a distraught Doreen gets away as soon as possible. Poor Doreen kisses her friend a final goodbye and runs off to find shelter [20].

Without Franky to guide her, Doreen is redundant. She makes her own way back to Wentworth and asks the gate guard to let her back in. On seeing Karen back inside the prison, Doreen immediately attacks her and blames her for Franky's death. She takes a tough stance on her return, obviously as a tribute to her fallen partner, and picks on anyone who crosses her. This tough and bitter act doesn't last for long and Doreen returns to her childlike ways [24] when she realises that it's not worth it.

Doreen becomes close to fellow inmate Lynn Warner but takes an innocent crush too far when she starts getting her into trouble on purpose so that her release is delayed. She intends that Doreen can spend more time with her on the inside, even letting Lizzie take the blame at times. When Lynn finds out she is furious and returns the favour by calling Doreen a worm and smearing mud all over her face [42]. Her current and past problems come to a head when she is questioned by Dr Peter Clements who delves into her past lesbianism and childhood. She becomes upset and distressed and runs out of the room in tears [45]. This results in a complete breakdown for Doreen and she's transferred to a psychiatric hospital on the recommendation of Dr Greg Miller. She returns to Wentworth but is still affected by the treatment and manages to stab herself in the foot with a garden fork while working outside [55] and she ends up back at hospital.

When she's released on parole to the care of the Halfway House [70] she finds it very difficult to adjust to life on the outside, even with the help of Karen who has been assigned the task of the house manager. It is during this time that she becomes friends with Alice Hemmings, a wealthy old lady who had visited her in prison previously. However, Alice is hiding a secret

Colette Mann in 1978

and she turns out to be Doreen's mother. She is dying of cancer and wants to see as much of her daughter as possible but doesn't want to reveal her true identity. Soon Doreen realises who she is but when she accepts the truth it is too late – Alice has passed away and Doreen is once again alone although she has been left her mother's house in her will.

Getting herself back together, Doreen begins to make a go of it on the outside and manages to get a job in a factory. It isn't anything too exciting, but for Doreen it is that first step to independence. She is even lucky enough to have some attention from Kevin Burns, the delivery driver who also works there. She is too scared to tell him her true identity and uses the name of Debbie while she's working there. Sadly for Doreen, Wentworth appears to be always on the horizon and, when she and Lizzie (who has also been released on parole) get drunk and try to steal some booze from the local liquor store, predictably the two of them are caught and sent back to the prison for breaking their parole agreement.

With Kevin wondering what has happened to Doreen, he eventually finds out that she is in prison but agrees to Doreen that he'll stand by her, no matter what. The guilt of letting him down is too much for Doreen and she gives him back the engagement ring that he had previously pleased her with. Kevin doesn't give up though, and the two are eventually married in a ceremony which takes place at the prison [116]. Meanwhile, new officer Jock Stewart has become aware of Doreen's mother's house and her refusal to sell it to a developer. Sharon Gilmour overhears Jock threatening Doreen and this ends up with Sharon being pushed down the stairs by him to her death. Jock is found out and, before it is too late, Doreen's house is safe.

Never thinking ahead, Doreen gets herself involved with the foreman of a local factory, Vince Talbot, where the women are working as part of a day release programme. He forces her to have sex with him [128] and Doreen finds out from him about a delivery tender

Left: Doreen during her work at the factory. Right: Doreen returns for the final time in 1984.

that she plans to pass on to Kevin so he can undercut the other applications. Vera finds out what she is up to and so she's removed from the programme. However, Doreen later discovers that she's pregnant and, with there being no chance of the baby being Kevin's, she is horrified to discover that Vince must be the father. Kevin finds out and, when Doreen admits that she agreed to have sex on more than one occasion so that she could find out information about the tender for him, he tells her that he wants a divorce. A confused Doreen tries to commit suicide by hanging herself in the laundry [139] but is saved by Meg and Vera. Sadly, just after she accepts that she wants the baby after all, she suffers a miscarriage through the night [142] and loses it.

Still probably subconsciously getting over the loss of her baby, while on the outside and working in the children's ward of the local hospital, Doreen kidnaps Elizabeth, the daughter of Chrissie Latham, when she finds out that there's a chance she may be placed in a home. She uses her mother's house to hide out at but, when Elizabeth becomes poorly, she is forced to bring her to the hospital for attention. Doreen is recognised and is swiftly returned to Wentworth [157]. This brings her face to face with an understandably upset Chrissie who vows to kill Doreen. Eventually Latham changes her mind when she hears Doreen's side of the story.

The famous tunnel escape [165-166] sees Doreen go underground in another crazy attempt to flee the prison. Unfortunately for Doreen, the walls literally come falling down on top of her and she is trapped under a pile of rubble with a suspected broken leg. The women are stuck for days, thinking about whether they will live or die. Doreen does a lot of soul searching while stuck and eventually, when they are found and rescued, she realises that she's left her famous teddy bear in the tunnel where he will stay forever. She admits that she has grown up and was thinking about getting rid of him anyway.

Life inside isn't all bad for Doreen. In fact, she has a lot of fun with Lizzie and they get up to all kinds of misdemeanours. She decides that she will somehow find love one way or another and writes an advert for herself to the local newspaper's 'Lonely Hearts' column where she is pleased to receive a reply from a Peter Hope [192]. She has no choice than to admit to Erica what she's been up to and, rather than stop it altogether, Erica makes Doreen go through with meeting Peter to reveal the truth to him. When they do meet, Peter turns out to be much older than Doreen but still very interested. However, Doreen isn't as keen and she is embarrassed when he turns up at Wentworth in front of all of the other women. Their relationship quickly fizzles out.

Doreen has to make a possible life-changing decision when Bea is seriously ill and in desperate need of a kidney transplant. Along with most of the other women, Doreen agrees to have tests to see if she could be considered to be a donor and is shocked when she finds out that her tissue samples match Bea's and she could go ahead with the donation [242]. When the other women find out, the decision is apparently taken out of Doreen's hands as everyone assumes that she is going to go ahead. What they don't know, however, is that she is petrified of the daunting operation and can't do it. Dor explains to the other women her decision and is then faced with the task of letting Bea know. Luckily for Bea, another donor turns up just in time and she's sent to hospital for the operation.

When Doreen and Judy are found out about their parts in forging the officers' work rosters, they are surprised to find that their punishment is much more than a slap on the wrists and loss of privileges – they are to both be transferred to Barnhurst [246]. They bid their farewells to the women and are carted away, just before a huge riot breaks out at Wentworth – arranged

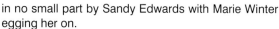

in no small part by Sandy Edwards with Marie Winter egging her on.

A surprise return for Doreen takes place when she is back at Wentworth, heavily beaten up by Marie at Barnhurst [253] for supposedly lagging. She makes friends with the new guard dogs who have been placed at Wentworth and trains them into understanding her commands. Dor uses this new skill to attempt another escape but, when the dogs escape and look set to attack officer Janet Conway, Doreen successfully calls them off [259]. With the dogs no longer fit for purpose they are removed from the prison.

Unluckily for Doreen, she is the first prisoner at Wentworth to undergo a Joan Ferguson-style body-search, complete with the famous black leather gloves [287]. The nickname of 'The Freak' was given to Joan by Doreen and stuck with her until the very last episode.

Finally, Doreen is released from Wentworth and lives at the new Halfway House under the care of Judy Bryant. She and Susie Driscoll go looking for work at the local shoe factory and Doreen is lucky enough to be offered the position which she happily accepts. Life at the house gets unbearable for Doreen, after the discovery of a gun on the premises which is the property of an undercover policewoman who is monitoring another resident. When a fire at the shoe factory causes Doreen to lose her job, she is back to square one but manages to be offered an alternative role as a live in home help. She isn't sure at first, but when she returns to the house to find a loud and uncontrollable drinking session taking place she makes the decision to accept and move into her new home immediately.

Doreen makes a brief return when Bea escapes and has relocated to Sydney [358-360] where she harbours her old mate until the police catch up with her. She also has a bizarre reappearance to catch up with some of her old pals at Wentworth, only to find that they've all long moved on and Helen Smart is the only person she knows [435]. She finds herself committing a crime just to get sent back into prison, so that she doesn't have to marry a man who is infatuated with her. In her final ever episode [446] she bids a last goodbye to her new friends by cheering them up with a funny message on the prison's intercom system.

'People do know me from that. It did make me a household name and I wouldn't be where I am today if it wasn't for Prisoner.*'*
Colette Mann, Prisoner documentary (unscreened)

Colette Mann's career started in 1971 when she worked in Godspell but *Prisoner* was her first television role, having only worked briefly on stage before then. A complete newcomer to life in front of the cameras, she quickly became very friendly with Sheila Florance who took her under her wing, sharing her many years of experience and tips for becoming a better performer.

'On TV, it was the first time women came out from behind the kitchen bench, cutting up carrots or putting on lipstick… it was the first show I'd auditioned for where I wasn't told I had to lose weight!'
Colette Mann – Sydney Morning Herald (03/03/2011)

A keen singer and stage performer, Colette teamed up with *Prisoner* actresses Betty Bobbitt and Jane Clifton to form the cabaret trio The Mini-Busettes. They performed regularly at Melbourne's Le Joke comedy club, various telethons and a number of Sydney League clubs between 1980-81. Colette also appeared in the music video for Jane's single 'Girl on the Wall'.

After leaving *Prisoner*, Colette continued to grow as a performer and appeared in a number of familiar Australian shows including *The Flying Doctors* and also *Neighbours* in 1995 when she stepped in temporarily at short notice to replace Caroline Gillmer as Cheryl Stark who was taken ill and it was too late to write her out of the series. She returned to Ramsay Street over 16 years later to grace the show with a long-awaited mature character in the form of Sheila Canning. The series is, of course, filmed where *Prisoner* was recorded all of those years before.

Colette is one of Australia's most well-recognised icons and has constantly featured in live theatre, radio and television. She has worked on the flagship shows *A Current Affair* and *Good Morning Australia* as well as various guest-hosting jobs for programmes including *New Idea's Saturday Kitchen* on Network 7.

In between acting and presenting, Colette has written two books, *It's a Mann's World* and *Give ME a Break!* She has also had her own column in *New Idea* magazine where she shared her family life with its readers.

Mann reprised her role of Doreen Burns as part of the 2006 Logie Awards ceremony in a 50-second tongue-in-cheek clip written by Val Lehman which saw Bea and Doreen discuss their chances of stealing an actual Logie award. Colette also joined in the celebrations at the Old Melbourne Gaol in 2011 to mark the return of *Prisoner* to Australian television in an unexpected re-run on the 111HITS channel.

As *Prisoner* entered 1983, Australia was gripped by the 1982 cliffhanger and on the edge of their seats awaiting Episode 327 going to air. Media critics, peers and audiences were left literally stunned following the epic battle between Bea and The Freak, as well as the awe inspiring performances of Lehman and Kirkpatrick as they cemented *Prisoner*'s place in television folklore. The weeks and months of tension rising between the two characters culminated in performances that even to this day are worthy of applause.

Following Wentworth being engulfed in flames, Ted Douglas arranges for the inmates to be transferred over to the male prison Woodridge, until Wentworth is safe for them to return. Bea quickly recovers from her tussle with the muscle. Back in the thick of the action at Woodridge, Bea is determined to find out which of her fellow inmates was responsible for the fire, which had killed Mouse and Barbara. Finally, it is discovered that the unpredictable actions of Margo Gaffney were responsible. Bea and Chrissie set out to take revenge on their fellow inmate's reckless actions. This heralded the end of Jane Clifton's performance of the brooding, selfish and nonchalant attitude of Margo. We would see her return to the series in the following year where a much tougher, sadistic and villainous Margo is brought back from Barnhurst. For the time being, Jane was about to enjoy a break for *Prisoner* and looked back on her time on the series with an honest and frank opinion of playing a Wentworth baddie:

I look back on my time on the show as regular work, regular income, and ensemble acting. I remember the fun atmosphere on set – hard working, occasionally snippy but mostly positive and a lot of laughs. The crew were a hard-working bunch of mostly blokes who were all extremely helpful and easy to get along with. Amongst the cast, it was Colette Mann who taught me when to shut-up and how to 'jog along'. I never actually auditioned for the role of Margo, I was just called in for a couple of days work playing an, as yet, unnamed character. Prior to joining, I was very happy singing jazz, doing plays at a theatre called the Pram Factory. As well

Far Left: Bea and Chrissie find out it was Margo who started the Wentworth inferno. Left: Firestarter Margo Gaffney

as doing solo shows at a theatre-restaurant in Melbourne called the Last Laugh.

When Prisoner came along, the job I was called in to do helped to move another character's storyline on a bit. Once established and named, Margo, was a daffy kind of dill who later morphed into something nastier. Highlights from my time spent in Wentworth include throwing Judy Bryant against the driers in the laundry when I knew she had a pacemaker. Getting tarred and feathered – Val and Amanda had far too much fun doing that. Killing Mouse! Doing the shower scenes in body-stockings that would fill up with cold water whilst the crew cracked up and cried 'Take 2!' The siege was fun. The concert was hilarious. Anything that took us out of the studio in Nunawading, so we could drive to the Forest Hills Shopping Centre for a proper coffee.

Looking back over my time on the show and its lasting appeal to the audience now, I think it's because the series is set in an anonymous place, with characters wearing uniforms. Like a good murder mystery, set on an island or a boat, the focus is on the story – family drama, life, love. It managed to transcend period stereotyping most of the time, except when one of us got a storyline set on the outside and had to dress in the current fashion and sport the latest hairstyle and make-up. Happy times.

After a monumental episode or conclusion of a gripping storyline, *Prisoner* fans would often be faced with a quieter spell of episodes where the inmates returned to normality. None more so than following the great fire, where some episodes at the beginning of 1983 created some softer, funnier moments within the show. Colleen Powell was faced with the prospect of a new love interest when Deputy Governor Geoff Carlson offers a massage to unwind from the tension of the Wentworth fire. Carlson, played by Danny Adcock,

provided an interesting approach to his counterpart Colleen – strict and stern with the inmates of Woodridge yet caring for some of the more vulnerable prisoners like Andy Hudson [Ric Herbert]. Andy is bashed in the prison and escapes from hospital where he rekindles his relationship with Paddy. Arriving at the Halfway House, Judy offers him only a few minutes of time with Paddy before putting her at risk should police turn up. Just then, police arrive at Driscoll House, seeing Andy and Paddy make a united bid for freedom. They are caught, signalling the end to their courtship. Andy is returned to Woodridge and Paddy is taken back to Wentworth and is given five weeks for aiding Andy's escape [329].

Terror was lurking in the shadows on Channel 10 during the evening of Tuesday 15th February 1983, when a mysterious Jean Carter arrives at the Halfway House [331]. This heralded the arrival of an actress well known to Australian television and highly respected amongst her peers. Carole Skinner brought a wealth of experience to *Prisoner* and a unique quality that would propel her to the heights of being one of the series' most celebrated villains. When viewers thought no more twists and turns could top the monumental fire episodes, Jean Carter, who would soon be revealed as double murderess Nola McKenzie, would bring a chilling reign of terror to thirty eight episodes of the series. Incidentally, look out for a familiar face serving Nola in Episode 333. It is none other than future bad girl Louise Siversen, who would in time bring her own breed of nastiness to Wentworth as Lou Kelly.

Carole recalls being Nola:

As you may know, I was originally offered the role of Bea Smith which I turned down. It was all over the money. Further down the track, this role of Nola was offered to me by Ian Bradley. I'd known Maggie Kirkpatrick and her late husband Norman for years. Maggie and I had appeared in several productions together for the influential

Right: Po can't say No. Far Right: Terror in the shadows: Prisoner's best loved villain makes her debut.

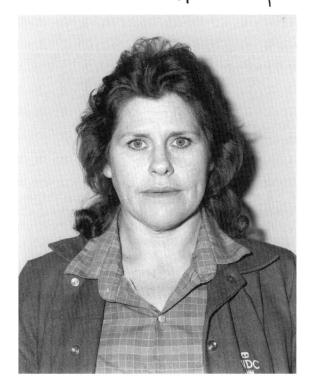

Left: Evil stares you in the eye – Nola McKenzie's Mug Shot. Above: Plotting and planning – Nola wastes no time sussing out how to survive on the inside.

New Theatre in Sydney way back in the 1960s and had remained good friends ever since. It was good having her there during those months. We could tart ourselves up and go out partying after all the intense intrigue at work. Nola was a nasty piece of work: a murderer who was wanted in WA where the death penalty awaited.

We were mostly theatre trained actresses when I was in Prisoner, which always makes for a good ensemble. Theatre is the training ground in so many ways, and being a part of a team is a strong part of that ethos. Dear old Sheila Florance was always suspicious of actors being flown down from Sydney. She could be quite vocal about them bringing outsiders into the Melbourne acting scene. We would have some good natured arguments about that. I loved all the insults that Nola used to throw at Sheila, 'Wrinkles' and 'Birdbrain'.

Even though they wanted me to stay on, I knew Nola had a shelf life. There is only so much you can do when all the drug dealing and murdering has been done. You just end up repeating yourself. The money was good and it is easy to be sucked into the regular work and become comfortable. I wanted a dramatic end for Nola. She had earned it! Hit 'em hard and get out is the best way with serial television I think. Typecasting in a profession such as ours can be a deterrent. The amount of letters I have received and having been stopped in the street

because of Nola, show that she has had some lasting impression with television audiences. I've done other soaps, such as Neighbours and Sons & Daughters to name but two, but nothing compares to the recognition for Prisoner. It was an amazing seminal series for women actors. We showed we could more than match what the male actors had to offer on prime time television given the opportunity. Many people remember Nola killing Paddy as a memorable moment. I got to work with the lovely Anna Hruby again a couple of years later on Harp in the South. Another lovely job.

I've got a long CV but if people want to remember me as Nola, that's OK. I have been lucky in playing so many wonderful theatre roles which have really stretched me. In a profession such as ours you have more to offer as the years go by. That contrasts with the struggle to get roles as you get past your thirties. And a lot of us are now well past that benchmark. I could probably be Lizzie Birdsworth in the new Prisoner series. The big bash in Melbourne for the 21st anniversary was extraordinary. I originally wasn't going to go, but my best friend Kirsty Child talked me into it. It reminded me what a landmark show the programme was for Australian actors. We were all lucky to be a part of it.

Contrasting with Nola's arrival is the reintroduction of Belinda Davey as troubled Hazel Kent. Hazel is almost tricked into admitting that she was responsible for the robbery Nola had committed. The women return to the newly refurbished Wentworth [333] featuring a new Governor's Office, a new reception and what appears to be a much smaller area of prison corridors, shot from different angles to give the illusion of other areas in the prison that have the same outlay. Erica

Top Left: Patsy King and Ian Smith in the new Governor's office. Top Right: Ferguson returns. Above Left: Judy is reunited with her sister, but all is not what it seems. Above Right: Amazing: Betty Bobbitt's stunning performance as heartbroken Judy.

is back at the helm, ready to deal with the barrage of wayward inmates in her path. A welcome back party is given to the inmates, whilst Erica is offered Colleen's resignation for her mistake in storage of the turps, which she declines. The welcome back party is halted with the return of The Freak, who stubs out a cigarette in the welcome back cake. The party is well and truly over. The gloves are off, or in this case the black gloves are back on!

On the outside, Judy receives a surprise visit from her sister Frances [335], played by Barbara Ramsay. Her desire to reacquaint herself with Judy is soon revealed as being a set-up, as Frances is purely interested in money. After Frances is found out for imitating Judy to get access to her inheritance, Judy attacks her in one of Betty Bobbit's most powerful scenes in the series. The rawness of Bobbitt's portrayal of Judy, effortlessly portraying hurt, anger and betrayal in these few scenes, distinguishes her from the rest of the cast in a heartbeat. Bobbitt is the epitome of fine acting and in this one episode conveys all what *Prisoner* stands for – the fight for freedom, respect and acceptance.

The introduction of Nola McKenzie was continuing at a pace, when she begins to mingle with the other inmates of Wentworth. Intent on prolonging her stay in the prison to avoid the death sentence awaiting her in Western Australia, the now blood thirsty McKenzie was like a cat among the proverbial pigeons as one of them was about to be brutally slaughtered. The survival of the fittest would see McKenzie remain in Wentworth at the peril of Paddy Lawson.

Paddy visits the shower block and is confronted by McKenzie, waiting for whatever prey walks into the room. Paddy is instantly backed into a corner and a ruthless Nola executes Paddy in cold blood by holding her head underwater. Anna remembers her final scene:

Poor Carole was so concerned that she might hurt me during that scene. At the end of every take she was immediately checking that I was ok, that she hadn't pulled my hair or knocked a tooth out. Honestly, I think fans would be surprised at how fabulous the creation of Nola was if they knew what a darling woman she actually is.

Working with Carole Skinner was one of the highlights of my experience on Prisoner. *Not only is she a wonderful actress, she is the loveliest, funniest, warmest woman and I adored her. I was lucky enough to work with her again a few years after* Prisoner *on a gorgeous mini-series,* Harp in the South. *Carole and Maggie Kirkpatrick were both extremely supportive of me during my time on* Prisoner *and they are the first two that come to my mind whenever I think about that period of my life.*

Bea walks in on Paddy's lifeless body lying on the ground of the shower block, with Nola smirking and boastfully goading the Top Dog: 'She was a pushover'. A fight then ensues between the two, separated by Colleen. Nola continues her reign of terror, and Bea's control and authority over the women is challenged.

At this point, Faye Quinn [Anne Lucas] returns and is quickly roped in by Nola to front her insurance racket to line her pockets. Anne's introduction to *Prisoner* came in Episode 285:

Faye's very early dialogue was actually written for Jane Clifton's character Margo. The Script Department came up with the name, which is a combination of Maura Fay from Casting and Betty Quin, a wonderful lady whom we all loved dearly, who was a major storyliner and writer on The Young Doctors. *Her favourite niece, Patrea Smallacombe, is a well known writer in the UK now, currently working on* EastEnders, *I believe. I was married to Ian Bradley and we were doing The* Young Doctors *when he was offered the chance of setting up a new production in Melbourne. So I lived and breathed* Prisoner *from the start -everything from the titles and the song to the characters and storylines. It was so different for its time; so brave. I often wondered if it would ever make it to air.*

Maggie Kirkpatrick was already an old mate, so we had fun with the scenes. One day however, my son, who was two at the time, was in the Green Room and saw Maggie beating me up on the monitor. He got terribly upset and poor Maggie had a hard time trying to persuade him that she really, really loved me. He calmed down after she demonstrated by nearly hugging me to death, but I'm not sure he ever quite forgave her.

Aside from playing Faye, Anne was also a writer and editor on *Prisoner*, with a couple of occasions having each title in one episode. Of all the characters she has written for, a special inmate remains very close to her heart:

All the women were great to write for because they were real actresses, not just pretty faces. Many had a depth of stage experience behind them so they could really handle dialogue and weren't afraid of showing emotion. Maybe Sheila Florance was my favourite. She could deliver a comic line or wring your heart with equal skill and she was as rascally as old Lizzie herself.

Having murdered Paddy, Nola continues to throw her weight around when she is returned to work with the other inmates. Bea tries to stay cool, but only has revenge on her mind.

She arranges for Babs [Marianne Brooke] to steal a soldering iron from the workshop. Ready to make Nola pay for killing Paddy and brutally bashing some other inmates, Bea brands Nola on her left breast with the initial 'K' for Killer.

Nola further enlists the assistance of Maxine in dodgy dealings. Bea eventually finds out and is furious with Maxine. Becoming increasingly frustrated with the women going behind her back and unable to defend themselves whilst Nola and The Freak tighten

Left: Paddy (Anna Hruby) takes her last breaths. Right: Anne Lucas replaces Margo as the resident bookie.

Above: "It isn't for kisses": Bea brands Nola with a soldering iron in revenge for murdering Paddy.

their hold over Wentworth, Bea seizes the chance to make a bid for freedom.

When a group of trainee officers visit the prison, Bea realises it's her perfect chance to escape. Stealing Joan's uniform from the staff room and dyeing her hair black, the Top Dog carries out the perfect escape of the series as she walks through the front gates.

In Bea's absence, two new inmates cause a bit of a stir in H Block. Marina Finlay arrived playing Lainie Dobson, joined by her partner Alan who manages to get himself inducted to Wentworth as a female. Val Lehman was so aghast at this that she asked for Bea to go on the run rather than take part in such an incredulous storyline. It was a memorable acting debut for Marina:

Prisoner *was the first professional job I was given. I had just graduated from the three year acting course at NIDA. I was twenty years old. I didn't audition for the role of Lainie. My agent rang me and told me that they were offering it to me. When I arrived in Melbourne to do the shoot, I felt particularly shy and vulnerable as it was really my first time away from my home in Sydney. Looking back, all the feelings of being a bit overwhelmed (it being my first job) suited the role very well, so I am sure it helped in my portrayal of Lainie.*

Lainie was shy, innocent and very frightened about finding herself in prison, a little like me at the time. I remember the atmosphere on set as being very jovial yet at the same time, quite intense as there was a lot of work to be done. My director, Kendal Flanagan, was very kind to me. He took me under his wing and looked after me. We became good friends during the shoot. Amongst the cast I adored Carole Skinner and Maggie Kirkpatrick. I found them both very kind

to me and they seemed to understand that I was very young and vulnerable.

The strongest memory I have of the storyline for Lainie was when she wanted to get rid of her tattoos, by putting her arm in caustic soda. It was very challenging to try to act how it would feel to put your arm in a bucket of caustic soda that would burn your skin so deeply to remove a tattoo. It was a stretch of the imagination. I also remember that I had a tattoo of a heart on my cheekbone which I thought was very unique and daring. My lasting memory from the time I spent on the series is probably the wonderful inspirational friendship of Kendal Flanagan. Also the intensity of the scenes I shared with Maggie Kirkpatrick will always stay in my memory.

Free from Wentworth, Bea makes her way to Sydney to track down old mate Dor. Doreen has been doing well for herself, employed in a clothing store and having left her days inside behind her. Naturally Bea is the last person she expects to see, but in true Doreen style she supports Bea in her plight to remain AWOL [358].

Bea enjoys a catch up with Doreen, but knows she can't wait for long as the police will be eager to trace her footsteps. She is caught and returned to Wentworth [361].

The arrival of Zara Moonbeam predicts further trouble for Bea, as Nola and Ferguson's coalition has been further heightened in her absence. Initially Bea appears dismissive of anything the two plan to do or operate within Wentworth, but the Top Dog has been weakened after her experience on the outside. A taste of freedom gave Bea the chance to see where her life could have gone had she not been incarcerated. With Debbie weighing heavily on her mind, an opportunity for Nola and Ferguson presents itself to bring Bea down. Ilona Rodgers was pivotal to the storyline as psychic Zara, and she remembers well bringing Zara to life on the set:

Before Prisoner, I had been working in The Sullivans*, playing Kate Meredith for two years. I had worked for the producer John McRae in New Zealand. He had seen me working on* The Sullivans *and suggested me for the part of Zara Moonbeam. Lisa Crittenden of course had played my daughter in* The Sullivans *– a sweet little girl – now here she was in* Prisoner *playing a bikie!*

Having just played a genteel forties woman in The Sullivans *with Mrs Jessop, to be with Carole Skinner, Val Lehman and Maggie was a huge culture shock. Oh boy, life had changed from the 40s!*

Sheila Florance was my favourite amongst the cast. What an actress. She had so many stories about theatre work at The Melbourne Theatre Company. Every lunch time she would sit there with her Guinness, or was it stout? John McRae adored her.

Joan and Nola prepare Bea's suicide: what could go wrong?

Everyone on that show were good actors so when it came to the scenes with the séances, they were great fun to do. I look back on that time with great affection, hearing lots of gutsy laughter.

A combination of prank stories and visits to her cell late at night leaves Bea close to breaking point at the hands of Joan and Nola. Zara pretends to imitate Debbie's voice and slowly Bea begins to doubt her own sanity. She is driven to the edge of despair and when a gun is planted in her dressing room pocket in the hope she will commit suicide, Bea's saviour is long term pal Lizzie who discovers the zip gun and is able to explain everything.

Bea is taken to the infirmary whilst Joan and Nola celebrate their victory. Lizzie is granted permission to see Bea and is able to explain how the two had concocted the plan. As Bea begins to realise how easily they managed to weaken her, she is immediately filled with rage. Armed with the zip gun Lizzie has brought her, Bea summons Nola to be brought to her.

'Debbie and Paddy... they're both waiting... both waiting... for you'

Bea pulls the trigger and Nola is shot between the eyes, falling to her death. The new Governor, Ann Reynolds [Gerda Nicolson] is faced with her first murder at Wentworth. Nola's body lies in the infirmary revealing to the staff the horror of the K branded upon her left breast. Carole Skinner's superb and chilling performance throughout her time on *Prisoner* would mark her out as one of the truly great villains, making Nola an undisputed entry into the *Prisoner* Hall Of Fame.

Maggie May Kennedy's [Davina Whitehouse, 371] arrival sees Lizzie recognising a face from the past. They were acquainted over forty years ago, bringing some much needed comedy for the two older actors. Brandy Carter [373] brought a unique characterisation to the 1983 season, with Ros Gentle portraying split personality sufferer Brandy / Laura. It was yet another instance of *Prisoner* welcoming a brand new talent as Ros explains:

It was my first role outside of NIDA. Whilst I had done a lot of commercials and extra work before NIDA, I hadn't really had a major role like Laura / Brandy / Susan! And on a show that was even then only a couple of years into its run, already an iconic show on which every actor wanted to land a role.

I remember feeling shocked and excited and terrified all at once. Shocked that I had landed a great long running role, although very short in terms of others, in a highly respected and watched television series and at my first audition out of NIDA. Excited that it was a role of

multiple personality, so I was not going to be put in a box in terms of 'type' in the eyes of casting people. Unless that put me into three boxes that is. And terrified that I had only a few days to prepare such a role and that I would be in a different state away from my friends and family for a few months. Though in reference to being put in a box I must say I did get a couple of roles for 'criers' shortly after. And as for preparation time and research, I had about three days to do some research and study the character, but also to get myself ready for being away from home for three or four months, the organisation and packing that entails.

Unfortunately, the research for television is very minimal, unlike film, as you get only days rehearsal; even on THE day sometimes before you shoot, unless it's for a series regular. I remember calling a couple of mental health institutes and speaking with people there and discussing the symptoms. But it was cursory to say the least for such a mysterious and debilitating illness. Above all however, I was thrilled at the prospect of having so much fun with such a flamboyant character: a timid mousy librarian, a loud mouthed prostitute and an altogether proper socialite. All in one! And it was fun. It was like shooting three different shows in one day at times. I arrive in the morning wondering which character was up first. I have to admit I enjoyed Brandy the most. There was something very satisfying about a good girl (me) playing a bad girl (Brandy) in a space where she can really do no real harm, in a game of pretend.

The atmosphere on set I recall as being fast and furious. I was living in a motel, so at times I was a little lonely when not on set. I loved going to work to be with friends and 'play' all day. It felt more like a family, the regulars were wonderful, friendly and approachable. 'Great gals'. I do remember a beautiful letter from the writer of the final episode, where all the personalities are in therapy and they all talk to each other and eventually kill off Brandy. She thanked me for adding so much to what she had written and said that she hoped they would put me up for an award for that episode. They didn't of course, but it was a beautiful letter and very reaffirming and encouraging for a young actor. I nearly died when I saw the script of that scene. It was about five minutes of dialogue – well a long monologue really, and we actually only did two takes of that scene.

There was also of course, the usual TV Week and other promotional articles in newspapers and

Top: Maggie gets re-acquainted with old pal Lizzie. Middle: Protest outside Wentworth to free Maggie. Bottom: Ros Gentle is inducted to Wentworth as Brandy Carter.

Left: Brandy settles into life in Wentworth. Or is it Laura? Centre: Dr Weissman searches for the truth behind Brandy's behaviour. Right: Powerful performance: Ros Gentle stuns audiences with her portrayal of multi personality sufferer Laura Gardiner.

magazines. Plus some fan mail. I have to say the most consistent fan mail over the years has been from the UK. Prisoner was an incredible 'out of the gate' experience I will cherish forever. And to get to play such a variety of characters, what a gift. And Brandy, a prostitute, was a character I would not normally be cast as, so she was especially fun.

I do remember the day poor little Laura decides to take her life. The actual attempted suicide scene came at the end of a long day and we were already running into overtime, which wasn't unusual. The Unions wouldn't allow us to go past a certain time. So I was given all these tricky directions that included lots of props, breaking a glass and manifesting blood. Because of the lack of time, it all had to be done without rehearsal. So the pressure was on, and on me, as I was the only one in the rather long scene. Fortunately it went off without a hitch and we all went home with the crucial scene in the can. But the adrenaline was pumping and my mind was working overtime to redirect the fear and doubt. This was years before I started meditating.

Right: Judy McBurney arrives as Pixie Mason. Bottom Row: Pixie's many men.

Driscoll House welcomes Sandy Gilham [377] seemingly with a string of husbands in tow! Each man turns up looking for Sandy. One of the series' most loveable characters had arrived. The police soon catch up with Sandy and reveal her true identity as Pixie Mason. Judy McBurney charmed everyone as the wedding obsessed bigamist and Pixie's zany personality dominates many of the storylines as the series approaches its 400th milestone.

A bomb scare with Bea stuck in solitary and an outbreak of a mysterious disease further propel the

Top Left: Bea seeing you: Bea's days are numbered at the hands of Ferguson and Sonia. Left: Tina Bursill lands behind bars. Above: Val and Sheila relax together prior to filming Bea's imminent departure.

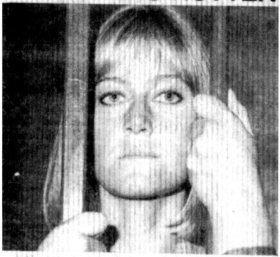

TINA TURNS ROTTEN

series towards its 400th outing. The landmark episode would prove memorable for the fact that the first and best loved Top Dog would finally lose her crown. Queen Bea's reign over Wentworth was coming to an end and not a moment too soon for The Freak.

Ferguson forms an alliance with 'ice lady' Sonia Stevens [Tina Bursill] and as part of their plan to take over the running of Wentworth, it means they must somehow dispose of the mighty Top Dog. After many failed attempts, the opportunity to set Bea up is finally within reach. A final battle in the corridor of solitary takes the story of Joan versus Bea to its conclusion.

The damning evidence is aided by Joan herself. Inflicting a scar to her left cheek and intimating to Mrs Reynolds that Smith attacked her, seals Bea's fate. Had Erica still been in charge it may have been more difficult for Ferguson to get away with her plan, but Ann supports the decision and Bea is transferred to Barnhurst leaving long term friend Lizzie alone.

Bea's departure changed the series on a number of levels. It was a daring move to remove such a well established character, but after four years Val Lehman had decided it was time to hang up her uniform. Explaining she felt Bea had become like a 'sucked orange' and there was no more to learn from her, Wentworth would continue without the red head Queen of the Steam Press. A huge number of dynamic characters were already being created to ensure that fans of the series couldn't spend too long mourning the loss of its greatest inmate, for the action continued at a pace as the end of the year approached. Running parallel to Bea's final moments was the masterfully played out Euthanasia storyline, which saw Judy Bryant return to Wentworth for the mercy killing of Hazel Kent. Writer Coral Drouyn crafted an exceptional piece of television in the wake of Val Lehman's departure from the series, which was softened by the phenomenal performances of Bobbitt and Belinda Davey in these haunting few episodes. Judy is arrested and taken back to Wentworth.

Nearing the end of 1983, the series presented more unpredictable characters to keep the audience in suspense. Babs McMillan won the role of Cass Parker arriving in Episode 401, and by the end of the

Hazel (Belinda Davey) pleads with Judy to help her. Right: Randi's slaughtered body lying hidden in the boiler room.

year her character would play a key role in the finale. Babs was a stalwart of many theatre productions as well as the final year of *The Young Doctors* where she was suitably severe as Sister Erin Cosgrove. Babs offered these recollections of her time as Cass:

> *I was thrilled when I landed the role of Cass. I loved the show and knew many of the actors in the cast. I'd already worked with Colette Mann in* Godspell, *Judy McBurney in* The Young Doctors, *Tina Bursill, and of course Betty Bobbitt and Anne Phelan. Annie and I shared a dressing room for twelve months when we worked for the Melbourne Theatre Company. Hilarious!*
>
> *Cass was complicated and very simple, driven by emotion rather than clear motivations. She could be funny and fun as well. I remember the atmosphere on set being focussed but relaxed, we all knew every week we had a big job to do. Two hours of television is a slog so we prepared which meant we were on top of the work, usually. Annie and I had been friends for years and I also had a lot of laughs with Reylene Pearce, Maxine, and Judith McGrath. Maggie Kirkpatrick and I had toured together for months in the late 1970s and she was always ready to work and play.*

Following Val Lehman leaving the series, only a few episodes later we would bid farewell to the lovable old lag Lizzie Birdsworth, who had been such a monumental part of *Prisoner's* early success.

To see Lizzie off in style, a certain male officer arrives from Woodridge in Episode 408. Immediately he is very friendly towards Lizzie and all the other inmates, but Officer David Bridges would take 1983 to a gripping conclusion.

Ridding Wentworth of Bea meant the inmates decided to take revenge on The Freak. A group of prisoners led by Phyllis Hunt and Bobbie Mitchell overpower The Freak and attempt to hang her in the shower block [412]. In a clever twist, it is Mr Bridges and Pixie who discover Joan hanging and try to help her. Whilst our attention is diverted by the sight of Ferguson hanging, the audience easily overlooks the fact that David is able to cut her down by producing a pocket knife. Ferguson is saved, but the hanging is purely a device to let the audience sense all is not what it seems with Officer Bridges.

With their leader gone, it doesn't take much for the women of Wentworth to put their trust in such a caring officer. The true David Bridges is in fact a psychopathic killer, offering the inmates the chance to be set free…

As several of the inmates begin to disappear, it's assumed that David is helping some of the women escape. The first glimpse we get of something being wrong, is when Randi Goodlove's body is seen slouched high upon one of the boilers in the boiler room, with a calm and collected Mr Bridges standing guard beneath her. Zoe Bertram was cast as the doomed Randi. Zoe recalls her fate:

> *Poor old Randi, disembowelled and slumped over pipes in the boiler room. I don't think anyone in* Prisoner *land ever found out what had happened to her! My memory of that day was climbing up and perching on that pipe, I don't think it was too precarious or high, but involved a bit of squeezing in the narrow space. It was filmed in the real Channel 10 boiler room and it was cold away from all the studio lights. To get the effect of dripping blood running down my arm, the make-up artist put fake blood in a condom, pin pricked the top to allow for slow dripping blood and concealed it up my sleeve.*

Top: David Waters is cast as David Bridges. Bottom: David Bridges' original prop ID badge.

Well at least Randi was colour co-ordinated – those yellow 'streaks' in my hair matched the yellow in the shirt. The other memories are of course of the great cast and crew.

Lizzie's final moments in Wentworth were also to fall at the hands of Mr Bridges. While Lizzie waits in the prison grounds for news of her parole, she drops her cigarette on the grass. Kicking through old newspapers amongst the grass, she sees a human hand emerge. David approaches Lizzie and offers his support. In a chilling scene he pulls a knife from his pocket and offers to set Lizzie free for good.

Actor David Waters was given the plum role of Wentworth's deranged new staff member, as he explains here:

Prior to Prisoner *I had my own national children's television show called* Match Mates *and had just finished the film* The Killing of Angel Street. *After this I went to Melbourne to audition for the role of David Bridges. I knew some members of the cast so it was an exciting time.*

The memory that stands out the most was getting my dinner in the canteen, covered in fake

Top: Sheila Florance reads over her lines during Lizzie's final year on the show. Middle: Sheila chats with newcomer Babs McMillan. Bottom: Sheila deep in thought as Judy poses for the camera.

blood after my head had been severed by Cass. The Director who had just arrived from New Zealand, who filmed my final episode, approaching me and saying 'Your character is coming along very well and I will be looking forward to working with you next year'. Which you can imagine left me a little gob-smacked. I am still waiting to return to the series as David Bridges' twin. I will always remember Sheila Florance with her morning tea of paté and a Guinness and of her wonderful stories of when she was working in the theatre in London during the Blitz. My lasting memory of that period was being the only male in the cast surrounded by the wonderful, strong and at times, daunting women. I loved every minute of it!

1983 had seen so many dramatic events on screen, culminating in the loss of its original Steam Queen, Val Lehman. The series faced the post Bea era with some trepidation, but a face from the past was to be welcomed fully into the bosom of the Wentworth ladies as a strong new leader waited in the wings for 1984 to dawn.

Above: Ferguson stands victorious after a successful year. Left: Tina, Gerda and Judy celebrate Episode 400 in style. Below: Joan disposes of Bea but her troubles are just beginning: an LSD trip sees Ferguson in her worst nightmare. Rare cast shot from filming the dream sequence.

The Ballad of Bea Smith

> *You are a mixture of anger and fury and a lot of strengths. You are a survivor. But you've still got a lot of softness, and honesty and warmth. A woman like you is never going to know what it's like not to feel...*

Ken Pearce to Bea Smith

Val Lehman played the original Top Dog Bea Smith to meticulous perfection. Lehman displayed such a firm grip on what was expected of her in the role of 'Queen Bea' that she became legendary among fellow cast members for her ability to look at a script, memorise it word for word and cast it aside not needing it again. Her confidence in the role was evident from a very early stage. Yet the ability to portray one of Cell Block H's toughest inmates was not for the faint-hearted. There had to be a vulnerability and insecurity to the character. On the surface Bea was very fiery tempered and quick to pounce on those who needed pulling into line, but the softer and quieter sides helped to display a more three-dimensional woman. The brief and isolated incidents of tapping into the more vulnerable side kept audiences enthralled to know more about Bea and how she became the person she was when the series first began.

Bea lived for her daughter, Debbie. Her strength in the prison ran simultaneously with a strong desire to care for others. Debbie meant the world to Bea. The fact that Val's own real life daughter Cassandra was chosen to play Debbie for flashback scenes brought a wonderful dimension to Bea's character. The real

life connection between mum and daughter shone through instantly, and helped the audience see Bea as an earth mother figure. Bea's life obviously revolved around Debbie and she would move heaven and earth to protect her daughter before looking after herself.

Despite the strong, steely exterior within Wentworth, Queen Bea was entirely different on the outside – a fish out of water. As the series progresses and we get to see Bea attend work experience, and also a daring escape to Sydney, she is frightened and alienated from the outside and how fast the world was changing without her. Never more so was the title of the series more pertinent. Our heroine had finally experienced a taste of freedom but the reality of being free was bittersweet. The title of the series would appear to follow Bea wherever she went.

The scenes with Bea attending work release are especially poignant. Bea befriends a woman named Cookie Brodie, played by musical theatre legend Judi Connelli [315], a wonderfully conceived plot to show Bea trying to cope with life on the outside but all the while mirroring her emotions with the events going on in Cookie's life at home. Effectively, Cookie could have been Bea had she not ended up in prison. Bea was

Left: Bea fends off the paparazzi. Right: Bea Smith.

Val celebrates with Patsy King

able to see the life she could have had, devoted to her daughter and still in a position to reach out and help her, without losing her temper and acting on impulse. The scenes with Bea and Cookie are played so sensitively and expertly handled, and show brilliantly the different paths one can choose in life. A much weakened Bea regrets her life choices and is able to see a glimpse of an alternative self in Cookie.

Beatrice Alice Smith ruled Wentworth for the best part of 400 episodes, bringing her fiery red headed leadership to the prison. Her presence as a figurehead for both the inmates and the series is without equal. Val Lehman made sure the opportunity to rule the screen was felt off the Richter scale. Within a short time Lehman made the journey from relatively inexperienced screen actor to multi-Logie Award winner. One thing is certain, the women at Wentworth need Bea's drive and commitment to stop them from ripping each other's throats out in the cauldron of emotions that result from incarceration. Bea can play the prison system better than most. She has had enough time to perfect it, that's for sure. She is intelligent, and this is her trump

card in the hierarchy of the jailbirds she commands. Some have muscle, some have intelligence. Very few have both. However, in many ways Bea is a sad figure clinging to her power base at the exclusion of all else. She often revels in conflicts with those who oppose her. The boredom of prison life obviously made more exciting by physical and mental challenges. She is often too quick to judge newcomers and can be a bully to get what she wants. But when Bea accepts that she has you on side and can fight your cause, it's the authorities who run the gauntlet of her campaigns. Her relationship with Lizzie in particular is worthy of note. It is akin to a long-standing mother and daughter relationship. Quite often, they would annoy the hell out of each other, but deep down there is a love and respect that is rock solid. It is a relationship that would entertain and delight viewers throughout Val and Sheila's time on screen together.

Bea enjoys rallying against the system. She is the only prisoner who can get away with calling Miss Bennett by her first name. She is certainly not on first name terms with Joan Ferguson. It is hate at first sight. Ferguson has the same ego problems as Bea, and there is never going to be enough room in a mere state prison to house these two forces of nature. Something has to give. The dynamic between Val and Maggie Kirkpatrick is worthy of a book in itself. The two actors connected in a way that took *Prisoner* to new heights. Their work as nemesis to each other has catapulted them both to legendary status within the Australian television firmament.

There is no denying that Val's charismatic presence on screen shone through always. No matter what dialogue Bea had, or what scene Val was given, she would rise to the challenge and carry it off faultlessly. Val created a template of quality in her playing of the Top Dog which would set the standard that subsequent Top Dogs would have to try and emulate. Recording two hours of fast turnaround television, often working long hours, is a feat of endurance. That Val gave such a sustained multi-dimensional performance during such a long period is a testament to her strength as an actress. The Logies that line Val's bookshelves are evidence enough that she delivered something very special to the television industry.

Valerie Kathleen Willis was born in Perth, Western Australia, on 15th March 1943. By 1962, Val had married her first husband and together they produced three children: Joanne, Cassandra and Jason. Val's husband being an army officer meant they were stationed at various points around the globe including Singapore and the United Kingdom. It was during this period as a mother and 'army wife' that Val's interest in amateur dramatics blossomed. While her husband was stationed at the Royal Military College of Science, Val appeared in the college reviews and directed her first play. She immersed herself in acting, writing and directing for amateur theatre companies

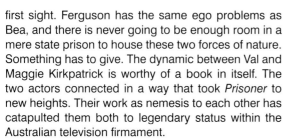

SANDRA LOUISE MASON "PIXIE"

Played by Judy McBurney

First Episode 377
Last Episode 511
Total Featured: 96

Sandy Gilham arrives at Driscoll House protesting that she is on the run from her husband. Bubbly and vivacious, Sandy's story continually changes depending on who she meets. The name of her husband changes and it becomes evident that she has been involved with a number of different men.

When her true identity is revealed, Pixie is arrested for bigamy and fraud and taken to Wentworth on remand [379].

With a string of men coming to visit her, Pixie is besotted with each of them and provides some welcome comic relief around the prison. When she tries to blame her crimes on her 'twin' sister, the judge sentences her to five years imprisonment [380]. With her bubble burst, Pixie continues to contact men through a lonely-hearts column which is smuggled out of the prison. Pixie leaves and re-enters the series several times throughout the 1983 season, striking up a close bond with Judy.

When she re-appears in Episode 442, it prompts Judy to write "Pixie's Song", which Pixie finds and realises that Judy's feelings are more than just friendship.

Joan catches her with Yemil in Lou's cell where they have uncovered a stash of drugs [505], prompting Lou to bash Pixie. She prevents Yemil from committing suicide [507].

When the three male prisoners of Woodridge arrive at Wentworth, Pixie takes an instant liking to Matt Delaney. As the men's stay at Wentworth progresses, they are allowed to mix with the women with tragic consequences. Pixie is raped by Frank Burke [510] and subsequently suffers a breakdown [511]. Despite our never seeing Pixie again, several references are made to her. "Pixie's Song" is played over the closing credits of Episode 534 when Judy is released from Wentworth for good. When Ann visits Ingleside to investigate Reb's treatment, Pixie is mentioned and we assume she must still be undergoing treatment there.

and when the family returned to Australia, Val had decided where her future interest lay. She wanted to be a full time actress. Separated from her husband, Val balanced duties as a single mother with trying to gain more valuable acting experience. Eventually, Val gained her first professional acting experience with the Children's Arena Theatre (CAT), a subsidised Theatre in Education company touring to schools with productions to aid the school curriculum. It was during this period that she was spotted by an ABC TV producer and cast in her first ever television role, the drama series *Obsession*.

Val Lehman herself takes up the story of her journey to the steam press:

I'd worked for five years in a Theatre in Education company called Children's Arena Theatre. During that time, I had gone from TV extra work to some small roles in television

productions. I decided to quit CAT and my agent suggested I audition for a new series set in a woman's prison. She said, 'I think you might be ideal for the Gestapo type prison officer.' Like hundreds of other actresses, I had an appointment at what is known as a 'Cattle Call' where you have ten minutes to 'sell yourself'. Fortunately, the casting director, Kerry Spence, had seen my screen work and said, 'No, I think you are Bea Smith material. Could you come back and read for the writer, director and producer this afternoon?' Having never read the character break-downs, I had no idea who Bea Smith was. When I went back in the afternoon I was introduced to Graeme Arthur, Reg Watson and Ian Bradley. I was told who Bea Smith was and given a script to look at briefly. Then I read for them. I noticed, out of the corner of my eye, the three nudge each

Val with Tom Oliver

other when I delivered a threatening look. They conferred and then said they wanted to screen test me. This happened several weeks later. I screen tested with Colette Mann, and afterwards we kept in touch. Colette heard way before me that she had been cast. I remember very well the phone call from my agent, Beris Underhill, telling me I had been successful. The role of Bea Smith was mine. They had apparently dropped her age five years so that I could play her.

The first time the cast met was not on set. It was for a read-through of the script at the studio. There was a great buzz and delight that it was a cast of so many women. I was immediately struck by the fact that most of us were stage actors and how diverse we were in type. Afterwards, we were taken for lunch at a local Chinese restaurant and Carol Burns said, 'We have to elect an Equity union representative. I nominate Val Lehman.' No one ever wants to be a union rep and I had done it for five years at CAT and knew how to read a contract and negotiate with producers. I agreed. I was told that despite the fact Bea was not originally an instituted criminal, she had committed a murder and been inside for ten years. She was the most powerful of all the prisoners, always had the last word, was protective of the weaker women, was never senselessly violent and was determined to defend her place against all comers. Sheila Florance became a close friend. She and I shared the same agent. It was Beris Underhill who told me Sheila rang her and asked where she had been hiding me. The truth, of course was, when it came to the profession, I had done very little. I was acutely aware that occasionally an incident in an episode had Bea doing or saying something that directly opposed an opinion expressed by her in a previous episode. How to cope with that was a skill we all had to develop. Sometimes I simply suggested an alternative, but I also learned how to deliver a line and play a different intention! The thing that disappointed me most was the fact that in the beginning it had been firmly established that the prisoners were territorial, and you can understand why. It was a pecking order 'power' thing. That should have been developed and protected, not ignored. 'You can't sit there, that's Bea's chair'- that sort of thing. However, we constantly had to fight directors who wanted us to sit somewhere else because it made a better shot. Soon, all that part of playing a prisoner disappeared. Shame. I'm told a genuine Top Dog would have taken up command of the kitchens and the food, not the laundry.

As long as they are not competing for male attention, I think women work well in groups because there is less of a power struggle than there is with men. There is, of course, nearly always one person in a group who, for whatever reason, behaves poorly. However, this is no threat when it is out in the open. It's the sly ones who do the most damage. Certain people became very territorial in the Green Room. I was not one of them as I spent more time on set than most. Our crew at Channel 10 were the best. They taught me all I know about cameras. We loved and respected them, socialised with them and on one occasion some cast even took them as partners to the Logie Awards. I recall those ceremonies very well. My first acceptance speech was 'I would like to thank Grundy for giving me the opportunity to bash almost every other actress in Australia!'

I left Prisoner when I was not enjoying it any more. Despite having been told I could be replaced overnight by Grundy, and that the audience would forget me, I was asked back to the show three times. Something I never considered. While we are on the subject, and just to set the record straight, I had to threaten to sue a very minor cast member for spreading the lie I was sacked from the show.

Bea has been a two-sided coin for me. She brought me to the attention of a lot of people. But sadly no one has ever had the nous, foresight or guts to cast me in another sustained role in television. Something I am asked by fans all the time is, 'When are we going to see you in another big role?' However, the powers that be in the industry in Australia are not known for listening to the opinions of fans. One of the biggest things I learned while in Prisoner is that networks regard drama as the gap between commercials. I take with me the memory of being involved in one of Australia's most ground-breaking and successful television dramas, worthy of a place in the Hall Of Fame because it always stayed true to itself. Unafraid to discuss pertinent women's issues in a down to earth manner, it pioneered the Australian accent and idiom in the US and never apologised for being hard hitting and earthy.

Since her days on Prisoner, Val has appeared in a huge amount of prominent theatre roles both in Australia and the UK. These have included Trafford Tanzi, A Streetcar Named Desire, Lady Chatterly's Lover, Driving Miss Daisy, Misery and the pantomime Aladdin with Michael Barrymore. She has also been seen in a number of high-rating television dramas such as City Homicide,

All Saints, *Secret Bridesmaids' Business*, *Blue Heelers* and, of course, the big screen adventure *Kitty and the Bagman*.

Val delighted fans by returning very briefly as Bea in a special skit for the 2006 Logie Awards, set in the laundry room. She was joined by Colette Mann in a scene scripted by Val herself.

MARGARET (MAGGIE) MAY KENNEDY NEE MULLINS

Played by Davina Whitehouse

First Episode 371
Last Episode 376
Total Featured: 6

Having known Lizzie in New South Wales in the early 1930s when she cooked on her husband's station, Maggie arrives in Wentworth on charges of being a drug runner. She becomes reacquainted with Lizzie and admits she knew that she was carrying heroin but was driven by her payment. Bea is quick to see through the act, but Maggie continues to proclaim she is innocent. Eventually all the women find out she was lying and are told she will be extradited to the United States to serve her full sentence. A brief and at times dull storyline only brightened by some great comedy moments with Lizzie, but mainly served to reiterate Bea's stance on drugs, regardless of age.

BEHIND THE CAMERA: Ken Mullholland's Memories:

1983: CHANGING CORRIDOR DOORS

John McRae was a somewhat 'theatrical' kind of Director. One of his pet sayings, when asked if the scene about to be taped would be difficult to get right was, 'It'll be a piece of piss!' And, whatever he actually meant by that (contemptible or too easy) he was certainly a capable Director, if somewhat abrasive at times.

I fell afoul of him, for some reason or reasons I cannot remember, and made the mistake of bad-mouthing him within his hearing. He took it on the chin and gave me as good as I'd given him, with that kind of acid-drop venom well known to old pros. That, in turn, stung me. I wanted to make him realise that I wasn't just a negative, anti-him cameraman.

I did a bit of deep thinking, and then went to Ray Lindsay, who was the head Floor Manager on *Prisoner* and asked him a question. 'Is there a three dimensional model of Wentworth Prison? Or some guide-lines as to how the corridors and cells, stairwells and floors work?' Ray made enquiries and came back with the answer. 'No.'

So, I produced some drawings for him to look at. My idea was that an extra dimension could be given by adding mock doors in the walls which actually backed straight on to the red brick walls of studio B. Now you know what was behind the mock brick corridor walls: enough room for the sand-bagged wooden set braces and the real brick walls that you see in the external shots of Wentworth.

I can't say for certain, but I think I might have suggested using the real stair well (One of two that led up to either end of the studio control room.) as the prison stair well.

In any event I did come up with the door suggestion and we took the idea to John. As I explained to him, the doors could actually be practical and there was just enough room behind for them to open wide enough to allow extras or actors to emerge. I didn't hear anything further about it until one morning I arrived in the studio to find the corridors suddenly had all these new doors.

A Bridge Over Troubled Water

> *Nola: What the hell am I supposed to do out here?*
> *Colleen: Well, you can start by pulling out the weeds.*
> *Nola: I wouldn't know a weed from a gum tree!*
> *Colleen: That's easy. If you get a hernia, you've pulled*
> *out a gum tree!*

Episode 341 – Colleen shows Nola McKenzie she's no push over

Left: Perfect as Powell: Judith brought a touch of excellence to her portrayal of Colleen. Right: "Should we make this a union matter?" Judith chats with Maggie.

From her very first introduction in Episode 48, Colleen Powell makes it obvious that she is no Meg Jackson, but also she isn't another Vera Bennett. Colleen's approach to her job at Wentworth is clear – the 'firm but fair' method. Her initial appearances [48, 65 and 111] are brief. However, her first major storyline sees Colleen in the role of union rep for the officers and results in the resignation of prison teacher David Andrews, showing the other staff and inmates just what she is capable of achieving [194].

Christened 'Po Face' by the women, Colleen's career is very important to her and, to begin with, it seems that she will do almost anything to better it. When new prisoner Kate Peterson arrives, Colleen foolishly agrees to arrange extra visits and special favours for her [244] in return for information about the

other prisoners and indeed the officers which help her score points with the Governor.

During the riot arranged by Sandy Edwards, Colleen shows she's made of tough stuff when she agrees to swap places with Kate who temporarily leaves the riot to discuss the prisoners' demands [248] with the authorities – and Bea Smith who is in hospital recovering from an operation. Colleen sees first-hand the state Wentworth has been turned into but keeps her cool when faced with a mob of angry women during the short exchange. We see that Colleen isn't worried about upsetting any of her fellow colleagues, especially Meg who is understandably shocked at having to face another riot: 'A good officer never forgets how to behave in an emergency,' she tells Meg, but her clinical attitude is slightly frowned upon by Erica.

Judith with co-star Elspeth Ballantyne.

When the position for Deputy Governor becomes available following the departures of Vera and Jim, Colleen and Meg go head-to-head for the role. Colleen continues to use her dealings with Kate to help her get noticed by Erica and, when the job is offered to her after Meg's refusal to accept it, she couldn't be happier [261]. It is at this point that she realises how dangerous collusions with an inmate are and so her dealings with Kate end for good – she has got what she wanted, for now.

Colleen's character really starts to develop properly following the arrival of Joan Ferguson. While Joan is clearly corrupt, Colleen conversely is a dedicated and respected officer who might have only bent the rules on occasion to better herself – the only similarity between their respective approaches turns out to be the uniform. Meg's relationship with Colleen improves greatly. This is partly, perhaps, because they find themselves united against the ever present threat of Ferguson. Certainly, the famous Powell put-downs find themselves a ready target in the arduous daily dealings with The Freak.

'I'd like to remind the bitch... with a sledge hammer!' (Colleen discussing Joan Ferguson with Meg).

When Colleen's daughter Jennifer recognises one of the men involved in an armed robbery, her life is turned upside down. Jennifer is kidnapped [275] and Colleen finds herself completely helpless, frantically worried about the welfare of her young child who is being held hostage. Colleen is relieved when the captors contact the prison to let her know that Jennifer is still alive. Unable to work due to the trauma, Colleen takes time off while the police track them down. An exhaustive search is arranged which finally finds Jenny safe but not before she has been brutally raped and assaulted by one of the men. The girlfriend of the man, Carol, is later caught and arrives at Wentworth as an inmate.

Colleen is forced to see Carol every day at Wentworth and, although Erica and Meg have their doubts about how Colleen will handle it, she is nothing less than calm and efficient towards her. However, the hatred and resentment do finally surface and she makes things difficult for Carol whenever the opportunity arises such as reversing the cleaning in the Rec Room. The women are totally sympathetic as to why Colleen is doing what she is doing and, before things get too out of hand, Carol is sentenced to three years for manslaughter and swiftly transferred out of Wentworth to Barnhurst prison [284].

A small mistake by Colleen almost sees her responsible for the burning down of the prison and the deaths of two of the inmates. She arranges for some cans of turpentine to be temporarily placed in the storeroom while she sorts out a mistake with the order. However, the very same store room is used by Margo Gaffney who hurls a Molotov cocktail into it which sets the prison alight [326]. The combination of the fire and the turpentine accelerates the flames and burns through the electrical circuit boards which are also located in the same room, bringing all of the prison gates to a locked position and thereby stopping people from escaping who don't have the keys. Inmates Barbara Fields and Heather 'Mouse' Trapp perish in the blaze. A detailed investigation by the fire department sheds light on the fact that the turpentine was stored in a place where it shouldn't have been. Colleen's professional and personal careers are in jeopardy but some quick talking by the Department sees that Colleen's name is left out of the final report, saving her job but shifting the blame to the very two inmates who lost their lives.

After 16 years of marriage, Colleen's relationship with her husband Patrick reaches a crisis point. Colleen is bored and moves out to gather her thoughts in order to assess the long-term future of the relationship [343]. She stays with Meg for a short time and, during some renovations being done at the flat; she builds up a friendship with the joiner Chris Young who also happens to be the husband of one of the inmates at Wentworth. This turns into an affair but when Chris' wife Janice finds out that she's been interfering with his family life, Colleen receives a slap across the face [351]. This seems to bring Powell to her senses and, thankfully, the affair is brought to a swift end.

The arrival of new officer Rick Manning causes one of *Prisoner*'s most tragic storylines. Rick's involvement in the underworld makes him the enemy of some of the city's biggest criminals and a contract is put out on his life. A bomb is placed in his car but when he finds that the car needs to go to the garage for repairs Patrick offers to take it for him, thinking he can drop off the kids at school on the way. When Patrick starts the engine, the car explodes into flames killing him and both of Colleen's children instantly [433].

Devastated by her loss, Colleen starts drinking heavily. Meg offers her sanctuary as Colleen can't face living in the family home without Patrick and the kids being there. She returns to work quickly but it is agreed that Meg temporarily takes over as Deputy Governor until Colleen is in the position where she is strong enough mentally and physically to take on the position again. The women recognise the immense grief that must be consuming Officer Powell and even cover for her when her drinking threatens to get out of control.

With time to come to terms with what has happened Colleen makes the life-changing decision to sell the family home, leave the prison service and travel the world. She resigns and begs for Meg to come with her but ends up having to find a new life for herself on her own… but not before one final drama on her last day when she is faced with a gunman in the prison [456] and is taken hostage by him. All turns out fine in the

Left: Rehearsing with Maggie Kirkpatrick and Elspeth Ballantyne. Right: Judith relaxes in the sun during a break between scenes.

Judith McGrath was perfect as Officer Powell.

her move to London to work for BBC Radio before returning to Australia and getting seriously involved in theatre for a number of years with the Melbourne Theatre Company and Playbox Theatre Company.

One of her earliest credited screen works is the 1969 film *Age of Consent* which also featured a young Helen Mirren. Judith was credited as Judy McGrath and played the small role of Grace. She later went on to play guest parts in classic Australian series *Bluey*, *Skyways* and *Young Ramsey* before joining *Prisoner* in 1980 for 263 episodes as the firm but fair officer Colleen 'Po Face' Powell.

Judith has worked extensively since hanging up her prison officer's uniform. On leaving *Prisoner* she jumped straight into theatre work and starred in Neil Simon's play *Last of the Red Hot Lovers*, playing the roles of all three lead female characters. The zany production couldn't be more different from her television role and although Judith enjoyed working on *Prisoner*, she longed for a new challenge:

'I desperately wanted to do something different... the nice thing about this play is that it has a beginning, a middle and an end.' – Judith McGrath: *TV Week* (11/08/1984)

Judith returned to television with small guest roles in *Neighbours, The Flying Doctors* and *Round the Twist*. These paved the way for a long-running role in the award winning *A Country Practice* where her character of Bernice Hudson proved popular and she stayed with the production during 1992-93 for over 140 episodes.

Undoubtedly, Judith's biggest television role to date is in the long-running hospital drama series *All Saints*. Her portrayal of Yvonne 'Von' Ryan saw her stay with the series from beginning to end with almost 500 episodes and with Judith appearing in every single one. While *All Saints* went though many changes of cast, production and even the very name of the series in the later days, Judith was employed on the show between 1998 and 2009, in the process becoming one of the most recognised faces on Australian television. In 2007 she was nominated for the prestigious Silver Logie award for 'Most Outstanding Actress'. Judith returned to the stage with the Sydney Theatre Company in early 2013 in *The Secret River*.

end, however. With help from the prisoners, the siege is quickly over and Colleen leaves Wentworth for the last time to embark on her new future.

As she is packing up her things, Meg tells Colleen that one of the women said, 'The place won't be the same without old Po Face,' and how right she was.

'I went out the next day and had all my hair chopped off. I wanted a completely different look. Colleen had served her time. I enjoyed being with the show but it had lasted long enough.' – Judith McGrath: *TV Week* (11/08/1984)

Born in 1947 in Brisbane, Judith McGrath joined the world of drama from the age of seven when she began taking drama classes at the Twelfth Night Theatre in her hometown. Her early career saw

HAZEL JEAN KENT

Played by Belinda Davey

First episode: 143
Last episode: 399
Total featured: 64 episodes

First appearing in 1980, Hazel stood out from the crowd as someone who always seemed to carry the world on her shoulders. Established as being among Bea's acquaintances, she was quickly accepted as one of the core group of inmates. Hazel's troubles would continue at a pace, being involved in the thick of the action in the prison. Despite the traumas inside Wentworth, Hazel was a devoted mother and longed for her freedom. Life on the outside became so alien to Hazel that her only glimpses of happiness were when her two children visited the prison. When her husband George wins custody of the children, Hazel's world is torn apart. She attacks Officer Bailey [267] and taken to solitary where she is sedated.

Returning to the series in 1983, Hazel has been released from Wentworth and spends time at Driscoll House. When she discovers a bag of stolen money owned by Jean Carter, she takes some herself and becomes embroiled in a robbery and returns to Wentworth [336]. Meg and Judy find Hazel drunk in a bar and it becomes clear her troubles are far from over. She spends time at the second Halfway House [343] before disappearing from the series again.

Hazel's final stint in the show is one which is particularly heartbreaking as she is suffering from a terminal brain tumour. Deciding she can't go on any longer, Hazel asks Judy to end her pain for good [399].

TED DOUGLAS

Played by Ian Smith

First episode: 61
Last episode: 382
Total featured: 52

Pompous and taking great delight in issuing orders, Ted was Head of Department of Corrective Services. Making fleeting appearances throughout the series whenever any drama occurred, he would often clash with Erica's vision of how Wentworth should be run.

He supports Vera in applying for the position of Governor at Barnhurst [219] and oversees Meg's reinstatement as an officer following her time in Wentworth as a prisoner. Frequently manipulated by Joan Ferguson, Ted saw this as a strength in her character and saw her as a potential candidate to take over from Erica who resigns from Wentworth [361]. He later announces the new Governor as being Ann Reynolds.

When the Lionel Fellowes drugs storyline progresses, Ted becomes mixed up in dodgy dealings and finds himself being blackmailed by Bea. He attempts to flee from the authorities but is caught and arrested at the airport [382].

CHAPTER EIGHT

1984
Episodes 417 to 505

> *Sheila's first words to me were: I hope you don't mind, but I have rewritten the script over the weekend...*

With David Bridges bringing 1983 to its gripping conclusion, viewers were left wondering if Lizzie's ticker would hold out past the opening credits of Episode 417, having lost her best friend only weeks before and then being faced with the gruesome sight of fellow inmates' body parts littered throughout the grounds of Wentworth. While Lizzie would indeed muster up the strength to pull through, viewers were able to sense that without Val Lehman it meant part of Lizzie also left with Bea, such was the bond they had created from the word go.

Lizzie had become a shadow of her former self in Bea's absence, yet the introduction of Roy Edmunds who was asked to play the role of Lizzie's long lost son, Arthur Charlton, gave rise to some lovely sensitive scenes between mother and son. These brought a rawness to Sheila's performance in her last few episodes as her departure from the show was just around the corner. Roy Edmunds remembers with vivid delight the time he spent working with Sheila, and describes the unfaltering fighting spirit that Sheila brought to her performance as she prepared to bow out of the show for good:

I was so chuffed when I was asked to play the role of Arthur. Lizzie was a big loss to the show as she carried a big audience. The magic of a character that jumps out of the little screen at you is something of a mystery to most actors. If it were that simple to do it, then we would all be A-list actors. Sheila was a serious actor, a total professional who might have been a little impatient in dealing with those who were not as devoted to the art without really knowing it themselves, as she felt the craft demanded. Many actors did not go on to greater things after making a start with Prisoner, *others did. Sheila was never a 'hack' and took the opportunity to*

make the most of a soapie but on her terms, and they were tough. Maybe that's what makes an A-lister.

Other things I remember are that Sheila liked a Guinness. I attended her funeral. Sheila had planned it. It was very moving and, at the end, we gave her a standing ovation as she made her final exit.

All in all, Sheila caused me to understand just how tough it could be in this industry. Something akin to the tensions and battles which were acted out in the Prisoner *scripts themselves, it is not an industry for the faint-hearted really, a rare example of someone who took on the powers above her and made it work on her own terms because in the final analysis the viewers were on her side. She had an audience which gave her the power and she never forgot that. In keeping with the integrity of her character, she felt she was keeping a bond with her audience in turn.*

I have many memories of Sheila. She impressed me greatly. I am thinking about my role as her son only. I arrived on set to begin work. When Sheila arrived, we were introduced and I was immediately taken by her voice which was clearly quite melodic and English and nothing like her character.

Her first words to me were as I recall, 'I hope you don't mind but I have rewritten the script over the weekend.' I replied that I didn't mind at all, which was true. I had my own concerns.

Sheila had a very clear understanding of her character and fought ferociously to protect the integrity of her character. I cannot recall the exact line changes although I do recall the furore it caused. But this was normal with Sheila. Meetings were hurriedly called to work out script changes that were forced into the next drafts.

Young people, with whom she was very popular, instinctively understood this in a way that I experienced directly in the street. I was doing a horse-drawn wedding one weekend (being a carriage driver), and was loading the carriage by myself onto the trailer. Some young kids recognised me and stopped to chat. They asked questions about Lizzie and I realised they totally believed in her. They believed she was who she was. That's a great compliment coming from young kids. But it was certainly no accident because Sheila got her way with her character right to the end. Even when she was leaving, they had no choice but to change everything as a result of her insistence. She could argue why her character would act or react a certain

way because she had detailed the history and background of her character and the writers, had they done their homework properly, should have known they were crossing the line. Sheila told me that what we would experience together was nothing compared to what could be explored in theatre. She was a supportive and enthusiastic member of the cast right to the end. A powerful lady in a tiny frame.

Everyone's Grandmum. Although she was in the slammer, it didn't matter; she was the Grandmum to the inmates and a very professional actor.

With Sheila's departure coming as a huge blow to the series, fans were left wondering if *Prisoner* would survive another year. Who could ever replace such an iconic character as the rascally old lag who found her way into people's hearts? Queen Bea had been transferred to Barnhurst where her renewed battles against Vinegar Tits and the likes of Marie Winter would keep her memory alive without being seen on screen, offering a glimmer of hope that we may see the great Top Dog return once more. Fleeting references to Bea would follow throughout 1984, but it was clear that *Prisoner* had ventured into a new era. Uncertain as it may have been, the likes of Betty Bobbitt would

Opposite: The inseparable duo: Prisoner was about to find out if could survive without Lizzie and Bea. Above: Roy Edmunds with Sheila. Right: Living legend: Sheila's legacy would never be forgotten.

prove that Judy was able to hold centre court herself and lead the viewers through a troubled year into a new chapter which would bring a host of new faces. 1984 was just warming up with trouble in the form of a James Dean wannabe, love for Joan Ferguson and a new Top Dog that would see one of Australia's finest character actresses emerge as a worthy successor to Queen Bea.

Casting supremo Jan Russ would play a vital part in ensuring that *Prisoner* would continue to employ the best acting talent in Australia and maintain the trend of excellence within the casting department that had been evident since day one. Jan chose Janet Andrewartha to play the role of tough new inmate Rebecca Kean. Modelling herself on James Dean, the hard exterior housed a delicate soul tortured by a troubled upbringing and resentment towards her parents. Jan would later cast Anne Charleston to return to *Prisoner* in the role of Reb's mum, to portray a convincing mother-daughter relationship struggling to reconnect in a world that had torn them apart.

Thirty-one-year old Janet was appearing in a play at the Universal Theatre in Melbourne which brought her to the attention of the producers of *Prisoner*. Originally screen tested for the role of Bobbie Mitchell, it was felt Janet was too old to play Bobbie. Convinced they had found a new star, the role of eighteen-year-old Reb Kean was created for Janet. A quick tug of her collar is all Janet Andrewartha requires to take her right back to 1984:

I often tell the story of my Prisoner *debut to acting students because it's worth going to a screen test, even if you think you are not quite right for it. It turned out to be a very lucky break for me as I hadn't done any screen work*

before. They then wrote a screen test for the Reb character. I had to cut off all my hair even though I only had a few weeks work initially. But I stayed a full year in the end.

Luckily, I knew some of the people, which was very fortunate to me. They were a very friendly bunch. A very welcoming environment. I had seen the show beforehand. I was in awe of some of the cast, I thought they were amazing. Still do. There were some very experienced older actors there at the time. I was the first to put my hand up and ask advice. I now encourage the kids to do that.

I am guessing my initial contract was eight weeks. It might have been thirteen, but I rather think it was eight. The three-camera process was completely foreign to me at first. I thought I was doing all right though. Then one day Maggie Kirkpatrick said to me, 'What you are doing isn't too bad, but it might be nice if you didn't have your back to the camera. The audience might be able to see what you are doing.' It is

New 'Prisoner' cuts locks

It was a big decision for Janet Andrewartha to accept a role in the television series, "Prisoner".

It was not the money or the part. Janet had to have her waist-long hair (above) cut after 15 years.

A hairdresser this week gave Janet, 31, a James Dean-style haircut — short and cropped around the ears (right).

"It was a hard decision to get my hair cut," Janet said.

"I wanted the role, it had to be done." Janet will play the part of an 18-year-old Rebeca Kenan, a great fan of the 1950s actor James Dean.

"Rebecca has a lot of problems, she has been rejected by her family," Janet said.

As an escape, the character cuts her hair like James Dean and imitates the legendary movie star.

Janet has had minor roles in some Australian television series including Carson's Law, but this is her first regular part.

She has been an actress for three years, since graduating from the National Theatre at St. Kilda.

Above: Janet cut off her waist-long hair for the role of Reb.
Right: James Dean wannabe Reb arrives. Bottom Right:
Backed into a corner: Reb freaks out.

difficult with three cameras. You are not just doing your performance and reacting, you are trying to keep an eye on where the cameras are, where the sound is and which angle they are getting you from. There is a light on the cameras but sometimes, because of problems with reflection, they will turn the lights off so it is pretty impossible to know which camera they are feeding from. You have really got to be aware of what the director will be going for in the scene.

I remember Chris Adshead, Steve Mann and Kendal Flanagan being particularly helpful directors. There were many good directors on Prisoner and, because I was a beginner in telly land, they were all pretty useful to me really.

I suppose the drugs storyline was a pretty memorable one for me. I think it was crack. I did like the 'Dad dying' moment. It allowed me to show a more vulnerable side to this little toughie, you know. I liked it when the rich tall character came into the show [Leigh Templar played by Virginia Hey] because, apart from her being a nice lady to work with, it allowed me to show another side to Reb. I just liked the things that showed other colours within the character. Stuff I did with my mother in the show was fabulous, too. So many good storylines, I was so lucky. Almost killing Phyllis. Yay !

It was the nature of the Rec Room and the canteen scenes that everyone was in studio all

Above: Make-up artist Doug Glanville prepares Janet for her debut. Right: Janet enjoys the Melbourne sunshine whilst reading over lines.

day. If you were unfortunate enough to have Friday afternoon in the canteen you were there until 7:30pm or whatever it was. You may have no lines, it may be very debilitating and your scene might not be until the very last shot of the day. I think in the case of playing Reb she had a certain energy about her which helped, but I am sure there are many, many scenes where I did not achieve the optimum result because of the long hard-working days. The scene where Reb was pushed over the stairs was, in fact, a stunt double. She was so like me. I saw that very scene last night and I thought it was me. They copied the way I did the socks over the trousers. She was very well padded with a big body suit. A very impressive stunt.

What they used to do with contracts in those days was renew every thirteen weeks. By the time they got around to renewing for the last time I had started to get some offers as an actor that I really wanted to explore. When you are young also you are looking for some variety. Grundy wanted me to stay on but I had taken the decision to say yes to a stage role at the Melbourne Theatre Company. It turned out to be the right thing to do, you grow and change. My lasting memory of my work on the show is the camaraderie. It was a really good ensemble.

I do have fond memories of Sheila Florance even though we never worked together. One night I arrived at a dinner party and Sheila was

Below Left: Tough at the top – Reb picks on Pixie. Below Right: Pillow talk: Reb seldom let her guard down. Bottom Left: Janet with Maxine Klibingaitis. Opposite: Reb with Pixie

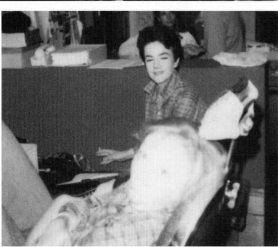

there. I was offered a wine and I said, 'I'll just have water, thank you.' Sheila said very grandly, 'WATER? Darling, fish piss in it!' She was an amazing woman as well as an amazing actor.

I am extremely flattered to be recognised as Reb still. It is a peculiar feeling; a feeling of appreciation for the appreciation, if you like. *Prisoner* will always be a special job for me. The reason mainly was that the writing was especially good for television. You don't get those sorts of characters and that sort of energetic writing on television, especially for fast turnaround television. You did have it before *Prisoner* and we haven't had it since. Sometimes when I was working on *Neighbours* I longed for a script like I got in *Prisoner*.

What became of Reb? I kind of didn't like her chances. She was fairly smart but, at the

same time, just so damaged. And she so enjoyed the wickedness. She had a spirit for it. I don't think she could have gone down a straight road in her life. Having started in life with a dreadful relationship with her mother is a really tough one to overcome.

Carl Bleazby is re-introduced as Major Ferguson, father of The Freak in [423], during Joan's stint as Acting Governor. Longing for the acceptance of her father, the Major visits Joan at work and witnesses the women humiliating her during an inspection. With Reb's storyline unfolding at the same time, the Major becomes mixed up in a plot to free Reb from Wentworth and he is kidnapped by Gary Wilder (424). Ferguson would never forgive Reb for the risking her father's life, and a battle line was drawn.

Episode 424 heralds the surprise return of Erica Davidson, now working for The Department and visiting Wentworth following a report submitted by Meg. One of Erica's iconic glares waits in store for Joan, who opens the door of the Governor's office to reveal her mighty ex-boss. Gone was the bouffant we all knew and loved. In its place a much trendier (it's the 80s, keep up) softer hairdo, but firmly encased in typical Davo-style mint-green frock, pulled tighter than the glare upon her face. Joan's brief reign of acting Governor was under immediate scrutiny and with no-one better to question her authority than the former Governor herself.

Maxine Klibingaitis looks back on 1984 with much affection, playing the mischievous tearaway Bobbie Mitchell:

In the audition scenes and character breakdown, Bobbie was a streetwise punk who was very aggressive and damaged. I think that because I am a softie, I naturally gave her a different heart. The schedule was intense. My mum used to leave my evening meal on the kitchen sideboard at the end of each shooting night. I must say she was a bit of a whinging bitch (Bobbie that is, not my mum!)

My first day on set was overwhelming. Everyone else seemed to know what to do. I was not nervous; I come from family stock with good reserve, so I simply rolled with any (gentle) punches. I visited the studio the week before I started to have my long hair cut and dyed, so I appreciated a kind of taste of what to expect.

I was made to feel at home from the very beginning. The hair and make-up and wardrobe and props departments respectively and collectively were my first friends, followed by the cast. The floor crew were and remain friends. Jen Williams, our vision switcher for the duration of the show remains one of my best friends. I love her; quite a few of the directors remain in the social connective. I rang and spoke to Annie Phelan just the other day for her birthday. Tina and Elspeth were especially welcoming. All of my Prisoner *friends are friends with my son who turns 20 years old this year. My son is working for actor/producer Cameron Nugent. I met Cameron working on a film called Boronia Boys which also stars Tim Burns and Desiree Smith. It featured as well* Prisoner *pals Elspeth Ballantyne and Reylene Pearce who I met on my first day on the* Prisoner *set. The film is a big hit here and is out on DVD release now.*

Sheila Florance immediately took me under her wing, because that was in her nature and we had a geographical connection in that her then late husband was Polish and I am Lithuanian, so we were neighbours by proxy. Sheila used to call me her 'Little Neoli', Polish for violet. It's also my favourite colour. Sheila was, and remains, very well loved. I think of her often with love, terrific fun and hilarious. Reylene Pearce once hid a condom in Sheila's bag as she flew to Sydney and, to pay for an in-flight beverage Sheila pulled out the condom. She thought it was a bank note.

SARAH HIGGINS

Played by Nell Johnson

First Episode: 416
Last Episode: 499
Total featured: 10

Sarah 'Justice must be seen to be done' Higgins was introduced in Episode 416 when she was chair of the parole board hearing for Phyllis and Lizzie. Described by Phyllis as a hard-faced bitch who drinks battery acid for breakfast, Miss Higgins is heartless personified. She returned in Episode 471 to pass further sentences on several of the inmates and recommends that Marie Winter is transferred to Blackmoor. When she is caught for accepting cash payments in return for lighter sentences, Sarah finds herself on the other side of the bars. With the majority of prisoners out for blood, there is no shortage of suspects when she is found with her throat cut. After a process of elimination, Myra discovers Frances Harvey as the culprit, but nobody is charged for the murder.

I have so many wonderful memories from my time in Wentworth. Among them, there also remains in my memory bank Janet Andrewartha's very fine work as Reb going through an intense drug-infused rampage. Bobbie was locked in the cell with Reb. Anything with Genevieve Lemon. We got into trouble all of the time and apparently we thought we were hilarious. The crew did also. I can definitely say I enjoyed working with Genevieve the most. Because I started in the show before Gen, I got her into trouble almost as if we were at school.

When it came to my leaving the series, I chose to leave. I loved and continue to love Bobbie. I wanted to explore other opportunities and some very welcome prosaic-style experiences in both film and television came my way. I also wrote and performed in a long-running radio comedy show, amongst some seasoned actors. So with this artistic freedom I have also moonlighted as a stand-up comedian. I have been working in independent film with an extraordinary ensemble of actors that I love and it has been fabulous working with other Prisoner *cast who weren't in Bobbie's time.*

After narrowly escaping death at the hands of David Bridges, Tina Bursill continued in the role of ice lady Sonia Stevens, caught up in dodgy deals with the other women after being dethroned from the Top Dog position by Minnie Donovan. Tina was perfect for the role of the bitter and twisted Sonia, her height often used to intimidate the other women. A further series of near death encounters await Sonia when new prisoner Belinda Johns arrives in Wentworth. Belinda, played by Jane Turner who would later go on to find fame in *Kath And Kim*, is intent on killing Sonia and sets up a number of traps to lure the ice lady to her death. She is stabbed in the back by a piece of broken glass [420] but recovers, and narrowly escapes another attack in the library when a mysterious figure turns out the lights.

A new male officer graced the corridors of Wentworth in 1984. Ex-policeman Rick Manning, played by Andy Anderson, caught the eye of more than Pixie Mason when he arrived at the prison. Rick

Janet relaxes in the green room with Anne and Betty

would later go on to develop a relationship with one of the inmates, be a shoulder to cry on for officers and prisoners alike, but was a welcome addition to the cast in a year that was jam packed with PMT.

Andy recalls one particular day sitting quietly in the Green Room where the atmosphere could be every bit as snippy as on set:

It was a shock to the system joining Prisoner. *The cast were all amazing, strong personalities. Not a shrinking violet in the bunch. It was terrific and a bit scary.*

I always thought that we should have filmed the Green Room, where we would hang out between scenes. On most days, there was more drama, and humour, going on there than on the set. Colourful and boisterous. Brian James was the other regular male actor when I was there. A lovely man, he played a kindly, older warden. Brian and I would usually be found sitting on the couch in the Green Room playing Scrabble. Most of the time we were part of the general raves but other times it was purely women's business. One day the air was particularly blue, some disagreement. Brian and I kept our heads down. Things got more strident and raucous, then at one stage Elspeth came over, crouched down next to us and said quietly, 'Brian, I am sorry about the language'. It was hilarious. The exact opposite

of most work places I've been in. We poor wee things who had to be protected. But I loved working on the show. The ladies were incredible. Took me in, made me feel welcome; always there with a kind word, a reassuring pat on the arse. I never knew from whom. Many laughs.

Brian James had arrived to play officer Stan Dobson, an older gentleman reaching retirement age. This produces several remarks from fellow officers about his suitability for the job and being able to cope with all it entails. Stan brings in his pianola for the women to use, but a heart condition is revealed when he tries to push it. It becomes apparent he relies on medication to survive when Reb kicks his tablets out of reach.

Annette Andre was cast as Camilla Wells [429] who acts as being socially aloof and initially belittles the inmates in their desire to lead a normal life on the inside. However, she later gains the respect of the women when she tricks the officers into letting her phone her radio station to let the world know of inmate Mo Maguire's plight.

An attempt to kill Rick Manning [433] ends up changing Colleen's life forever when her husband Patrick borrows Rick's car to take their kids to school. A bomb has been planted in the car which detonates, killing all of Colleen's family instantly. The impact of the scene was brought further to life by Judith McGrath's

Left: Major Ferguson. Right: Down but not out: Maggie and Carl relax during the kidnap storyline.

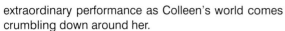

extraordinary performance as Colleen's world comes crumbling down around her.

While Sonia is up to her eyes in fighting off revenge attacks, a new cellmate arrives after killing her husband in Episode 435. We are treated to Anne Phelan's return to Wentworth as Myra Desmond. Myra gets a brief reintroduction on the outside as a devoted mum to Kay and Alan, pushed to the brink of despair by her husband Bill. It was a welcome return to the series for Anne, restoring viewers' faith in the continuity department, investing time and effort in resurrecting a key (albeit peripheral) character from the show's earlier years to redevelop and flourish when the time was right. 1984 was the perfect opportunity to showcase Anne Phelan's versatility and experience as an actress, with *Prisoner* set to offer Anne the challenge of becoming the new Top Dog, a challenge which would see Anne take the show to new heights in a masterful portrayal of former PRG leader, Myra.

Also returning in Episode 435 is the wayward Doreen Burns who arrives to visit her old cellmates. Doreen runs into The Freak, and is disheartened to find out that many of her old friends are gone.

Twenty-one-year old Tottie Goldsmith had a brief stint inside playing Gloria Jean Payne, former girlfriend of Myra's husband Bill. Gloria is inducted into Wentworth by Joan Ferguson charged with possession of drugs. Joan seizes the opportunity to set Myra up and lures her to have a violent confrontation with Gloria. Despite their on screen battle, Tottie was thankful that Annie was on hand to help the younger actors feel at ease. She recalls:

Being in Prisoner *was a very memorable time for me. It was my second TV show, I was under skilled and totally intimidated by these larger than life women that I was suddenly sharing a Green Room with. I think most of them stayed in character in between scenes! I wanted to run for the hills until the beautiful Annie Phelan introduced herself and took me under her wing, showing me the ropes and much needed warmth. Annie and Maxine Klibingaitis were my saviours. I feel blessed to have been part of such an iconic Australian TV show and wish I had had the maturity and acting chops I have now. It took me 15 years to ever wear denim again and I still can't wear a denim frock!*

Margo Gaffney returns to Wentworth [442] although this time we see a much darker and sinister side to Margo, whose life now revolves around drugs and supplying drugs to young inmates trapped in the penal system. Joan suspects the Fellowes gang are behind Margo's transfer to Wentworth in order to start peddling drugs there.

A transfer to Barnhurst for Bobbie and Sonia for their own safety sees the two inmates end up in

MINERVA EDITH DONOVAN "MINNIE"

Played by Wendy Playfair

First Episode: 405
Last Episode: 437
Total Featured: 33

Inducted by Joyce Barry, Minnie arrives at Wentworth charged with inspiring to commit theft.

She knows Governor Ann Reynolds from Ann's days working in child welfare and attempts to rekindle their friendship. Lizzie provides her with information about who to be careful of in Wentworth, starting with 'the 'Ice Lady', Sonia. An expert in pick-pocketing, she organises some classes for the women. When some of them start disappearing, Minnie believes Mr Bridges is helping them to escape. She calls a halt to the exodus [413] and has a narrow escape from being next on the hit list. Minnie steals The Freak's keys [417] but Joan exacts her revenge by poisoning her [418]. When Reb arranges an escape, Minnie and Bobbie go on the run for a couple of days [435] but the fun is soon over when Minnie takes the blame for the escape and is transferred to B Block [437].

Top Left: Make-up artist Caroline Garbett perfects Bobbie's punk image. Top Right: Maxine with Nigel Bradshaw who arrives to play Dennis Cruickshank in Episode 457. Left: Maxine lands the role of newcomer Bobbie Mitchell. Above: Moody blues: Bobbie was capable of a tantrum or two.

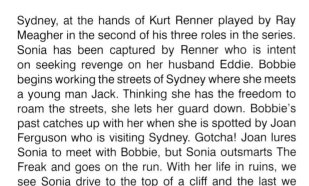

Sydney, at the hands of Kurt Renner played by Ray Meagher in the second of his three roles in the series. Sonia has been captured by Renner who is intent on seeking revenge on her husband Eddie. Bobbie begins working the streets of Sydney where she meets a young man Jack. Thinking she has the freedom to roam the streets, she lets her guard down. Bobbie's past catches up with her when she is spotted by Joan Ferguson who is visiting Sydney. Gotcha! Joan lures Sonia to meet with Bobbie, but Sonia outsmarts The Freak and goes on the run. With her life in ruins, we see Sonia drive to the top of a cliff and the last we see of the ice lady is a shot of her staring down to the waves beneath her.

Bryan Marshall joins the show playing psycho psychiatrist Jonathan Edmunds who is conducting experiments into behaviour modification in Wentworth. Jonathan knew Ann Reynolds from years ago, and his return to Wentworth looked certain to reignite some love for the lonely Governor. However, he also has his sights on Meg, and no amount of behaviour modification can prevent the mighty Morris from seducing the male talent of Wentworth. Both Ann and Meg go head-to-head to vie for the attention of Jonathan, but Ann is unaware that he has already begun changing Meg's behaviour through hypnosis. Eventually he is revealed as a villain when Ann finds his dicta-phone and overhears his work with Meg under hypnosis.

Episode 451 saw Polish actress Agnieszka Perepeczko playing the role of East German illegal immigrant Hannah Geldschmidt. Hannah is inducted by Colleen Powell on the charge of attacking a man who Hannah claims was a Nazi.

A Polish-trained actress with extensive experience in television and film, Agnieszka was forced to leave her home country due to the political situation at the time. Having previously visited Australia as a model, as Polish ambassador for the Australian Wool Corporation, Agnieszka fell in love with the country and decided to settle, being granted citizenship some years later.

Agnieszka started her own photographic business in Australia which eventually opened doors to some contacts who persuaded her to screen test for *Prisoner*. Agnieszka recalls:

> *Don't call us, we'll call you, I was told after the test. A typical reply to be expected in such circumstances. Six months went by and I had all but forgotten about* Prisoner *when suddenly, out of the blue, the phone rang. 'We would like to offer you the part of Hannah Geldschmidt, a Jewish woman, and four months work.' I was ecstatic.*
>
> *In Poland, I work not only as an actress but also write books for women. In one of those I described my first impression of meeting with the cast, and especially with the prisoners. The day was full of emotions and sympathy from my Australian fellow actresses lamenting my situation: a husband and family in Poland, loneliness and political servitude and the part of poor Hannah. All that meant that I was at once accepted by my fellow actresses who sincerely felt sorry for me, which did not prevent me from dressing up after she shoots and looking the best as I do in everyday life. Betty Bobbitt and Maggie Kirkpatrick became my closest friends and helped me with everything. Maggie was especially fantastic. She taught me English, took me out to various events and parties and attended those we organised at my place. I especially fondly remember one such party I organised, and which was attended by Don Dunstan to celebrate the arrival in Australia of my husband Marek Perepeczko, a famous and extremely popular Polish film actor. I still cherish the many photographs with Maggie which had been taken at the event.*
>
> *In order to get the prisoners to get to like me I devised a little trick. I attended the first meeting dressed very shabbily as Agnieszka / Hannah. I also told them a true story about how lonely I was here, in Australia, how I longed for my family back home, with whom I had no contact, because of the martial law imposed in Poland – this made both the girls and me cry our eyes out. And from the very start they began to love Hannah! It was a wonderful time with stories both happy and extremely sad, but wonderful reminiscences, nevertheless. My husband, a very severe critic and theatre director as well watched all the* Prisoner *instalments in which I featured and even praised me – something very unusual and exceptional for him!*

Louise Siversen began to emerge as one of the latest heavies of H Block, alongside Lois Collinder as Alice 'Lurch' Jenkins. Their torment of Hannah would signal the beginning of a deadly partnership for the pair that would continue for over a hundred episodes.

Rick Manning develops a crush on a girl in the newsagents, Rachel Milsom [Kim Trengrove], and they end up going on a date. When her father is knocked down by a drunk driver and found not guilty of manslaughter, Rachel runs him down outside the court. She is inducted to Wentworth in Episode 458 and continues her relationship with Rick until he leaves for pastures new.

Andy Anderson recalls a period of the show filled with humour and camaraderie behind the bars as he prepared to hang up his uniform:

> On my last day I had a scene where my girlfriend had been locked up for murder and poor old Rick had to do this long, distraught walk down the hallway. I was fighting back tears, doing my best heartbroken acting. Then I look up ahead and there was Anne Phelan at the end of the hall, off camera, blouse up, flashing me. Well, poor old Rick suddenly saw the hilarious side of his one and only love being locked up for the rest of her natural. I've always thought how superb it would have been if they'd only whipped a camera around and caught her. Alas, it remains one of those magic, missed screen moments. For Anne and I alone. Priceless.

When Myra receives a visit from her daughter Kay [455] she can sense all is not well at home, and confides in Judy that she's no longer able to reach out and help her family. Worried that Kay has fallen foul of drugs, Judy advises Myra to speak to her old pal Wally for help. Playing Myra's daughter Kay Desmond was Sally-Anne Bourne. Sally is the daughter of Ernie Bourne, later in the series to achieve fame for wooing Joyce Barry as Mervin Pringle. Now a star of many West End and Australian musicals, here Sally recounts her days being banged up with the girls:

> I had played Annie as a child. Done a few TV series and at the age of 17 I got an audition for *Prisoner,* which was pretty huge then. I went along and did the screen test. I felt I did pretty well. I remember not hearing anything for ages. I had pretty much forgotten about it when I got

a call saying that I had got the role. I was so chuffed. I did love the show and just wanted to meet Maggie Kirkpatrick, whom I ended up getting along with famously. So I was pretty excited. I was 17 and had just got a role on one of the hugest Australian TV shows of the time. So it was a pretty cool thing to tell my school friends.

All my first shoots were on location. We were setting up how Myra got into jail. I only worked with a few of the actors and wasn't in prison as such. It felt like I was on a TV show but not the iconic laundry or corridors of Wentworth. Annie Phelan had worked with my dad so I had met her. In fact, I saw her just last month. She is still a great mate 30 years on. She was amazing to work with, so natural and just got on with it. You reacted with ease to her dialogue. It was always just like chatting filming scenes with her. I should say arguing as a lot of our stuff was screaming at each other. I adored working with her.

I knew Kay was the crux of the storyline as to how Myra ended up in jail. I did all that storyline and knew it was a few months' work. I only learned months later, when Annie had to do a play and so needed to be out of the prison in order to film lots of episodes quickly so she could have time off, that we were doing the whole Kay-on-heroine storyline.

I did a bit of research on the drugs issue. Watched videos and read stuff. Looking back, I was pretty young to delve into that stuff. I have always found that costume and make-up are a great 'hook' into a character. Three hours in the make-up chair with yellow skin, shaded cheekbone and sunken eyes really helped. I remember filming those 'cold turkey' scenes with Annie and Alan Hopgood. We were in rural

BEHIND THE CAMERA: Ken Mullholland's Memories:

1984: FREAK OUT
The episode where the Freak goes completely haywire in her home and regains her senses only to realise that she has killed her pet dog, which was a pug from memory. The episode was directed by Kendal Flanagan, and the dog was trained by its handler and did what was required very obediently. However, when it came to the shot of the dead dog, which had supposedly been battered to death, Kendal wasn't sure how to approach it. Hardly a make-up job, although he was contemplating a pool of fake blood with the dog's head lying in it, but wasn't sure whether he could get away with that.

I'll say one thing about Kendal, he was always open to advice and suggestions. So, I suggested to him that we could underplay it and have the trainer get the dog to lie down beside a couch or armchair, and the shot could be taken of the motionless hind quarters with the head masked behind the furniture – chilling enough without wasting much time.

The cut back to Maggie's slow realization of what she'd done was powerful enough to get the message across.

Above: Bosom buddies: Maxine grew close to Genevieve Lemon. Top Right: Genevieve and Maxine amongst the Prisoner uniforms in the Channel 10 wardrobe department. Right: Genevieve and Maxine.

Victoria and there had been massive bush fires a few years before, so it was all pretty sparse. We were very hot and crammed into a bedroom with a camera, lighting and sound. I was on the bed with Annie and Alan wrestling me down as we fought and screamed at each other. The scene ended with Annie slapping me. I can tell you she really slapped me. Hard! We did it so many times and it was physically draining, apart from being insanely hot. When you see the scene where she slaps me and I collapse, it was very real and I sobbed and sobbed. Probably the most real moment I had as an actress up to that point. I almost couldn't move. It was hard but I learned a lot from it. I had to fill my mouth with cold tea before filming me vomiting over the side of the bed. It wasn't my favourite moment. Working with those people was amazing training for a young actor. They can be hysterically funny and when they call 'Action'. It all kicks in and, take after take, they are fantastic.

What can I say about my dad, Ernie? He was an amazing actor and company member. Everyone who I have ever met, who worked with dad, loved him. They always remark on his wicked sense of humour and amazing characterisations. Sadly, we never worked together. Although we did used to go and sing together for old folks when I was a teenager. He loved being in Prisoner *and it became a great family for him. He knew a lot of the cast already*

and always enjoyed the immediacy of working on television, its time pressures and disjointed scenes. Always a great challenge for an actor. I believe there is an episode we were both in [524] but we didn't do a scene together. My dad was simply one of a kind. A brilliant actor, singer, comedian, person – and dad!

Having lived in the UK for 13 years, I totally get why Prisoner *is still so huge. Even though it's quite camp and raw, it's really fantastic entertainment with magnificently strong characters. I loved doing* Prisoner. *It was amazing. I had always been a bit of a 'child star' although hopefully not an obnoxious one. I felt like, and was treated like, a grown-up for the first time doing* Prisoner.

Now on her own, Colleen decides it's time to leave Wentworth for good. The strength of her hair clasps are put to the test one last time when a mysterious Peter Secker visits Wentworth to see Hannah. When Hannah does not recognise him, he pulls a gun and threatens her in German. Colleen is taken hostage while Hannah runs to beg the women to hide her from certain death. Colleen's clasps hold up well and she

Above: Andy arrives as Rick Manning. Top Right: Tina Bursill as Sonia Stevens. Bottom Right: Brian keeps Tina locked behind the bars.

finally bids farewell to years of dedicated service and looks forward to a future of travelling the world.

Leigh Templar [Virginia Hey] is inducted to Wentworth charged with the murder of her manager, with officer Dennis Cruickshank [Nigel Bradshaw] also arriving in Episode 457. Resplendent in designer clothes, and her best 80s hairdo, Virginia portrayed troubled Leigh with a calm and confident approach to life behind bars. But, according to the now legendary star of *Farscape*, Leigh's confident manner was far removed from how she really felt arriving on set for the first time:

I was living in Sydney prior to being cast for the role of Leigh Templar in Prisoner. *I had only just finished my very first acting role in a film called* Mad Max 2 *(*Road Warrior *in the US). I was a well-known fashion model for a decade before I ventured into film and TV acting. I had experience with video and film cameras because of all of the television commercials I had been in, 57 in all. But the actual craft of dramatic acting I had no experience of at all. I was terrified when auditioning for* Mad Max 2 *and absolutely horrified to death when going up for* Prisoner. *The show was very established by the time I auditioned in 1984. It was sitting at the top as Australia's television award-winning dramatic series for years before I entered the picture. The thought of joining the cast seemed unattainable to me. Only very highly skilled theatre, film and television dramatic actresses were invited onto*

Left: Perfect casting: Anne returns as PRG leader Myra Desmond. Right: Caroline Garbett prepares Colette Mann for her final appearance as Doreen.

Prisoner. I was a fashion model. Gulp! There was NO WAY in heaven I would be invited. Lo and behold, I was. I nearly fainted. I auditioned for the role of Leigh Templar, and I won the role. God knows how. How daunting to step I into an ensemble of Australia's most brilliant and highly acclaimed, multi-award-winning dramatic actresses. If Prisoner was an American series it would take a very long wall to hold all the Emmys.

My first feelings were absolute fear. A fear so great I actually developed a dreadful rash on my side from terror. Thankfully, no one saw it and it wasn't on my face. All the actresses had been warned that a 'model' was coming in to play a role and I am certain many a lip was curled into a sneer. In Australia, if you are not highly trained you are not always welcome on set, as I was to find out later in my career many, many times. There was a real meaty disgust in Australia until fairly recently, brought about by the thought that any actress who was trained at NIDA should be sitting unemployed while a 'model' or someone non-NIDA trained took a place in line for an acting pay check. The lynching mob of 'git cha' didn't exist on the set of Prisoner thankfully. I think my absolute 100% devotion to absorbing as much as possible, and learning whatever I could from everyone really shone through. They all settled and embraced me. I was VERY lucky and loved. I'm certain that, if I hadn't proven myself, the knives would have been out (figuratively speaking). My love for them all, for

their welcome and kind embrace, will live with me forever. To this day, I use techniques that they taught me.

I worked most closely with Maggie Kirkpatrick, Betty Bobbitt and Janet Andrewartha. They knew I was serious about learning the craft of acting as best I could. I was in the show for 14 episodes [457 – 470] which I think from memory took three and a half months. I didn't have any input into the character. In fact, I would have fainted if a director or writer had invited me to make suggestions to build my character. I wouldn't have known how to at that stage. I did however have input into the visual aspects of the character since she was a model and so was I. I was required to wear model-esque make-up, hairstyles and the latest fashions of the day. So I had very definite input in those areas.

The Prisoner set was exactly the same as any professional working set on a fast-paced television series – very focused, exquisitely organised and orderly. Fans often fantasise that all the sets are playgrounds for actors who jump about and play pranks, behaving like toddlers all day. I suppose that is due to the light-heartedness of the publicity machine, but really, if only they knew. It's extremely hard work and the pace is tremendously fast. On film, it is a much slower pace. After all, it takes on average six months to shoot an hour-long feature. In episodic television, you shoot an hour's worth in four to five days. All the actors and actresses behave like professionals as in any skilled job. Occasionally, when an actor fluffs a line or makes a mistake, the actor can burst into laughter and that creates some fun for the moment. In actual fact, there is a first assistant director whose job it is to keep the pace up, make sure we are all moving along according to schedule and keeping time. So much work must be completed each day or the overall job will run over time and over budget, creating mayhem.

Every day that I act, and do a good job, it is because of Maggie Kirkpatrick and Betty Bobbitt. They opened doors to the magic of the craft for me and I will NEVER forget them and never cease to grateful. One of my best friends was Arkie Whiteley, who was also in Prisoner. *We met on the set of* Mad Max 2. *She was one of the closest people to me in my life. We shared flats many times over the years in London. Sadly, Arkie died a few years ago. She was so dear to me. I have kept in touch with Maggie Kirkpatrick, I also adore her. The last time I spoke with her was on the phone earlier this year.*

Prisoner *continues to endure because of the bloody BRILLIANT writing and best cast ever seen in any TV series on the planet!*

Back on screen, Myra escapes from Wentworth in order to find Kay, narrowly avoiding her escape being thwarted by Reb. Reb later attacks Phyllis by hitting her over the head with one of the statues from the fete, ending Reylene Pearce's time on the show, having made her first appearance in Episode 49.

Marie Winter is transferred back to Wentworth [461] after tension between her and Bea meant the officers had to separate them. Maggie Millar effortlessly recreated the now infamous swagger and cackle, and Winter immediately seized the Top Dog position from Judy.

With Myra on the run and Cass having been committed to the state hospital for the criminally insane for a vicious attack on Dennis, Judy was powerless to stand up to Marie. The new Top Dog soon enlists Reb to assist her with supplying drugs in the prison, threatening both officers and prisoners who stand in her way.

The arrival of Vivean Gray in the role of Edna Pearson [463] would be memorable for the wrong reasons. She has been found guilty of attempting to murder her husband, Harry. The storyline would later cause headaches for producers when a member of the public, Emily Perry, accused them of portraying events that occurred in her own life. With matching initials and a warning of an ensuing

Rare ariel view of the Prisoner set: Colette chats with Props-man Tom Heading

lawsuit, Grundy were forced to take action. Script editor Coral Drouyn remembers:

Well, the story was based on a woman in Adelaide, charged with poisoning her husband but he didn't believe she was guilty. Unfortunately, I chose the same initials as the woman concerned, Emily Perry. She took legal action rightly so, since in the show Edna was very definitely guilty and Emily Perry was acquitted. The story had gone to air in Australia (at least part of it had) but then had to be pulled so it made very little sense. I am told Grundy had to pay compensation so I was not in their good books. Today, of course, the story would have gone to the legal department who would have knocked it on the head, but we didn't have such luxuries back then.

Arriving into the series at the same time as Vivean Gray was a young actor who would go on to be remembered as 'the boy who tames The Freak'. Rob Summers was chosen from a cattle call of other boys to become Shane Munroe, a young tearaway on the run from the cruelty of his father and seeks refuge on the sofa of the fearsome Fergo. Of all the sofas in Melbourne...

Almost thirty years later, his episodes playing Shane are held very dear to his heart. The *Prisoner* experience afforded him the chance to be treated as an adult even at such a young age, such was the way the other cast embraced him. While The Freak may have towered over the youngster, Rob's memories of Maggie, the Green Room and a certain drain-pipe storyline all remain vivid in his mind:

I auditioned for the role in November 1983. My agent called and said there was a part in Prisoner *that she thought I should go for. I was sent part of the script to memorise and read to Jan Russ who was the casting agent. When I got to the Grundy offices, there was a cattle call, a term used when you arrive and find twenty boys sitting there to audition for the same role. You could cut the air with a knife. When it was my turn, I read for Shane with Jan reading for Joan as a video camera filmed it. I didn't hear anything – Christmas and the New Year came and went. I was preparing to start high school that year. Then, out of the blue, in late January, my agent called to say I got it. I nearly fell of the chair – so often you don't hear back and you learn to accept rejection. The irony was that I wasn't allowed to watch* Prisoner *until I got the role.*

The first day I was really nervous. My dad came with me, which at twelve I found

Top: Myra squares up to Gloria. Middle: Tottie Goldsmith with Prisoner icon Maggie. Bottom: Myra comforts Hannah.

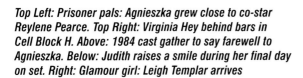

Top Left: Prisoner pals: Agnieszka grew close to co-star Reylene Pearce. Top Right: Virginia Hey behind bars in Cell Block H. Above: 1984 cast gather to say farewell to Agnieszka. Below: Judith raises a smile during her final day on set. Right: Glamour girl: Leigh Templar arrives

embarrassing but secretly was happy he was there. Arriving in the Green Room, Maggie introduced herself and really made sure I was at ease. When it was time for our first scene where she finds me asleep on her couch after breaking in, we went on set. As we marked through the scene, where to hit certain spots for the cameras, the director kept saying, 'On the day, we'll cut away to you on camera two'. I was confused. On what day? I thought we were shooting the scene. Do we come back another day? Then Maggie explained it meant when we go for a take. The Prisoner week went like this: studio run through on Monday and Tuesday to mark everything out with cameras, lighting and set. Then on Wednesday and Thursday they'd film early in the morning to late at night like a well-oiled machine. In those two days they'd film two full hours of Prisoner, the amount aired each week. Friday was location day. They had to make sure all location scenes were done in that day, come hail, rain or shine. Filming in studio was so tightly scheduled, sometimes if you fluffed a line, or stumbled, they'd just carry on with the idea that the viewer wouldn't notice in the bigger scheme of things. Maggie soon told me that if I wasn't happy with my performance, then really stuff up the scene so they'd have to go again. That was good advice, and I did that once or twice, albeit with a sly wink from Maggie.

Maggie was the main person who took it upon herself to really look after me. She'd give me tips, especially saying when my voice started to sound a bit high or if I tended to deliver my lines with a whine. I took it all on board. She actually used to drive me to location if we were coming from the studio. I still remember sitting beside her in her cool white Alfa Romeo. We really bonded and she always looked out for me. I felt comfortable with her – there was no ego, as she'd tell me about her daughter Caitlin and other non-showbiz talk. That was Maggie, and the reason people warmed to her. We connected in some way; it's hard to define why exactly. My life was full on. I'd get a cab to the studio and be on set at 6:00am. I'd then get a cab to school, and have one waiting after school to take me back to the studio where I'd be till late at night. I lived on the other side of the city so it took almost two hours either way, which was the perfect time to revise lines. The only other two actors I do remember taking me under their wing were Maxine Klibingaitis [Bobbie Mitchel]) and Genevieve Lemon [Marlene Warren]. I think they took to me because I was the only regular child actor. Who really knows? They were really great, and a heap of fun to be around.

I don't really remember many other story lines being filmed. Usually I was watching on the television in the Green Room. They'd have a monitor showing what was being filmed, so you knew how long until you were needed. Usually, I was reading my lines for a final time, or I was needed in wardrobe or make-up. It is funny how blinkered you were to your own part. I honestly can't remember other scenes being filmed. Other than going on set between takes and realising how fake the prison looked. The bricks were chipboard, and the gates plastic, and they'd overdub a metal gate being closed if my memory serves me right. I do remember watching a scene in the laundry and watching the press in action, then realising out of shot was a stagehand shooting steam from a concealed hose on cue. The press wasn't hot at all. Lucky for the actors that had their hand or head 'burnt' in the various story lines.

For the scene where Joan has to slap Shane right across the face, we both decided for my authentic reaction she should really slap me. I think we did a few takes with a fake slap, but my reaction was forced. Plus it looked good when her hand print actually showed on my face. We did laugh about that.

Looking back, it was a bit strange, all of a sudden people yelling out 'Auntie Joan'. A lot of people would come up to talk to me, which I was fine with. I'm not sure I was a 'child celebrity' as such, but I did get quite a lot of fan mail. My school friends were fine, they knew me pretty well. Some of the teachers gave me a bit of a hard time, thinking I might be a prima donna, but that settled down pretty quick.

As for working alongside The Freak herself, I have loads of memories working with Maggie. Apart from looking after me on set, I remember she bought me a Fox FM sweat shirt for my birthday which I loved. Another memory was when we filmed at McDonalds for my screen birthday. We both had so much fun, and I think I ate myself sick. You can imagine a twelve-year-old let loose in a closed McDonalds. My main memory was of a very kind, giving person. When I finished Prisoner, I remember missing her. It's funny, you're filming for months all these crazy hours mainly with Maggie. Then all of a sudden it stops.

Filming the drain storyline is the thing I remember most. It starts with me on location following my dog Nicky into a drain. They had big fire hoses to make it look like a huge downpour. All of the scenes with me stuck in the drain were filmed in the studio in a large cylinder which was about three metres long. I'd climb in from a top

Top Left: Virginia poses with crew members after an outside broadcast shoot. Top Right: Robert Summers. Middle Left: She's back: Maggie Millar returns to stir up trouble as Marie Winter. Bottom Left: Robert holds his memories working with Maggie close to his heart. Above: A recent photo of Robert Summers, the boy is now a man!

Above: A boom-mic hovers over Maggie and Alethea rehearsing a scene in the recreation room. Below: Ready for take-off: Maggie and Maxine wait patiently for the Director to call action for Marie's helicopter escape. Top Right: Fire or no fire: we can't miss a chance of a photo with Meg! Middle Right: Life sentence: Anne would remain a prisoner at Nunawading studios for many years to come. Bottom Right: Life sentence: Anne Charleston poses in the infamous corridors.

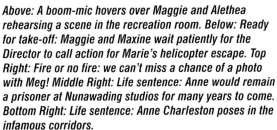

Top Left: Maggie Dence as Bev 'The Beast' Baker. Left: Kylie and Maxine show off their cuts and bruises following a scrap in the shower block. Above: Kylie Foster wins the role of Angel Adams

entrance hole and wedge myself into the wire mesh. The end of the cylinder was about a metre in front, where the camera was. They'd then force water through, as I gasped for breath and tried to stop from 'drowning'. The water had to be tepid, cold but not freezing. They tried warm water but it fogged the camera lens. Damn. So I'd shoot scenes in the drain, get out of the water, go to school, then come back in the afternoon and get back in again. It was all quite strange. When it came to the scenes where I was being rescued, we filmed that on location at night. I remember that was a really late night. I think we started at seven and finally wrapped at around midnight. There was a drain which flowed into a river, and Maggie was at the drain edge yelling into it, tying to keep me calm as the rescuers were 'cutting me free'. From memory there was a speaker in the drain and I was reading my lines near her into a mike. When we filmed the climax of me bursting out of the drain in a huge gush of water, it was my stunt double that flew out and landed in the

river. Then I had to get into the freezing river as I'm 'pulled from the water'. I remember one scene when the ambulance guy was putting an oxygen mask on me, which I didn't like at all. I was actually scared of having the mask over my face, and had to be coaxed into it. My parents laugh as they remind me of this from time to time, how I refused to put the mask on. I thought I was going to really suffocate. I do also remember for that whole night having the firemen with huge hoses pointed at the sky and blasting water to make it look like a big rainstorm. Maggie and I shot all our scenes in heavy rain. We were soaked!

I guess my lasting memory of my time shooting Prisoner is how lucky I was to be a part of it. At the time I was just focussed on learning my lines for the next day, making sure I was on time and hitting my marks. It was only after seeing the end result on television, and the recognition that came with it, that I realised how blessed I was. Not many twelve-year-olds have that kind of experience. It was also a huge learning curve,

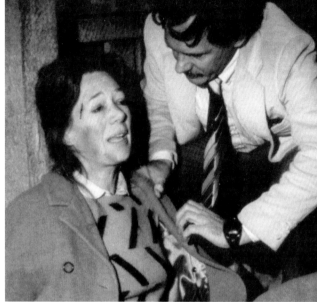

Top Left: Pyjama party: 1984 cast relax in the tunnel. Left: Maxine and Genevieve help Jill see a lighter side of her character's exit. Above: Explosive: Renno is rescued.

years later the long hours and hard work I did on Prisoner seemed easy because I really loved what I was doing. That's what I kept with me: love what you do. Actually I lie. One thing I used to dread was going into make-up. With all the bashings my 'father' dished out to me, and the drain drama, I used to spend hours in the make-up chair. Maggie Kolev, the make-up artist (who I coincidently worked with on another show the next year), was a genius at covering my body with massive bruises, my swollen lips oozing blood. Sometimes I'd be there for three hours before I was ready to shoot.

I kind of keep those special memories to myself. Obviously, people that have known me for a long time were there to see it for themselves, and we'll talk and laugh about it sometimes. However, it never really comes up in conversation with recent friends or work colleagues, and if they do find out they want to know all about it. Either that, or at some odd time in a group situation or party a friend will ask, 'Can I tell them what show you were in?' It doesn't bother me, but I keep it short so as not to look like I'm living out of that one experience. Silly, huh? In truth, I hold it dear and I love that people still remember the show so well.

and I grew up fast. I was never treated as a kid. If Maggie thought the way I said my lines was wrong, she'd tell me, as would the director if I kept fluffing my lines because time is money. The work ethic I learnt has actually stayed with me, which says a lot. I have Maggie to thank for a big part of that. She helped me adjust and pushed me forward. The best thing was memorising for exams at school and university, thanks to nine months of Prisoner scripts. I realised a few

In true Marie Winter fashion, the women of Wentworth are lead to riot [465]. Myra is back in jail after successfully aiding her daughter Kay to turn her back on drugs and is stuck in solitary when she begins to smell smoke from the cells below. When Reb backs out of Marie's threats to kill Myra, she is pushed over a flight of stairs and is found at the bottom by Joan Ferguson, with Bobbie standing over her.

The relationship between Deidre Kean and her daughter Rebecca was at a testing point too. Deidre turns up at Wentworth intent of reconciling Reb with her dying father. This eventually she does, and Reb is suddenly $200,000 richer at the reading of the will. But Deidre has gambling debts and needs money, so Reb trades off helping her escape with paying of her mother's debts. Thus, when she is in hospital after Marie's double cross, Reb gets maternal help to escape. However, it does not end well and both mother and daughter are brought into Wentworth. Kean junior vows to kill her mother. The role of Deirdre Kean was the third role in the show for soap legend Anne Charleston. She played Mum Brooks' daughter at the very start of the show, and then an unnamed policewoman who turns up at the Halfway House. Anne remembers her two later roles:

That police woman! It was one day's filming. So insignificant that I don't even recall anything

about it now. I often think 'What the bloody hell? How did the fans notice me?' Something I like to gloss over really.

Sheila Florance was a dear, dear friend and one of the funniest women I ever met. When my son Nick was very small I got a role in the theatre and, for some reason, my mum who used to look after him went away and couldn't. Sheila begged and begged me to let her look after him. 'I love babies,' she kept saying. So one afternoon I dropped Nick off and went to go to the show that night. The next morning I walked in to find Sheila opening a bottle of beer. 'Thank God you are here,' she bellowed. 'Christ, that boy is spoilt!' Another time Sheila and I were having an argument. As it went on and on, I was winning the war of words. Suddenly Sheila stopped dead, looked at me and declared, 'I can't stand your hair that colour. It makes you look hard!' End of argument. A fantastic woman.

Deidre Kean was a much better role, and something that I enjoyed doing. I had a mixture of studio and location stuff doing her. Working with the likes of Janet Andrewartha and Louise Siversen was great. They are good actors and playing scenes with them was always fun to do. I was supposed to be in it longer, I think. Janet

Above: Wendy Playfair. Right: Back on top: Anne effortlessly takes over from Val as Top Dog.

was brilliant as Reb, I thought. I worked with her later in Neighbours, of course. They (Grundy) pulled me out of Prisoner to do another new series called Possession, an espionage drama, but it wasn't a success and was cancelled after six months. Shortly after that, they offered me Madge in Neighbours and my soap pedigree was cemented.

I think Madge is the best thing I have done in soaps on television. Soap is not my life however, even though I have done quite a few. I would like to do a sit-com, a one-off play. I had a guest spot in Holby City which was a lovely role. Television is nice to do if it's a good role. However, I don't want to be defined as an actress by my work in soaps.

With the riot intended to undermine Ann's abilities as Governor, it seemed Joan had taken one step closer to the Wentworth Governorship. Myra is returned to the other women and begins to restore calm to the prison after the mayhem caused by the riot. Marie is informed she will be transferred to Blackmoor, affectionately referred to by other inmates as 'the black hole', but before the white-haired rioter extraordinaire bows out of the show for good, a certain helicopter was arranged to take Marie over the fence in one of the most over-the-top escapes ever witnessed in any television show.

With Marie having left the series, producers wasted no time in drafting in yet another villain as the 1984 season hit Episode 472 – another creation which Coral Drouyn remains fiercely proud of. Coral was inspired by a book called The First Deadly Sin, about a man who killed strangers just to witness the expression in the victim's eyes. With the producers hoping to find an actress that would be a physical match for The Freak, Maggie Dence was chosen to bring Bev 'The Beast' Baker to life. Recalling some of her favourite times on the inside, Maggie Dence remains surprised that her character had such an impact on the show, and fans still write to her with compliments:

A clear memory I have of the first day I walked on set was thinking how bunker-like the Green Room was. Not very impressive and the make-up facilities were not exactly glamorous either! Everyone in the cast and crew were very welcoming to me, particularly Anne Phelan. I

Left: 1984 Season opener: David lures Cass to her death. Below Left: Make-up artist Caroline Garbett uses close-up shots of David Waters to create a prop head for the beheading scene. Below: Too gruesome: David's decapitated head was cut from the final scene

Above: Trouble looms for Hannah. Top Right: Maggie poses with Agnieszka's leaving gift. Right: Vivean Gray arrives for a controversial storyline.

also got to know Genevieve Lemon because of Prisoner and we have worked together on both stage and television since then. I didn't actually base her on anyone; I just took the thought that she was a psychopath with no redeeming features at all. Nearly all female murderers poison their victims, so Bev was unusual in that she used physical means.

I had rarely seen any of the show prior to being cast as Bev. This was the time when we didn't have recorders and also my main work in those years was on stage so I have actually not seen many shows that were popular in those years.

One particular memory that stays in my mind is being very embarrassed that there was a big dancing scene and, influenced by Genevieve, it was decided to do it just like the opening of The Muppets. *With every one dancing in a circle, Bev was to burst in to disrupt it; unfortunately I burst in and promptly 'dried' so it all had to be repeated. It was quite complex for the cameras so I was pretty mortified!*

With Bev wreaking havoc in the prison and getting pleasure from inflicting pain on her fellow inmates, Maggie found it quite peculiar when the character was written out as quickly as she had arrived.

I had originally signed a contract for three months but it was abruptly terminated when the producers felt the character was too violent and

unsustainable. I have no idea what the writers thought about this. I just was told I would be no longer required – end of story. I can't really recall anything much about Bev's demise. I appear to have done it rather badly actually. From a photo I once saw I appear to be sticking the needle through my shirt sleeve. Less than realistic, I'd say. And it didn't take long to shoot. Nothing did, the show never had the luxury of much time for recording.

It's still a source of wonderment to me that there is such a following for Bev. It really was only a month's employment and the first and last weeks were such brief appearances.

Not as obviously monstrous, but infinitely as evil, Angela 'Angel' Adams, played by Kylie Foster, is first seen in Episode 477. Angela's child-like innocence masks a darker nature that would prove her to be one of the nastiest and devious inmates to appear in 1984. News reaches the women that Marie has been caught and is sent to Blackmoor. Romance blossoms between Dennis and Heather, while plans for a waltz marathon get underway. Angel begins to show a more manipulative side, and even tears her uniform to blackmail The Freak. Since everyone thinks she's an angel by name and nature, she would be able to fool people into doing anything she wants. During the dance marathon, Angel puts a magnet in her pocket as she dances close to Judy, dangerously affecting her pacemaker. Judy eventually feels ill and has to take a rest. Angel shows the true extent of her evil ways when she arranges for Meg to be raped.

Kylie Foster was 23 years old when she was cast as Angel Adams. In terms of characters we can loathe, Angel is up there near the top. Kylie has since gone on to appear in many other television series, including stints in *Neighbours* and *Home and Away*, but she recalls her enduring nastiness as Angel here:

I was offered the role of Pixie but could not do it, so I thought I had no chance of getting offered another role. Pixie would have been great but Angel was less like me, so more challenging. I recall being a little nervous, unlike with other shows, as I was actually a fan. It was the only show that I was in that I actually was a fan of. That was back in the days when my boyfriend Nigel was in Split Enz. Before I played Angel I would watch the show with Nige, Neil and Sharon Finn. The boys went on tour in Europe and we gals taped some audio cassettes of the show with narrative like 'Meg is walking down the corridor'. I have no idea now why we did not send videos but it was very funny. I was nervous, too, of so many women in the cast. I thought they may be bitchy and mean, but nobody was. Quite the opposite. If anyone was nasty to me personally it went over my fluffy blonde head. It was easy to settle in because everyone was fun. I really liked Maxine, Betty and Elspeth who was especially lovely. Of course The Freak was very cool! I remember Maggie and I went out in character one day to a shopping mall somewhere. The reaction of the shoppers and shopkeepers was great fun and I guess she enjoyed the looks on people's faces as much as I did. I had to post something so I queued up. When I got to the counter I was my real nice and smiley Kylie self, but the woman serving was not buying it. She refused to serve me. When I asked why, she said, 'I know what you did to poor Meg Morris'. I exclaimed that I did not do it really, it was my character in the show and I just wanted to post a letter. 'No, I'm sorry. For you to do that to Meg there must be something in your (real) character that means you are capable of evil things like that.' I realised she was serious so, bamboozled, I put my letter back in my bag to send from my local post office next day. I enjoyed all the story lines really. Being mean to 'Nana'

was so not me, but I think I managed okay. Being horrible to Dot and unravelling her knitting was fun! 'Stupid old goat' springs to mind. The Meg rape, stabbing The Freak and setting off Judy's pacemaker were all tremendous fun.

Peter Wright carries out the brutal attack on Wentworth's most beloved officer in a chilling episode [483], offering Elspeth Ballantyne the opportunity to remind everyone that, behind goody two shoes Meg was a brilliant actor who sadly to this point had become underused in the structure of the show.

As the 1984 season draws to a close, several attempts to set up Joan backfire. One incident ends up costing Heather her job. Lou, Fran and Alice emerge as the main troublemakers, with Lou attacking Joyce and escaping from Wentworth [491].

Jill Forster has a brief stint inside Wentworth as Kerryn Davies, whose troubled relationship with husband Lyle [Barry Hill] causes her to commit suicide by hanging herself in the conjugal visiting suite. When Stan Dobson suffers a heart attack, he warns Bobbie that new officer Len Murphy is a sadistic killer. Visiting Justice Sarah Higgins ends up on the other side of the bars, with the women vowing to take revenge for her treatment of them at the many parole hearings she chaired.

Following a series of letters terrorising Ann and threatening an attempt on her life, she receives a dead rat from someone intent on seeking revenge. Meg offers to let Ann stay with her, but this is not enough to prevent the perpetrator breaking into Ann's house and taking them both hostage. The kidnapper is revealed to be Brian Lowe, former boyfriend of Phyllis Hunt who wants to take revenge for Reb's attack on her which left Phyllis brain damaged [460]. Brian takes the two hostages to a disused building where he has set some trip wires to detonate bombs should they attempt to escape. Not realising how unsafe parts of the building are, Brian falls to his death leaving Ann and Meg trapped inside. The police receive a tip off from boys who are playing on bikes around the building and decide to investigate. They find Lowe's body but accidentally trigger one of the trip wires causing the building to explode with Ann and Meg inside.

Under the cover of darkness, three mysterious new inmates arrive at Wentworth. An explosive year ends with Ann and Meg being rescued, and the aforementioned new inmates being revealed as three male inmates transferred from Woodridge for their own protection. Two of the men would find love in Wentworth as the series moved into 1985, but another would destroy the life of one of Wentworth's most loved inmates.

Myra and Me

“ *My name is Myra Desmond. And anyone who doesn't do what I tell them get themselves out of the front door now. Now!* ”

Myra Desmond, 429

Left: Anne relaxes with the O.B crew during a break from filming. Right: Anne's original resume with Woods Agency.

Our first glimpse of Myra Desmond, a prominent light in the PRG – Prison Reform Group – occurs in Episode 154. Suggesting that she has served time for an unspecified crime in Wentworth, Myra's interest in the welfare of the prisoners of the State is born of her own experiences. She is known and respected among the old lags, but also has the earned trust of Mrs Davidson. This is evident by the ease with which Myra calls the staff by their first names. Myra's charisma and confidence were evident in the few short episodes she was given and thus it was perhaps a logical step to re-introduce the character in 1983 when Bea Smith dramatically exited the series.

When we next see Myra, she is helping run Driscoll House along with her son Alan. However, Myra's relationship with her 15-year-old daughter isn't as harmonious. Kay is being a rebellious teenager and spending too much time with her drunken father Bill and his new girlfriend Gloria. Myra is worried that Kay will be drawn into Bill's world of a drunken good-for-nothing. 'I'd let Bill give me a black eye if it would make Kay see what a bastard she has got for a father,' she tells Alan when her son has returned, sporting the bruises of a physical tussle with his Dad. The unfortunate chain of events then moves quickly. Bill and Gloria turn up at Myra's house, having been kicked out of their own by the landlord and a heated argument ensues. In the heat of the fight, Myra smashes a bottle over Bill's head and accidentally kills him.

'Look at me on the outside, telling people how to run their own lives, and look what I do to my own two kids'. – Myra, Episode 432

Returning to Wentworth as a prisoner once more [432], Myra is immediately caught up in the dark politics of prison life. The Freak, having rid Wentworth of the troublesome Smith, is not keen to see a woman of Myra's reputation land on her doorstep just as she is finally getting Wentworth as she wants it. Myra doesn't want the Top Dog position but, as time goes on, it is clear that to protect herself and the other women she has to show her proven leadership qualities once again. Having known the other inmates over the years, she can clearly see that life under Freak rule means the prison is entering decidedly dangerous waters. Realising that she will soon have to face the consequences of her actions with Bill, it becomes apparent to Myra that in order to survive she has to try and take control of what is happening around her.

Myra is convicted of murder with little chance of parole until she has served at least five years, and it is at this point that Myra knows she needs to restore the status quo to a prison which is being terrorised by the underbelly team of Sonia Stevens and Ferguson.

With Sonia transferred out of the prison and the re-arrival of Margo Gaffney who seems set on pushing drugs at Wentworth, Myra makes her feelings known straight away. The women need a new leader and Myra seems the obvious choice. She's also quick to work out that Joan is trying to set her up to bashing Gloria, who has now also arrived at the prison. She quickly takes the place of spokeswoman for the others and demands from the Department better conditions for the prisoners [443].

After receiving too many bashes to the head during some of Wentworth's famous scuffles, Myra is warned by doctors that if she continues to get into fights it could leave her in serious danger. Judy agrees to take over as Top Dog until Myra is fully recovered but has to fight off the likes of Reb Kean who has her heart set on the coveted position [450].

When Myra's daughter Kay visits her mother, Myra becomes increasingly concerned about her state of health and mind. She looks dreadful but tries to convince Myra that it is due to her trying out a new diet. Myra doesn't believe her and knows something is wrong. She tells Judy that she's going to have to plan an escape [456] to try and help her. Myra makes her way out of the prison during a special fête where she wears the most ridiculous hat and poses as a visitor, somehow managing to walk out of the grounds unnoticed, until a handsome stranger spots her and offers her a lift in his car [459].

While on the run, Myra catches up with son Alan and they both track down Kay who is living with some friends but in a very bad state. She gets kicked out of the house and Myra takes her to a hide-out in the countryside in an attempt to clear her system of the drugs and alcohol she has been abusing her body with. They end up contacting Wally who suggests they go to his friend's house that he is looking after while they are on holiday. Getting Kay to stay at the house is another challenge as she makes numerous attempts to escape but, with Wally's help, they manage to see it through. Myra makes the mistake of phoning Ann at the prison to tell her that she's going to turn herself in, but Ann hears Wally's voice in the background and realises that he's been helping her. She returns back to Wentworth [465] just in time for a riot to break out when she's in solitary.

On losing support from the women, Myra decides to stand down from the Top Dog position and names Reb as her successor [502], but this new management is short-lived when Myra finds out that Reb has been working with Joan and pushing drugs in the prison. Myra's very much of the 'Bea Smith rule of drugs' and believes that the prisoners should not have access to them at all, especially after seeing the damage they caused to her own daughter. The walls come crashing down on Reb and she's transferred to Blackmoor

MARLENE WARREN

Played by Genevieve Lemon

First Episode 461
Last Episode 534
Total Featured: 74

Prankster Marlene "Rabbit" Warren is imprisoned in Wentworth for throwing stones at a car which lead to a man being killed. Her immature behaviour continues behind bars, playing jokes on officers and inmates alike. Fixing Marie Winter's bed to collapse earns Marlene her first taste of Wentworth muscle, but Marie puts pressure on her to spill the beans on what she knows about officer Heather Rogers. Marlene is poisoned by devious new inmate Edna Pearson who attempts to shift the blame on to Bobbie [468].

It's love at first sight for Marlene when she meets Matt Delaney, sharing their first kiss [505] and, after some squabbling, they eventually tie the knot in one of Wentworth's best-loved weddings.

After a touching farewell, Marlene is released from Wentworth and Matt is transferred to a prison farm.

Left: The Glitter Sisters: Anne performs with Prisoner colleagues Betty and Collette. Right: The Village People surprise the cast with a visit to the Prisoner set and a rendition of YMCA.

prison [506], leaving Myra happy to take over again, this time with full support from most of the women.

During a particularly far-fetched storyline, Myra finds love at Wentworth in the form of Geoff Macrae who is one of three male prisoners transferred to the prison from Woodridge for a short period. Initially quite hostile and rude to the men, Myra and Geoff become good friends. They are counterparts to each other, both having the same attitudes and beliefs. They have an affair and, with the help of a secret master key, they manage to spend time together alone without being disturbed. When Geoff is released on parole [534], Myra is heart-broken but tells him there can't be any future for them together as she is going to be stuck in prison for years. He insists that he'll wait for her.

With Myra seeing off attempts on her life through framings and bashings, the arrival of new inmate, Ruth Ballinger, sees her begin a new battle which sadly she is not going to win. When terrorists break into Wentworth in a bid to break Ruth out, the plan turns into a siege that lasts for a number of days. Armed with guns and knives, the men make demands which are refused by the prison authorities, so they begin killing the inmates to show everyone that they mean business. Faced with an impossible dilemma when the tables are turned on Myra, who is forced to choose which of her fellow prisoners will be the next one to be killed, a fight breaks out and Ruth decides that it should be their mighty Top Dog who the women will lose next. As she is saying goodbye to them, she is shot mid-sentence and drops to the ground – killed instantly by the gunshot [552].

Myra's final episode ranks among one of the best in the series with fans. A true feeling of shock was felt across the *Prisoner* community when they first learned of Myra's demise. At this point in the series' life it was important, after the loss of such an impressive character, that someone else equally as strong should replace her. Sadly, this wasn't to be and the next 30 or so episodes were seen to be some of the series' poorest until the arrival of a certain 6 foot tall bikie-girl [585].

Anne Phelan remains one of the most respected actresses in Australia. She was born on the 2nd August 1948 in the Salvation Army-run Bethesda Hospital, Melbourne. Anne lived with her parents James and Laura in the working class suburb of Fitzroy. Her wider family mostly lived in rural Victoria which meant the school holidays were spent on farms throughout the state which Anne delighted in. The family was something of a musical one, every Saturday night being spent at the Phelan family home. Mum would be on piano and Dad on the concertina or spoons. Little wonder the young Annie developed a taste for performing. Having moved to West Melbourne at the age of eight, she finally flew the family nest, aged 22, and started on the path to becoming a professional actress. Gaining her all-important Equity union card in 1968, an impressive array of theatre credits were soon notched up along with a leading role, Kate Murray, in ABC's major soap *Bellbird*. Further screen work followed in *Homicide*, *Matlock Police* and *Skyways* before *Prisoner* was first seen on the impressive CV. Anne is briefly seen as Officer Manson [17] and further appeared as a rather gawky uncredited lag, Bernadette [94 & 95], before making her impressive debut as Myra Desmond [154]. Although a relatively small role, Myra returned for a further six episodes over the next two years before being handed the ultimate *Prisoner* accolade, prime position on the steam press as a *bona fide* Top Dog. We asked Anne what she recalls of her time in *Prisoner* starting with those small roles in the early days:

 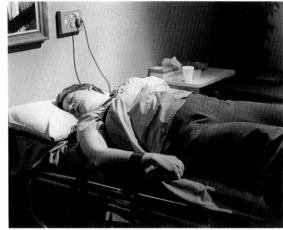

Left: Anne with Maxine Klibingaitis. Right: Myra recovers from a near death encounter with Ruth Ballinger and The Freak.

I can't remember anything of those early roles to be honest. Knowing the quality of the people involved, I can imagine I would have felt very comfortable on set. It's always difficult going into a show in a guest role but all the actors had great respect for each other. I certainly have no memories of needing counselling after my first encounters with the show.

I had no idea whatsoever when I went in for my first appearance as Myra Desmond that it was going to develop as it did. I was just glad I had a week or two's work to be honest. I was mainly working with Betty Bobbitt at that stage, I think. I am always one to look for the negative professionally so I don't get disappointed and probably thought, 'Oh no, they won't want me to come back after this job.' And certainly it never entered my mind that if they did bring Myra back it could be as a prisoner. The idea of being a Top Dog just didn't enter the equation. I know some people thought of Myra as a Bea Smith clone, but I never consciously did. In retrospect you realise Prisoner has between six and eight characters that are continually replicated. I didn't think Myra was anything like Bea Smith except she was Top Dog, anti-drugs and had a daughter. Because Myra was first seen outside the prison and established herself there, the comparisons with Bea never entered my head.

I think Prisoner worked so well because it was just solid ensemble acting. We were all, by and large, theatre trained actors in the early days certainly. They used people who have never done TV before, but were very experienced stage actors. Betty Bobbitt I had worked with long before Prisoner. Our characters were good friends fortunately, so that mirrored real life in a way – the same with Judith McGrath,

whom I had known for years. At one point, there were six of us who had appeared together in Bellbird including Elspeth, Maurie Fields and Gerda Nicolson. I never had too much input into Myra's storylines. I am quite forthright though, and will always debate a point of view if I feel it is necessary. One thing I was quite vehement about was the bruises. You could have the shit kicked out of you in one episode and in the next one there were no bruises at all. I used to fight for some continuity to it; the violence was something that shouldn't be glossed over. Prisons are ugly places – and I have been involved in drama workshops in prisons so I have seen it myself. If Myra had a black eye in one scene, I insisted it stayed for a couple of days recording (which was a couple of weeks on air). The violence should not look pretty. Not that I thought the violence was gratuitous. Quite the opposite, in fact. Today violence on TV is ten times worse. You must be careful to portray both the physical and psychological pain. It's very important. Fans often ask me about the lampshade hat. That was the silliest thing in the world. Ludicrous. A great green walking mushroom! I used it to escape in order to look after my daughter played by Sally Bourne. I worked with her father Ernie [Mervin Pringle] in Bellbird and it was terrific working with Sally on Prisoner. I had known her since she was a baby. It was great having another mate Alan Hopgood around for that storyline. I was lucky that I managed to escape the typecasting trap that you could get into.

It is well-known that I asked for a pay rise and was refused so I handed in my notice. It cost them more to write me out than it would have done to keep me. I would have stayed if they had upped the money but I would have missed out on what became one of my very favourite roles, Mamma in the telly movies of Harp in the South and Poor Man's Orange. Harp completely broke the casting trap of Prisoner because there were absolutely no comparisons between Myra and Mamma. I know others from Prisoner did suffer from typecasting after they left the show and could only do theatre. So, in retrospect, I am very glad they turned me down for the pay rise. To be part of two classic Australian novels adapted for the screen was very special to me. It was meant to be. Was Prisoner just another job? It is a very special 'just another job' is the only answer I can give. I would never negate what Prisoner has done for me. I have just moved house and one of the young men doing some concreting for me wasn't even born when it originally went out but he has seen Prisoner and knows who I am. It means producers also know you have a following. At the time, it was just a well-paid job.

I now use the Prisoner connection for my charity work for Positive Women. I am currently in a show called Winners and Losers for Channel Seven. What is fascinating is that young members of the crew are watching it on Foxtel. So the following keeps perpetuating itself and finding a new generation. Like other actors, I did go through

a stage when I would think, 'I wish people would stop talking about Prisoner.' But I was part of Australian TV history and you have to embrace that. I was on the organising committee for the big 21st Anniversary Reunion event in Melbourne. It was terrible leading up to the event. A lot of people booked very late. I was exhausted by the time it actually happened. On the night, Babs McMillan was force feeding me a falafel as I flitted about from A to B because she was worried I wasn't eating. Then there was that beautiful moment when the actors started arriving. We had 120 cast members from the complete history of the show. It took eight months to organise. Even the actors replied very late, some phoned up just a few days before and said they would be able to make it. I am getting goose bumps just thinking about it. George Mallaby turned up in his wheelchair, but he was there. It was so special. Then the moment when everyone was on stage singing the theme tune. It was mind blowing. Frank Van Straten, the theatre historian, said to me, 'The moment the screen went up you realise what the show Follies was all about. Every single TV show in Australia was represented on that stage.' They had all been in Prisoner at some point. I think my most vivid memory of the whole time was when Myra was killed. I had to spend two filming days under the blanket on the floor playing a corpse

PHYLLIS HUNT

Played by Reylene Pearce

First Episode: 49
Last Episode: 460
Total Featured: 138

Although loitering in the background for some time, Phyllis is first credited in Episode 49. She emerges from the group of background inmates to become eventually the instigator of a number of deadly plots, particularly the attempted hanging of The Freak [411].

A sidekick of Reb Kean's for much of the 1984 season, the pair frequently quarrel as Phyllis usually ends up being used by those who befriend her. When Reb escapes from the Glee Club outing, leaving Phyllis behind [434], she takes a young girl hostage. She is returned to Wentworth where she attempts to blame Judy and Cass. Joan uses Phyllis to goad Bea into attacking her in the Rec Room, leading to Bea's final exit from the series [400] and is later used to frame Myra when she pours boiling water over Gloria [443]. When Phyllis fails to assist Reb with smuggling drugs into Wentworth, she is branded a liability and brutally attacked by Reb in the shower block [460], suffering brain damage. Although never seen again, later in the series her boyfriend targets Ann Reynolds in a revenge attack for Phyllis' injuries.

while the siege was being acted out around me. But what very few people know is that, although I was wearing the uniform blouse, underneath the blanket that covered my bottom half I was in black mesh tights, 'fuck me' high heel shoes and had a can of beer. I even wanted to go to Myra's funeral in disguise, just in the background. I was all set to do it then a gig came up and I was not available. It was just the best time.

Since her *Prisoner* days, Anne Phelan has remained one of Australia's busiest actors. Her stage work includes the musicals Guys and Dolls, Fiddler on the Roof and Sweeney Todd as well as countless plays. On TV, her credits are equally impressive and feature *The Man from Snowy River*, *GP*, *Blue Heelers*, *Neighbours*, *Marshall Law* and *Family and Friends*. She is a multi-award-winning actress, having been honoured with a Variety Club Award, a Green Room Award, two AFI Awards and four Television Society of Australia Awards. Anne was awarded the Order of Australia (OAM) in 2007 for services to the Arts and her work in the community.

Winter Wonderland

"*'How far is too far when you're aiming for the top...?'*
Marie Winter"

'Right-o, you lot!' – Marie's first words in Episode 197 of the 1981 season and a catchphrase that would stay with the character for a further two memorable returns which would see her become one of Prisoner's all-time favourite villains. When Maggie Millar landed the role in 1980, she was given a brief description of her character:

Marie became a bikie's moll at 14, and spent three years in and out of trouble with the police. In the vain hope of getting away from the gang scene, she married a truck driver, became pregnant by him and tried to settle down. But her husband bashed her and she lost the child. She roped in some of her old bikie friends to beat him up. Satisfied, Marie rejoined the gang and became involved in a rival bikie clash. She accidentally let off a shotgun three times, killing one person and injuring two others. She was then arrested and given a life sentence for murder.

Nemesis and mortal enemy of Bea Smith, Marie subsequently became a survivor of the prison system. Nothing or no one would stand in her way for the glorified Top Dog position. We first see Bea lock horns with the infamous Marie Winter when Bea is transferred to Barnhurst [197 & 198], a lower security country prison that would become the second main prison in the series. Initially, life at Barnhurst appears calm and relaxed with inmates spending their time gardening or making baskets. Bea discovers that all is not as it seems when inmate Frida (played by Aussie TV

stalwart Esme Melville) informs her that inmates at the adjoining male complex take part in a working party out of the prison, with a couple of female prisoners going along to make their lunch. However, lunch with a difference is served at Barnhurst, as the inmates on work release use the opportunity to smuggle magic mushrooms back in the food containers. The mere mention of drugs is enough to make Bea see red, and an initially friendly welcome from Marie soon turns sour. The gloves are well and truly off.

In their quest to disempower their impetuous rival, Marie and Janie, played by Alix Longman, arrange for Bea to be drugged. Bea's stay in Barnhurst was to be short-lived, but not before the mighty Queen embraced her nemesis in a headlock and warned Marie that she had met her match. With the brilliant Maggie Millar making her chilling debut in the series and realising they had tapped into the makings of an iconic villain, it was without question that the producers would want the character to return at some point in the future. Marie's next appearance in the series would come at a time when *Prisoner* was at its strongest, when Millar's performance, accompanied by that of Louise Le Nay and Olivia Hamnett, would provide the backbone of the 1982 episodes and pass into the realms of television history.

Marie is brought back to Wentworth by order of Ted Douglas [245] in an attempt to restore harmony in the prison following Bea's admission to hospital. 'What's that bitch doing here?' are Bea's parting words as she is carried off on a stretcher. With Bea removed from the series, the viewers are left with an

Above: Maggie presents Olivia Hamnett (Kate) with a pencil portrait she has drawn of her. Left: Top Dog wannabe Marie Winter.

Left: Marie Winter played by Maggie Millar. Right: The look that could sink a thousand ships – don't get on the wrong side of this Top Dog!

uneasy tension as Marie makes her presence felt and clashes with Top Dog Sandy Edwards. With riots her speciality, mayhem soon breaks out at Wentworth as the women take over the prison [246].

With her trademark swagger and thumbs in her pockets, Marie's second stint in the series was more powerful, with Millar relishing the opportunity to unleash her versatility as an actress into the cold and unremitting Marie. The trio of Marie, Sandy and Kate brought a new dynamic to Wentworth, with the rivalry between Marie and Sandy providing a marvellous juxtaposition for Hamnett's unforgettable portrayal of psychotic Kate Peterson.

The tension played out between the ensemble during 1982 is worthy of a book in its own right. Marie stays as a catalyst for the action until she is transferred back to Barnhurst [269]. We hear nothing more of Marie for some time, until she is returned to Wentworth [461], and with the help of a bent policeman, who feigns having searched her, manages to smuggle in cocaine by way of her soap dish. By this time, Judy Bryant is acting Top Dog of the prison and, of course, Joan Ferguson's reign of terror has been going great guns for some time. Winter sided up with Reb Kean in order to distribute the coke through the prison, with Marie's power games soon being felt, not just in the main body of the prison but also for the staff of Wentworth. After Kean backs out of helping Marie kill

Myra in solitary, she is rewarded with a hefty push from Winter down the stairs which lands Reb in hospital. Joan is blackmailed into helping Marie escape in a daring helicopter snatch which would prove one of the most memorable moments in *Prisoner's* history, perhaps not for the right reasons though.

The character of Marie Winter on paper is a stereotypical villain. It is, however, with the deft playing of Maggie Millar which breathed a fearsome, evil quality to the scenes. Her brooding laugh and cocky swagger would raise the playing of Winter from merely a plot device to a performance of great energy and intensity. The appearances of Marie Winter were to receive plaudits from both fans and fellow actors alike.

Maggie Millar was 39 years old when she was asked to play Marie. She had already played some prominent roles on Australian television, including Dr Georgia Moorehouse in the ABC's *Bellbird*, and later as Elizabeth Bradley in Crawfords' hit *The Sullivans* and *Homicide* for which she won a Best Actress Logie.

Maggie Millar is undoubtedly one of the most fondly remembered of *Prisoner's* long list of villains, and here she strolls down memory lane and remembers her time as one of Wentworth's toughest characters:

I had watched it now and then, having been asked originally to play the role of Franky, played

so brilliantly by Carol Burns, but I had a small child at the time, and turned it down. It wasn't till a couple of years later that I was asked to play Marie Winter. It was good to have some wonderful women to work with like Janet Andrewartha, Maggie Kirkpatrick, Olivia Hamnett, Louise Le Nay, Genevieve Lemon, Judith McGrath... I could go on and on. But some things, like the wobbly sets were a bit of a worry. We often had a good giggle, very important when working such long hours! I didn't have any input into the scripts but I did have what I thought was a great idea at the time. Marie had a twin sister who was a real goody-two-shoes, a social worker who comes to the prison to see another prisoner. I submitted it to the producers but without success. That's showbiz, I guess.

Playing Marie was fun sometimes but, given the totally unremitting evilness of the character, I saw my job as an actor to make her believable – not always easy. I especially enjoyed the storylines involving some of the above mentioned ladies: Louise's character ending up in the garbage disposal unit was pretty full-on! As was Marie's belting up Lizzie. I didn't dare go out the day after that episode was shown. But it's so long ago. I can't honestly remember all that much. And I have done lots of other things. I don't really like violence and found some of the stuff I had to do quite difficult. The great helicopter escape had to be filmed twice. I had a double to do the over-the-fence sequence the first time, which all worked well. I actually grabbed the skids on the helicopter with bloody hands (I mean totally unbelievable!) and the rest of the scene was cut together featuring a blow-up doll dressed in prison garb and a wig hanging on the skids, and being lifted high up into the air. Unfortunately, whoever had decided that this would work, forgot that something filled with air tends to sway in the breeze. So there was 'Marie' swinging about like a trapeze artist hundreds of metres off the ground. It all had to be done again, a few days later, with said dummy now half filled with water.

Prisoner has achieved longevity for many reasons, I think – strong roles for lots of great actors and over-the-top storylines. The women in a

Maggie poses with one of her paintings in 2012.

Melbourne prison were fans, and thought it was a hoot apparently. Plus it's very cheap for the people who buy it, so it can be shown again and again for very little cost. None of the actors receive a cent.

Maggie is an Honours graduate of RADA in London. In her graduation year she won the Gertrude Lawrence Award for Best Performance.

Maggie has won several acting awards, including a Best Actress Logie; has performed on stage with many theatre companies including the Old Vic Company (with Vivien Leigh Directed by Sir Robert Helpmann), Elizabethan Theatre Trust, Melbourne Theatre Company, J C Williamson, Playbox, La Mama; and has appeared in the films *Phar Lap*, *Bushfire Moon*, *The Bit Part* and *Pieta*.

Maggie served on the Women's Committee of the MEAA (formerly Actors Equity) being especially interested in the portrayal of and opportunities for women in the entertainment industry. With a reduction of good roles for women her age throughout Australia, Maggie retired from acting at the start of 2000. When an English friend visited Australia in 2002 and asked if it would be possible to visit the *Neighbours* studios, it led to Maggie being offered a role in the show. A yearlong appearance as Reverend Rosie Hoyland in *Neighbours* followed. Maggie now devotes her time to art work, with a special interest in painting portraits of tigers, cheetahs, snow leopards and panthers, with regular exhibitions held in Melbourne.

A two-month break in Australia during the festive period left viewers waiting with bated breath to find out what had happened to Pixie who was suffering a bashing by Lou, Alice and Frances. Luckily, they didn't put up much of a fight when Myra and Judy turned up thanks to the help from 'Jane', now revealed as Yemil, who had spoken for the first time since arriving and probably saved Pixie from a hospital visit.

For actress Maria Mercedes the role of Yemil was a welcome return to the show, having previously played the character of Irene Zervos back in the early days. It was a time that would leave lasting memories with Maria:

I loved the role of Yemil. I loved the thought and care that went into her development, sensitive to the cultural background of Islam. I connected to her back-story of leaving her beloved country and family. The scene I did for the audition was her describing her homeland and her heartache to the rest of the inmates. The tears came easy; I just thought of my parents leaving their homeland and the sacrifice they made. I also loved the fact that Yemil was so gutsy, totally destroying Frank Burke's prison cell because he had torn up her Koran.

Maria had noticed a definite change in the way that the series was made, over six years after joining the show for her first stint, along with the memories of working with Maggie Kirkpatrick who left a great impression on her:

Obviously, the difference was in script and production values; they continued to grow and develop. By now we all realised what a unique, brilliant piece of Oz TV it had become, and totally driven by the female force which was a first in the world.
Maggie was no push over! She is a gutsy, honest human being and a great talent. I told her the story of my first foray as Irene and how

difficult I had found fitting in, along with the usual politics of being a newcomer in a TV show. Plus, the awful status quo of keeping the 'non-speaking' extras away from the rest of the cast. I never liked it, I found it ludicrous. Let me tell you, it didn't stop me from hanging out with the 'NS' extras. She made sure to let me know that now she had joined the show, she wasn't going to put up with any bullshit, so I guess Maggie was a guardian angel for a lot of us on Prisoner. She has my respect to this day.

Filmed in 1985, some of the cast celebrate the 500th episode.

Left: Jackie Woodburne, Maggie Kirkpatrick and Dorothy Cutts mark another celebration. Centre: Terri Malone – one of Joan's only loves. Right: Maggie and Margot joke in between filming their scenes.

My lasting memories will be the camaraderie, the women, the laughs, the set at Channel 10 and the toasted cheese crumpets at the canteen. What an amazing opportunity us lucky actresses had in creating characters, a genre and a show that people have loved right around the world. The fact I still get fan mail is a testament to the impact Prisoner had on viewers and I will never forget my time behind the bars.

The first shake-up for this year sees Reb transferred to Blackmoor prison after slapping Joan in front of the women. Joan had intervened to stop Reb and Lou from attacking Myra [506]. Order returned to the prison with Myra taking over as Top Dog while Lou stepped up a gear and filled Reb's shoes as chief troublemaker along with the ever-faithful Alice as her loyal and trusty sidekick.

With Meg and Ann recovering from their kidnap experience, the acting Governor's position is up for grabs with both Joan and Len vying for victory. Cue a fabulous fight in the corridors between the two of them when Len accuses Joan of setting him up after he visits Lou's cell for some hanky-panky [507]. The women are alerted to the fact that the two officers hate each other. When Len is made acting Governor, the power struggle picks up pace and Len's time at the top is to be very short-lived. Joan finds out that Len's past saw him suspected of being involved in a number of suspicious deaths at his previous prison, with Geoff backing up the claims – an incident that would return to haunt Len later this year.

The men at Wentworth find themselves in trouble when a threatening note is found in the prison gardens after being thrown over the fence. They decide to go on strike until Len grants them permission only to work inside the prison as they begin to fear for their lives. Geoff, meanwhile, begins to romance Myra and, after

a particularly shaky start, the two of them retreat to the comfort of an empty and unmanned cell following the discovery of Reb's master key which effectively has given them free access to roam the prison as they like. Anne Phelan recalls that *Prisoner* gave her the first sex scene in her TV career although viewers were not treated to much more than a quick look at Myra's naked shoulders and a glimpse of Geoff's chest – the series did go out at prime-time after all! When the two are eventually forced to part following Geoff's release [534], the moment becomes a real tear jerker. Providing one of the most natural and heartfelt breakdowns of any of the Top Dogs, Anne told us how the director of the scene was about to ask for it to be shot again as Myra had her back to the camera when Geoff walked away. He was unaware that Myra would then turn back to face the audience in floods of tears. He congratulated Anne on how brilliantly she played the scene which was one of the finest moments he had witnessed. Indeed, it was pivotal in proving Myra was not only a worthy successor of Bea, but Anne Phelan's powerful portrayal of Myra Desmond demonstrated that *Prisoner* could indeed live without their beloved Queen Bea and was in the very capable hands of an astonishing actress.

As the show tried to keep up with current trends and fashions, following the arrival of punk-styled Bobbie Mitchell previously, the series is introduced to Boy George fanatic Lexie Patterson. Her impressive dress sense and make-up style an obvious homage to the 80s star, who was extremely popular in Australia during this time, although a character like this may have been best suited to an earlier year when Culture Club were at their peak. Lexie doesn't go down particularly well with the inmates and staff but she settles in quickly, having already known Bobbie on the outside. The newcomer is introduced as an early replacement to her friend who would soon leave to be

Left: Len Murphy roughs up poor Jude. Centre and Right: Filming Bobbie's final scenes.

paroled into the care of Stan and Edie Dobson [513]. Played by Penelope 'Pepe' Trevor, Lexie injected huge doses of energy to the series on her arrival and initially caused friction between Bobbie and Marlene while impressing everyone else with her knowledge and talent with card games. Pepe is the daughter of *Prisoner* writer/producer Marie Trevor who also worked on the series during this time. There was no special treatment for Pepe however, who had to audition as normal for the role. Marie was responsible for bringing the controversial idea of introducing the three male prisoners to the series and was one of the most experienced producers in the country. She passed away in Australia on 7th June 2000 at the age of 77. Her input to the series was invaluable as she also helped seal the fate of The Freak, co-writing the final episode with Ian Smith. Pepe has largely stayed away from television work since, having turned her hand to writing and has had two novels published.

In a particularly disturbing storyline, sex-addict Frank makes a move on Pixie and attacks her in the corridor. When she puts up a fight and punches him in the face he drags her off to the library and brutally rapes her [510]. Pixie somehow manages to make it back to the laundry and arrives in a confused state. She appears to be in complete shock and in a world of her own, not knowing who or where she is. When Joan finds out what has happened she uses the opportunity to frame Len for the attack. Myra reluctantly agrees that they will move Pixie back into her cell and have

Len turn up on cue so they can blame him for Pixie's condition. The plan works perfectly with Len even being witnessed punching Myra when he realises that he has been set up. He is swiftly frogmarched out of the prison charged with Pixie's rape and attack. Sadly, Pixie is catatonic and there is no alternative than to transfer her to a psychiatric hospital. A very depressing end for a character that was so positive and full of life. The true rapist, Frank, is later punished by Myra and Geoff who brand the letter R on his forehead [518] as a permanent reminder that he is a rapist. He hides the letter by burning himself further with cigarettes which leave nothing but a nasty scar on his face for the rest of his life.

Another long-standing character in the series would also soon say goodbye to loyal viewers. Betty Bobbitt had played Judy Bryant since 1980 and had appeared in over 420 episodes but the moment had come for her to bow out gracefully. Filmed at the beginning of 1985, it would take six months before Judy eventually left Wentworth for the final time on 11th June on Melbourne television. It would have been too much to have both Pixie and Judy leave the series under a cloud so a happy story was developed instead and this was appreciated by everyone involved. With Judy distraught at the loss of her special friend Pixie, she decided to put music to a poem that she had written about her. When musician Sheila Brady [played by singer Colleen Hewett] arrived at Wentworth, the two of them wrote a beautiful piece of music which

Left: Here come the boys! Matthew Delaney, Geoff Macrae and Frank Burke arrive. Centre: Geoff and Myra grow close.
Right: Mother and Daughter: Marie and Pepe Trevor.

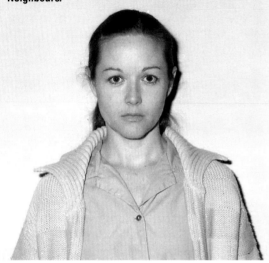

Julie Egbert played by Jackie Woodburne, best known as Susan Kennedy in the long running soap **Neighbours.**

later became *Pixie's Song*. Sheila was swiftly released and the song was suddenly heard playing on the radio. Sheila came back and, as luck would have it, Judy was also released and the two of them drove into the sunset, free and with a lucrative music recording deal to look forward to. Judy's final episode [534] was very special as, for the only time in the series' history, the usual closing theme tune was replaced with *Pixie's Song* (the real title was *I'm Missing You*). The song itself was chosen as a result of a competition that the TV company had arranged. However, copyright issues meant that it would never be released to the public and it has only ever been heard over those closing credits. Betty was treated to a special farewell party to celebrate her time on the series. Familiar faces from the past including Sheila Florance, Colette Mann, Val Lehman, Fiona Spence and Patsy King all made an appearance especially to wish her the best of luck in her future career.

Episode 534 also continued the series farewells with Marlene Warren, played so vigorously by Genevieve Lemon. Marlene found a happy ending marrying Matt Delaney in the grounds of the prison. Genevieve has gone on to become a major star of stage musicals in Australia including *Priscilla, Queen of the Desert* and Mrs.Wilkinson in *Billy Elliot – The Musical* which she has played in Australia and London. In addition to an award-winning career on the stage, Lemon also boasts a host of impressive small and big screen appearances to her name. It was a stage appearance with another *Prisoner* legend that led to Marlene, as Genevieve remembers for us:

I had already done one Grundy soap, The Young Doctors. *The producer was Sue Masters, a bit of an Australian television legend. I was touring in the play* Steaming *with Amanda Muggleton, and Sue came along. We caught up afterwards over a drink. She asked if I would be interested in coming into* Prisoner. *Well, I had never watched it much but it had an amazing reputation for having great actors, so naturally I jumped at the chance. Prisoner was the most fun I ever had in a long-running series. Those girls were such fun. Has anyone ever told you how much fun doing those dining room scenes were? I just remember doing ANYTHING to make the other actors laugh. Using the food they gave us in the most revolting ways imaginable. Doing unspeakable things with spaghetti! I'm surprised I wasn't sacked, although I did get into trouble a lot of the time – ridiculous behaviour actually which must have been highly annoying. Betty Bobbitt was the most fun, and she could get away with murder, so was Nigel Bradshaw. I remember Nigel had a line, 'It's a chopper.' I think we were all highly emotional, exhausted after a very long day. For some reason it struck us as the funniest thing we had ever heard. We said it for years, apropos of nothing, in very bad Yorkshire accents. I miss Nigel. A very funny man.*

My main memory of Maggie Millar is how sweet she was, extremely gentle and softly spoken; nothing like Marie Winter at all. Shows you what a great actor she is. I admired her a lot, and we used to have many quiet D and M's. I still see Betty Bobbitt and Maxine Klibingaitis. They are two of my best friends. I see Maggie Dence, too. She's absolutely hilarious; we have worked together a lot including Neighbours, *and we are*

Left: Genevieve rests her sore feet while filming her on-screen wedding. Centre: Pepe, Joy and Anne sharing a drink. Right: Ruth Ballinger's arrival is set to cause waves.

still very close. I also loved working with Judy McBurney, a very funny girl. Such a great cast. I still see Maggie Kirkpatrick and Carole Skinner; we are all Sydney girls.

The marriage to Peter Bensley, playing Matt, was so much fun. We were both playing virgins which, if I knew Bensley, was hilarious in itself. All we did was laugh. But especially as Marlene's farewell to Matt actually coincided with my leaving the show. A sad time for me. Without fail, whenever I visit Melbourne, someone will recognise me from Prisoner. *It has happened in the UK too.*

A number of smaller stories were devised to take the focus away from the cast members who had moved on. Inmate Sam Greenway is mistakenly killed by Lou and Alice who are trying to get Myra [521], Ettie Parslow tries everything she can to get sent back to Wentworth in a storyline not dissimilar to a certain Lizzie Birdsworth's, and Dennis becomes romantically involved with Meg. Even the ever-present Joan Ferguson has to face a serious operation when a brain clot is discovered which results in life threatening surgery [535]. She returns to the prison far too quickly [539] with her only war wounds being a slightly shorter hairstyle. The blacked gloved tyrant is back to her old ways soon enough.

In the middle of all this, a guest writer by the name of William Shaw is credited with co-writing Episode 530. This was a fairly important episode with Dennis being arrested for murder. Ettie moves into a retirement home and Joan is attacked in the library resulting in a bookcase being pushed on top of her. So who was this William Shaw that we never saw mentioned again? The answer couldn't be any closer to home in the form of actor Nigel Bradshaw who had played the part of Dennis Cruickshank since Episode 457 and stayed with the series until Episode 560, albeit with a short break. While we were not to see Shaw again, it cemented Nigel's ability to write a cracking episode of the series. Nigel left the show when his character, nicknamed

'The Yorkshire Pud', became kneecapped as a result of Frank having escaped from a prison farm. He proceeded to terrorise Meg and Dennis, leaving Dennis with terrible injuries after shooting him in both legs. Confined to a wheelchair for the rest of his life, Dennis couldn't bear to put Meg through looking after a cripple so their relationship ended and Meg was once again left alone. She stayed single for the rest of the series. Nigel remembers being a Pom among the prisoners:

I was new to Australia and went along to see Grundy. I did a general audition and screen test for them. They were looking for a new 'regular screw'. They asked if I would be interested. When I said yes, they created the role of Dennis for me. I must admit I was a tad intimidated making two hours of television a week, but there were so many great character actresses in the show they all helped put me at my ease. Gerda Nicolson certainly helped me settle. She was a wonderful actress, very strong and focussed. I enjoyed working with so many of the cast at that time: Gerda of course, Elspeth Ballantyne, Annie Phelan and Genevieve Lemon. Regarding writing for the show, I had a chat with Ian Smith who was at that time the senior script editor on Prisoner, and I expressed an interest to him about writing for the show. He asked me to do a test script and, on the strength of that, he commissioned me to write four episodes. He didn't want the rest of the cast to know I was writing for the series, so I wrote under the pseudonym of William Shaw. My main memory though is working with all those great Aussie actresses. Prisoner *gave them the opportunity to show the depth of talent that was around.*

Episode 536 might on the surface seem to be a weak excuse for some cheap flashbacks but it actually sets Wentworth up for the greatest off-screen departure in the series. Myra and the girls reminisce about old times with scenes featuring Bea, Judy, Jock,

Franky, Lizzie and most of the old favourites making an appearance. There are some inconsistencies, however, with Lou and Alice suggesting that they have been inside for much longer than we had originally thought while Lou even tells the women that she helped dig the famous escape tunnel of Episodes 165-166. However, nothing prepares the viewer for six words uttered by Ann Reynolds at the very end of the episode. She gets a phone call to advise that there's been a devastating riot and fire at Barnhurst Prison with a number of the prisoners being burnt alive – 'one of them was Bea Smith'. And with that, Queen Bea's fate was finally sealed. A wave of new blood was to arrive at the prison in the following episode – Willie Beecham, May Collins, Nora Flynn, Daphne Graham and Julie Egbert, all freshly transferred from

a fire-damaged Barnhurst. The 'Laurel and Hardy' antics of Willie and May, the cool and calm mannered Nora, the young and immature Daphne and the very clever but quiet Julie could almost be carbon copies of any of the characters that the series had seen previously. The show was beginning to look well and truly tired with recycled storylines doing the rounds until it was to find its feet again. A burst of energy and glamour suddenly appeared with the arrival of the wife of a ruthless crime baron, Ruth Ballinger, played by Lindy Davies:

I was offered the role of Ruth by my agent and said yes to the job for many reasons. I was very broke as I was working with a company doing classical theatre, but television meant

RUTH BALLINGER

Played by Lindy Davies

First episode: 538
Last episode: 552
Total featured: 15 episodes

The wife of crime baron Arnold Ballinger, Ruth joins Wentworth complete with fur jacket and numerous cases of clothing and accessories [538]. Ann is instructed by the Department that Ruth is to receive special treatment, as the Federal Police will be using her to try and find out more information about her husband's exploits in the world of drugs. She immediately demands a larger cell and more furniture and, much to Ann's dismay, she gets everything she has asked for, including a private telephone in her cell.

Ruth asks Lou for the names of any young attractive inmates who are due to be released soon so that she can arrange for them to work for her, with Lou receiving an expensive bottle of perfume in return [541]. When she decides that she wants to bring drugs into the prison, Myra firmly denies her that request; however, Joan is later bribed into helping Ruth and Myra ends up drinking a cup of coffee which is spiked with acid [543] as payback.

When Joan finds out that Ruth has been heavily involved in child pornography, she makes no attempt in hiding the fact that she has just bashed her [544]. She tells Ann exactly what she has done and challenges her to sack her. For once, Ann sides with Joan, and Ruth's bashing is explained with a supposed fall in her cell.

Things begin to snowball for Ruth. Her drugs are found and she starts to get framed by the police with a newspaper article suggesting that she has spoken out about her husband to the press. An escape plan is hatched for Ruth but this time it will be different. She won't escape from the prison on her own; a group of terrorists will break into the prison and simply snatch her away. It, of course, doesn't go to plan. The break-in turns into a siege and when the terrorists' demands are not met they start killing the women – including Top Dog Myra Desmond.

They manage to leave the prison with Ruth, but have Joan as their hostage. They end up at the airport and plan to jump on a plane to flee the State. However, the police are one step ahead of them and the bus they are travelling in has been booby trapped. With Joan in possession of a gun, Ruth's time is up and she's almost shot dead by Joan who takes some talking down by the police to spare her life [552].

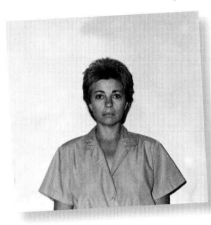

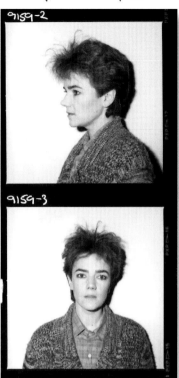

Above: Unused mugshot of Nora Flynn.
Right: Reb's unused mugshots from her
second stint at Wentworth. Far Right:
Unused mugshots of Willie and May.

money and security for six weeks. It also provided
me with the opportunity to work in a medium I had
never experienced. It was my first job and I was
extremely nervous and stumbling over my words.
Elspeth Ballantyne and Joy Westmore were very
patient with me on my first day.I was struck by
the commitment of the cast. I also thought their
working conditions were appalling. Everyone was
crammed into a 'demountable' in the middle of
a warehouse; there was no privacy. There was
no running water so the water for tea and coffee
had to be decanted and brought in from outside.
There wasn't enough room for everyone and it
was often very cold.

It is no secret that Anne Phelan had made her
feelings known about the extra workload that she was
to undertake, now that the strong character of Judy had
left the show. Anne's contract was up for renewal and,
because Betty Bobbitt was on more money than Anne
but was now gone, Anne thought it only right that she
should deserve a pay rise following the extra storylines
which would be given to Myra. She asked for her salary
to match what Betty had been on when she left but
this was refused. So Anne decided that this would be
a signal to leave the series and the task was made to
write Myra out. When four armed mercenaries broke
into the prison in an attempt to rescue Ruth, this was the
beginning of Myra's demise. In a number of extremely
tense and violent episodes, all of the women are held

hostage while Ruth's captors work out a way of fleeing
the prison with her. The Department and the police
don't play ball and this results in a serious threat – the
men will shoot a woman every hour until their demands
are met. They go through with their plans and Tammy
(an extra who we have never seen much of previously)
is the first unlucky one to receive a bullet and her body
is thrown out of the prison to show they mean what they
say. Myra, however, is faced with an impossible task –
Ruth challenges her to choose who the next casualty
will be. In a surprise move, when Myra attacks Ruth she
is shot dead in front of the shocked women. Their Top
Dog has gone [552]. Lindy Davies recalls working on
the series at such a crucial time:

Filming the last few episodes was very
problematic as there was a great deal of tension
as a much beloved actor and character was
leaving for contractual reasons. I think there was
an ambivalence about my character because
of the dastardly deed she was about to do. I
was also given the privilege of wearing smart
clothes and make-up in a context where others
were forced to be drab. Shooting the siege was
extremely difficult, involving night shoots in a very
wet and cold situation.
The environment certainly was not friendly.
I was in a strange position, an extremely
experienced classical actress but a complete
novice in terms of television. It must have been

Left: Myra is about to meet her maker in one of the series' most shocking stories. Left: The women mourn the loss of their Top Dog Right: "My work here is done!" – Anne celebrates filming her last scenes, and now she only has to play dead.

frustrating for the other actors because only one of them [Louise Siversen] was prepared to go over lines with me. I think they were not used to rehearsing. I became confused when they said no to going over scenes. I was also confused by the fact that half way through the shoot the script was changed and awful scenes inserted such as Ruth being a child porn perpetrator. I particularly minded a scene being inserted which involved Ruth having her head pushed into a toilet bowl. All these scenes were added after I said yes to the job. I definitely wouldn't have agreed if those scenes had been in the original script.

I don't believe the management looked after the actors and those night shoots were particularly difficult. They required a lot from the actors who were committed and worked beyond the call of duty. I remember asking the union rep to intervene as I was being required to work without a ten-hour break after night shoots and she was loath to act on my behalf. Management wouldn't be able to get away with that behaviour nowadays but we have to remember that Prisoner happened before the era of celebrity. The actors had no power; a pity as the network has benefitted enormously from their unwavering dedication.

Nora Flynn, played by Sonja Tallis, was to become Wentworth's latest Top Dog with varying degrees of success. Although Nora's time was to be fairly short-lived in comparison with previous Top Dogs, Sonja was thrilled to be part of one of Australia's longest running dramas:

When I landed the role it was an exciting time – to be in such a fantastic show, a great cast – many I knew, and to be in something that was on-going. It meant going to another State, away from Sydney, but a dream come true. Prior to that, I had been doing stage work and guest appearances on other TV shows. It was a 'general audition' with a selection of women to play according to type and age. We had a script to learn, two actors at each time; we played the character, were given pointers and redid the audition. It was a good atmosphere – no pressure.

I bonded with Anne Phelan when she was 'killed'. I took over from her but I didn't know when I joined the cast that this was to happen. We talked a lot about being a Top Dog. I didn't feel I was physically strong-looking enough for Top Dog so I spoke to the producer and I suggested I be 'strong' internally and she said, 'OK, give it a go,' and I did. I felt it worked well. Strong will, mind, purpose and the physical side took a back seat.

I remember a complex scene, lots of characters, and I was holding a baby. Many things went wrong – camera positions, new lines just written, which led to a lot of tension on set. One thing after another kept going wrong and the more this happened the more the nerves started to get to us on all levels. It was take after take. The director was a perfectionist and everything had to be right. Many on set were tense and one of the extras started to cry but we finally got it done. By this time, the baby I was holding felt like a lead weight; my arms were almost falling off. The next day in the Green Room, the producer came in and said, 'Well, that was a record on the number of takes,'- when I asked him how many, he told us it took a total of 47 before the scene was done!

I think that Prisoner 'pulled no punches' – it was confronting, challenging. It was about the bonding of women, their struggles, why they were in prison. Maybe it brought up some small aspect of the viewers and they could relate to it. Maybe they saw another side of prisoners and felt compassion for them. Viewers bonded with

characters, prisoners spoke out, a voice to be heard. It was demanding of viewers.

I was part of a great cast and crew and a show that made an impact of a great impression to the audience. It seemed to touch them in so many ways. When people come up to me, they are overwhelmed when they talk of the show. It touched them on a really deep and personal level that has lasted for years and years. It has a lasting memory with them and to be a part of that it something very special. There is a lot of work we do and it is forgotten, but to be part of a lasting memory, that is wonderful. To be in Prisoner *was a great and important time of my life. I learnt so much about being in front of a camera, the finer details, to have an awareness of the camera and work with it. The value of stillness, that less is more. Not just learning lines but knowing that silence can also be incredibly strong and can sometimes say more than the words. This was achieved by being in a show each day and always learning the craft.*

A change in direction on how the Top Dog should take command was introduced by writer Coral Drouyn in the form of a 'Prisoners' Council' which would feature a number of 'members' who would act on behalf of the prisoners and talk about any issues that affected them, rather than deal with them using violence. The Governor and an officer would also sit in on these meetings. As is the true Wentworth way, not everything would go according to plan. Viewers also began to notice that the usual dynamics of the series had gone adrift and this had come to the attention of those behind the scenes, too. There was a chance that the series could have finished for good right there. Coral revealed a few secrets when we spoke to her about that period:

This is something very few people know. I thought the show should have ended in the mid-500s. It was tired. We'd lost most of the main cast and I had said pretty much all I wanted to. I don't think Nora's reign and the Prisoners' Council worked, though I had high hopes for it. I proposed to the producers that we should wind the show up in its two-hour format and replace it with a series of ninety-minute telemovies which showcased the stories of individual prisoners. The Bea Smith Story, The Lizzie Birdsworth Story, The Judy Bryant Story, The Myra Desmond Story, and The Nola McKenzie Story and so on, the

The set for the workshop.

From Left to Right: Daphne Graham, Willie Beecham and May Collins

premise being that the telemovie would show the life they had before they went to prison the first time. Then follow their first stint in prison, release and end with them being in Wentworth, a complete journey for the character. The idea was knocked back and within six months I was gone and the show continued for nearly a hundred more episodes which a lot of people really love. I never saw any of them, so obviously I was wrong, but I still think it would have been an interesting idea.

The arrival of new officer Terri Malone sees Joan finally get something positive happen to her life, having being devastated by the death of her father earlier in the year. Terri is much younger than Joan but their friendship quickly develops into a relationship. Sadly, Terri's parents are horrified and can't accept that she is living with another woman. Terri resigns from Wentworth in an attempt to avoid any further upset between them, but when Joan arrives home from work early and finds Terri in bed with her new male boss Barry, their relationship becomes strained and the pair split up after a blazing row [576]. Coral picks up the story:

We couldn't take the Joan / Terri storyline as far as we wanted, and a story about middle-aged transgender seems to have wound up on the editing floor. We were getting a lot of flak from the Gay and Lesbian community about Joan being so evil.

Storylines outside of the prison featured heavily during this year and it often shows when watching them back today how dated the series becomes when Wentworth isn't involved. The first of these introduces four young delinquents to the prison in a 'scared straight' type of programme which attempts to show the young girls who are about to go off the tracks outside,

showcasing that this is how they could end up if they don't think about going straight. The main toughie, Nikki Lennox [played by Vicky Mathios], is identified as being the one to crack so a crazy plan is arranged that on the outside she would get involved with some (fake) underworld dealings which would hopefully make her see the error of her ways. For schoolgirl Vicky, life working on *Prisoner* was to be very exciting:

I remember the nerves I felt; I believe I was one of 40 to audition. They were impressed with how fast I memorised my script. I miss the atmosphere on set so much, it was go, go, go! The cast and crew were wonderful, every single one of them. Each in turn giving me pointers and lots of help along the way. I remember a couple of funny stories on set. I had a take I did 25 times, I just couldn't get the words out: 'I'll make you whistle God Save the Queen through your belly button'. I'll never forget it. The other one is when Lou and Nikki are arguing in the cell and Lou slaps me. That slap is not a sound effect. She actually connected and you can see her reaction for a split second before I choose to keep going. I was told that my role would be a permanent one just before it was axed, which was a little disappointing – but I'll never forget it.

The plan works and all of the girls leave the prison with, hopefully, their paths veering towards the straight and narrow. May and Willie also experience some time on the outside when they are asked by the police to help them catch a wanted criminal. Apparently, the skills of these two middle-aged women are second to none and they are the only people fit for the job although we weren't treated to any examples of this during their stay in the prison. Sadly, May is killed when the robbery they are involved in goes wrong, leaving Willie to receive a free release but to face the world without the woman she loved to hate. This

JANICE MARY GRANT

Played by Jenny Ludlam

First episode: 514
Last episode: 528
Total featured: 15 episodes

Solicitor Janice Grant is sentenced to a three-month stay at Wentworth for driving while under the influence of alcohol. She starts asking around for booze and she turns out to be a very well served alcoholic.

In desperate need of a strong drink, Jan makes her work colleague smuggle in some money for her so she can buy some contraband from Lou. It turns out to be a homemade recipe of methylated spirits mixed with liver salts which she calls 'bush champagne'. When Yemil later visits Janice to ask for advice about her trial, she is found to be drunk and the task of sobering her up is left to Lexie [515]. As a result of the booze, she suffers hallucinations in her cell after lights out but this only makes her further determined to buy more.

Ettie is moved in with Janice and manages to give her something to take her mind off her addiction – Ettie's original crime. Janice believes that Ettie has never been to court and has been stuck in Wentworth for over 40 years, in a storyline not dissimilar to Lizzie Birdsworth's. Janice manages to kick the booze habit and finds out that indeed Ettie was never tried for her supposed crime [519]. Ettie instructs Janice to handle her case, which she accepts but is warned by Myra not to mess things up. She does have a relapse however, drinking furniture polish which almost kills her [524].

While Ettie is successful in her case against the Department, sadly Janice's alcoholism causes her to need serious treatment which Ettie demands that she funds in return for all of the work she has done in getting her case heard. She leaves the prison for a private medical sanatorium where it is hoped she would make a full recovery.

causes a major headache for Ann who is blamed by the inmates for May's death.

The character of Willie saw another recognisable face return to Wentworth in the form of Kirsty Child who had played a number of smaller roles in previous years although this would probably be the one she is most remembered for. Kirsty spoke to us about her final visit to Cell Block H:

I was very pleased to be joining the show again with an on-going role. I think the producers wanted to introduce a few new characters and Billie, Sonja, Debra, Jackie and I started at the same time, perhaps even on the same day. We all met on our first day together, all terrific actresses and great women. I worked mostly with Billie as we were playing partners and got to know her well.

I don't remember anyone I did not enjoy working with, including the crew who were

terrific. The best thing to come out of Prisoner *for me was the dog that one of the floor managers brought in one day to 'give to a good home'. I took him (Ralph) home as a companion for our lovely female dog and it was a great decision!*

Towards the back end of this year, some further new characters are introduced. Eve Wilder [Lynda Stoner] convinces everyone, including her lawyer, that she is innocent when in fact she is as guilty as hell and starts playing the women off against each other. When Joyce suspects that her relationship with lawyer David is more than professional it results in an horrific attack on Joyce at the hands of Eve. Officer Barry is hospitalised, fighting for her life. A surprise return in the form of Reb Kean also takes place; however, she appears to be a completely different person from the baddie that we used to know. She has experienced some unorthodox electric shock treatment while at Blackmoor prison and Meg believes that this has

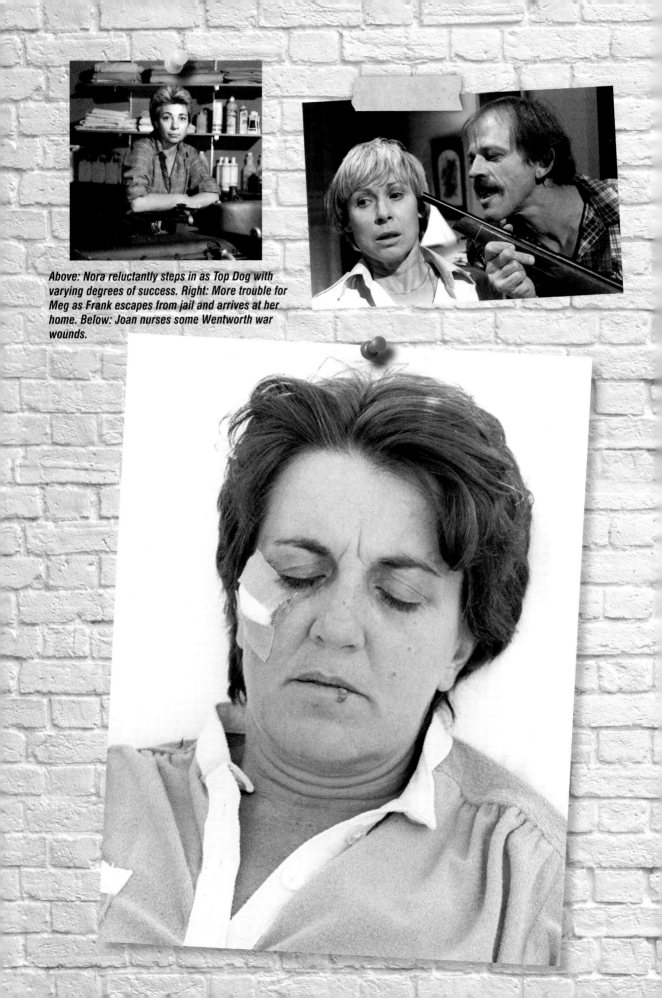

Above: Nora reluctantly steps in as Top Dog with varying degrees of success. Right: More trouble for Meg as Frank escapes from jail and arrives at her home. Below: Joan nurses some Wentworth war wounds.

caused her to have a complete change of character. The women nevertheless tread carefully around Reb who is very unpredictable and keeps suffering flashbacks from her previous time at Wentworth. The return to her old stomping ground was welcomed by actress Janet Andrewartha who managed to sandwich the role in between other work:

When Reb came back and was a changed person due to the ECT, the writers did a lot of research for me. I arrived at the Grundy offices to have a meeting with the writer and she had masses of material that she had used when she actually wrote the scripts. So I didn't have to do much research, it was all waiting for me.

There was a lot of discussion about whether Reb was faking or not when she returned. It could have gone either way. Because of the theatre commitments I had already made, I could only stay the six weeks on Prisoner *when I came back. We had to make a decision about what would be the outcome and originally I think they had wanted Reb to be revealed to be faking it, and slowly the old Reb would creep back in. But with only six weeks available we went for an open ending – let the audience decide if she was or wasn't pulling the wool over their eyes.*

Viewer favourite Daphne Graham finally gets some good news and is released after it is found that she has been suffering from PMS and cannot be held solely responsible for the crime that she had originally committed. She is one of the few ex-inmates to be seen about to 'go straight' as she looks forward to working in her ideal job at the local gardening nursery. Actress Debra Lawrance, later best known as Pippa from *Home and Away*, has happy memories of her time working on *Prisoner*:

I enjoyed the challenge of playing Daphne, with her low IQ and basic approach to life. It pointed up the fact that there are some people who fall between the cracks without proper parenting and social support. My favourite storylines were the ones where her irrationality due to her PMT was played out: burning herself, getting up on the roof. It meant that when she was finally diagnosed and released, the audience were relieved that she could stop inflicting damage on herself and others. A Prisoner *success story.*

The roof scenes were thrilling, but my frustration was that I said to the director that I was prepared to stand right out on the edge so he could get an authentic shot. I trusted our stunt trainer who had rigged a rope from a harness under my clothes and was holding on to that rope at all times out of shot. When I later saw it on screen, the director hadn't used any of the footage that showed it was actually me standing on the edge; the whole thing looked like it had been done by a stunt woman!

The prison is turned upside down when a certain bikie by the name of Rita Connors arrives as Glenda Linscott makes her mighty presence in the series felt for the first time. Rita turns up to Wentworth in the usual paddy-wagon which is escorted by her bearded biker gang The Conquerors who gave her a terrific welcome when she steps out of the van, revving their engines and sounding their horns [585]. Immediately, we see that Rita is a force not to be messed with as she shrieks what would become her famous bikie salute-call back out to them. During her induction by Joan, the two lock swords immediately when Joan rips the chains from her leather jacket. Rita has arrived at exactly the right time for the series and Wentworth is to change forever with her presence. In a complete contrast, another new arrival is Barbie Cox [Jayne Healey]. Barbie by name and Barbie by nature, she looks like a child's doll and only manages a few words – mainly 'naughty, naughty' and 'hi de hi'. Although Joan and Meg appear to be shocked by her crime during the induction, it is never mentioned on screen and to this day nobody knows why Barbie has been sent to prison.

With the arrival of Rita, the current Top Dog Nora suddenly disappears without trace with everyone wondering how she has escaped. Meanwhile, Eve's lawyer David finally works out that she has been using him. The guilt becomes too much for him, having believed everything she has said and becoming infatuated with this beautiful woman, that he can't take it anymore. During a private visit in the interview room, he reveals all and, before Eve has a chance to persuade him otherwise, he shoots himself in the head in front of her. An explosive end to what was a very mixed year for the series. However, the new energy that this year closed with left viewers with an exciting wait and high expectations of 1986. They weren't going to be disappointed but had to prepare for a shock as the inevitable future of the series was due to become a reality.

The Rise and Fall of Lou Kelly

" *'What's this I hear about that fat cow Jessie being your mother?'*
Lou Kelly (tact was never her strong point) **"**

Louise Jane Kelly – one of Wentworth's mysteries. Originally serving an eight-year sentence for armed robbery, she stacks up an impressive list of additional crimes during her time as an inmate including murder, assault, illegal possession of a firearm, kidnapping and so the list continues. Her first appearance as an unnamed background character [385] sees her return to be credited as Tammy Fisher [399] before finally being known as Louise five episodes later. It takes a further handful of appearances until she develops into the Lou Kelly character that she is remembered for. For Louise Siversen, the entry into television through *Prisoner* was one she remains grateful for as she explains:

> *I did an audition for Grundy which was really like just a general casting for nothing in particular. It led me to playing Lou Kelly from virtually the next week. There was never any character breakdown or a plan, I just arrived and next thing away we went with Lou developing as time passed. I don't ever remember speaking to, or hearing from, a writer about where I was going. I was just given a script and did as written, unless instructed otherwise. To this day I have no idea what her original crime was but it became fairly evident quite quickly that what they wanted was vicious and heavy so that's what I gave them. And let's face it – that is fun to play. I think she committed more crimes inside than she ever did on the outside!*

> *My first day on set was thrilling and terrifying. One of my first scenes was with Val Lehman and*

that in itself explained the order of things. I knew what I needed to do pretty quickly and did it. Most of the women on the show were gorgeous and welcoming and still remain great friends of mine to this day. Maggie Kirkpatrick, Glenda Linscott, Deb Lawrance, Jackie Woodburne, Pepe Trevor – so many wonderful friends come from that show. It was a great baptism into series life and I loved it; every moment, every year, was utterly wonderful. I am so lucky I got to be part of such an iconic show that will never be repeated, and I got to play Lou – one of the all-time great baddies a woman could ever hope to play.

During German prisoner Hannah Geldschmidt's time inside, Lou torments her with her future partner in crime Alice Jenkins. The two baddies taunt and tease her about being a 'Kraut' and when Hannah takes extreme measures to ensure she's not deported, she stirs Lou and Alice so much that a heavy beating by the duo is the response [453]. This leads to a stay in hospital for Hannah – thus prolonging her time in Australia. This first proper appearance as one of the bad girls sees Lou regularly involved in future bashings and general wrong-doings and she sides with whoever the current leader of the opposition is – Reb Kean for example – but with very little lines.

Lou continues to work her way up the ranks and sides with Reb, even thinking she can take over the drugs business in Wentworth now that Phyllis Hunt is out of action. Hunt is living the rest of her life with serious brain damage thanks to an attack on her in the

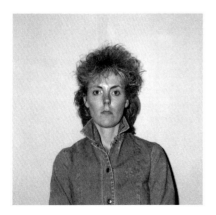  

Left: Lou's mug shot, never actually seen on screen in the series. Centre and Right: Promotional Shot.

shower block by Reb. Enter Marie Winter, the snowy-haired ex-Wentworth inmate who arrives back at the prison just in time to start another riot in a conspiracy with Joan Ferguson to see governor Ann Reynolds lose her job. With the assistance from the ever-present Alice, Lou is given the chance to beat up Joan [466] while Marie takes over the prison with her growing gang of rioters. When Marie demands that Reb help her kill Myra Desmond during the commotion, Kean refuses, resulting in a shove down the stairs by Marie in the hope that this will finish her off.

With the riot over and Marie still making further demands, Lou helps plan her escape by arranging a diversion in the garden while Marie makes a run for it to a waiting helicopter [471] in one of the series' most spectacular escapes. Lou now has the chance to take over, seeing as both Marie and Reb are out of the way. Her first moneymaking idea is to arrange a raffle with new and scary inmate Bev Baker who has a fascination with torture and seeing other people suffer. While Bev doesn't want to make any money from the 'Numbers Game' she does request Lou to help her obtain some special items including a knitting needle which she later uses to stab a prison social worker to death. The combination of Lou and Bev appears to be a winning one with all of the other women too afraid to get on the wrong side of them, fearing what might happen. Bev takes her own life by injecting air into her bloodstream [476] and Lou returns to become the muscle for Reb who has returned after escaping from hospital during her recovery.

After a crazy idea to get involved with blackmailing the Governor goes wrong, Lou decides that she needs to escape Wentworth and demands that Reb helps her. Her first attempt doesn't go quite according to plan. She attacks social worker Phil Cleary during a softball game but is stopped in her tracks by none other than Marlene Warren and is swiftly sent to solitary [490]. Unknown to Officer Joyce Barry, Lou has a razor blade hidden in her shoe which she uses to take her hostage, collect a gun from the armoury and escape the prison via Joyce's very own car. When she has travelled far enough, she ties up Joyce and puts her in the boot and leaves the car abandoned next to a graveyard.

Still armed with the gun, Lou makes her way to the home of Reb's mother Deidre where she demands money from her. Deidre tells Lou to wait until the morning when she can get to the bank but, during a scuffle, Lou is injured in the arm when the gun goes off [492]. She isn't seriously injured and, after stealing the money from Deidre, the runaway gets as far as Adelaide but is the victim of a theft herself. A man she has made friends with takes the money for himself during a dinner date which leaves Lou unable to pay and the police are called. A return to Wentworth is imminent [495].

The arrival of male officer Len Murphy sees Lou involved in the plans of the other inmates and Joan's bid to get rid of him. Wentworth isn't big enough for two corrupt officers; however, plans on both sides fail. With the resignation of Myra as Top Dog, Reb decides to take control of the women but Len is too smart for them all and Lou is forced to have sex with him [503] when things don't go according to plan.

Being raped by Len Murphy was hilarious as was Maurie Fields. A beautiful, funny, kind man who made me laugh out loud all the time. He farted the whole way through that scene and I couldn't stop giggling. Hilarious! Maurie was a showbiz great and I worked with him, and I am grateful.

It is from this point that Lou's devious ways really bring her character to life. She ends up in hospital when a homemade gun goes off in her hand [517] which was meant to be used to kill Joan. When she has recovered, she vows to kill Myra and makes plans to electrocute her in a bizarre attempt to wire her cell door up to the electricity supply. Tragedy strikes when Samantha Greenway is killed by mistake. Lou and Alice make her death look like suicide [520] by stringing up her body from the ceiling. When Myra finds out, she tricks male inmate (and another of Lou's gang) Frank Burke into thinking that Lou was going to frame him for Samantha's murder, so a bashing is due when Frank catches up with her [522]. It has to be noted that the more devious she became, the more her impressive hairstyle reflected that too!

I did Lou's hair from day one. They used to say it was 'a two shot – Lou and her hair', but it was the era of the punk and so I just kept developing her love of spray. I went through cans of it. The hair got bigger as it got longer and I got better at getting it to stand up!

An interesting claim made by Lou during the infamous flashback episode [536] is that she has been in Wentworth along with Alice for much longer than she has been seen on screen. She tells the other women that she helped build the tunnel which Bea, Judy, Doreen and co. used to try and escape from the prison. This episode sees a shift in storylines with the arrival of a selection of new characters who have been transferred from Barnhurst where the mighty Bea Smith lost her life during a massive riot and fire.

I laughed more on that show than any other before or since. For many reasons, not just that they were a great group of people but the time I spent (around three years) made for familiarity and that makes for 'in jokes' and 'known behaviours'. When certain actresses came together they just have chemistry. Jackie Woodburne and I are two of those people. I was always having terrible trouble laughing when I worked with her. We could not stop laughing! There is something terribly funny about pretending to be vicious and threatening, particularly when it is someone you know well. She is small and I am very tall; the height difference always makes it seem funnier. I seem to remember a director coming down on to the floor and threatening the two of us with some punishment if we didn't stop. What punishment he was hoping to inflict I am not sure, but I guess he, too, was at his wits' end as to what to do to stop us.

Lou is heavily involved in the siege, although she tries to help the terrorists. She is forced to side with the prisoners who are scared for their lives. She manages to sneak some knives and skewers from the kitchens and attacks one of the men in his leg [551]. They are still too strong for this attempt to swing power back to the women. When their beloved top dog Myra is brutally murdered in front of them, they all realise that it could be any one of them for the chop next. The siege ends without any further killings but the effect on many of the women will never be forgotten.

Lou: Anyone who doesn't pay me a dollar will suffer a nasty accident!
Jenny: But I haven't got a penny to my name!
Lou: Well, you'd better change your name then because I don't give credit!

The various power struggles continue with Lou fighting against whoever is in the Top Dog position and becoming more and more psychotic with every move. She eventually forces her way to the privileged position herself. When new Governor Bob Moran arrives, temporarily replacing Ann, Lou convinces the women to take part in a hunger strike against him and his new rules. She also finds out that ally Eve Wilder is revealed as Wentworth's 'phantom lagger' and responsible for a lot of secrets getting spread around the prison. Lou and Alice hold a mock trial for her in the Rec Room during a riot and hang her

JENNIFER HARTLEY

Played by Jenny Lovell

First episode: 540
Last episode: 588
Total featured: 45 episodes

Friend of Pippa Reynolds, the Governor's daughter, Jenny lives in a large mansion with her wealthy grandmother who appears to be very poorly and generally confined to her bed. She has tirelessly looked after Mrs Hartley for a number of years and the old lady has come to depend on Jenny much more than she actually needs.

When Jenny arrives home to find her grandmother brutally murdered – bashed on the head with a table lamp – Jenny becomes the prime suspect and is arrested and swiftly sent to Wentworth [548]. She is in a completely different class to the majority of the other inmates and it takes her a long time to find friends. She is thrust straight into the famous terrorist siege which sees the death of Top Dog Myra Desmond and scares the women beyond their greatest fears.

When her trial ends up with a hung jury, May Collins suggests an alternative lawyer and finally some new evidence about her grandmother's murder comes to light. Her uncle Steve Formby is arrested for the murder of both his own wife and Jenny's grandmother in the hope that he will be left with all of their riches. He admits everything and Jenny is released. She sticks around however, staying friendly with Pippa and also attending her wedding. She is last seen in Episode 588 as she leaves to search for a new home and the start of her new life.

Left: Heavily involved in the siege, Lou wrestles with one of the terrorists. Centre: Louise Siversen. Right: She's alive! Louise poses as Lou during a rare visit to the UK and it looks like she has made a friend… a lethal combination!

in front of everyone present [600]. With the riot in full swing, she arranges for a fight between new inmate Rita Connors and Joan who have quickly become enemies. With both women fighting to the death, Bob manages to step in at the right moment armed with a gun and Meg, and the riot is over. Rita takes over as the new Top Dog and teaches Alice and Lou a lesson by organising a fake hanging for them both [603]. Writer Coral Drouyn particularly enjoyed writing Lou's scenes:

> *I was always looking for the humour in things, sometimes unexpected. I was reading a script of mine the other day – the first time in 30 years – and Lou says about Lurch, 'She can only type with one finger, and that's the one she picks her nose with!' and I chuckled out loud. It was just Lou being a bitch, but it was funny!*

The relationship between Lou and the gullible Alice finally comes to an end when Alice sees the light and decides to move over to the other side, headed by Rita. Becoming even more maniacal, Lou decides that she's going to have to escape from the prison again in order to survive, so fakes a suicide attempt which results in her being sent to hospital where she manages to escape [607]. She makes the journey to Alice's family home in the country where she is looked after by Alice's mother but is raped by Sean, Alice's brother. When Lou hears them talking about killing her, she manages to get one step ahead and shoots them both dead and runs off further into the country [612]. She is recaptured and returned to Wentworth. Louise recalls working with Lois and the unusual combination of Lou and Lurch:

> *Lois Collinder and I were a great team – polar opposites and it worked. She is such a beautiful woman, full of kindness and generosity and always was. We got on well and were great friends at that time. I think we made a funny visual*

gag with her being even taller than me, and playing the bumbling incompetent one and me as the heavy still makes me laugh.

Stacking up an impressive episode count, Lou Kelly lives on as one of Wentworth's most-loved baddies. Louise Siversen was only 23 years of age when she joined *Prisoner* – the series which would reward her with her first main television role in one of Australia's most popular dramas at the time of airing.

Born in Melbourne in 1960, Louise initially had a career as a model with dance training in classical ballet and jazz behind her also. After leaving school, she studied law but decided to train as an actor after attending a careers day that made her re-think her future.

She appeared in guest roles in series including *The Sullivans*, *Cop Shop* and *Carson's Law* before making her first guest appearance in *Prisoner* as a nurse [169]. She had further guest spots in the series as a camera shop assistant [333] and was also credited as character Tammy Fisher [399] before the Lou Kelly role became hers.

The vicious character that she portrayed couldn't be any further to the opposite of Louise. She played the part so well that understandably some viewers weren't able to tell fact from fiction and in 1984 Louise arrived home after going out for lunch to find her flat had been broken into and ransacked.

> *They had scaled the side of the building to get in, so obviously knew whose flat they were in. The police said it could have a lot to do with my* Prisoner *character being so nasty.*
>
> TV Week (15/09/1984)

This didn't put Louise off however, and she stayed with the series until 1986. On leaving *Prisoner*, Louise joined the cast of *The Flying Doctors* between 1986 and 1989 in the recurring role of airline pilot Debbie O'Brien. She also won small guest roles in *Neighbours*,

House Rules and *Sugar and Spice* towards the late 1980s. Louise explains her departure from the show:

> *I wanted to go on to other work. Be with other stories and discover other roles. I was young and wanted to move to something new, and I did. I'm still moving on 27 years later. I have never done anything but be an actress and I still love it. Still learning and discovering. I understand it a lot better these days and am more skilled than I was then but the joy is the same – just the same if not more so, because now I know so much more and understand how to use it.*

The 1990s saw Louise take to the big screen where she appeared in *That Eye-The Sky*, *Shine* and *Crackers* with regular voice-over work also becoming a welcome addition to Louise's versatile talents.

Theatre is another of Louise's loves and she has worked extensively for a number of companies including the Melbourne Theatre Company, La Mama and Zootango. Her work has been both on and off stage as Louise is also qualified to direct as well as write work to be performed by others. She has also been a drama teacher at the Victorian College of Arts

and has a wide range of interests to keep her occupied when she is not working.

She won nominations for the Silver Logie Award for her roles in current affairs series *Backburner* and drama *Janus*. Louise has continued to work with appearances in *The Secret Life of Us*, *All Saints* and *MDA* in the mid-2000s. Most recently, she had recorded roles in *The Eye of the Storm* and *House Husbands* in addition to working regularly in the theatre.

Louise travelled to the UK in 2010 for some rare public appearances for her British fans who had patiently waited for their chance to catch up and meet the lady behind Lou Kelly.

> *I feel enormously fortunate that I was part of so many extraordinary series that will never be repeated,* Prisoner *being one of them. It was irreplaceable and always will be and I was blessed to be part of that, in a time when TV was inventive. It has been great for me to look back on the work and celebrate it due to the continuing fan support. My lasting memory of all my work is the joy I had, the friends I made and all the lessons I learned about acting from the work and other great actors. I am grateful, pure and simple.*

SHEILA BRADY

Played by Colleen Hewett

First episode: 519
Last episode: 534
Total featured: 11 episodes

When musician Sheila Brady arrives, the women can smell her before she even enters the room due to her poor personal hygiene and unwashed clothes. With her guitar never far from her side, the women realise that she's a talented performer after she belts out a blues number following lights out [519].

She makes friends with Judy and falls in love with 'Pixie's Song', which Judy is composing. The two of them work on the song together and eventually a full melody is written and the song is finished. Sheila's own compositions, however, are not quite up to the same standard.

The women try to think about the best way of telling her about the smell which travels with her and Lexie offers her some of her own clothes which Sheila loves [522].

Not expecting to get released after her trial, Sheila gives Judy her faithful guitar to look after until she returns but she is surprisingly released and the women think that's that. When Judy later hears 'Pixie's Song' on the radio some weeks later, she thinks that Sheila has ripped her off so she arranges to contact the record company. Sheila returns [532] and apologises to Judy explaining that she didn't steal her song on purpose but wanted to record it straight away because everyone loved it. She also proposes that she and Judy work together to write a whole music album. No sooner is that suggested then Judy is also released. The two of them leave Wentworth for the final time, looking forward to their future together as recording artists.

The Reynolds Girl

" *Ann: I'll make this as short as possible, Ferguson. I will put up with and excuse many things in this prison but if I ever hear a repeat performance of what I've just heard, I will do everything in my power to remove you.*
Joan: I think I have a right to...
Ann: NO-ONE has the right to sabotage the working authority of this prison. If you haven't got the guts to come to me with your complaints, either go to the Department or keep your mouth shut... UNDERSTAND? "
Episode 460 – One of the many rounds of Ann Reynolds vs Joan Ferguson

With the surprise departure of Governor Erica Davidson in 1983, Wentworth is in need of a new leader. When Ann Reynolds appears [364], both staff and inmates are shocked at the Department's decision to bring in someone from outside of the prison service especially when Colleen Powell, Meg Morris and Joan Ferguson are all favourites to win the position following some gruelling interviews.

Ann makes herself clear from the very beginning: 'I'm not Mrs Davidson,' she snaps at Colleen when her predecessor is mentioned. She also upsets Lizzie on her first day when Erica's name crops up again. It seems that Mrs Reynolds has a lot to live up to if she's going to be a hit at Wentworth.

Joan is quick to strike up a friendship with her new boss in an attempt to earn some early respect and possibly stop any whispers of corruption reaching her by the other officers and inmates. The two colleagues spend some time together after work going through the prisoners' files and Joan makes every effort to subtly criticise Meg and Colleen. Colleen's initial relationship with Ann gets off to a rocky start with Colleen's understandable disappointment at not being promoted. This causes some tension, along with her trying to cope with Ann's views on completing paperwork given precedence over looking after the prisoners. However, Ann is quick to realise that the two will work together well, so any initial issues are soon ironed out and a more professional teaming begins.

Firm but fair, Ann Reynolds is no pushover.

Life outside of Wentworth is introduced quite quickly with Ann's character. She is very much a working mother with two grown up children and lives in a modest house which is part of a larger property. When Judy's friend Wally Wallace meets Ann, she suggests that he moves into the attic at her place when he is looking for somewhere to live in the city [377]. Her photographer son Paul helps Wally move in, but when he takes an innocent photograph of Department head Ted Douglas appearing to take bribes from a big crime boss, Ann is attacked in her home by part of the Fellowes gang in an attempt to steal the negatives. Ted is soon found out by the authorities and arrested just as he is boarding a flight to make a quick getaway. Unfortunately for the prison, the Fellowes gang don't go away as easily and punish the inmates by planting a bomb which kills one of the bomb squad and injures Bea Smith. Ann is made the scapegoat and blamed for poor security at Wentworth. Coral Drouyn helped bring this impressive new Governor to life:

I have to confess I HATED Erica. I thought she was two-dimensional and unreal, like the headmistress of a private girls' school. I'm sure Patsy King did the best she could but the character didn't work for me and ultimately became an icon just because she was so camp.

Maggie Kirkpatrick, Anne Phelan, Louise Siversen, Marie Trevor and Gerda Nicolson celebrate.

I wanted someone earthier, more believable; someone who had sensitivity but could be tough as nails when it was called for. All of my characters have elements of me, I guess because I know myself better than anybody else. I'm much more volatile and unreasonable than Ann (at least I was in those days) but I can be super tough on the outside while being a total sook underneath. I was raising kids alone and holding down a reasonable job. I took all of those things and used them. Then I added elements of women I admired, and Ann evolved.

Ann's approach to managing Wentworth is different to Erica's. She is passionate about reform and improving conditions from the beginning. This doesn't go down too well with Joan who immediately starts working against Ann rather than with her when their initial friendship wears off. She is furious with Joan for arranging Bea's transfer to Barnhurst while she is out of the office [400]. Unfortunately for Bea's cohorts, Ann's hands are tied when she returns to the prison and there's no chance of a transfer back to Wentworth. While Joan scores herself a point in getting rid of her biggest enemy, the mood changes at Wentworth with new Top Dog Sonia Stevens working with a further corrupted Freak and so begins the many attempts to bring the prison crashing down around Ann, with Joan always behind the plans.

Life for Ann is turned upside down when she discovers a lump in her breast, just as her relationship with Wally is turning serious. Like many women faced with the same worry, she puts off going to visit the doctor but is convinced by Colleen to get things checked out properly. During a biopsy [417], the surgeons perform a mastectomy which devastates

Ann. While she is recovering in hospital, she also has to deal with a further serious blow – Paul has been shot on the orders of Lionel Fellowes and is in a critical condition [422]. Ann is discharged from the hospital to recover at home, and considers giving up her job at Wentworth to look after Paul who is going to need a lot of support to help him walk again following his horrific injuries from the gunshot which damaged his spine. Wally steps in to nurse Paul back to health, meaning that Ann can return to Wentworth and comes back as Governor [429], where the battle between her and Joan is set to continue.

When Ann starts receiving threats on her life, she moves in for a short time with Meg who has become good friends with her. One night after work, Ann is followed home to Meg's place by Brian Lowe, a relative of ex-inmate Phyllis Hunt who was seriously bashed by Reb Kean, resulting in permanent brain damage. Lowe shoots the policeman outside Meg's house and tricks his way inside, shooting a further policewoman and holds a terrified Meg and Ann hostage. He forces Meg at gunpoint to drive the three of them to an old disused warehouse in the middle of nowhere. There he ties them up and leaves them there, the only company being the rats who live in the old building. Their attempts to escape prove fruitless as Lowe has booby-trapped the whole building with trip-wires which would detonate a series of bombs if a foot is placed in the wrong position. When Lowe returns in a rage [499], he forgets about the staircase and is caught out by one of his own traps as the steps give way and he falls to his death, giving the hostages the chance they need to escape. Tired and exhausted, they make their move but the whole building explodes when an unsuspecting policeman sets off one of the bombs.

Amazingly, Ann returns to work soon after her kidnap ordeal [504] but on this occasion has pushed herself too far and is forced to take further time off when she collapses while back on the job.

Ann's daughter Pippa makes a surprise appearance in Episode 540 and reveals that she is having an affair with a married man, much to the disappointment of her mother. She returns later and starts working at Wentworth to teach the women screen printing, with Lexie Patterson making an impressive

collection of t-shirts that are snapped up by a major supplier. She later gets married to Ben Fulbright and Ann happily attends the occasion which is unfortunately disrupted by the bikie friends of new inmate Rita Connors.

A brief fling with priest Dan Moulton shows another side to the face that most people only know as Mrs Reynolds or 'Renno' as the prisoners have nicknamed her. While Dan's feelings on religion are quite clear, he is also a bikie and good friends with Rita and her gang The Conquerors. He and Ann spend a lot of time together and she is quite happy to be a passenger on his motorbike. Their relationship ends after Dan's injury at Wentworth during an escape attempt by

Promotional Shot.

ANITA SELBY

Played by Diane Craig

First episode: 526
Last episode: 536
Total featured: 11 episodes

One of Wentworth's unusual prisoners, nun Anita is arrested following her involvement at a nuclear disarmament rally and is the series' only Sister of God to be inducted. Frank doesn't waste any time and attempts to assault her until her notices the crucifix hanging around her neck.

Anita's strong values are often challenged by Lou who makes every effort to break what she believes in. Lou slaps Anita across the face twice in the hope of some retaliation, without success [527] and fazing Lou considerably. However, when Lou suggests that Anita is a lesbian it causes the mild-mannered worshipper to almost lose her temper.

She becomes friendlier than most of the inmates with Joan who has recently lost her father. Some of the other women, including Lexie and Marlene, also turn to Anita for some friendly advice although when she offers to help Lou, Anita's efforts are quickly rejected [533].

When the women set up Joan to be caught bashing one of the other prisoners, when in fact she is suffering black-outs from a medical condition, Anita tells them that she cannot go along with their plans. They set Joan up as planned [534] and she is all set to lose her job; however, Anita can't bear this on her conscience and lags on the women so Joan's job is safe once more.

With the church having paid Anita's bail fee, she is released and leaves Wentworth under a cloud because the other women are set to be in serious trouble as a consequence of their actions with Joan. Anita visits a recovering Joan in hospital after her operation and suggests that, when she returns, she tries to help the women rather than work against them [536]. It appears to work but not for long and soon Joan is back to the old routine as if nothing has changed.

Bongo Connors to get Rita out of the prison. Dan falls in love with one of the nurses [648] and Ann is again left single but handles the whole affair with dignity, although when Joan provokes her about the relationship it is responded to with a sharp slap across the face – a truly brilliant moment.

Prison reform is the way forward for Ann towards the end of the series. She finally gets some of her wishes and conditions at the prison begin to improve. A punishment cell and reward area are introduced, along with a more relaxed environment and further enhancements to Wentworth. As always, trouble is never far away and she is sacked by the Department [671] when Joan plots with ex-Blackmoor Governor Ernest Craven to get rid of her. Their plan backfires however, when an exposé is revealed on national television about Craven's corruption and the Department is forced to re-instate her.

The series ends with Ann's report on prison reforms being accepted by the Department and Wentworth is rid of its biggest sources of evil forever.

Gerda Nicolson was born on 11 November 1937 in Hobart, Tasmania and acting couldn't be any further from her mind when she grew up wanting to be a successful architect. In fact, she studied architecture but when she became involved in amateur dramatics during the early 1960s it was clear to see that Gerda's life was to head in a different direction.

For Gerda, the acting profession ran in the family although she was a bit of a latecomer to the scene with her first professional stage production taking place in 1962. She performed in one of the lead roles in *A Woman in a Dressing Gown*, which she took to the road on tour around Australia and New Zealand. Incidentally, Googie Withers was among the cast at this time and little did Gerda know that Googie was later to be linked to a television role which Gerda would be most remembered for.

During her working life, Gerda skipped between television and theatre work quite happily although a lot of her stage appearances were during the 1960s where she was involved in productions including

Left: Gerda and the rest of the cast play up for the camera, a certain Ian Smith is lurking in the corner too!. Right: Anne Phelan, Les Dayman and Gerda Nicolson.

Devil's Disciple, *The Private Ear and the Public Eye*, and Shakespeare's *Hamlet* in 1964. In the same year, Gerda would join the cast of the long-running TV crime series *Homicide* where she would later go on to return a further four times to play a different guest role on each occasion.

Bellbird was Australia's first soap opera and ran between 1967 and 1977 for an impressive 1697 episodes. Gerda joined the series in 1970 and played the part of Fiona Buckland, who later became Fiona Carstairs, then Fiona Davies. She stayed with *Bellbird* until 1976 and worked with many other familiar faces including Alan Hopgood whom she would later join again as her career progressed.

Throughout the 1970s, Gerda extensively worked in Australian television dramas including *Bluey, The Sullivans* and *Cop Shop*. She played a guest role in *Prisoner* in 1981 as Officer Roberts – the Barnhurst version of Vera 'Vinegar Tits' Bennett for two episodes, but in 1983 she joined the cast as new Governor Ann Reynolds, a significant role for Gerda as the series was at the height of its popularity during this time and audiences were remaining strong. Perfectly cast as Wentworth Detention Centre's new head jailer, Gerda stayed with *Prisoner* until the series ended in 1986 and stacked up 316 episodes to her credit.

Further TV and stage work came Gerda's way during the late 80s and an appearance in *Neighbours* as Robyn Taylor saw her working with some old friends again. She was a love interest for Ian Smith's character Harold Bishop although her time in Ramsay Street was only a short one.

In the summer of 1992, during a preview performance of the theatre production *Mary Lives!*, Gerda collapsed in her dressing room while the interval was taking place. She died on 12 June 1992 from a sudden stroke which claimed her life far too soon. Her death was a shock to the Australian acting industry who remembered her for many years to follow with the introduction of the prestigious 'Gerda Nicolson Award for an Emerging Actress' which was given as part of The Green Room Awards in Melbourne every year. Following the death of Gerda's husband, Julius Szappanos, the award is no longer included in the ceremony. However, plans are taking place to reintroduce it at some point in the future to celebrate the life of this wonderful, respected and much missed actress.

LOIS COLLINDER:

Gerda was the most beautiful person. So professional. A gentle, refined, beautiful woman. Her husband Julius worked at that time for a food importing company. Every time we had a party, he would supply us with a big stinky smelly cheese which was so powerful it would make everything in the fridge smell. It was one of those things that smelled really bad but was delicious to eat. Gerda was just really happy that someone else liked this cheese as much as she did. A special lady.

ELSPETH BALLANTYNE:

I first met Gerda in 1962 at The Union Rep Theatre Company. She was a graceful, charming

fellow performer, and we instantly became friends. From then on, we constantly worked together either in TV or the theatre. Our first foray into TV was a series called Bellbird *at the ABC – a homespun family soap which captured the hearts of rural Australia for 10 years. Gerda played the wife of the local policeman, and soon was a favourite with the thousands of viewers. Later we met up again in Prisoner. I was thrilled, we were social friends as well, both of us attending each other's weddings and we lived just a suburb away from each other. Gerda took her work very seriously, always extremely well prepared, yet happy to join in any fun and games. A consummate, intelligent, thoughtful and insightful actress she often left me in awe of her capacity to learn long difficult speeches with technical data that she delivered without flinching, no mean feat when you had to turn up five days a week. I miss Gerda very much. She left us too early. She had many more fabulous performances in her. Gerda's dignity, wisdom and charm will never be forgotten.*

MAGGIE KIRKPATRICK:

Working with Gerda Nicolson was a joy every day. She was one of the most gracious women I have ever met. Every scene with her was a joy to do – always spot on, prepared and challenging. In her quiet, caring way, she made

her presence felt in a most positive manner. My fond memories of her include watching her do Tai Chi in the lunch break...kitted out, focused and graceful in the cold empty studio... an oasis of serenity. A true 'one off' and gone far too soon from this world.

LOIS RAMSEY:

In the beginning I had very little to do with the beautiful Gerda, until my last two weeks, where Gerda had lots of difficult dialogue and asked if she could come to the flat where I was staying and do the lines with her. She came with a vase from her home and a large bunch of camellias from her garden. It brightened the rather stark flat. A typical thing for Gerda to do, such a gracious and elegant person.

LOUISE SIVERSEN:

Gerda was a woman of tremendous grace, dignity, humour and exceptional talent. I loved her and her beautiful husband. Both were incredibly kind to me as a young actress starting out. She was never threatened by the younger cast members. Gerda knew who she was and was proud of that. She was a 'class act' and I was lucky enough to work with her and receive that understanding. Now I see her even more clearly and I am grateful I had that time with her.

The suicide of David Adams at the climax to the 1985 season of episodes made for a suitably shocking end to a troubled year for *Prisoner*. But change was afoot. The programme marked its seventh year on screen with a new run of episodes on Thursday 16th January 1986, sporting a bombastic new character while saying goodbye to a couple of old favourites. Reb Kean, so wonderfully played by Janet Andrewartha, bows out in the first episode of the new year by being vindicated of the charge of attacking Joyce Barry. She is seen leaving Wentworth, her future uncertain.

A final chat with psychiatrist Doctor Weissman shows the rebel is now without a cause and facing the first steps into the world at large with a new persona and new challenges ahead. But this is *Prisoner*, and a gap in the prison system won't take long in filling. The future Dame Pat Evison arrives to play former prostitute Jessie Windham, real life mother of Lexie Patterson. Jessie is aghast to find Lexie's adopted mother Lady Giddings arrive and washes her hands of Lexie once and for all. Jessie schemes with her friend Mabel [Val Jellay] to get herself arrested in order to spend time in Wentworth getting to know the daughter she had adopted so many years before. But Lexie is a wild card, and won't take easily to the new prisoner who is seemingly taking an unhealthy interest in her. Everything turns out OK for Lexie though. She has a baby and leaves Wentworth to start a new life with Jessie, a real family at last.

Julia Blake returns to the *Prisoner* fold, in the wake of her previous visits as poisoner Evelyn Randall and Alice Dodds, to deliver her finest and best remembered of her three *Prisoner* roles. This time she is Nancy McCormack, trapped in an abusive marriage to husband Joe and defending her son Peter against victimisation by his father. Following another attack on his mother, Peter has finally had enough of his father's bullying and retaliates. Joe falls and hits his head on the coffee table. Rather than just being dazed and bruised, he is dead. Nancy is desperate to keep her son from the full wrath of the law, and decides to

offer herself up as the guilty party. But instead of the manslaughter charge she has been expecting, she is, in fact, charged with murder. Thus, a stay in Wentworth Detention Centre is assured. Debra Lawrance makes her final appearance in *Prisoner* visiting Joyce Barry in hospital [590], finally a firsthand account of Daphne's happy ending. Joyce, though, is still in a bad way following the bashing from Eve Wilder, but has the delightfully rugged young Doctor Steve Ryan [Peter Hayes] to watch over her. After hearing Joyce's stories of the prison, he has plans to further his psychiatry studies by getting a little closer to the women of Wentworth.

Although Lou Kelly is marching around the prison proclaiming Top Dog status for herself, the imposing bikie newcomer Rita Connors is clearly not going to be pushed around by anyone. Within a few episodes, Connors has shaken up Ferguson and decreed that anyone who messes with her, prisoner or captor, will feel the full force of her Conquerors' justice. Glenda Linscott's arrival in *Prisoner* was the blast of fresh air it had been needing. Finally the producers had dared to veer away from the Bea Smith clone template and go for a bold, striking figure who could hold her own physically with anyone in the prison and yet still have a caring nature that made her the perfect choice to look after those less able to deal with the politics of prison life. Glenda Linscott was undoubtedly the series' secret weapon in its final year as she acted her socks off to bring the more vulnerable elements of Rita's

complex persona to the fore. In doing so, she was the springboard for some terrific scripting and some memorable moments for one of *Prisoner's* greatest regulars. Rita's feud with The Freak developed in intensity to rival the golden days of Bea Smith's hatred for the uniformed dictator. It was the tonic the series needed, struggling in the ratings against other more glamorous rivals from *Sons And Daughters* to US import *Dynasty;* neither of these fellow soapies was able to deliver the high energy bruises and banter that this, by comparison very downmarket, setting could deliver.

Episode 600 was celebrated in style with a full-scale riot. Lou Kelly is bordering on madness as she barricades the women in the prison with Joan and Mervin Pringle among the hostages. Kelly has a plan.

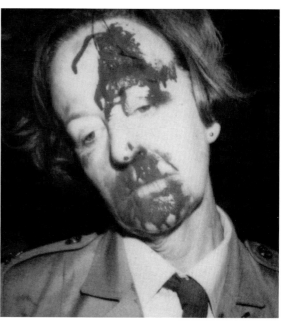

Above: Ernie Bourne and Joy Westmore relaxing at the 600th Episode party. Below: Eve Wilder (Lynda Stoner) drags the unconscious Joyce Barry (Joy Westmore). Right: Joyce's injuries.

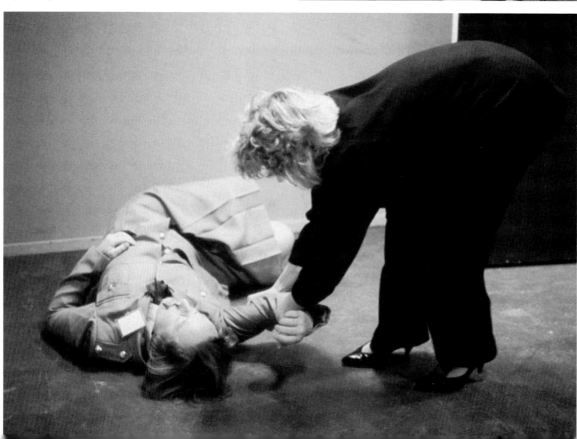

She is going to unleash Ferguson and Connors on each other: a fight to the death in the laundry, with the women baying for blood like Romans at the Coliseum, while Bob Moran hatches his plan to get inside the prison through the air conditioning ducts. The brutal fight between the two gaol gladiators is a thrilling spectacle and it's only the arrival of gun-toting Moran that stops the carnage. This physical showdown proved a fine device to hot up further tensions between Connors and Ferguson. The war between them was far from over as the coming weeks would prove.

The stunt co-ordinator for the showdown scrap in the laundry was Glenn Ruehland. Glenn had been responsible for many sequences since he joined the show, and here he recalls his time tutoring the 'ladies who punch':

I was taken on as regular stunt co-ordinator around 1982 or 83 and I was with the show until the end. I knew most people behind the camera

but the 'girls' were very enthusiastic and great to work with. Very welcoming and glad to have someone look after them for their stunt and fight sequences. I enjoyed all my work on the series but I guess because of their characters, Maggie, Glenda and Louise were the most memorable for the aggressive quality of their characters.

The fight between Glenda and Maggie would have been rehearsed over one or two days so the actors could get into the fight. The two ladies were always great to work with, very industrious and eager to learn and listen. Once they were comfortable with the scene we would amp up the violence and the energy levels to 80% and then we'd leave it at that until the actual shoot day. On the day itself, we would run through the fight two or three more times before going for a take. I encouraged the ladies to go for 110% commitment for this. On most fight sequences, we would run on three cameras so there was

Left: Nancy McCormack (Julia Blake) contemplating her incarceration. Below: Warriors! Rita The Beater on the war path. Right: The Freak encounters Rita

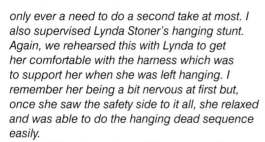

only ever a need to do a second take at most. I also supervised Lynda Stoner's hanging stunt. Again, we rehearsed this with Lynda to get her comfortable with the harness which was to support her when she was left hanging. I remember her being a bit nervous at first but, once she saw the safety side to it all, she relaxed and was able to do the hanging dead sequence easily.

I still have to get even 20 years on with Maggie Kirkpatrick for one particular scene. I think Louise Siversen's character had to whack her on the back of the head with a breakaway chair. We had padded Maggie up and rehearsed it OK as usual. Unbeknown to me, Maggie had set me up. We did the take and, as she got smashed in the back, she went down and landed on the mat as planned. I thought all was fine. I was first in after the stunt as usual. 'Maggie, are you OK?' No response. 'Maggie, are you OK?' Again no response. I started to get a little worried. I bent down to check on her, thinking she might have been knocked out. 'MAGGIE, ARE YOU OK?' Then she suddenly rolls over and says, 'Haaa! Got ya!' She had arranged for the camera guys to be pointed at me to get the reaction on my face. I had started to freak out thinking I was responsible for the lead actress being injured or knocked out. A stunt co-ordinator's nightmare. Very funny. Not.

The good thing about working with women and stunts is that unlike men, they don't pretend to know it all. Hence, they listen and take direction for the fights and stunts better than men. So overall, the cast were a fantastic bunch of women to work with. Over the years, I have come to appreciate what a unique experience it was to work with such a great bunch of ladies. Women have a different way of viewing the world than men. If a new cast member came into the Green Room, they would be very conscious of a man in the flock but I think it was Elspeth who said one day, 'Oh, don't worry about Glenn, he's just one of the girls'.

Lou Kelly is now completely deranged and manages a daring hospital escape, only to find her way to the home of Lurch's family. Having been raped by Lurch's brother Sean, she shoots both him and his mum dead. Upon capture, there are so many people vying for Kelly blood, and when she is found dead in her cell in solitary there are no shortage of suspects. It turns out that Janet 'Maggot' Williams [Christine Earle] is the culprit. This, in effect, is something of a cop out, Williams has only been around for a few episodes and has done little more than a bit of posturing and whining. Having such a glorious character as Lou Kelly done away with by such a seemingly ineffectual character is not doing justice to the wonderful work put in on the series by Louise Siversen over the years. But this is not a perfect world, far from it.

Channel 10 received a very special visitor to the set in February 1986, none other than legendary Rat Pack entertainer Sammy Davis Jnr. Davis had declared himself a fan of the show, and especially of one particular cast member as Maggie Kirkpatrick explains:

Sammy was doing the Hilton Cabaret circuit and began saying in the shows that he was addicted to watching Prisoner, and always wanted to find out what The Freak was up to. Naturally, it was too good an opportunity for the publicists at Channel 10 to miss out on. They flew him by helicopter out to the studios. I had seen Sammy perform in my teens in Sydney and I was in awe of him. When we met, I was just a giggling schoolgirl again, but he said some really nice things about my performance, not in a campy way but as an appreciation of me as an actor. He was genuinely interested in the show and how it was made. As a result, a handful of the girls were invited out as his guests at the show the following evening. It just happened to be Valentine's Day and I said I would only come if he sang 'My Funny Valentine' to me on stage. Of course he did and it was a very special moment. When Prisoner *had finished I flew out to Los Angeles and was entertained by Sammy and his wife at their home. He also took me to a recording of* The Cosby Show *and introduced me to his friend Bill Cosby. It was all too brief a friendship as he sadly passed away in 1990. My memories of him are to be cherished – a legendary entertainer and a dear man.'*

A rather complex character entered the Wentworth roll call in Episode 601, her name Katherine Maxwell played by Kate Hood. When we first see Maxwell,

Lou Kelly lies dead.

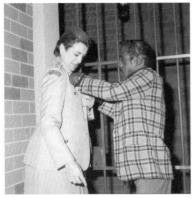

Sammy Davis Jnr meets The Freak.

she is at the end of her tether. Her daughter Linda has a condition which sees her in constant pain and getting weaker. With a marriage that is falling apart, Kath turns to a family friend Bob Moran for support. However, completely traumatised by watching her young daughter in so much pain and with no hope of any relief, Kath administers a mercy killing in order to stop Linda's suffering. Naturally, she finds herself in Wentworth, but it is here, trying to cope with the guilt of her actions, her grief and a struggle to cope inside a penal institution, that Maxwell channels her darker side. Her one motto is do what you must to survive. She becomes embroiled in prison politics and decides to fleece the women to make as much money as she can for whatever the future can offer. Her saviour, in many ways, arrives in the person of Merle Jones [625]. Merle has learning difficulties and has the IQ of a child. Having spent her life in institutions, she had suffered sexual abuse by a foster father whom she nearly killed. Merle is a big strong girl with a keen temper who does not know her own strength. She is transferred from C Block to H Block and immediately befriends Maxwell who, having lost a daughter, is drawn to Merle's childlike qualities. Kath becomes Merle's protector, the mother she never had and, in all her dealings with the women, which would involve some rather dark and dangerous deeds, her one aim is to keep Merle safe and well. Rosanne Hull-Brown was faced with

the difficult task of portraying Merle's innocence to a believable degree, and Hull-Brown's performance hits just the right note. She manages to convey the child within and also a deeper inner turmoil when Merle knows things are not right, but just doesn't have the intelligence to work out what is going on around her. Jones is haunted by the nickname 'Looney', given to her by a less than sympathetic element in the prison, and fears constantly she will be transferred to the mental institution Ingleside. Both Kath's and Merle's emotional journeys through their time in Wentworth add a fascinating layer to what is an exceptionally rich year for Wentworth Detention Centre. Here, Rosanne shares with us her journey to the gates of Wentworth:

Acting the role of Merle Jones in Prisoner *was a memorable experience for me. From childhood, I have been involved in a wide range of roles in the performing arts from ballet, music and drama, to musical theatre and melodramas. I presented music and ballet concerts for my own students and toured as an accompanist with the drama students of the Victorian College of the Arts. I was invited to be part of many wonderful productions through some of those clever and creative people. One of these included writing and performing a one-woman show at the La Mama Theatre in Melbourne where I also enjoyed*

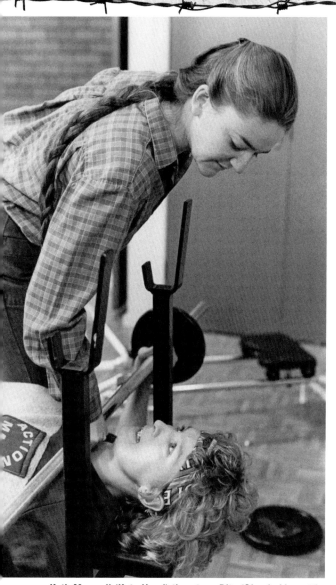

Kath Maxwell (Kate Hood) threatens Rita (Glenda Linscott)

'goodies and baddies' in her comic books. The character of Merle seems to have touched a chord and audiences have found empathy with her situation. She shows a trusting nature and an air of vulnerability in contrast to the bleakness of the conflict and violence that exists in her world. In her mind, she is a super-hero, out to save the world. I thoroughly enjoyed working with such a talented cast, particularly with Kate Hood who played Kath Maxwell. I feel very fortunate to be part of a television series that has remained so loved. The loyalty of the fans is extraordinary, keeping the show alive after all these years.

A familiar face to Australian television viewers was to grace the corridors of Wentworth from Episode 623. Paula Duncan had served seven years in a major success by Crawford Productions, but now found herself transformed into con woman Lorelei Wilkinson. Lorelei had been a friend of Joan's lover Audrey Forbes at the Queensland jail where Audrey was murdered. She is pleased to see Joan, who was a very different person in Queensland, but soon finds out that Ferguson has morphed into something quite different, and the women's loathing of her is something that Lorelei comes to appreciate all too keenly. Paula Duncan herself relives the memory of being Lorelei:

I was a leading role in the very successful series Cop Shop. *The role rewarded me with seven Logie Awards during my time working on that series. During my time on* Cop Shop *there was a producer, Marie Trevor, who was quite a fan of mine. She approached me to play Lorelei. She said it would certainly help me to stop the stigma of 'type-casting' which was a fear after playing such a very much-loved and publicised character like Danni Francis. The two shows were the absolute opposite on and off screen.* Cop Shop *was glamorous; it incorporated comedy, drama, and the private lives of very 'good' people. These cops wanted nothing but the best for everyone. We looked after characters with disabilities, had empathy with those with mental illness, helped local communities, promoted multi-culturalism and always brought the criminals to justice. The feeling behind the show was that of a family; we were all in love with each other off and on the screen. To this day, we are the best of friends, godparents and husbands and wives to some of us. A real family. But the environment was so different too. Our hours were ironically longer, but we worked in and out of the studio, saw daylight and had heaps of light and shade, both on and off the set. In contrast, the prisoners had come from*

participating in experimental theatre with Liz and Lloyd Jones. To this day, I appreciate the experience gained during these times. More recently, as well as teaching music, I have been creating and producing children's musicals for festivals.

At first glance, the role of Merle appears to be challenging but I based my interpretation of this character on my observation of children drawn from years of teaching ballet and music. I approached the role of Merle as an example of a childlike mind in a character most people treated as a volatile and dangerous adult. Merle sees life through the prism of a child's innocence. Life is black and white to her, much like the a bad place; they had tragic backgrounds, some disadvantaged, some just 'bad people'. We never saw daylight. It was a cast of primarily women, who were isolated each day from the community. Living with nothing but violent thoughts, pain, revenge and mostly no hope. Prisoner really required the truth of the actor; there was nothing to hide behind, no make-up and no wardrobe, although my character was an exception there. It was in the writing, the anger, the fear, anxiety. The characters fought each other on a regular basis in the series and often off the set. I found at times it could be

quite hostile even though there was a respect for the actors' worth.

After Cop Shop, whose characters were joined at the hip, it seemed quite lonely but this was probably just how it was for me. My character was very vulnerable; she lived with the devastation of the loss of her child. She definitely suffered with a mental illness and these days would probably be described as bi-polar. Very up and down. I was breast-feeding my daughter Jessica at the time and was suffering with swollen breasts and no

Below Left: Rita rejects Dan Moulton's (Sean Scully) advice. Below Right: Merle's mugshot makes her look more scary than she actually was. Bottom: Merle Jones (Rosanne Hull-Brown) makes a new friend with Tommy.

Left: Paula Duncan having a mad cap moment as Lorelei Wilkinson. Below Left: Michael Winchester as the third Marty Jackson. Below Right: The 1986 staff in-take: Marty, Rodney and Delia (Michael Winchester, Philip Hyde, Desiree Smith.

sleep. When I first got on to the set of Prisoner *I was really scared, all these women who were very strong. Very opinionated, too, politically and intellectually. Glenda Linscott was truly wonderful to me and, above all, I was the only character that The Freak ever loved, so Maggie Kirkpatrick took me under her wing, both on and off the set. I hadn't long come out of giving birth to my daughter Jessica, a very long birth too, and Maggie understood that I suffered the guilt in not being able to deliver a normal birth. That's what happened in those days if you had a caesarean, it was frowned upon. Maggie helped me emotionally get through a lot of that time. Ironically just as she did for Lorelei in the prison. Maggie was the major teacher for me and I am proud to have worked, known and love her on and off the set. The cast were just fabulous, disciplined, direct and talented. Just look up the names in that series. Just the best cast ever. My rape scene was horrendous and scary but, in fact, many experiences were on that set. It was probably more frightening when I stabbed Ray Meagher's character to revenge him.*

Prisoner was and probably still is a success because of the nature of the characters. It can't really date. There is no fashion and no real technical magic – just a whole lot of miserable people struggling with each other and their destiny, living in hope that they will see daylight. These people are all from different backgrounds, ages, ancestry and with totally different dreams. It makes great drama. Amanda Muggleton, Maggie and I got together for Richmond Hill, promoted by the brilliant Brian Walsh. Very different again, and the axing of Richmond Hill was political. I don't have much to say about that except it was so unfair. However, I have learned it can be the nature of this unpredictable business and Richmond Hill was extremely popular.

The changes were truly ringing at Wentworth with the return of Meg's wayward son Marty [625] who reveals he has packed in the Navy. What he doesn't tell his mother at first is that he is training to be a prison officer and sure enough he turns up in Episode 630 with two other trainees, Rodney Adams [Philip Hyde] and Delia Stout [Desiree Smith]. Actor Michael Winchester was the third actor to play Marty Jackson, and turned out to be the longest-serving. Now a drama teacher, director and, by contrast, an organic beef farmer, Michael remembers his time in uniform well:

I was asked to do it by the producers. They had seen my work on TV and in other soaps like Sons and Daughters *and* A Country Practice, *I guess, so I was fortunate enough not to have to audition. I was particularly pleased that I got the role because Glenda Linscott, whom I shared a house with in Sydney, had only recently got her role as Rita, I think it was about a month or so before me. I only watched the series when Glenda started working on it so I can't say I was a fan of it. My first impressions of the cast were very friendly. It was obvious that there was a very strong sense of ownership among the long-standing cast members. I also recall how the non-speaking roles also exuded a sense of ownership too, although when the main cast were around there seemed to be a definite delineation between the main cast and the non-speakers. There was a very professional respect for the main roles from the non-speakers. Quite a few of them had been there longer than many of the major players. They tended to keep to themselves. I can't recall ever hearing any of them speak disparagingly about the main actors and vice versa. Elspeth was very welcoming and warm and encouraging and helpful and down to earth. She was always a friendly face and you got the feeling she was on your side.*

I never researched the role of Marty other than what Elspeth told me, which she thought was rather funny because, if I recall correctly, the character had been in the series before but disappeared. Besides, he looked nothing like me, but the impression I got was that the writers and producers didn't seem to think it was an issue. It was a well-oiled machine and you felt you were a cog with a particular role to play which was fine. The scripts weren't rocket science but it was very good formulaic writing – a particular genre that was done well in Prisoner's case. I saw my job to serve that genre and that formula as best I could. That was my role as a professional actor and that's all I wanted to do really and do it well. The structure of doing the OB stuff first (week A) and then into the studio to shoot the interiors (week B), all within that two-week time frame, established a certain rhythm in terms of learning your lines and making sure you were ready and pacing yourself for the performance. I felt my training at the Victorian College of Arts gave me the tools to deal with the framework: offer a character within the constraints of TV given the script and lack of time. I do recall a memo being sent from the producers that too many cast members were not adhering to the script as written. I didn't think this applied to me because I don't think I purposefully tried to change words. I did think it was a silly way to communicate with

Top Left: Lois Collinder relaxes on The Wattle during a break in filming. Top Right: The crew on the beach filming the ladies in the water. Above Left: The crew on The Wattle recording a scene in the water. Above Right: Rita and Lurch in the water.

your cast. I would much rather be told privately to keep to the script if that's what needed to be said rather than be unsure whether or not the memo applied to me personally. It was like being a student at school, not very mature, I thought. I did have a run-in early in my time there with one of the directors who told me on set and in front of the cast and crew that my 'drunk' acting was piss-poor. I got quite upset about that and told him back to his face that I didn't appreciate the way he spoke to me and that, if he didn't like what I was doing, to give me some direction and offer me some constructive means by which to improve what I was doing. I felt basically he was only having a go at me because his ego had been hurt somewhere along the line by something I might have said or done which was totally unbeknown to me. Anyway, he never spoke to me like that again AND it was Elspeth who came up to me and reassured me that he had been out of line.

With Gerda Nicolson I always thought, 'You can do this standing on your head, why are you on the set of Prisoner?' Very presumptuous of me, mind you, and I only say this because I thought

she was a fine actor. The same with Julia Blake. I now know that both these ladies had worked in theatre and were extremely gifted and talented actors. Who was I to question on why they were working in Prisoner? And what was wrong with working on Prisoner anyway? Maggie Kirkpatrick was a little distant from me; I think that was the way our characters reacted to each other as well. So I was happy to go along with that because it made it easier to act alongside of her. Maggie was very professional, though, and very good at what she did. I respected her because she knew what had to be done and did it really well. Likewise Elspeth, she didn't muck around, she knew what had to be done and did it without any fuss. She was also a lovely person. Maybe because she played my mum I have this soft spot for her? Seriously though, she was just a lovely person, the kind of mum anyone would want.

Just like the previous year, April's annual Logie Awards was surprisingly *Prisoner*-free. Despite some first rate episodes during 1985, the programme was not nominated at all in the 'Most Popular Drama Series' category. The winner for the second successive year, *A*

ERNEST CRAVEN

Played by Ray Meagher

First Episode: 665
Last Episode: 672
Total featured: 8

Ernest Craven can rightly be counted as probably the most corrupt person in the prison system. He stands for everything that is old school in the penal system. The rulebook is thrown out of the window in Blackmoor, his own private playground for crims. When Rita Connors arrives at the hellhole he already knows of her reputation and sets out to break her. But Rita shows Craven she is a match for him. When Rita lays siege to Blackmoor, it is Craven who gives word that that her brother Bongo should be shot dead. This results in the inmates, led by Rita, torching Blackmoor and then in the aftermath being transferred to other state prisons. Craven arrives at Wentworth with an agenda, he knows he must silence Connors. In league with The Freak, they conspire to rid Ann Reynolds of the Governor's chair but Ferguson is determined she will be the next Governor of Wentworth and Craven has to make do with Deputy Governor. An attempted assassination of Rita with a makeshift crossbow is foiled. When Craven has two notorious sex offenders, Stud and Billy, rape Lorelei Wilkinson in solitary even Ferguson is appalled. When he threatens Lorelei's daughter this is the final straw and Wilkinson plunges a dagger in his stomach. It is the end of the line for Craven, his reign of terror finally over.

ROSE 'SPIDER' SIMPSON

Played by Taya Straton

First Episode: 649
Last Episode: 686
Total featured: 37

Spider Simpson is aptly named. She spins intrigue around her, with her own heart of stone beating at the centre of it. Spider sees herself as the business mogul of Wentworth. Whatever you want, Spider can get it – for a price. Her ginger frizzy locks, which cascade from her head, disguise a singular brain which is never more at its nastiest than when her business plans are threatened. The major thorn in Spider's side is Kath Maxwell with the combined forces of The Freak and Rodney Adams backing her. However, when Simpson tries to burn the shop down to stop the contraband being sold under the counter, Joan orders Rodney to teach her a lesson and she is viciously bashed [661]. Spider will stop at nothing to make sure those who have crossed her get their just desserts. When Spider's stash of contraband is found in the grounds by Maxwell, the articles are offered around the prison by Kath but without knowing it, Spider has injected some sweets with poison which subsequently are given to Rita. Spider knows that Maxwell's weakness is Merle so she and her consort Vicky McPherson make Merle believe Ernest Craven's ghost is haunting Wentworth. A constant troublemaker, Spider is transferred to Barnhurst shortly before the end of the series.

Left: Rita gets ready to kill Ferguson. Above: Rita is pulled to safety by her arch enemy.

Country Practice beat its fellow nominees *Neighbours* and *Home and Away* to the post. *Prisoner* was still a television force to be reckoned with and its poor showing at the Awards perhaps saw the Logies wanting the young pretenders to get a look in. The single *Prisoner* nod was for Maggie Kirkpatrick whose continued fine playing of Joan Ferguson saw her earn a nomination for 'Most Popular Actress' which she subsequently lost to Anne Tenney of *A Country Practice*. It remains a great injustice that Kirkpatrick never won a Logie for her stretch of quality performances in *Prisoner*, but that is showbusiness. Kirkpatrick was to reap her reward for continued great playing by an invite to London's West End some years later.

Despite the lack of recognition from Australia's most prestigious television awards, *Prisoner* was to prove it was not finished yet. In an attempt to bring some of Australia's beautiful coastline into the show, the prisoners are allowed to go out on a working party on a boat. All is going well until Rita activates her plan to kill The Freak. Roach Waters [Linda Hartley] uses her charms to let persuade the skipper Mick [Nick Carrafa] to take the boat out onto the open sea. Rita sabotages the engine and radio; she knows that this is

her chance to finally kill Ferguson. When Joan decides to take a lifeboat to shore in order to find help, Rita jumps in and swims after Ferguson with Nancy and Lurch in hot pursuit in a second lifeboat.

The filming in the beautiful waters off the coast of Melbourne certainly brought further glamour to *Prisoner*. Michael Winchester remembers the recording of these memorable scenes, with his character ending up in the water trying to rescue fellow officer Delia Stout:

I remember that day quite well. I was asked to do my own stunt which required me to dive off the back of the boat. For some reason the stunt man didn't show so the producers wanted me to do it but, strictly speaking, it was against union rulings and some of the older actors were a bit disapproving that I was breaking union rules. I didn't really care because I had always fancied myself as a bit of a daredevil. Anyway, in the end I did it but I recall the captain of the boat coming up to me just before they called 'Action'. He said to me, 'Listen mate, no one has bothered to tell you this, but you make sure when you dive, you dive far enough out from the boat because the power of those propellers will drag you back under and into them if you are not careful'. There was a moment of doubt and then thankfully I heard 'Action' so I just went for it. Needless to say, there was no problem but for a moment I did flinch.

Lisa Mullins is inducted and charged with prostitution and blackmail. [651]. It was the second appearance for *Return To Eden* star Nicki Paull, who had previously enjoyed a brief stint as Dennis Cruickshank's wife Doris [478 – 481]:

> I recall absolutely nothing about Doris. It was my first professional role out of drama school, and it felt like such a big deal to be working opposite REAL actors and the like, instead of my student buddies. I had no idea how television worked, as we were trained in theatre, and I didn't know what I was doing. I was terrified. All I remember about it was some critic saying it was a memorable performance – for all the wrong reasons. Not a very salubrious start in the industry, but I survived it.
>
> I can't recall if I auditioned for the role of Lisa Mullins or if I was offered it straight after the success of my appearance on *Return to Eden.* Actually, I think it might have been the only time I have not had to audition for a role. I had a bit of star cred at the time. I had been having trouble with a stalker during *Return to Eden, and when* we finished filming I went out and had all my long, permed hair cut off and dyed blonde to escape from his clutches psychologically. There is a thing called 'rushes clearance' which requires

actors to be ready for a re-shoot until such time as the producers give the all clear that the right stuff is in the can. I knew nothing about this. They nearly died when I turned up at the finishing party in short blonde hair before rushes clearance had been given. But the blonde, spiky hair cut was perfect for Lisa. Now that twenty years have passed, I can be honest with you. No, the cast were not all friendly, and the pecking order backstage was pretty much the same as it was on set. The bullies were the bullies. I don't see any

Below: Rodney Adams (Philip Hyde) welcomes Lisa Mullins #1 (Nicki Paull) to Wentworth. Right: Elspeth Ballantyne goes through a script with Lisa Mullins #2, Terrie Waddell.

Top Left: Maggie Kirkpatrick and Ray Meagher get ready to record a scene. Left: Ray Meagher without Craven's trademark sunglasses. Above: Recording Bongo's ordeal going cold turkey. Below: Brumby Tucker (Sheryl Munks) threatens Blackmoor's Deputy Governor Terry Walters (Bruce Kilpatrick)

Above: Marty Jackson tries to reason for Bongo's life. Top Right: Rita comforts a traumatised Lorelei. Right: Ernest Craven gets his comeuppance from Lorelei. Below Left: Stud Wilson (Peter Lindsay) threatens Rita. Inset Below: Roo Morgan played by Sally McKenzie. Below Right: Spike Marsh played by Victoria Rowland

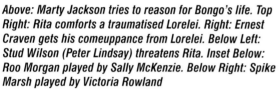

of them anymore so I can say this without fear of retribution. There were a few notable exceptions of course, but I felt very unwelcome when I first arrived. It was like being in prison. Plus the Green Room was almost as cold as the set, which was kept absolutely freezing for the sake of the lighting grid. Cold rooms, cold dynamic. But, most of all, I remember the nightmare of getting sicker and sicker in that freezing environment in the middle of winter and still having to get up at 4am and get myself to work every day. I have always been asthmatic and had a weak upper respiratory system. Well, I went from one chest infection to the next until I was delirious and ready for hospitalisation with pneumonia and pleurisy. It was hell. We had the scene of the breakout by the prisoners, where we covered ourselves in mud to avoid being identified. It was shot mostly outdoors in Melbourne, which is almost as cold as London. Covered in wet mud. In the studio, for these scenes, we were still covered in mud, and the make-up girls would spray us all over to keep the mud wet. So there were days and days of being kept wet with mud in freezing temperatures. It's a wonder we didn't all die. Well, I nearly did, and it was a race against time to get me out of my contract and into hospital. The scripts were obviously written some time ahead, so I had to hang on for a few weeks while they figured out a

storyline that would work. Rather than kill me off, they found another actress with short hair and had my character dye her hair dark and emerge from it looking and sounding like a different person. It was ridiculous but we were all in a bind and the viewers accepted it. Plus, Terrie Waddell was a lovely actress. We went to college together. How they coped in The West Wing when a cast member died at the height of his storyline I can't imagine.

And so, by the miracle of soap, Terrie Waddell was transformed into Lisa Mullins via a particularly powerful hair dye [657]. But a show that had had three Marty Jacksons and two lots each of Tracey Morris, Lorraine Watkins and Brenda Latham to name a few, was not going to baulk at getting another make-over for a character.

The difficult subject of racism was tackled head on when Sarah West [Kylie Belling] arrives at the prison [658]. Aboriginal Sarah is a wild child, with foster parents and authorities unable to control her. She is the subject of racist abuse from the likes of Spider Simpson and Rodney Adams, which only makes things worse. Sarah is brought into Wentworth at the behest of Ann Reynolds' friend and Aboriginal social worker Pamela Madigan [Justine Saunders] who can see that, if nobody can get through to Sarah, she is headed for a life of crime and institutionalisation. Ann knows that Rita would be good for Sarah, and it is pointed out that Sarah cannot embrace her Aboriginal heritage. Over the course of a number of episodes – and some hard-hitting racist taunts along the way from the more unsavoury characters –, Rita proves that black or white, inside everyone is the same. It is the start

Left: Set of the bar in Wentworth town. Below Left: Tuck Shop set. Below Right: Inside Blackmoor set

of Sarah's metamorphosis. Once she has accepted Rita and the Warriors as her friends, her ability to look at herself and her strengths is heightened. By her departure from the prison, Sarah is a changed person. She embraces her heritage, her white foster parents, and heads, we hope, to a positive future.

June of 1986 saw the entire *Prisoner* unit decamp to the Spotswood Pumping Station in Booker Street to film some of the most hard-hitting scenes ever attempted. Blackmoor Prison had been referred to many times in the scripts and was where the very worst of Cell Block H's wild women were dispatched to at the end of their stint in the series but, for the first time, this hell hole of the prison system was being depicted on screen. In the show, Rita Connors is hurriedly transferred to Blackmoor by Joan Ferguson as acting Governor while Ann Reynolds is away. And so the bikie skyscraper finds herself at the very worst place in the penal system. The highly suspect Governor at Blackmoor is one Ernest Craven. This proved to be Ray Meagher's third and greatest contribution to the programme:

I had absolutely no hesitation in accepting the role of Ernest Craven when the offer was put on the table. He was such a lovely, kindhearted person to play! We filmed the Blackmoor scenes at an old disused gas works. The location was sensational. It was so dark and austere that we could easily have been in an old high security prison. The funny thing about that week was that one day we heard a sort of popping in the distance, and thought nothing of it. It turns out, when we watched the news that night, a real armed robbery had taken place at the shopping centre a couple of miles away where an armoured car had been held up and shots were fired. So it really was a case of life imitating art. Craven wasn't based on anyone I knew. It was my idea for him to constantly wear his dark glasses to create a feeling of detachment. With the audience not being able to see his eyes, it created a feeling of fear because people automatically judge emotion by looking at the eyes. Remove that and it is quite scary. The long thin cigarettes were my suggestion, too.

My roles in Prisoner *were very welcome jobs for me. The directors were good and I thought the finished result was always of a high quality. Craven is the* Prisoner *role that is mentioned most often in fan mail I receive. It seems to have been the one that the Prisoner fans have latched on to the most. I am happy to be remembered for playing him. I didn't know a lot of the actors I worked with on* Prisoner *because a lot were Melbourne-based whereas I was always Sydney-*

based. I have over the years kept in touch with Maggie Kirkpatrick. Back in 1978, we both appeared in The Cassidy Album, a trilogy of plays at the Adelaide Festival. Then we took the whole lot to Sydney. It was very heavy and intense stuff. The schedule was punishing with the first play opening on Monday; then the second play on Tuesday then you would repeat those two and on the Friday open the third play. You would then perform all three in a sort of nightly repertory season, sometimes doing two of the plays in one day if you had a matinee. It was really exhausting. But Maggie and I had a great time doing it, and I also knew Maggie from The Strand pub. So it was a real pleasure to work with her again all those years later in Prisoner. *I found Elly Ballantyne delightful to work with, too. Of course, Fiona Spence went on to become my sister for three years in* Home and Away. *I love her to bits, she's very special.*

The Grundy unit was at Spotswood for a week as they shot the all-important scenes including Rita's induction, the courtyard fight with Roo Morgan [Sally McKenzie] and the dramatic highpoint, the shooting of Bongo Connors [Shane Connors]. It was a very gruelling week of recording with long hours, perhaps the greatest pressure being on Glenda Linscott herself who needed to be present for most of the scenes recorded that week.

The razing of Blackmoor proved to be not only memorable moments in the story arc of Rita Connors but some of the most hard-hitting, dramatic moments of *Prisoner's* six hundred odd episodes. It was also instrumental in introducing a number of prisoners who would be transferred to Wentworth following the fire. Naturally, without a prison to govern, Ernest Craven turns up in Wentworth. He is determined to kill the woman who has been responsible for Blackmoor burning down, but it is Lorelei Wilkinson who engineers his downfall. Having already been raped at Craven's behest, when he threatens the life of her daughter Zoe, Craven sees the most powerful force in nature: a mother protecting her young. Lorelei sticks a knife into Craven's stomach, ending his reign of black deeds for good.

In early August, the news broke of the decision by Channel 10 finally to bid goodbye to *Prisoner*. Although the ratings were still very strong in Melbourne, they were wavering in other crucial cities such as Adelaide, Brisbane and, most crucially, Sydney. Long-term producer Marie Trevor told the Sydney Morning Herald:

I believe that when some of the stuff coming up hits Sydney, the ratings will go up. I think

Sydney goes for the harder line. When we have a riot, or even if it's only implied violence, Sydney reacts very well. Melbourne is much more consistent but, if you have a soft story, Melbourne people will love it. Melbourne must see justice done. Sydney is just happy to see the reaction regardless of whether it is justified or not.

Prisoner's other long-term contributor Ian Smith offered:

We realised how powerful the show could be because people were imitating what our prisoners were doing, especially in prison. We were told this by Correctional Services. There was a Governor of one prison who said he was glad the prisoners watched because then he knew what was going to happen in his prison during the next week. The minute we found out we realised we couldn't do this, couldn't do that. About three years ago, we had to send Maggie Kirkpatrick out to different schools to say: 'Look kids, we're acting'. You have to find a way of keeping the stories as strong without being so blatant. It's a powerful medium and you have to be responsible. We were allowed to show blatant lesbianism – that is, a woman saying 'I love you' to another woman – but we are not even allowed to suggest it now because the Board says we have to protect children. They're right, we do. But we brought lesbianism out into the open. We tried to show the naturalness of it. When we first started, the inequality of women in the workforce was much bigger than it is now. We showed women in the workplace being sexually harassed. We covered areas that you could read only on Page 3 of the tabloids. Inequality was so accepted that it was never front page. But we never dropped the entertainment to carry a social

Top Left: Ferguson escorted to her cell by Meg and Joyce. Middle Left: How did you know? Bottom Left: Recording Rita and Joan's final confrontation. Below'' Joan alone in her cell hears the chanting: "Ferguson! Ferguson!"

message because messages can be boring.

Prisoner creator Reg Watson also stated that the show could have gone on and on:

> *It was obvious that, although there are only so many crimes, there are thousands of permutations of these crimes. We could have gone on quite happily. There is no way we were running of out of ideas. And it's one of the best stories ever to go out on, a most gripping story, especially if people watch the last six weeks. I am positive we will go out on a very high note.*

Certainly, had the show been re-commissioned, it might have done so without some of its major players. Maggie Kirkpatrick again:

> *I knew pretty much that Joan Ferguson's race had been run. There is only so much the writers can do with a character, and I had done everything I could with her by then. I had already asked my agent to start looking for other work when my contract came up for renewal. Elly Ballantyne felt the same. We were both planning to leave at the end of the year. As it turned out, that decision was taken out of our hands. In a way I am glad it was, because those final episodes proved to be some of the best I was involved with. A rather lovely lap of honour for those of us who had been around so long.*

As *Prisoner* worked out its notice, there was to be no let up in the action. C Block was now housing men from Blackmoor Prison, and this included the two men that had raped Lorelei: Stud [Peter Lindsay] and Billy [Glennan Fahey]. When Alice arranges a meeting with her potential new beau Harry Grosvenor [Mike Bishop], the unsavoury pair of rapists believe their luck is in. They knock out Harry and set to push themselves on Rita and Lurch. However, they are not reckoning on The Beater. They are overpowered and transferred to a storeroom. The women vote to permanently scar them for their part in Lorelei's rape but, just as Rita arrives to do the deed, Stud and Billy have freed themselves of their binds. It is only the arrival of Merle who bashes them both with a steel bucket that saves the two Warriors. Meanwhile, Marty Jackson has been set up and accused of supplying his old school friend and new arrival from Blackmoor Spike Marsh [Victoria Rowland] with heroin. Kath escapes, thanks to a deal for setting up Spike and Marty, but, in the confusion, has to leave Merle behind. It is a gut-wrenching moment for both of them. Merle is transferred to Ingleside. Kath realises she has been set up herself and breaks free from the villains holding

her to go to Ingleside to help Merle; it is there she is caught and returned to Wentworth. But reconciliation between the two is not going to be easy.

After her short spell in the Governorship is terminated by an exposé on television, Joan opts for long service leave and then resigns as she tries to find an alternative job. Firstly, she finds herself with a trial as a restaurant manager where she deals with a difficult customer in her own firm way. When she applies for a job as a Security Officer however, she runs into an unexpected boss. Willie Beecham [Kirsty Child] is now a respectable head of a security firm, and threatens to blacklist Ferguson from every employer in town. This she does with surprising ease. Ferguson has no choice but to blackmail Minister Dwyer back into her old job. Tired of Wentworth, Joan needs to find a way out of the rut she is in. Rita has non-Hodgkin's lymphoma and the prospects don't look good. But she strikes a deal with Ferguson, both of them conspiring to pull off a big robbery – one last act of bravery for the ever weakening Conqueror – and they both stand to be very rich at the end of it. But can Ferguson trust Connors and vice versa?

The final day of recording was set for Friday 5th September 1986. The recording began at 8:00am with the scene involving John McTernan [new teacher Tom Lucas], Kate Hood and Rosanne Hull-Brown. The tired cast at the end of a long week didn't have time to be too emotional as scenes had to be recorded on time and everyone involved was required to be focused. It had been planned that the final studio scene ever recorded for *Prisoner* would be the final scene taped for the day. At approximately 6:45pm the studio went quiet and Joan, now going quite psychotic, is served a tray of food in her cell by Rita Connors. The trap had been sprung and Rita is shown to have won the war. At 7:15pm, a final wrap was called and that was it. *Prisoner* had finished. The final transmitted scene of the women's recreation period, with Joan being led away to the waiting police car, had been recorded the previous week. Maggie Kirkpatrick has vivid memories of the last day:

> *It was pretty much 'business as usual' although the final scene in the cell with the chanting of 'FERGUSON, FERGUSON' and the appearance of Rita and Meg Morris was somewhat spine tingling. Hopefully, it added to the dramatic impact. As for any emotional atmosphere due to the ending, I can't say that I felt too down in the dumps. We were concluding a part of television history, something that had set the bar very high indeed for writers, producers and actors to come. It had come to a conclusion and not just 'axed'. For that, one has to thank the powers that be at Channel 10 and Grundy. They*

PLEASE COME TO OUR

PRISONER

WRAP PARTY

DATE: FRIDAY SEPTEMBER 5

TIME: 6.30 P.M.
(If taping finishes on time!)

VENUE: STUDIO B

The invitation to the wrap party following the recording of the final scene.

paid the appropriate respect to a show that had gone where no others had dared. As to leaving all those people behind? I was not too morose about leaving other actors. Those who had become close friends, still are. To me the rest were simply colleagues on a most interesting, rewarding journey. It was sad to leave the crew, though, because they were the ones who actually taught me the techniques of television acting. They were a remarkable bunch of people and they have my eternal gratitude and respect.

The final garden scene – recorded the week before the studio scenes – afforded a tribute to the regular non-speaking artists who had worked regularly on the show since the very early days. Barbara Jungwirth is seen in the very earliest episodes and had risen in the rankings to become a speaking artist with her character given a name, Lorna. Similarly, Hazel Henley had become Tina Murray, another example of a non-speaking artist rising through the ranks. The last episode allowed them, and others, well-earned close-ups in recognition of their service to *Prisoner*.

The directing honours for the final two episodes were awarded to long-term director, Sean Nash, who had also contributed some scripts to the show. Sean has gone on to write and direct for *All Saints* and *Home and Away*, but here he recalls bringing *Prisoner* to its conclusion:

Twenty-six years after directing the final episode of *Prisoner: Cell Block H*, it was a pleasure revisiting it via *YouTube*. I was reminded of the enormous talent and commitment of everyone involved. I do recall a general feeling of sadness and disappointment among the cast and crew that a show, pulling rating figures a network would kill for now, was being cancelled. And there was an enormous amount of pressure to ensure it got shot. With the sets being pulled down – and destroyed – the moment we moved out of them for the last time, there was no going back for re-shoots if it wasn't all successfully in the can. Not only was the studio already booked for other things the following week, the contracts of the cast and most of the crew expired on the final day of shooting. Each two-hour block of *Prisoner* was completed over a four-week period. One week of prep, one of shooting on location, the third week spent in the studio, the fourth in post-production. The fact this was happening simultaneously meant that, screen-time wise, a feature-film-length block of *Prisoner* was

Above: Director Sean Nash. Right: Two friends celebrate as the series draws to a close.

being produced each week. Quite extraordinary and something I've found people overseas – particularly in the States – find hard to believe. When Sammy Davis Jnr., a huge fan who had episodes of the show flown out to him wherever he was performing in the world, visited our set and he sat with me in the control room – a real buzz for me. He was astounded to discover we produced two hours of the show a week. The fact was that this last location week was pretty big by regular standards of Prisoner – night shoots, windows being smashed, buildings being scaled, shooting on roof-tops. It put extra pressure on us all to not only complete the schedule in the time allowed and from memory I think they might have given us an extra day, but also make it look the best we could for our go-out. The script for the final episode was co-written by producer, the late Marie Trevor and by associate producer Ian Smith. It afforded the cast and crew a real opportunity to strut their stuff one last time. A co-writer credit on Prisoner wasn't unusual; scripts were contracted in half-hour increments, and often one writer would write the first half of an episode and another the second. In particular, the first segment of the final episode was dialogue free save for one brief exchange, drawing in audiences around the world by telling the story with an evocative music track, edited by John Clifford White. It was an action-packed story devised by Alison Nisselle, Tony McDonald, John Coulter and Robert Greenberg. It was shot mainly on location by a talented but shivering crew over a number of cold Melbourne nights and performed predominantly alone by Glenda Linscott playing dying bikie Rita Connors. The location for the ASA Finance company that Rita

robbed and where Joan Ferguson was arrested was also used as the police station where Joan was finger-printed. This location was the then offices for Grundy Television in the Melbourne suburb of Richmond. The smashing of the window was the real thing. A real chair through real glass, and not special fx breakaway sugar glass. Safety officers wouldn't allow that today. A glazier was on standby to immediately replace the shattered panel so the Grundy staff (accounts department, from memory) could use their office again first thing in the morning. Small piece of trivia: the double for school teacher Tom Lucas (played by John McTernan, a hugely talented and under-used film and television actor in this country) when he rode Rita Connors around Ann and Meg on his Harley-Davidson, was stunt and safety officer Glenn Ruehland who later worked on Moulin Rouge, Superman Returns, Scooby Doo and The Great Gatsby. In the final scene of Joan Ferguson being walked past inmates and staff of Wentworth Detention Centre to the waiting police car, I went to the trouble of shooting close-ups of all the background players. The same non-speaking players would come in every week for group scenes in the Rec Room, or out in the grounds, and I did this as a mark of respect for those women. A couple had been with the show since the beginning. At the end of shooting that sequence, one of them sought me out to give me a bollocking for not remembering all their names. Rightly so. Back then as a much younger director I was totally focussed on getting two hours of television a week in the can, sometimes to the exclusion of social interaction on the set. Social interaction after we wrapped for the day was very much a different thing, though. That cast and crew certainly knew how to party. And a final piece of trivia: I can confirm it WAS Ian Smith doing a Hitchcock as the driver of the police car Joan is put into after being arrested at the finance company.

The one person who might have felt the loss of the show keenest was Elspeth Ballantyne. Of the 692 episodes broadcast, Elspeth had appeared in 669 of them. She is the only major character to have appeared in both the first and last episodes, and what an epic journey she undertook on screen as Meg Jackson / Morris. Elspeth sums up her feelings on that final day:

My last day was a mix of emotions. Great relief that I was to start a new life and enormous sadness that I was leaving a crew of men that I had been with every day bar the weekends for eight years. Men whose lives I had been sharing, hearing about their first girlfriend to their wedding, then on to their first child. That was my problem, and it kept choking me up to the extent that the cast for me meant very little as did the scenes I

was in. The actors were always going to be in my future. I knew Maggie, Glenda, Lois et al. would be on my radar forever, but crews have to move on. So I was very much in turmoil about them. Having been in the job for so long, although very respectful of the privileges it provided me, I was happy to let it go.

Permission had been sought from Channel 10 to hold a huge party in Studio B following the recording. The sets had been pulled down when work had finished on them throughout the day and now just a bare studio was left where Wentworth Detention Centre had once stood. For eight years the cameras had rolled in Studio B, but now there was one final riot happening, a riot of celebration as all involved in the making of the show gathered to party and say their goodbyes. According to the printed invitation to the wrap party in Studio B, 6,480 actors, writers and directors and 784 crew members had worked on *Prisoner* since it began production in October 1978.

The Australian premiere of Episode 692 went out at 8:30pm on Thursday 11th December 1986 for Melbourne audiences, who had remained devoted to their local drama heroines. This was in stark contrast to the schedulers of Channel 10 in Sydney. They cut down the transmissions to one hour per week. Then, they rested it for a short while before seeing out the episodes in slots around 11:00pm. Sydney fans had to wait until August 1987 before they witnessed the fate of Rita and Joan. Thankfully, the last few episodes had at least been granted a traditional 8:30pm airing. Even before Sydney viewers had a chance to take in the ramifications of the last few episodes, the rumblings of a distant riot could be heard. Original inhabitants Bea, Franky, Vera and Erica were about to get a whole new lease of life with telly-obsessed Brits who were embarking on their own life sentence. *Prisoner*-mania was waiting to be born on the other side of the world.

The final episode wrap party

The Oldest Biker In The World:
A Warrior's Lament

Rita Connors' war cry as she exits the security van as she arrives at Wentworth [585] is emblematic of her attitude to life. A biker's moll, her world is one of gang culture. You are either with her, or against her. Together with her boyfriend Slasher and brother Bongo, Rita is part of The Conquerors, a notorious biker gang whose bitter rivalry with The Eagles is to prove fatal for Slasher as tensions hot up. At six feet two inches tall, Rita Connors is an imposing sight. Not that this cuts any ice with a certain Joan Ferguson who, within a couple of minutes of Rita landing in reception for her induction, manages to put herself right at the top of the towering figure's hate list when she rips off Connors' jacket chains. Rita has been sent for remand prior to trial for assault after she discovered Slasher in bed with another woman. The 'other woman' came off an unhealthy second best in the ensuing showdown. 'I know scum when I see it, and right now I am staring it in the face...,' sneers Ferguson as she delivers Rita to her cell. But she gets an early inkling of the Connors grit when the The Beater grabs her by the lapels, staring Ferguson straight in the eye and spits, 'That's funny,

so am I.' Joan is shaken at the sheer brazenness of the physical skirmish. It is at that moment Ferguson realises that Rita Connors is in a whole new league of lag. Cracking the new arrival is going to be one of The Freak's greatest challenges.

Rita arrives at Wentworth at a time of great change; she has only been there a short while when Ann Reynolds resigns and in steps Bob Moran [Peter Adams], a tough no-nonsense figurehead who wastes little time in putting up hard measures for the women. Rita is initially not interested in the Top Dog position. She just wants to be left alone as her trial approaches, but the machinations of Lou Kelly make that almost impossible. Rita is only in Wentworth for a short time before Lou and her henchwoman Alice Jenkins try to bash the bikie. But she is not known as 'Rita the Beater' for nothing. This lady has been in many a scrap and not always facing women either, so she sees off the ambush with relative ease [585]. This only causes the humiliated Kelly to redouble her efforts to rid Wentworth of Connors whom she recognises will never bow to her steam press authority. Rita's Aunt

Above: Rita examines a note hidden in her food. Top Right: Rita arrives at Blackmoor. Bottom Right: The 1986 cast.

Ida [Paddy Burnett] sneaks in a CB Radio which Rita uses to contact Slasher to keep up to date with news of the outside and to use the radio as a way to keep the airwaves hot with talk of amour with her boyfriend. But, when Joan slashes Rita's beloved leather jacket [593] with a scalpel, Rita finds a whole new use for the CB. She arranges for The Conquerors to pay a visit to Ferguson's house where they trash all of Joan's most-treasured possessions [594], a warning from the leather-clad bikers to stay away from Rita. But they severely under estimate Ferguson's wrath. The cunning keeper visits The Conquerors' hideout, douses it in petrol while they are inside partying and sets fire to the building [596]. Thinking it is the work of their arch-rivals The Eagles, a bitter gang war breaks out and Slasher is killed. Biker and Minister – yes, there is such a combination [Dan Moulton played by Sean Scully] – arrives at Wentworth to deliver the devastating news [598]. Worse is to come when Lou Kelly organises a riot in order to stamp her authority on new Governor Bob Moran. She hangs phantom lagger Eve Wilder [600] and locks arch-rivals The Freak and The Beater in the laundry, ordering them to fight to the death [601]. Thankfully, the riot is quelled before the two mighty combatants have to reach the final decision, but it is an epic struggle and both women are forced to acknowledge the sheer stamina and strength of each other. Had the situation been different, they might admire each other. But the battle lines have been drawn. There is no going back. Ferguson now knows that Connors can match her physically but, as ever with the black haired behemoth, The Freak intends to outsmart her new rival. It has worked in the past and it will work again.

Sentence having been passed, Rita realises she is staying in Wentworth for some time. In order to satisfy her craving for gang culture and to raise the spirits of her friends, she forms the Wentworth Warriors. Lurch Jenkins [Lois Collinder] is now firmly on Rita's side, along with Julie Egbert [Jackie Woodburne] and newly arrived Nancy McCormack [Julia Blake]. Stepping easily into the mantle of Top Dog, Rita has whisky hidden in tennis balls which are thrown over the fence. She intends to make her stay in Wentworth as big a party as possible. But the spectre of Ferguson won't go away. The arrival of Kath Maxwell [Kate Hood] at Wentworth for the mercy killing of her daughter Linda brings fresh trouble for Rita. Merle Jones' [Rosanne Hull-Brown] transfer from C Block sees Maxwell bonding with the poor unfortunate whom she vows to protect and it is a desire not to hurt Merle that often has Rita holding back in the tussle for supremacy between the cunning housewife with the impossibly long hair and the leather-loving lanky lady. When Rita learns that Ferguson was responsible for the fire that led to the gang war in which Slasher died, she vows to kill Ferguson. Rita arranges for Ferguson's house to be burned down and knowing The Freak will come after her in the dead of night, Rita is waiting. With Lurch's help, they drag the warder up to the roof, threatening to throw her off in order to give her a real fright [623]. Rita decides not to kill her arch-enemy. She is not prepared to spend the rest of her life in prison but she knows the day will come when Ferguson will be hers. As time passes, we see Rita transform. Freed of the social pressure to be seen to be a tough biker, we come to see a warm and caring nature for those less able to cope with the stresses of prison life. Her own family values are strong, she cares deeply for her brother Bongo who is going off the rails swiftly. Being powerless in prison, when she could be helping him fight his demons, is reminiscent of the plight of Bea with Debbie and Myra with Kay. This Top Dog feels the hurt; she struggles to be able to show emotions other than anger but her heart beats loudly and strongly for those she likes and feels are worthy of her friendship.

A plan forms in Rita's mind when a working party is required to be taken to a boat, *The Wattle*, for cleaning duties. Persuading Mick, the skipper's mate, to take the boat out into the open water, Rita sabotages the engine and the radio. Out at sea there would be no escape for Ferguson. Disposing of officers Marty Jackson and Delia Stout in the water, it is the intervention of Nancy McCormack which stops

Left: Lois Collinder, Glenda and Maggie Kirkpatrick celebrate the 600th Episode. Below: Glenda Linscott goes glam.

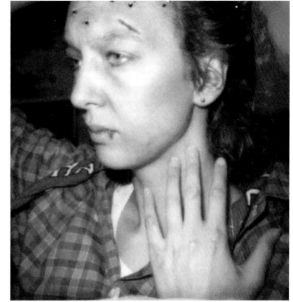

Continuity stills for make-up.

Rita from committing murder. But Rita is not finished yet. Ferguson dons a lifeboat to row to shore to get help, and Rita swims after her. On an isolated spot of coastline Rita secretly tracks Ferguson and just as she is about to make her move Connors trips over the edge of a precipice [643]. A startled Ferguson grabs her and pulls Connors back to safety, much to the shock of the Warrior Queen. It is an unexpected helping hand, and with 'one all' on the score sheet the battle lines remain drawn but not crossed.

Ferguson thinks she has won the war when she transfers Rita to Blackmoor behind the back of Governor Ann Reynolds [664]. However, despite the appalling physical and psychological punishment meted out to Connors, she strengthens her resolve to smash the corrupt system. The true horror of Ernest Craven's administration is felt when Rita's junkie brother Bongo is paraded before her and shot dead [667]. The murder of her brother sets off a volcanic reaction within The Beater and she leads the torching of Blackmoor, resulting in its being gutted. Rita's emotional scarring at the death of her brother is a wound that cannot be healed.

It is the diagnosis of non-Hodgkin's lymphoma that finally flaws the irresistible force. With her strength being sapped daily and embarking on a gruelling course of chemotherapy, Rita even starts to alienate those around her, especially her best friend in the prison, Alice. Apparently siding with Joan Ferguson, the women are at a loss to know just what has come over the once mighty Beater. But Rita has one final ace up her sleeve which would change Wentworth forever...

Just as Joan Ferguson arrived in 287 to give *Prisoner* a whole new lease of life, so the arrival of Glenda Linscott to the series injected the show with a mighty pump of adrenaline when it needed it the most. Most of the true high spots from the final year of *Prisoner* can be pointed squarely at Linscott's exquisite portrayal of this impressive new inmate.

Born on 6th September 1958, Glenda takes up the story of a birth in a perhaps unexpected location:

I was actually born in Zimbabwe (then called Rhodesia) in a tiny little village called Zvishavane. We moved to the UK in 1965 for eighteen terrible months when the British Government refused to recognise Dad's thirteen-year service in the British South African Police where he had been an Inspector. He had to go back to basic training. My youngest brother was born with clubfeet and life in the UK was very miserable for us. So we took advantage of the £10 Pom ticket and emigrated back to the sunshine. My brothers and I all grew up in the land Down Under.

From an early age, Glenda had a yearning to be an actress, having started with a youth theatre company in Adelaide. When she was old enough Glenda enrolled herself into NIDA (National Institute of Dramatic Art) for formal training. At over six feet tall, Glenda was never going to blend into the background. Upon graduating, she returned to South Australia where she gained some valuable Theatre In Education experience. But work was not easy to come by, agents were not too keen to take such a tall actress onto their

Played by Kate Hood

First Episode: 601
Last Episode: 692
Total featured: 82

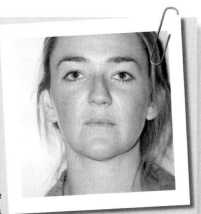

Kath Maxwell spends most of her time in Wentworth consumed by an almighty guilt at having killed her own daughter. When she first arrives she is reviled by the women, as anybody committing an offence against a child always must be. Her platonic friendship with Bob Moran sees him trying his best to protect her from the wrath, but when the women find that she is friends with the Governor, it makes the situation worse. Kath has, though, a survivor instinct; she is drawn into Maggot Williams schemes for dealing drugs; it is an unwise alliance. Fate is not kind to Kath during her stay in Wentworth. When Ferguson uses Nancy McCormack's diary to spy on the women, Kath mistakenly gets the blame and is bashed by Rita and Lurch [620]. When Kath destroys a videotape of the Pringles' wedding, she is then sprayed with a fire extinguisher for her trouble by the Wentworth Warriors. It further escalates the war between Maxwell and Connors. Ferguson – realising Kath's physical disadvantage against the towering duo of Rita and Alice – has Merle Jones transferred from C Block. Merle has learning difficulties but has a nasty temper and is very strong. But Kath – who is still inwardly grieving for the loss of her daughter – finds that she likes the troubled soul that is Merle, drawn to her childlike innocence. So begins the extraordinary relationship between the pair. Kath becomes fiercely protective of Merle against the cruel taunts of 'looney' and the attempts to take advantage of her by the more unsavoury women in H Block. Maggot convinces Merle to attack Rita, something Kath would never do for fear of Merle being transferred to a psychiatric institution and, in the chaos, pregnant Lexie ends up getting thumped. And so the war goes on between Maxwell and her conspirators and the Warriors. Things reach a turning point when, in return for setting up Marty Jackson and Spike Marsh in a drug bust, Maxwell is hijacked out of Wentworth to a remote location. In the confusion of the snatch, Merle is left behind and transferred to Ingleside. With the guilt of leaving Merle behind almost unbearable, Maxwell escapes from the villains harbouring her and goes to Ingleside to see Merle, whereupon she is promptly arrested and returned to Wentworth. Merle is now completely anti-Kath for leaving her behind, and refuses even to talk to her best friend. It is new teacher Tom Lucas that forces Kath to face up to the terrible emotional trauma of her crime and to see that, in Merle, she has a second chance to be a mother figure. Finally, the pair are reunited, both needing the other equally. The last we see of Kath Maxwell in 692, she is Top Dog – and, with no other agenda than helping Mrs. Reynolds implement her reforms, Rita gives her a seal of approval.

books as they knew casting people in television and theatre would see it as a big disadvantage. Taking a backpacking trip through Europe at the age of 21 en route to visit her grandmother in England, Glenda was inspired by seeing Greek theatre and knew in her heart her journey to be an actress was not over. A spell in London was spent working and saving money in order to pay for classes at the Actor's Centre in Sydney. It was after a full five years of slog to become established as an actress, and with Glenda's hope of decent theatre roles waning, that *Prisoner* came knocking at her door. With only a handful of small

television roles to her credit, again Glenda reveals the importance of *Prisoner* in her career:

I'd virtually given up hope of getting any work, let alone any television work. Then I was called in to audition for Prisoner, *the first audition I had done since leaving drama school five years earlier. I didn't know much about the character but just went for it, and they said, 'That's it, that's who we want'. Apparently, they had been looking all over Australia for Rita and they knew straight away they wanted me to play it. That's*

Glenda poses as Angela for the Prisoner play, 1989.

actually arrived in the studio for the first time, I had thought a lot about Rita's world, what went on inside her head. She was very much a three-dimensional person to me. I think the writers then fed off that. We became good for each other.

Working with Maggie Kirkpatrick, which I did so much in Prisoner, was a joy. I remember when Ferguson slashed Rita's leather jacket and I was stood at the security gate screaming for her to stop. At the end of the take Maggie announced to everyone, 'At last, a bloody theatre actress', and that was a huge accolade from Maggie. She always stuck up for me. When we went to do all the scenes for the Blackmoor storyline I was featured in virtually every one. We did such long days, I was totally exhausted and, in fact, I collapsed towards the end. Maggie really hit the roof. 'What are you trying to do to her? She needs rest, for God's sake.' She really let the production team have it. And she was such an experienced actress that you could only learn from her. Sally McKenzie who played Roo Morgan in the Blackmoor storyline was in the year above me at NIDA.

what happens in our profession sometimes, they are looking for a certain something. A look or a personality and the minute you walk into an audition they know you are right or not. For once, my height counted in my favour. At that stage, I had no idea that Rita was going to become such an important character. I was just so excited to get the part. Had I known that she was going to be so significant for me as an actress and was to become Top Dog, my agent might have got me some more money. I signed up for Equity minimum (the lowest an actor can earn under union rules) for the whole of my stint on the programme. When the deal was done, I then started to think about the character. I was determined to find out about life for prisoners so I arranged a discussion group at Mulawa Detention Centre in return for some drama lessons. I put the character on the table and asked everybody to discuss what motivated Rita and how she would cope on the inside. So that was an interesting discussion and gave me some thought processes to carry into work with me. So by the time I

The fans seem to remember that physical fight in the laundry as being a highpoint. But it was so well choreographed, like a dance. It was determined very early on that Rita and Joan would fight like men. Full on. I think the fight went on for something like 11 minutes of screen time. Someone pointed out that we would probably both be dead after an encounter like that. Our stunt co-ordinator Glenn Ruehland was really brilliant. I learned so much about performing stunts from him. He had our safety in mind all the time but managed to put together a routine that really leapt out through the television screen. When he showed me what he wanted me and Maggie to do I just got a massive fit of giggles. I thought, 'I can't do that'. But, of course, in the hands of such an expert teacher anything is possible. The arrival of Rita also spelled good things for Lois, too. They teamed Lurch up with Rita. Lois and I developed a close relationship which lasts to this day. We had so many wonderful scenes to play together, both comic and dramatic.

After Prisoner finished, I was out of work for 18 months. I had won a Penguin Award for my role in the series but it seemed I was back to square one. Struggling to get work. I decided to get married, and, soon after, my husband was offered work at the BBC in London so I went along to see what would happen. I had only been there a day, I think, when the phone rang and a voice asked me if I would be interested in being part of the stage version of Prisoner. My character had not gone to air in the UK at that point so they gave my character a name, Angela Mason. I was really playing Amanda Muggleton's role from those early episodes. The tart with a heart. To be honest, although I was billed on the poster as being from the TV series I was glad nobody really knew me. The crowds used to follow Elspeth and Patsy. It was frightening. Every night at the stage door there was what seemed like a mob. The two ladies would be engulfed by people wanting autographs. I had great fun being on the road with all those English girls playing the other roles. We toured to some absolutely beautiful theatres, I was sat in Cliff Richard's dressing room at the Dominion Theatre in the West End. It could not have been more exciting. Down the track I then became a mother, my marriage ended and I started my own business. But the spectre of Prisoner would not go away. In 2009, Barry Campbell contacted me about flying to the UK to appear for the Prisoner Fan Club. It was the most marvellous experience ever to know that my work twenty-five years before is still being enjoyed on DVD. We took it one step further the following year and I performed a one-woman show, Retrospectively Rita, in which Rita is the catalyst for lots of different characters that I have played on stage over the years. Maggie Kirkpatrick was there too, so the fans just lapped up seeing the both of us together on stage. I had become quite down about my career prospects and it made me doubt my talent and the whole experience lifted me, made me feel some self worth. Made me believe in myself again. The fans of Prisoner have done so much for me, and to think Rita means so much to them, it is just very special.

Post-Prisoner, Glenda has had great success on stage with productions such as Steaming, Scenes From An Execution, Daylight Saving, Shirley Valentine and Bad Blood Blues for which was she nominated for a Green Room Award. She has continued to work in television with a regular role as Dr. Tootsie Soames in Murder Call to her credit, along with guest appearances in many series including All Saints, Underbelly: Infiltration, MDA and as Dr. Jessica Girdwood in Neighbours. Glenda also runs her own public speaking and performing courses under the name Perform with Confidence.

Left: Maggie and Glenda reunited in the UK, 2010. Above: A portrait of Glenda taken twenty five years after Prisoner had finished.

Living Next Door To Alice

Who the **** is Alice ?

She's not the most subtle operator in the prison. She is clumsy and men visitors to the prison have to have guards just to keep them safe from her lustful attention. Alice Jenkins is one of the real backbones of prison life. Not that this is always a good thing. She doesn't always side with justice and is easily led, but for the most part she is 'fair dinkum'. Nick-named after the impossibly tall ghoul with the hangdog face in the 1960s television comedy *The Addams Family*, Alice seems to have had a hard life. Her mother raised her and five siblings alone with their father having abandoned them. Being raised on a farm, Jenkins had little chance to develop social skills. The art of courtship was lost amid a constant struggle of keeping the farm going and earning enough to put food on the family table. Alice sadly, lacks the ability to really determine what is the winning side during her early time in Wentworth. Her size and natural strength are sought by the likes of Reb Kean and Lou Kelly

to act as regular 'muscle' as they bully the women into doing their bidding. Lurch even falls prey to Lou Kelly's machinations when she is forced into admitting to the murder of Sam Greenway. Although Alice is first credited in Episode 448, she actually doesn't get her first line until Episode 509. Inherently Alice is a good person, and following the riot in Episodes 600 and

Below: Lois Collinder as Alice cleaning The Wattle. Right: The classic Carmen Miranda song. Bottom Right: Rita and Alice pose on The Wattle.

601, the women teach Lou and Lurch a lesson by having a mock hanging. It is at that point that Alice knows she has to keep clear of Kelly. It marks the start of her friendship with Rita that was to develop greatly over the final year of *Prisoner*, and by the end they are the very closest of friends. It is Lurch who becomes confidante to Rita when she learns she has cancer.

Lurch is always up for a lark, none more so than when the Wentworth girls put on a fashion show with entertainment [582]. Lurch's star turn as Carmen Miranda remains a fan favourite moment within the show, and was specifically designed to incorporate Lois Collinder's skills as a singer and dancer in stage musicals. The song itself, 'Down South America Way', was written for the musical It Happened in Tanjablanca by Grundy's executives Don Battye and Peter Pinne, later responsible for the *Prisoner* musical.

Jenkins suffers the loss of her mother and brother at the hands of Lou Kelly when the mullet-haired bitch escapes and heads for the Jenkins farm for shelter. Raped at the hands of Alice's brother Sean, she shoots him dead followed by Alice's mother Flora [611]. Naturally, when she is returned to Wentworth, Jenkins vows to kill her. But fate steps in, and Janet Williams is eventually collared after Kelly's dead body is found in solitary [615].

Lurch also finds a love interest in the final days of the show with Blackmoor transfer Harry Grosvenor (Mike Bishop). They initially meet at the connecting security gate between the blocks where the men are working and quickly the mutual attraction grows between them [679]. Harry is in for rape, but it transpires that he didn't actually physically rape the victim but watched the events unfolding, making him a party to the crime. When Harry is transferred to Barnhurst, Alice is offered a transfer too, but she knows she can't. Rita is dying and Alice knows she needs to be with her best friend until the end. But the signs are good for Grosvenor and Jenkins; they are in love and we hope that Lurch finds a happy life with a man to care for her in the blurry landscape beyond Episode 692.

Lois Collinder had mostly amateur stage experience as an actor before *Prisoner*, but found herself being put forward for a role in the massively popular series. Lois takes up the story:

I originally went for a general audition for Grundy. I didn't know quite what they were looking for but they did send me, through my agent, a couple of scenes. They said they wanted me to play such and such in those scenes. So I

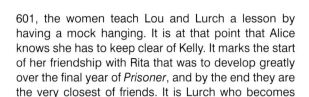

RODNEY ADAMS

Played by Philip Hyde

First Episode: 630
Last Episode: 692
Total featured: 56

Rodney Adams is part of the new intake of recruits along with Marty Jackson and Delia Stout. Adams wastes little time in sucking up to Joan Ferguson and, as such, gets drawn into her bogus schemes and cruel vendettas. Rodney develops an almost schoolboy crush on Kath Maxwell while at the same time baiting her adopted friend Merle Jones, whom he frequently calls 'Looney'. Mrs. Reynolds sees through Adams very early on, yet, like Ferguson, she cannot prove his misdeeds; otherwise she would have him marching out of the gate with his notice in his hand. When Spider Simpson steps out of line, it is Adams who finds himself having to bash the prisoner in the dead of night in a hard-hitting end of episode moment. The women strip Rodney and borrow his uniform when they want to make a video to send to Nancy McCormack; Rodney narrowly avoids being caught out by Mrs. Reynolds over the theft of the uniform. When the women have Adams followed by a paroled Lisa Mullins, they record his romantic speeches from The Importance of Being Earnest which he is performing with a local dramatic society. The women play it over the prison intercom system causing Adams to smash the cassette recorder in fury. Mrs. Reynolds catches him in the act and forces him to replace the recorder out of his own pocket.

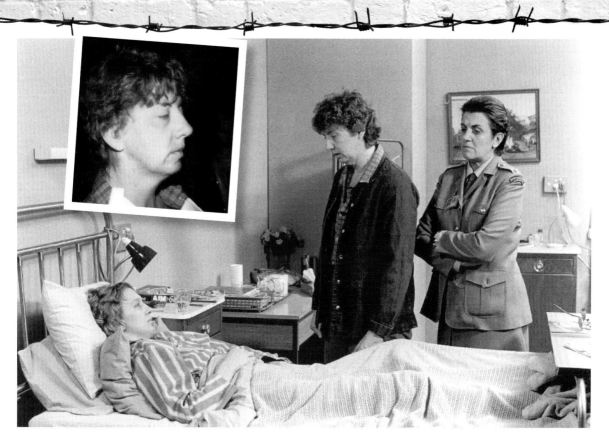

Inset: A make-up continuity still. Above: Lurch visits the bedside of a very ill Rita in a touching moment from the last days of the show.

went along with about ten other women; Jan Russ had just started casting and the previous casting director was also there. I did the audition and, probably the next day, I got a call from my agent to say they loved the audition but they didn't have a role suitable in the scripts that had already been written to be able to introduce me into the show. They asked me to come into the show in a non-speaking role. In time, I would get lines, they said, and my character would grow. So that's what happened for the next year to eighteen months, I would be in scenes, have a few lines. I was working for two or three weeks, then I wouldn't hear from them for a while. Then I would get a script, a contract for maybe four weeks and the character would be a little bit bigger. They began to work me in as Lou Kelly's sidekick, which sadly meant that Reylene Pearce [Phyllis Hunt] disappeared. I was the perfect size to be a heavy. I had to learn to bash people up with the stunt co-ordinators. I did stunt classes to learn how to throw a punch, and react to a punch as well. That went on for quite some time. So I was working for three or four weeks, then nothing for four weeks. On and off. I was just trying to keep going, paying the rent with some training films and voice-overs

in between the calls for Prisoner.

We would be called at 7:00am, as filming always started at 8:00am. The studios at Nunawading were quite a long way from the city, a good 45 minutes drive depending on the traffic. Then you would put on your denims, add the smelly runner shoes you had to wear, a dusting of powder and that was it – you were ready and filming would start. At least two days a week you would do the outside scenes [OB] which meant you were filming in the grounds. One day a week, usually Monday, was rehearsal day for all the inside scenes that the director was working on for the week, blocking the moves for actors and cameras. Tuesdays, Thursdays and Fridays we filmed inside the studio and we worked on four episodes at least, always. Two episodes you were working with the director on the outside broadcast and then another director who had already recorded his OB material would be working with you in the studio. Then, if for some reason you didn't get all the scenes in the can for the previous week, you could be picking up scenes for a further two episodes. I always spent a long time at the weekend writing out my running sheet, so I knew what scenes I was

Top: Rita and Lurch. Above Left: Lois Collinder, 1986. Above Right: Lois, Rosanne Hull-Brown and Kate Hood celebrate the success of the series, 1986.

in and what had happened before in the script because we never filmed anything in order. We would do all the Rec Room scenes, then the Dining Room scenes, then the Muster scenes and so on. I learned a lot from all the actresses on the show. Watching how they worked, how the director worked. You would watch which of the actresses were more professional than others and why that was so. There were so many really good actresses that came through Prisoner, some of the best actors in Australia. I used to hate anything that had anything to do with physical sporting things. I am not a very sporty person anyway. The days were tiring enough without having to spend energy on physically playing games or roller-skating, that sort of thing.

Often, if one person got a cold or the flu, it would go through the whole cast. There were times in those cells when there were actresses in those beds because they were not well and they were fetched from the bed to do their scenes when required. The worst time I think was in the days when Pepe Trevor was there. We all got this really bad flu and I think production had to stop for a couple of days. But you had to be on your death bed before they would consider such a thing. We were not consulted a lot on our characters, although you were encouraged if you had any ideas to write them down and send them to the storyliners. Having said that, if the writers were aware of your talents they would try and work something in. I remember that Pepe Trevor was the only person who could roller-skate. They wrote a whole big storyline where we were all roller-skating around the prison and that is scary, as anyone will know. You try and get about on skates and they just go from under you. Sometimes we would pick up on inconsistencies in the script for our characters. When you were saying one thing one week and then contradicting it the following week. But they generally said, 'Oh, don't worry about it, no one will remember so just go with it.' Occasionally, we would fight when we felt the script wasn't quite right, and the director would ring the office and put your case. But they didn't like to change things too much as it disrupted production.

I'm not sure why Prisoner has proved so popular over the years. There is something fascinating about women in prison which people seem to like. It also has the elements of melodrama about it. There are goodies against baddies and we all like to see the goodies win. A lot of really good actresses went through the show which helped enormously. When the core cast was strong the show itself was very strong. My favourite scene is the scene I did with Nancy after Lurch's brother and mother had been killed. I had a long monologue about how my brother would take me to the circus when it came to town. It was an emotional moment for her. Lurch was often silly and dumb but that scene allowed me a really dramatic moment and is some of my best work in Prisoner. That and, of course, the Carmen Miranda number, that was such a hoot to do. And the really funny lead up with Lurch trying to find the fruit. Another thrill was Sammy Davis Jnr.'s visit. He was a huge fan of Maggie's and they became quite good friends. He came out to the studios as he wanted to see us and meet us. To me he is the ultimate entertainer; I have his recordings on my iPod now. I had finished my scene, and was in wardrobe changing; when they said he was on set. I ran back into the studio. He had been introduced to the main cast so I came running up rather late to join the group. He turned around and said, 'Here's a face I recognise,' and I was just beside myself as he shook my hand. He then went up to the control room and watched us shoot a scene in the corridor.

One vivid memory is those scenes on the boat. I remember being just so exhausted. We had to be on the boat for 6:30am so The Wattle could be out in the middle of the bay for 8:00am to start filming. It would take an hour and half to get there. We would not get back until 7:30pm and then you had to get home. It was lovely to have the chance to do something different, but we paid the price. The following week everyone was just so tired and exhausted. Similarly, filming outside Channel 10 in the winter was just so cold, with the temperatures in the minuses with the wind factor. Sometimes television can take a long time to do a couple of minutes, so under those conditions it's exhausting. I remember being on the roof of Channel 10 when we were trying to throw The Freak over the edge. You can imagine the wait we had while they rigged Maggie up so she was secure. That seemed to take hours as we were freezing in the dead of night. Those were the things that made it tough. The times when you do a take first time and it's all fabulous, that is when it's the most rewarding. I was very happy with the way the series finished. Especially for me having the romance with Harry and all those fabulous scenes I got to play with Glenda. I loved the fact that we got The Freak. That was something I think all the fans wanted. She had gotten away with murder; literally, so many times so it was great she got her comeuppance. If the series had gone on, I would have been

happy to continue with it. Lurch had gone from non-speaking to a major character and a Top Dog. It was a unique journey. I always loved the comedy; I fell into that so easily. I can do comedy instinctively. I don't think playing Lurch affected my career to any great degree. I went straight from Prisoner *into a children's pantomime, then not long after I was cast in the musical Nunsense. So I went from being a prisoner to playing a nun.*

Following *Prisoner*, Lois returned to the stage playing a singing dancing nun in both *Nunsense* and *Nunsense II*. Most recently, Lois has turned her hand to directing with a production of Alan Bennett's *Habeas Corpus*.

On the small screen, she has been seen as recurring character Mabel Jeffries in *The Flying Doctors*, *Something In The Air*, *Blue Heelers*, three different characters in *Neighbours*, *Underbelly* and an incontinent woman in *Kath & Kim*.

When The Saint Goes Marching In....
Meg's Life Sentence

She has been referred to on more than one occasion as 'Saint Meg' and it is true. Meg Jackson has shown courage in the face of adversity more times than anyone else in the series. That's hardly surprising though, as Meg is the only character to have survived the full 692 episodes.

Meg's history is revealing. She was born in a prison and taken from her mother to an orphanage only to be shunted about care homes during her childhood before taking the plunge and deciding she wanted to play a part in rehabilitating women like her mother. This led her to the prison service where she and her husband Bill are first found, Bill being the prison's psychologist. It takes only four episodes before Meg has her first taste of tragedy. Bill is killed, having been stabbed with a pair of scissors in his chest, by Chrissie Latham it later emerges. It is then we get a taste of the despair and loneliness Meg feels, with a rebellious son Marty hardly helping the desperate situation. For someone who lacked childhood security to suddenly find her husband tragically murdered must have been a cruel blow twice over. It sends Meg into a spiral of grief, while she desperately tries to hang on to the normality of working in the prison as a cushion against the emptiness she feels inside

By and large, Meg is not fuelled by the prison power games that obsess Vera and later Joan. It is a chance to reform lives which keeps driving Meg as she sees cases parade before her of abandonment and despair. She knows that, given the chance, she might be able to make a difference to the women, helping them find a path of honesty and self-respect, which they have frequently denied themselves. It has to be this driven ethic that helps Meg forgive and mentor the very woman who killed her husband. Chrissie Latham turns to Meg for both advice and help as the birth of her daughter Elizabeth approaches. This is perhaps

the start of public canonisation as 'Saint Meg', for very few of us could muster such kindliness in the wake of the crime.

Another chance of personal happiness is offered with Bob Morris, father of drug smuggler inmate Tracey. Bob is a successful businessman who fell for the charms of a woman he knew was a good screw. For a while, Meg was granted the domestic bliss that had eluded her since the death of Bill but, as ever, happy endings do not a ratings hit make, so the marriage fell apart. This left the sexy siren in uniform to play the field which she did successfully for a while; however, getting romantic with Meg did shorten the odds somewhat of a full life. Boyfriend Phil Cleary was shot and potential husband number three Dennis 'Ey up lass' Cruickshank had his knees blasted off by Frank Burke. The message being that involvement with Meg was in fact quite dangerous and a pointer to a termination of contract for any actor playing romantically opposite Elspeth.

Perhaps one of the most harrowing of all the storylines to feature Meg was her brutal double rape. This is engineered by the odious Angel Adams, and this sequence is probably as shocking as the producers ever allowed on screen. Although the act itself was not portrayed, the sheer terror conveyed by Elspeth Ballantyne to the viewer both during the attack and then later the shock that engulfs her, mark it out as one of the defining moments of *Prisoner* acting. There are very few sequences during the whole eight-year run that rate alongside this scene to equal the show being at its most raw and disturbing.

It is true to say that 'Mrs M', as she becomes known to the ladies of Wentworth, is seen as a fair and decent officer. Certainly, when Meg finds herself serving a short stint behind bars for perjury in court and is bashed by Margo Gaffney, the women in H Block are incensed. Seeing someone so fair with them given such harsh treatment, would not be tolerated. Bea and Chrissie tar and feather Margo to avenge the treatment she has dished out to Saint Meg.

Elspeth Ballantyne was an established and recognised actress, both on stage and television, by the time *Prisoner* casting directors turned their attention towards her. Born in Adelaide, in 1939, Elspeth's father was a prominent local thespian and director.

Initially, she wanted to be a laboratory assistant; however, her father was keen that his daughter should follow him in his love of the theatre. Elspeth's first taste of fame was as a long-standing cast member of ABC's seminal soap *Bellbird*, in which she appeared with her husband Dennis Miller.

Elspeth's agent at the time managed to secure her an audition with Ian Bradley and Reg Watson for the role of Meg Jackson. Elspeth explains:

The auditioning process was simply a matter of reading opposite someone who was playing the Governor and I had to audition reading a scene with her in the Governor's office. I was called back again because they thought I might be a bit too young for Meg, but thankfully they decided I wasn't! Auditions are always nerve wracking; you always go in thinking 'as soon as I get out I will put it to the back of my mind' because you won't get every job you go for. I suspect that with Prisoner I will have been thinking 'Oh, that would be nice, that would be very nice to do.' On the first day of rehearsals I was

Elspeth Ballantyne surrounded by fan mail.

most impressed. I was delighted to see Sheila (Florance) there. I had known Colette Mann previously and also known Patsy King before Prisoner *started. I found I had an instant rapport with Fiona Spence, so I felt really good about it all. Denise Morgan had a very, very strong idea of each and every one of these leading characters and she had it very clearly written down how she thought they should be. Denise had done a lot of research and each of the leading cast members had to go through the process of attending women's prisons and talking about those sorts of situations in preparation for doing it. The first week of recording was an enormous adrenalin rush. I remember the first week being desperately long, thinking 'will this ever end?' It probably took six weeks before we got into the rhythm.*

Like all actors on the show, Elspeth started off on a 16-episode contract which was extended and generally increased by six months and eventually year-long periods. With so many episodes to her credit, keeping some kind of continuity to characterisation is vitally important to any actor serving long-time contracts in soaps, as well as having to deal with an increasingly changing array of producers, directors and writers.

That does become frustrating. You open a script and it could be different to how Meg had behaved two weeks previously. You can't really go back to them [the writers] and argue too much. You can make suggestions but once a script is out there and ready you can't mess about with it too much. I don't remember any stand-up fights about them. After the first four or five years Meg didn't play such a central role, she would bounce back every now and again, but one of the challenges of soap opera is making the ridiculous believable. That was my job.

The stamina of recording two hours of television a week is something that many actors who have appeared in *Prisoner* have commented on.

The schedule would be two days of rehearsals, two days of taping and one day for outside broadcast scenes. You had to be

Top: Inventor Dick Smith visits the Prisoner set. Left: The original Jackson family, Meg, Bill (Don Barker) and above Marty (Ronald Korosy). Right: Meg in court await the outcome of her rape ordeal trial.

Opposite Top: Meg and Marty number 3 (Michael Winchester). Opposite Bottom: A lighter moment during rehearsals for Maggie, Elspeth and Joy Westmore wearing THAT wig! Left: Meg and Vera. Right: Rebecca Dines (Vicki), Rosanne Hull-Brown (Merle), Elspeth and Maggie sign a souvenir.

at Nunawading for 6:30am for make-up and wardrobe and there would be a schedule of scenes you were to do. You had to get your head around the fact that the scenes could well be all over the shop. They might do all the bashings first thing in the morning but then do the scenes leading up to the bashing later in the day. For an actor it can be nerve wracking to find out about a sequence and find out just how everything is going to be shot. For instance, all the laundry scenes would be done at once and well as the dining room, so the prisoners could well be eating three different meals in a row. Occasionally they would have plastic bags below the tables.

Elspeth had a unique 'ground floor' perspective of all eras of the show, from the days of Franky Doyle and Bea Smith through Myra Desmond and the male prisoners to the dramatic ending with Rita Connors. Did she feel at all that there were periods when the show lost its way, or the magic wasn't working as well as it could have?

Perhaps around the time of Pepe Trevor and Paula Duncan's characters arrived. There was a great deal more levity among the prisoners and it seemed to me the dynamic between the inmates and officers changed and the inmates were running the prison. I didn't like that and I used to wonder where it came from. But again, it was probably generated from ideas around the storyline table. New producers come in, that sort

of thing. It had become a bit more glamorous, but I think they [the producers] wanted it to be so to some extent. So everyone was happy to go with it.

One of the biggest changes among both cast and characters was the arrival in 1982 of Maggie Kirkpatrick as Joan Ferguson. This impacted in a huge way on the show, with many storylines revolving around this sensational new arrival.

The cast weren't suspicious in any way of the new arrival or worried. We knew of Maggie's reputation as an actress which was quite formidable, and when she arrived on set her presence was felt immediately. That added a huge injection to the show too, and I'm sure will have helped the ratings.

Similarly, the series lost its original Top Dog which paved the way for a succession of power struggles for the steam press. Elspeth played opposite all of the infamous Top Dogs throughout the series.

Without Bea Smith there was a tangible difference in the playing of the Top Dog, I felt, but that in itself was good. I felt it was good for the rest of the cast as there is only so much a Top Dog character can do and when a new one arrived I think everyone responded very positively to it.

It has often stated that Elspeth championed the

extras or 'supporting artists' as they are now known during the long run of *Prisoner*.

> *We had a Green Room for the actors; in fact we had a tunnel to start with, then we got our own Green Room but even then it wasn't large. If you've had lots of scenes and lots of tired actors, one half of the room would seem excessively full. Some cast members were not as thoughtful as they could be with the seating arrangements in there. I always felt that no matter who the person was, an extra or lead, after a long time standing on your feet everyone deserves a seat. I used*

> *to speak up for extras on that show and I don't believe in a strata system of actors.*

Since her days in prison ended, Elspeth has continued to play a wide variety of roles on stage and television. She was seen as Cathy Alessi in *Neighbours* for an extended stint. Other appearances include *The Flying Doctors*, *Blue Heelers*, *The Secret Life of Us* and *All Saints*. She has also been seen in the movies *Boronia Boys* and *Boronia Backpackers* playing Maxine Daniels. Elspeth brought Meg Jackson to the stage in 1989 when she appeared in the world premiere of the *Prisoner* play in the UK.

RACHEL 'ROACH' WATERS

Played by Linda Hartley

First Episode: 595
Last Episode: 643
Total featured: 26

Rachel 'Roach' Waters is the girlfriend of Rita Connor's wayward brother Bongo. She follows Bongo by aiding him in a daring raid and is subsequently caught and sent to Wentworth along with Ida Brown. It is here that she struggles to recognise Joan Ferguson, knowing there is something familiar about her. It dawns on Roach that she was at The Conquerors' hideout the night of the fire. Realising that Ferguson is indirectly responsible for Slasher's death causes Rita to go into overdrive to exact revenge. Roach becomes embroiled with Kath Maxwell's drugs schemes despite Rita's warnings about them. Roach realises that Bongo is never going to be the kind of boyfriend she wants, and when she meets Mick on the day release scheme she falls in love. The women engineer it for the both of them to sail off from Australia and start a new life together.

CHAPTER ELEVEN
PRISONER RECAPTURED

The gates of Wentworth had banged shut for good at the end of 1986. By rights, the show should have been consigned to the television graveyard. Just another soap that had shone brightly on Australian screens but which had now burnt itself out. However, fate had different plans for *Prisoner*. 10,000 miles away from Channel 10's studios, the United Kingdom was awaiting its sentence.

The BBC's main rival for dominance of the airwaves (before the Sky satellite revolution) was Independent Television (ITV), which had been formed in 1955. This was effectively a coalition of television companies which each laid claim to a region of the UK. Material could be networked across all channels or consigned to local broadcast. Locally transmitted material was usually reserved for news programming and lifestyle content, by and large. Every now and again, some imported drama would be inserted into the mix, and in this way *The Young Doctors, The Sullivans* and *Sons and Daughters* found a ready afternoon audience during early 1980s. Crucially, these programmes were never broadcast simultaneously across all regions; instead, each regional variation might have started a show earlier or later than its bedfellows and sometimes

Left: Val Lehman prepares for a UK press conference. Right: The cast of the 1989 Prisoner play. Left to Right: Glenda Linscott, Elspeth Ballantyne, Patsy King, Joanna Munro.

Top Left: A scene from the 1989 play. Top Right: Patsy King, Brenda Longman and Elspeth Ballantyne get ready for Christmas in Wentworth. Above Left: Britain's Bea Smith, Brenda Longman. Above Right: Jennifer Stanton as Joan Ferguson, 1989.

with more episodes a week. And so, depending on where you were in the UK, you were not necessarily watching the same storylines as relatives or friends in a different ITV region. The arrival of *Neighbours* on BBC 1 in November 1986 signalled an overnight obsession with all things Australian. Originally airing in the daytime schedules but swiftly moved to an early evening time slot, the Ramsay Street saga blazed a trail for Australian television product. It would take until February 1989 for its arch rival *Home and Away* to become a fixture of ITV, by which time Australian television was very much the order of the day with the soap-craving Brits.

It was deemed that, due to its often controversial content, *Prisoner* was suitable for a late-night broadcast slot. Thus in 1984, largely unnoticed, Yorkshire

Television became the first of the ITV consortia to bring the ladies of Wentworth to a British audience. It wasn't until the Central region of ITV, covering the large Midlands area, began showing *Prisoner* in April 1987 that the cult following started in earnest. It became apparent to Central bosses that the reaction being stirred up by the late night escapades was way beyond the response programmes in such a late time slot usually received. Central took the decision to show *Prisoner* three times a week. Although episodes would go out frequently past midnight, no matter how late they scheduled it, the feedback was vociferous. The postponement of an episode for a movie or sporting event would inevitably bring phone calls and letters of complaint from the increasingly devoted following. The same reaction was beginning to be

Left: Sheila Florance arrives at Manchester Airport for The Great Escape tour, 1990. Right: Amanda Muggleton is swamped by fans at the airport. Inset: Programme cover for The Great Escape tour.

EVE PROMOTIONS AND THE PRISONER CELL BLOCK H FAN CLUB PROUDLY PRESENT

THE ON THE OUTSIDE TOUR 1990

PRISONER

THE GREAT ESCAPE

OFFICIAL TOUR SOUVENIR

felt wider afield as more and more ITV regions joined the *Prisoner* party. From housewives to gay men and women to clergymen and labourers, *Prisoner* was becoming 'must see' TV. Work places across the land became hotbeds of Cell Block gossip as the latest episodes were digested, discussed and ridiculed over a tea break.

It was in this atmosphere of growing cult that two young ladies decided they would start the first fan club in the world devoted to the show. Roz Vecsey and Tracey Elliott lived in Derby, right in the middle of the Central region where *Prisoner* was hottest. They were enamoured enough to start production of a photocopied newsletter entitled *The H Block Herald*. From little acorns mighty oaks were sure to grow. The makeshift fan club that had started in the local pub suddenly hit demand on a national level. Hundreds of letters per week were pouring into Derby wanting to know about the stars of *Prisoner* and also to buy photos and merchandise. Vecsey and Elliott were happy to oblige. They even managed to get a small government grant for new businesses and rented an office in the local Council chambers. Their earliest coup was to make contact with Val Lehman who was keen to come back to Britain where she had spent several years of her married life, to meet the pommie *Prisoner* fans for the first time. Thus in April 1989, 'Prisoner' Mania' was truly born when Val descended on the UK for a round of interviews and personal appearances in gay clubs, bingo halls, shopping centres and any manner of public places as the demand to see Bea Smith in the flesh reached fever pitch. Mobbing was frequently experienced by the former Top Dog wherever she appeared. It was further

evidence that this schedule-filler was becoming so much more. The fan club was to repeat this success with tours by Betty Bobbitt and Judy McBurney, both receiving a warm welcome from the Blockies, as admirers were by now affectionately termed.

The cult following the series was attracting had come under the scrutiny of theatre producer, John Farrow. Farrow had been instrumental in reviving the fortunes of the Theatre Royal, Hanley (Stoke-On-Trent) by turning Richard O'Brien's cult B-movie homage *The Rocky Horror Show* from a small devoted following to a massive touring money spinner. He had followed this with a critically acclaimed production of the Kander and Ebb musical *Cabaret*, starring dancer Wayne Sleep, which had found its way to a West End home. Farrow had also been the first pantomime producer to bring over stars from another Grundy hit, *Neighbours*. Anne Charleston, Ian Smith, Peter O'Brien and future movie star Guy Pearce were all put before pantomime audiences by the forward-thinking Farrow. Thus Farrow was quick to notice the swell of popularity for *Prisoner* and recognised the beginning of a cult along the same lines as *Rocky Horror*. He reckoned a stage version of the new phenomenon was just what the Stoke theatre needed to swell the coffers. And so it was that John made contact with Grundy Television and Reg Watson, a man Farrow had known briefly from his days at ATV working on *Crossroads*. Negotiations ensued in order to bring the Wentworth warriors from screen to stage for the very first time. Launching the new production, Farrow told The Stage newspaper:

> *Not only will* Prisoner: Cell Block H *be an excellent stage drama, but it will also promote that wonderful excitement that makes going to the theatre such an exciting and special event. It is essential to the production that we have familiar faces from the TV series. Not only does this add to the appeal of the production for the millions of Cell Block H fans in this country but also makes it a real Anglo / Aussie production.*

Quick to put pen to contract were Elspeth Ballantyne, Patsy King and final Top Dog Glenda Linscott who was living in London at the time. Rita Connors was some months off appearing on British screens, so instead Glenda opted to play 'Angela Mason', a re-working of the Chrissie Latham 'tart with a heart' pigeonhole. Based on the first six or so episodes of the television series, the continuity was somewhat misplaced by having The Freak and Franky Doyle both inhabiting Wentworth at the same time. This didn't seem to bother the British fans who turned out in their thousands at major venues all over the country when the tour commenced at the Wimbledon Theatre in South London on 21st September 1989.

When the casting of the British Bea Smith came up for grabs, the role went to a quite unexpected source. Brenda Longman had, for a decade or so, voiced the role of Soo, Sooty's panda friend, in the classic children's television puppet series *The Sooty Show*. Brenda was a stalwart of many plays and musicals and now had the chance to turn her talent to Wentworth's fearsome Top Dog. Would-be Bea, Brenda Longman explains:

> *My agent asked me to audition; I think he must have put up several of his clients for the play. I remember my audition piece was performed before the director Stewart Trotter and producer John Farrow. They mostly seemed*

Top: Flyer for the 1989 play tour. Bottom: Flyer for the 1990 play tour.

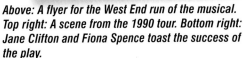

Above: A flyer for the West End run of the musical.
Top right: A scene from the 1990 tour. Bottom right:
Jane Clifton and Fiona Spence toast the success of
the play.

concerned that I would be able to dye my hair red for the part. I had been aware of the television series before hand. While I was appearing at the Salisbury Playhouse, myself and the artistic director David Horlock used to sit and devour it when we got in from the theatre. We both used to reckon it was because our resistance was at its lowest through tiredness that we became hooked on the exploits! I was told to completely forget about Val's performance even though I knew that the audience would be thinking differently.

When it got to rehearsals, the three 'stars', Elspeth, Patsy and Glenda, hadn't been doing the TV show for some time so it was a bit of a reunion for them. None of us was prepared though for the opening week at Wimbledon and the subsequent reaction to the tours. People offered to buy my old tights and someone even broke into my dressing room to get an authentic bit of 'Bea'

memorabilia. One guy dropped his wife off at the theatre and kept his car running thinking it would only be a 45-minute episode! We opened the same night as Miss Saigon in the West End and Ned Sherrin was bold enough to say that in his Times column that we were the theatrical event of the year, not Miss Saigon! One funny incident occurred at the stage door at Lincoln. As I made my way out of the theatre, stopping to sign autographs, a big noisy motorbike pulled up beside me. Off got a great hulk in leathers and came towards me. Taking off the helmet, I had a photo thrust at me and a gruff voice said, 'Please sign it to Debbie.' 'Is Debbie your girlfriend?' I asked. 'No – I'm Debbie!' came the reply.

On another occasion, a woman came backstage and told me, 'You saved my life!' It turned out that a fire had broken out downstairs and she had been upstairs watching Prisoner:

Top: The Freak reads the riot act to Lily in the 1995 West End Prisoner musical. Above Left: Flyer for the UK tour of the musical, 1997. Above Right: Promotional shot for the Prisoner musical. Left: Press cutting from 1995. Maggie Kirkpatrick on stage at the Royal Albert Hall with Kylie Minogue, Elton John, Lily Savage and Marc Almond among others.

Cell Block H. *As a result she was able to escape with minimal burning but had she been downstairs she would have burned to death. I tried to tell her that it was Val on the telly, not me, but she just kept saying. 'I know that, but you are Bea.' Perhaps the most remarkable event was when Elly went to speak to a lady in a coma who was a big fan of the show, hoping to get some reaction. It did, the lady opened her eyes and started to come round at the sound of Meg. That's the power of* Prisoner *for you! I felt the first tour worked better because it had never been done before; it created the most impact. We had to be shown out the side door of the hotel in Liverpool for fear of being mobbed. I even had people sleeping in the corridor outside my room in the hotel just wanting to be near us. I was quite ill during the first tour of the show. In Eastbourne, I was rushed to hospital and an ovarian problem was diagnosed, so throughout the first run I was battling ill health. Luckily, our 'Freak', Jennifer, had a cousin Stewart who was a gynaecological surgeon and he operated on me as soon as the first tour was over.*

I have retained some great friendships from that time, and I keep in touch with both Elspeth and Patsy with Christmas cards. It was fantastic being a small part of such a well-loved show. I enjoyed every moment of my time behind bars.'

With Maggie Kirkpatrick tied up in Sydney on the stage musical *Anything Goes*, a new Joan Ferguson was sought for the production. This was handed to experienced actress Jennifer Stanton:

John Farrow rang me at home. I had done pantomime several times for John as the Wicked Queen and he gave me a quick character breakdown over the phone of this horrendous person and followed it with 'I thought straight away of you!' So that's how you see me, is it? I thought. The strange thing was at the time two of my children were doing exams and they would come down after studying and watch Prisoner *in its late night slot. I have always found learning lines to be much easier at night, so if I had scripts to learn I would take a break and sit and watch it with them, never dreaming I would be part of the line up one day. Having auditioned for the director and been given the role, we rehearsed at an old synagogue in Dean Street (London, W1). We conducted rehearsals very seriously. We played the show completely straight; it was written as a drama after all. Imagine then the scene on opening night at the Wimbledon Theatre when we heard a lot of shrieking and screaming from*

the audiences as they waited for curtain up. Joan Ferguson was the first on stage, entering from the back and walking slowly down to the footlights. They starting boo-ing before I had opened my mouth and then as the play went on they laughed and called us names. Reg Watson came over and changed some of the dialogue which only seemed to make things worse.

Every performance there was an amazing audience who really threw themselves into the show and the characters. The fans were amazing, lots of wonderful gay men and lesbians, who were just so enthusiastic. There were huge crowds waiting at the stage door, mostly for Patsy and Elspeth, of course. Strangely, I never did get to see the original television 'Freak'. I based my version on my ex-sister in law! One of the great joys of the tour was sharing the dressing room with Stella Tanner playing Lizzie. Stella had been one of the singing Tanner Sisters who were quite famous in the 1950s. They appeared with loads of great performers such as Danny Kaye and Alma Cogan. Stella had a fund of theatrical anecdotes second to none and she was a great raconteur. One interval she told such a funny story we were still hysterically laughing as the curtain went up to begin Act Two. In this scene, I had to speak harshly to a prisoner who had her back to the audience supposedly crying. Well, she was actually laughing like a drain. Eventually, I succumbed too and broke out into laughter. The company manager of the tour, Sarah, went beserk, threatened that I would never work for the company again and that she was going to dock me a week's wage for unprofessionalism. Such a drama.

In Lincoln, we visited a real life prison which was rather strange. Overall, though, a lovely memory of the tour. Patsy, Elspeth and Glenda were all terrific to work with. I got on particularly well with Patsy who would ask me to join her for a coffee and a chat. Australian women I found are very forthright and tough but in a lovely way. It was a shame for Glenda as she was not on in the television series at the time so none of the fans knew who she was unfortunately. A great actress, though.

Industry newspaper *The Stage* was among the first to review the production as it hit the road. Maureen Paton praised Geoff Rose's 'excellent set design' and went on to comment of Longman that she 'shows spirit, though lacks the scowling presence of Val Lehman.' The article further appraised that 'Joanna Monro suggests real tragedy' and 'Jennifer Stanton makes a most hissable villainess.' Strangely, hardly

any mention was given to the three ladies topping the bill. One criticism Paton honed in on were the physical encounters, '... the fight sequence is the phoniest I have ever seen,' she concluded.

The logic saying the Fan Club would be delighted at seeing their favourite programme take shape on the British stage was pricked when Vecsey and Elliot came out publicly to oppose the new stage production. Their own reasons were not entirely clear; it seems some of the content was a bone of contention. 'You would never get drugs being stored in vibrators in the real Cell Block H,' Vecsey told *The Stage*. Farrow hit back defending the production as written by original series creator Reg Watson. 'I'm very glad the Fan Club exists,' Farrow told the press. 'I would be very happy to meet anyone from it, providing they come and see the show.'

Vecsey and Elliot were happy to put their money where their mouths were in the spring of 1990 when a large-scale chat-show theatre presentation was announced. *The Great Escape* promised live music plus four *Prisoner* legends in conversation. Carol Burns and Val Lehman had now both made their homes in the UK so were readily available. Flown over

especially for the tour were Amanda Muggleton and the ace card of loveable old lag Lizzie herself, Sheila Florance. The tour was scheduled to open in Derby and thereafter to hit the road and visit Stockport, Cambridge, Glasgow, Wimbledon and Newcastle upon Tyne. However, when Florance arrived in Britain it was obvious she was not well. Within days, Sheila was rushed to hospital and it began to look unlikely that she would make the big launch of the show at the Assembly Rooms. By the skin of her teeth Florance rallied and joined her former colleagues and host, TV presenter Anna Soubry, on stage for a nostalgic homage to the series and its cast. Sadly this was to be the one and only appearance of the great lady and she was soon back in hospital and the tour was thrown into jeopardy. Fortunately for fans worldwide, the Derby show was recorded and later released as a VHS videotape thus preserving for posterity the reunion. It furthermore sought to demonstrate to *Prisoner* fans throughout the country that they had been cheated of an audience with one of Australia's greatest actresses through a cruel twist of fate.

A second tour of the *Prisoner* play hit the road in March 1990. The same Reg Watson script was its

PRISONER
UNLOCKS THE GATE FOR AIDS

COME AND CELEBRATE THE 21ST BIRTHDAY
OF THE LEGENDARY TV SERIES "PRISONER".
MEET THE CAST AND RAISE MONEY FOR AIDS.

SATURDAY 26 FEBRUARY 2000

COMMENCING 8PM

AT THE FORUM THEATRE
CNR RUSSELL & FLINDERS STREET MELBOURNE

*Be "On The Inside" and
meet the stars of the
award winning TV Series.*

*Top entertainment
provided by former
"Prisoner" cast
members & "Force 10"*

*Featuring an auction of
"Prisoner" memorabilia.*

*Come as a character or
come as yourself.*

*Buy a souvenir,
an autograph or a photo.*

Snacks and drinks included.

Bring $$$ for a worthy cause.

ALL TICKETS $75
AVAILABLE INTERNATIONALLY FROM

TICKETEK ▶

Phone 132 849 within Victoria
Outside Victoria Phone 1800 062 849
Outside Australia Phone 61-3-9299 9079
Or Book On The Web www.ticketek.com.au

An Oz Showbiz Cares/Equity Fights AIDS
Fundraising Event (CFN. 16667)

FORUM THEATRE
A Charity Event For OSC/EFA
PRISONER
UNLOCKS THE GATE FOR AIDS
A 21st Celebration
Sat 26 Feb 2000 8:00pm
SECTION
GENERAL ADMISSION 137 $75.00

TICKETEK ▶
EVENT
FMC26FEB
SECTION
GA
137
TMELG3
01DEC99
TN 13952
NO.

Opposite: The Magnificent Nine. A press call to mark the 21st anniversary at the former Pentridge Prison, Victoria. Above and Left: Flyer and ticket for the 21st Anniversary reunion event in Melbourne, 2000.

basis with revised casting meaning that only Brenda Longman as Bea was back for a second stint. Fiona Spence led the visiting Aussies scraping back her hair once more to become 'Vinegar Tits' opposite Jane Clifton's refined example of womanhood, Margo Gaffney. Further down the cast Jacqui Gordon was familiar as Susie Driscoll to fans of the series but instead appeared as inmate Kath Evans, the replacement character for Linscott's Angela Mason. Again the box office did well. However, the response from the media was a bit more muted than that of the first tour. Audience reaction continued to be highly appreciative with many fans returning for multiple visits throughout the trek around Britain. The production was rocked during the very final week of the tour in Hull by the sudden death of executive producer and driving force behind the production, John Farrow. Farrow had collapsed suddenly of a heart attack and died in hospital within hours. The shock wave that ran through the entire company meant a very downbeat, sombre end to the months on the road. So hands-on was Farrow with the play, personally supervising every aspect, that his production office just had not got the impetus to forge on with plans for a third tour scheduled for the autumn, even though Maggie Kirkpatrick and Colette Mann were waiting in the wings to make the

trip from Down Under. The *Prisoner* play faded away, having enlivened an evening for thousands of fans during its two celebratory romps around the UK.

It would be a full five years before theatre audiences would again visit Wentworth. In the interim most of the ITV regional stations had completed their first run of the 692 episodes in the *Prisoner* canon. Don Battye and Peter Pinne had long been a songwriting partnership outside of their duties as Grundy Television executives, and had written several successful musicals for the Australian stage on diverse subjects. They were not slow in spotting the potential of *Prisoner* as material for the musical theatre and set about writing a full-on musical production they called *The Wild Wild Women of Wentworth*. The script mirrored the series events with a *pot pourri* of songs from country and western to pop to big ballads. Finding backing for the show proved problematic until the duo approached Australian chat show host and media mogul Mike Walsh who, with his business partner Helen Montagu, began finding ways of presenting the show in the UK. This process plodded along for a couple of years until Mike had the inspired idea of approaching a drag legend who was rapidly becoming a hot property on television: Lily Savage, alias comedian Paul O'Grady. Paul had long been a vocal supporter of *Prisoner* and he was very definitely interested, particularly if he could play opposite his favourite actress from the show, Maggie Kirkpatrick. Kirkpatrick was an old friend of Walsh's and had been on board with the project from the early days with a view to Maggie achieving her long-held ambition to act on the British stage. Thus it seemed fate threw these wildly differing talents together in the latest incarnation of the soap that refused to die. On the back of O'Grady's involvement, the prestigious Queen's Theatre on Shaftesbury Avenue, in the heart

of the West End, became the home to the ambitious new production. All the characters in the show were spoofs of the original. British comedy icon Liz Smith, known to millions around the world as Nana in *The Royle Family*, added her immaculate timing to playing the Lizzie Birdsworth type role. Australian diva Alison Jiear unleashed her power vocals on saintly officer Mrs. Austin. Originally, the plan had been to have Bea Smith ruling Wentworth; however, with the arrival of Lily Savage, it was deemed that out went the flame haired guardian of the steam press to make way for the self-confessed box office-busting 'blonde bomb site'. The assembled cast, including the two leads, attended a read-through four weeks before the show was due to open. Until that time nobody had seen the script being prepared by Battye and Pinne; however, at the end of the first day both O'Grady and Kirkpatrick were unhappy with what they had read. Both felt that it lacked comic potential with some material completely at odds with a fun rock musical. O'Grady was quick to come up with the answer. Everyone was despatched to write their own contributions and the production would from then on be a hotch potch of ideas and dialogue with the songs of Battye and Pinne at the core of the piece. O'Grady introduced the 'Cell Block Tango' number from the musical Chicago to fill out the show while several cast members provided additional music and lyrics for the embryo piece. In the end, although Battye and Pinne were credited with music and lyrics, less than fifty percent of their original musical vision was used in the show. Perhaps wisely nobody was credited for providing the 'book' (script) for the show. At the heart of the entire production were O'Grady's razor sharp put-downs and frequent ad-libs. Maggie Kirkpatrick matched this with a Freak that went the full hog and became a high comedy Nazi commandant in all but name. It was literally a riotous production with the director (now Sir) David McVicar attempting to make sense of the chaotic vision.

Several preview performances were cancelled due to an injury sustained in rehearsals by O'Grady. With issues relating to script and songs still to be addressed, and not quite on schedule, the entire bold melee re-titled *Prisoner Cell Block H The Musical* was delivered to a live audience on Monday 30th October 1995. Any doubts that the *Prisoner* fans would not accept this boldly mocking interpretation of their beloved Wentworth were dispelled when O'Grady took a two-minute ovation as he appeared on the stage, and Kirkpatrick had the audience on their feet again as she slowly strode into view in full Wentworth regalia. It was clear to the entire company that this show was going to be a hoot from beginning to end from both sides of the footlights. Surprisingly, the broadsheet papers were very welcoming. The hard-bitten London theatre critics seemingly joining in the revelry with only a couple of tabloids blasting the show for its pantomime-style lack of subtlety.

Jack Tinker, Daily Mail:

Not being a devotee of the series, the true awfulness of the acting, the cheesiness of the plots and the flimsiness of the scenery was something one could only relate to having come across the occasional episode of Crossroads. Yet David McVicar's wilful direction manages to raise this to the level of pop art.

Charles Spencer, Daily Telegraph:

The amazing Maggie Kirkpatrick has been imported from Australia, where she starred in most of the original show's 692 episodes. You get the feeling she is taking gleeful revenge on a terrible programme that was once required to be taken seriously. The lesbian subtext of the telly version becomes hilariously explicit in the dykey power mad warder Joan ' The Freak' Ferguson. With her hair slicked back and her feet shod in Nazi-style boots, this hatchet-faced old boot sings a hilariously kinky ditty to her leather gloves and somehow contrives to keep a straight face while ordering prisoners to strip off for a strip search in the showers.

Vicky Powell, Gay Times:

The night I went, Prisoner provoked laughter and a great deal of audience participation, which was hardly surprising since most of the punters were gay men... Although the production was overlong, there were some tender moments like The Freak carrying out intimate body searches on the younger better-looking girls. Lily also gets a good going over but, as she herself says: 'I told her if she finds anything up there she's welcome to smoke it.'

Tony Purnell, Daily Mirror:

Strewth! Whoever decided the Aussie TV series Prisoner Cell Block H was West End material should be locked up. The late-night soap set behind bars in Wentworth Detention Centre for Women is noted only for its disastrous dialogue, awful acting and wobbly walls... Maggie Kirkpatrick flies halfway across the world to recreate the role of butch warder-from-hell Joan Ferguson nicknamed The Freak. But she needn't have bothered. She is out-freaked at every turn by outrageous Liverpool drag star and Big Breakfast

*favourite Lily Savage. Banged up for nicking a
fondue set, prostitution... and murder, Lily totters
around the stage in six-inch stilettos, giant wigs,
a denim micro-skirt and some glitzy outfits Shirley
Bassey would kill for.*

John Gross, Sunday Telegraph:

*There are some sturdy performances. Lily
Savage stands her ground and wields a mean
insult. Terry Neason (who also has a beautiful
singing voice) makes a formidable Steff. But the
evening belongs first and foremost to Maggie
Kirkpatrick as Ferguson, the part she created
on television. Striding around like a gauleiter,
launching into a hymn in praise of leather,
plucking hairs from her chin – whatever she is
doing she dominates the proceedings, and rightly
rouses a storm of pantomime booing.*

Such was the tremendous box office for the
London season that the show was sent out on
the road for two hugely successful tours in 1996
and 1997. A few cast changes were implemented;
Linda Nolan took over as the Governor, allowing the
show to crowbar in that favourite disco hit from the
Nolan sisters, *I'm In the Mood for Dancing*. Familiar
comedy stooge Bella Emberg slipped into the shoes
of Liz Smith as Minnie. The reaction from provincial
audiences at major cities throughout the UK continued
to be euphoric, a party atmosphere pervaded at many
performances. Maggie Kirkpatrick continued to have
a ball sending up Ferguson in this adult pantomime:

*It was a schlocky show, sure, but great fun to
do. I learned to be feed to a comic with that show.
Paul O'Grady has such a sharp mind and quick
wit that keeping up with him was a challenge. But
I think generally I gave as good as I got. One of
the first things we did together when I arrived in
the UK to do the show was a charity event at the
Royal Albert Hall for Stonewall. There were 5,000
people there and the moment I strode on they
started cheering, then the booing and hissing
started. I had to stand there for a full two minutes
before I could get my line out. They gave me and
Paul such a wonderful reception. We shared the
bill with Elton John, Janis Ian, Jennifer Saunders
and Joanna Lumley, Kylie Minogue, Julian Clary.
So many big, big stars. It was quite humbling
to be a part of it. Then when the season at the
Queen's Theatre got under way the reaction from
the audience was quite overwhelming for my
return to the role. There would be crowds waiting
outside the stage door each night. It was like being
a pop star. It was just the same when we went on*

*tour. O'Grady and I both liked to party hard, too. I
eventually had to go home to give my liver a rest.
But we work in a strange business. After all the
glowing reviews, audience reaction and Australian
television news programmes beaming live from my
dressing room in the West End, when I got home
it was still the same struggle for a mature actor to
get work. But at least I had my name up in lights on
Shaftesbury Avenue.*

The fans continued to get better organised as time
went on. When the original Vecsey and Elliot fan club
ground to a halt, it was replaced by S.O.A.P. (Save Our
Aussie Programmes). In turn, this led to *Blockade*, a
first class magazine-style tribute to the show which ran
for quite a few issues. Over in Australia Colin Gerrard
issued what must be regarded as the Bible of *Prisoner*
fan publications, *The Wentworth Star*, in August 1994.
This was a glossy publication featuring in-depth
interviews with the crème of *Prisoner* cast members
and many hitherto unseen production photos. These
issues continued until February 2000 and, like
Blockade, have now become collectors' items.

Just as *Prisoner Cell Block H The Musical* was
hitting the road for its final UK tour, the UK's newly
launched Channel 5 took to the air. They repeated
the show with episodes showing five nights a week
between March 1997 and February 2001, the only time
the episodes have been networked across the land at
the same time – and, to date, the last showings in the
UK for the series.

Prisoner celebrated its 21st anniversary in style.
The gates of Wentworth Detention Centre opened
once more, with over two hundred former cast and
crew members reunited in the one room, to raise
money for charity. The ultimate event in *Prisoner*
fandom was about to unfold, and was the brainchild of
Prisoner's much loved Top Dog, Anne Phelan.

At a committee meeting for Oz Showbiz Cares
and Equity Fights Aids, the assembled members were
discussing and debating over how best to raise funds to
support their charity. They are dedicated to mobilising
the unique talents within the media, entertainment and
arts industries in Australia to mitigate the suffering of
individuals affected by HIV/AIDS. Phelan informed
the group that *Prisoner* was about to celebrate its
21st anniversary, and suggested an event could be
organised in its home country to celebrate one of
Australia's most iconic television shows. This would
prove no mean feat, as the charity had little funds in
order to make their dreams a reality. The success of
Prisoner was still resonating around the world over
21 years later, but to arrange for a massive reunion
of cast and crew to come together for one night
only seemed incomprehensible. However, Phelan, a
staunch supporter of the charity for many years, was

Left: Maggie Kirkpatrick with Prisoner fan and former Doctor Who, Colin Baker. Right: Fiona Spence and Elspeth Ballantyne reunite for the 111 HITS re-run launch at the old Melbourne Gaol, 2011 (courtesy of Newspix / Julie Kiriacoudis).

determined to fight on and raise money and awareness to assist the growing number of women who were living with HIV/AIDS and woefully under-supported. Phelan's courage and determination is a testament to her reputation of being one of the most respected and highly regarded members of the *Prisoner* cast. With the overwhelming support of over two hundred cast and crew who turned out *en masse*, Annie was about to raise the roof of Melbourne's Forum Theatre.

The doors of the Forum Theatre opened at 7:30pm on 26th February 2000 with excited *Prisoner* fans flying in from as far afield as Scotland, Sweden and The Netherlands, reflecting the worldwide appeal of the series that continues to endure to this day. A specially selected group of twenty-one fans travelled from the UK to celebrate the 21st anniversary, as a pilgrimage for the (then) UK fan club *Blockade*. The gathering was advertised in several of the UK soap magazines which brought it to the attention of many fans in Great Britain.

The greatest surprise of the evening came right at the start when the assembled guests were invited to move down towards the stage area. Instead of one or two cast members taking to the stage to welcome everyone, instead the massive curtain rose to reveal every single cast member in attendance, united on the stage to sing the theme tune to the series, 'On the Inside'. As casting director Jan Russ noted, 'The moment that will stay in my mind forever is when the curtain came up, and the gasp from the audience was just fabulous. A beautiful moment.'

The evening got under way with all the cast members mingling with their beloved fans, some of the actors looking extremely perplexed as to why they were there, bearing in mind that, for many of them, they had moved on and were simply unaware of the continuing success the show enjoyed around the world. The MC for the evening was the wonderful Marty Fields, son of renowned Australian entertainers Maurie Fields and Val Jellay, who each graced the *Prisoner* corridors.

All assembled cast members were available for autographs and photographs in exchange for a token. A replica prison cell was created especially for the evening with the last few props from the series being donated from cast, crew, and the old Channel 10 studios in Nunawading. These included a cell cabinet, mirror unit and even a truncheon! To see part of the old set come back together proved simply magical for the hardcore following. As the fans began to queue for photographs in the cell, the cast members took it in turns to pose with the fans.

Highlights of the evening included the auction of original props and memorabilia conducted by Val Lehman. Memorable items on offer were the original officer's jacket worn by Joyce Barry, Joan Ferguson's ID badge, first and last episode scripts plus various T-shirts and crew member windcheaters. The last surviving props and costumes had been found and put up for auction to the highest bidder. The evening was a triumphant success with $35,000 being raised for charity. In 2002, in recognition of her charity work and outstanding efforts, Phelan was awarded the 'Activist of the Year Award' for outstanding contribution to the fight against HIV/AIDS.

Scott Anderson and Barry Campbell have continued to keep the *Prisoner* flag flying in the UK through their website *On The Inside* which has progressed to arranging regular appearances by the shows stars in the UK, the first cast member to fly over being Maggie Millar; this has continued with several eagerly anticipated visits including the reunion of Glenda Linscott and Maggie Kirkpatrick on stage which was subsequently released on DVD.

Prisoner has pervaded popular culture on both sides of the world. Celebrity fans have often made mention of the show; Dame Edna Everage herself staged a *Prisoner* sketch during one of her high-rating Christmas television specials. Influential BBC radio DJ Scott Mills appeared on the celebrity special of the cerebral television knowledge quiz *Mastermind* with *Prisoner* as his specialist subject. SBS comedy series *Pizza* and ABC's *The Librarians* have both directly referenced the show by having guest appearances by cast members and it has been frequently mentioned in quips by characters on many comedies and dramas. An ITV half-hour special *The Inside Story* was broadcast in the UK, looking at the mania around the country and meeting the cast of the first stage play version. Celebrity admirers are known to include Jonathan Ross, Lord Andrew Lloyd Webber and Sir Ian McKellen. The wonders of Cell Block H may even have extended to time and space. Former Time Lord, the sixth *Doctor Who*, Colin Baker, has outed himself as a fan:

> *We all have guilty secrets. I have many. One of my late night furtive pursuits in the 1980s, when returning home from theatre-land to a house full of sleeping family, was to watch* Prisoner *while eating my plated meal. It was only later I discovered I was not alone in my solitary vice and that there were many other similarly twisted folk who immersed themselves in the dramatic goings on in Wentworth. And as someone who played a rather dodgy art teacher in* Within These Walls *back in 1973, I was charmed to learn that Googie Withers – star of that series – was originally offered the role of*

Erica Davidson, eventually played, of course, with wonderful iron hand-in-velvet gloved-ness by Patsy King. Like all addictive series, it relied on strong characters and, by gum, there were plenty of them. Not just Top Dog Bea Smith and the charmingly named Deputy Governor 'Vinegar Tits', but also the double act between Doreen and the 'Dot Cotton' prototype, Lizzie the old lag. And I must confess to a crush on the wonderful squeaky clean, endlessly patient and eternally decent Meg Jackson. I'd volunteer for prison if she were my wardress! I hear it's being shown again in Australia. It's about time UK channels introduced a new generation to the charms of the shaking sets and fiendish villains – now which other series does that remind me of? I even got to see the stage show in which my good friend Brenda Longman got to play Bea Smith. That was a surreal experience. The vast auditorium was full of very vocal ladies brandishing handcuffs and looking very butch indeed. Maggie Kirkpatrick came to see me in a play not too long ago, so I got to meet The Freak afterwards. She's really a lovely lady. Prisoner *has stood the test of time as a cult favourite and long may it continue to do so.*

Val Lehman has been instrumental in campaigning to get the entire series released on DVD, which occurred in 2007. The Shock label released forty volumes of DVDs including one massive boxed set containing all 692 episodes. This was, at the time, the biggest DVD boxed set ever to be released. It also turned out to be Shock's biggest seller. These sets

The original cast are reunited by 111 Hits Channel to mark the re-runs on Foxtel.

have been repackaged for the British market in twenty volumes. The Brits even had a special release of the Edna Pearson episodes which had become the victim of the censor's scissors due to legal wrangling in Australia. In actual fact it finally proved that this much talked about storyline was in fact hardly worth noticing among the other events in the episodes, but one thing a cult series demands is absolute completion and the fans of the show were certainly glad to have the unedited (almost) episodes available to them at last.

The 111 HITS channel on the Foxtel satellite provider was surprised to find *Prisoner* among its most watched shows. They had reunited some cast members with a special lunch at the Melbourne Gaol prior to the repeat season which naturally attracted a large amount of media interest. Perhaps the biggest surprise came with an announcement in early 2012 that Fremantle had secured a deal with Foxtel to 're-imagine' the series for a new generation with a show entitled *Wentworth*. At the time of writing, this is recording in Melbourne. It is in itself a symbol of the timelessness of the original series. Whether this new incarnation of this much-loved Australian classic can live up to its predecessor is a matter for future debate, but it continues the legend for a new generation. Writer Pete McTighe explains his joy at being able to bring Wentworth Detention Centre to a new generation:

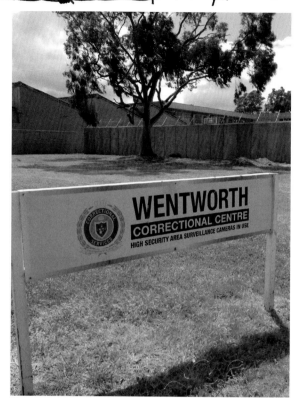

The setting for the new Wentworth series based on Prisoner.

In December 2011, I got a phone call. Prisoner *was coming back. Brilliant, talented people were developing a new take on an Australian television classic. I thought it was a joke. I'd been mulling this over for years. I'd even written my own pitch for it. See, I was a big-time fan. When I was a teenager, I was obsessed with it. I was one of those nutters who would rush out and buy the TV Times or TV Soap magazines just because there was a poster of Joan Ferguson. I grew up but I never grew out of it. Every so often, I would dust off my old VHS tapes and re-watch Episode 600 or 327 or 400. For me, it was a show that never died.*

And then on 1st January 2012 I had the giddy privilege of sitting down at my computer and typing the following words: WENTWORTH. EPISODE ONE.

It still gives me chills. And now it's all done. In a warehouse about half an hour from where I am typing this, talented actors, directors and crew are turning those words into a reality. Wentworth is a re-imagining of Reg Watson's original, fantastic concept. It's not a replacement for the original, and it's not a continuation. It has to stand on its own two feet. It has to come screaming out of the blocks like those early Prisoner episodes

did. Like the original, it has to push boundaries, usurp expectations, challenge and entertain its audience.

The original series we fans know and love will always be there. Available whenever we want it, on our DVD shelves. Nothing will ever take that away from us or diminish the enjoyment we've had from it. But now, we'll have a brand new series too. A contemporary re-working that maybe, if we put aside our prejudices and impossible expectations, we will come to love as well.

It is Melbourne, Australia, 2013. A woman is being driven in a police van to her new home – Wentworth Detention Centre. *That woman is Bea Smith. Her story is starting over. And you'll be meeting her very soon.*

So with the arrival of *Wentworth*, the walls of the prison will echo to new voices, new problems, and new adventures. *Prisoner* lives on. The phenomenon shows no sign of stopping. The cult status it has achieved ensures a never-ending supply of devotees. It remains a unique and much loved piece of television history. Long may it continue to delight, enthral, shock and surprise.

Top Left: Michael David Reeves with Pepe Trevor. Top Right: Robert Ivory with Lois Ramsay. Above Left: Karen Diston with Jacqui Gordon. Above Right: Iain Hayes with Carole Skinner. Left: Martin Duggan with Nigel Bradshaw and Genevieve Lemon

Top Left: Ellen van der Kraan with Fiona Spence. Top Right: Alan Alexander with Val Lehman. Above Left: Judith Hayeem with Jentah Sobott and Amanda Muggleton. Above Right: Jay Kelly with Maggie Millar. Right: Rachael Wallis with Louise Siversen.

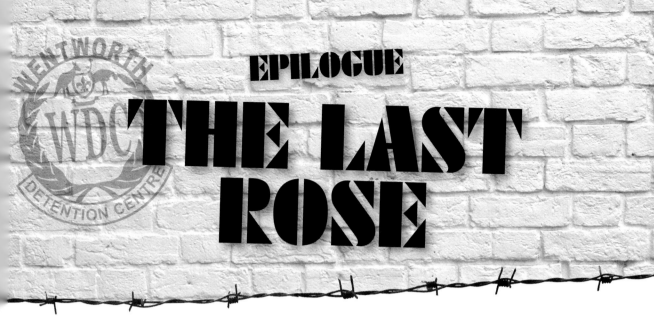

EPILOGUE
THE LAST ROSE

He used to give me roses. I wish he could again...

A **dark shadow began to descend over the corridors of Wentworth during *Prisoner's* final year. The series was drawing to a close and the prop gates were becoming harder to open. Producers reached a general consensus that the press had just about run out of steam. The various Top Dogs who commanded the audience from that very spot brought a rich plethora of talent and versatility, showcasing the Australian entertainment industry around the world. *Prisoner's* place in history had been sealed.**

Prisoner played its last trump card in the form of Glenda Linscott in her awe-inspiring role of Rita, and it was agreed that Rita would be the character who would take the series to its gripping conclusion. Despite a short stint as Top Dog by Kath Maxwell [Kate Hood], Glenda's performance of Rita brought together a culmination of aspects and behavioural traits displayed by her predecessors. However, her strength was conveyed not only through her height but from watching and listening, a tool many former Top Dogs failed to utilise in order to conquer, the now apparently indestructible Ferguson. The women had finally found the key to unlocking The Freak's weakness – to stand together and be united as one.

The surprising success of Prisoner has caused much speculation around the world. Media critics struggled to grasp what it was about this small Australian soap opera that would prove to be one of the most enduring and best-loved serials ever produced in its home country, creating massive impact around the world.

Unlocking the secrets of success can only happen if you are indeed a true 'Blockie', and have followed the series from beginning to end. Each era in *Prisoner* is separated by memorable performances by the Top Dogs. Some stronger than others, but each used cleverly by the writers to make the strength of their predecessor more incandescent, and help cement and crystallise their contribution to the shows energy.

It is without doubt that *Prisoner* stands at the top of all other television shows produced in Australia as the one which captured the hearts of the audiences and, to this day, receives the most requests for a sequel.

The talents of the *Prisoner* writing team, and the powerful performances of such actors as Val Lehman, Maggie Kirkpatrick and Olivia Hamnett, are worthy reasons why *Prisoner* has become so successful. Without their firm grasp on their characters or sheer level of charisma, we would have been watching a very different Wentworth. Their energy and ability to control and captivate an audience gave true meaning to the title of the series and now remains locked in the realms of television history.

Now, moved by the sheer level of devotion and loyalty of its fans, the cast and crew of *Prisoner* have helped us to look behind the bars, at a series that catapulted the Australian accent and idiom to worldwide stardom, in the process helping us to understand, from their own point of view, why *Prisoner* became the success story it did. The timeless appeal of *Prisoner* has brought us together to share with you some of the stories from the very people who were there when it all happened. The remarkable longevity of the series appears to run synonymously with a retrospective look back at a time described as a 'golden era of Australian television'. In a league of its own...

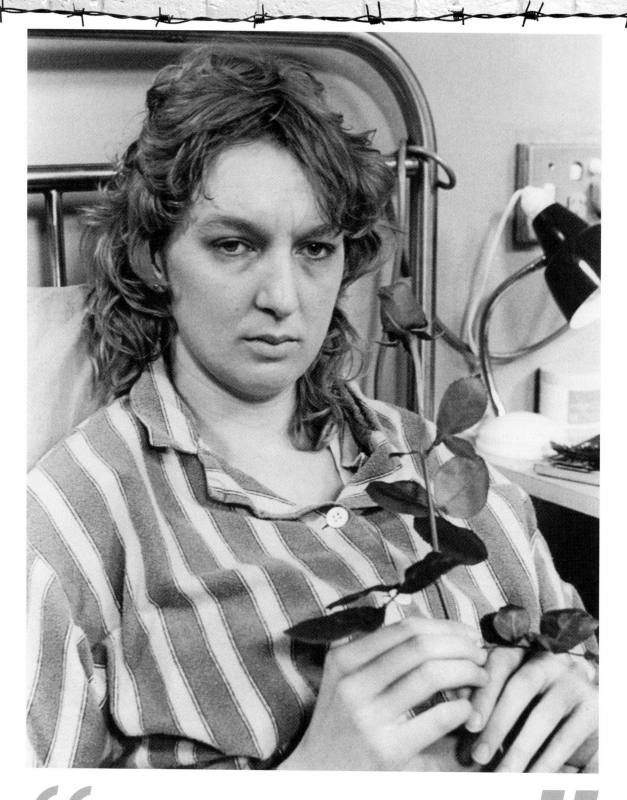

" *… and things were different, then.* "

APPENDIX

EPISODE SYNOPSES

Episode 1

Welcome to Wentworth – this first episode introduces us to some very familiar faces for the first time. New inmates Karen Travers and Lynn Warner are inducted and have to quickly adjust to life inside.

Episode 2

Top Dog Bea Smith and long term inmate Mum are released on parole while Lynn protests her innocence by going on a hunger strike. Bea's first day of freedom is short lived when visits her husband with a 'present'.

Episode 3

Franky Doyle takes over as Top Dog and starts stirring trouble immediately. Chrissie Latham unsuccessfully tries to seduce the prison social worker Bill Jackson. When Bea returns, a riot breaks out resulting in tragic consequences.

Episode 4

Bill dies in the ambulance and the women are determined to punish whoever killed him during the riot, while his wife – Officer Meg Jackson struggles to control her feelings following his death. Mum has an accident in her motel room.

Episode 5

Mum recovers at her daughter's house but isn't allowed to disclose her real identity to her grand-children. Lynn collapses following her hunger strike but is shocked to find out that she is pregnant when examined by the doctor.

Episode 6

Lynn is told she can't have an abortion so threatens to kill the baby herself. Still protesting her innocence she convinces Meg to investigate. Lizzie plans an escape but ends up drunk in her cell instead.

Episode 7

Lizzie finds a new friend in the garden but is devastated when things go wrong. Franky tries to control her temper in the hope she'll be released. Marilyn is tempted to return to prostitution when she can't find a job on the outside.

Episode 8

Marilyn gets as job working in a hotel. Celebrity beauty consultant Helen Masters is arrested and sent to Wentworth following a hit and run accident but makes a big mistake when she 'lags' on one of the other women.

Episode 9

Lynn's appeal is arranged thanks to the help of Helen, but Meg finds herself in trouble when details appear in the newspapers. Eddie accuses Marilyn of going back to her old ways. Lynn finally has something to smile about when she is released.

Episode 10

Helen convinces the women to protest about the prison food and offers to help everyone with their problems, but her promises are soon broken when she is released. Vera drowns her sorrows and makes a fool of herself when she gets drunk in a bar.

Episode 11

Vera forms an alliance with Graham and between them make Marilyn's life inside very difficult. Lynn and Doug run away from Lynn's parents' house. Franky receives some very bad news about her brother.

Episode 12

Karen talks Franky down from the roof. Meg notices that Graham is intimidating Marilyn and threatens to him and Vera that she'll report it to the Governor if it doesn't stop. Franky's advances to Karen are not reciprocated resulting in 3 of the women going over the wall…

Episode 13

Lizzie can't keep up with Doreen and Franky so ends up back inside in the prison hospital while the others find a barn to sleep in for the night. Lynn and Doug plan to get married but Doug can't resist one more robbery before they settle down.

Episode 14

The robbery doesn't go according to plan when the two men are shot. Lynn goes into labour but loses the baby. New social worker Jean Vernon arrives and convinces Judith-Anne to visit Mum again. Karen's mother visits and shares some home truths.

Episode 15

Doreen and Franky disguise themselves as nuns in the hope that they can raise some money for their own funds and find a new place to live. Lynn returns to Wentworth after being questioned about the robbery.

Episode 16

Miss McBride offers Doreen and Franky a room at her house, which they accept. Vera is set up by Bea and Monica while Mum and Marilyn are released again. Lynn is so depressed that she cuts her wrists – has Meg found her in time?

Episode 17

Lynn recovers in hospital. Erica is embarrassed when her niece Barbara is brought to Wentworth for drug smuggling. Vera is reinstated thanks to Barbara who tells Erica everything she hears from the women. Franky and Doreen go on the run again.

Episode 18

A young schoolgirl, Sarah, is raped and her mother is determined to get justice on the man responsible. When drugs are found by Vera in Monica's cell, she realises she has been set up by another prisoner.

Episode 19

Franky attacks Toddy when she realises that he's been bashing Doreen. Vera tells Bea why Barbara is really inside – for smuggling drugs. Sarah spots the man that raped her and calls her mother, who takes matters into her own hands and purposely runs him down in her car.

Episode 20

Catherine arrives at Wentworth but has she killed the wrong man? Franky and Doreen plan to rob a hardware store but things go wrong when shots are fired and Franky is hit. Doreen manages to escape but walks back to the prison announcing that her partner in crime is dead.

Episode 21

Doreen adopts a 'tough' image when she is returned to the other women and blames Karen for Franky's death. Lizzie finds out that her brother is dying and is allowed the chance to visit him. Barbara suggests that she's going to cause problems for Vera during her hearing.

Episode 22

Lizzie's visit to her brother ends up with a huge argument between her and Angus. Catherine is sentenced to 3 years after refusing to let her daughter testify. Karen finds out that her re-trial is closer than she thought.

Episode 23

Doreen and Barbara have a fight, resulting in Barbara getting drenched with a bucket of dirty water. Catherine is disappointed when her daughter comes to visit. Barbara causes more problems when she barricades herself in her cell, threatening to set the room on fire.

Episode 24

Lynn's father arranges a work placement for her in a friend's nursery. Karen's court appearance begins but is adjourned when she becomes too upset. Barbara is transferred to another prison and Doreen returns to her normal self.

Episode 25

A new inmate arrives at Wentworth but refuses to say who she is. Lynn's work release gets off to a bad start when she is accused of stealing money. Karen's mother gives evidence in Karen's favour during her re-trial.

Episode 26

The mystery woman is revealed as Susan Rice. When Vera goes to the local pub she bumps into ex officer Anne Yates who introduces her to her landlord George Lucas at a party. Vera arranges to see him again but all isn't as it seems.

Episode 27

Susan's odd behaviour prompts Meg into suggesting psychiatric treatment. George invites Vera to dinner and she discovers that he is heavily involved in drug dealing. Later he tells her that Anne has been arrested and he wants Vera to look after her if she's sent to Wentworth.

Episode 28

Doreen and Lizzie arrange to forge a work release document for Doreen. Anne is, as expected, brought into Wentworth as a prisoner and it doesn't take Bea long to find out why. Susan is released on a good behaviour bond and Anne demands more protection from Vera.

Episode 29

Susan attacks Jason live on television and life on the other side of the bars for Anne goes from bad to worse – she stabs Bea during a fight and runs off then hides in one of the dryers in the laundry, only to have the door closed on her when Vera walks past it…

Episode 30

Anne can't be found anywhere in the prison until Lizzie opens the dryer door to find that she has suffocated inside of it. Monica plans to take over as Top Dog during Bea's absence but Noeline wants the job and makes up a story to have Monica take the blame for Anne's death.

Episode 31

Clara Goddard confesses to adjusting her financial records and is arrested. Monica gets revenge on Noeline by scalding her in the shower block. Bea escapes from hospital and turns up at Mum's house but Meg later arrives so Bea has to hide.

Episode 32

Lynn's work release is stopped when her boss finds out she's attracted to his son. Judith-Anne arranges a disguise for Bea but she has to return to Mum's when things don't work out. Vera is left tied up in her flat when George and her split up.

Episode 33

Vera is found by Erica who is less than happy in her involvement with George Lucas. The women get bored of Monica and want Bea back, unbeknown to them that the police are already on her trail.

Episode 34

Bea and Val have a night out resulting in a very bad hangover the following morning. Lizzie is forced by Monica to make some of her famous brew but Noeline tries to muscle in on the production line. Noeline's bother makes a big mistake during a burglary.

Episode 35

Clara throws a party for the other women and manages to make even more booze but Noeline drinks the lot. Bea is concerned about the young girl who lives next door. Noeline's brother is shot dead by the police when his burglary goes wrong.

Episode 36

Bea's time is up on the outside and she's returned to Wentworth where she takes over as Top Dog, much to the dismay of Noeline and Monica. Meg is injured when Monica and Bea fight in the laundry over who is working the steam press.

Episode 37

Businesswoman Marianne de Vere has been persuaded to fund the Halfway House project so a celebration barbecue is organised for the prisoners. She also arranges a new colour television for the Recroom but Noeline ensures that nobody will watch it.

Episode 38

All privileges are cancelled by Erica, furious about being blamed for the television being smashed. New prisoner Irene joins the women but is likely to be deported back to Greece as her family are illegal immigrants. Bea decides she's in 'semi-retirement'.

Episode 39

The Department decides to investigate the running of Wentworth, which may result in some big changes. Irene gets some good news but Vera receives the complete opposite when she is called to the Governor's office following the investigation.

Episode 40

New Deputy Governor Jim Fletcher arrives at the prison but doesn't make any favourable first impressions with the other staff. When Lynn is searched on her way out for work release, Jim finds some letters in her bag. New inmate Joyce Martin is inducted.

Episode 41

Bea suggests to Monica that she sell her shop to Marilyn and Eddie. Doreen steals some pills from the prison hospital and sets Lynn up by hiding them underneath her pillow. Joyce's husband visits her and an attempt is made to break her out of the prison.

Episode 42

Jim is only slightly injured but ordered to have further tests at hospital. Lizzie confesses to framing Lynn so she can have her work release re-instated. Lynn later finds out that Doreen is the real culprit. Joyce asks Monica to move her money when she's released.

Episode 43

Monica refuses to be involved with Joyce's plans, but later agrees when she finds out her husband has ran up huge debts since she's been inside. When Monica and Lynn are released, Lynn is kidnapped by mistake instead of Monica.

Episode 44

Lynn (again) protests her innocence but the kidnappers don't believe her. Monica finds the money and moves it as agreed then pays off her husband's debts. When she gets home, Fred has stolen the rest of the money and is nowhere to be seen.

Episode 45

New prison psychologist Dr Clements arrives and begins studying the women, and staff. Fred's plans backfire and he returns home to be beaten up by Monica, who is then sent back to Wentworth – and meets up with Fred's 'girlfriend' Blossom.

Episode 46

Blossom is attacked by Monica. Lizzie has a bad turn during the fight, which is broken up by Vera and Jim. Jim reacts strangely when he sees the sight of blood on Blossom's face. Doreen has a breakdown. Has Jim stolen Joyce's key?

Episode 47

A metal detector is used to search everyone leaving the prison in case the key is smuggled out but Jim makes a deal with Blossom and offers his help for half of the money. Jim is suspended after Vera overhears his plans on the telephone.

Episode 48

Jim sleeps with Blossom and finds out where the key is – he reports this to the police but names Joyce as being the person responsible. Melinda blackmails Carol with the photographs but Tom arrives home too late – she has gone.

Episode 49

Melinda's plans crumble and she is arrested for blackmail when Carol calls the police in anticipation for them meeting. Bea finds out that Jim has a secret phobia. Edie dies on the night before she is due to be released.

Episode 50

Noeline is sent back to Wentworth after a failed burglary attempt with her daughter Leanne. Jean tries to help Noeline but her offer is refused. She gives Leanne her address at Meg's place should she need anything. Meg arrives home to find she has been burgled.

Episode 51

Bella Albrecht arrives as a prisoner, guilty of killing her own child. Her crime is kept secret from the women but Bea tricks Peter into telling her the full story, fooling him that she knew already. Bella is later attacked in the shower block.

Episode 52

Bella survives the attack and is sent to work in the garden with Martha Eaves, away from the other women. Peter's time in Wentworth is cut short by Erica. Meg agrees to allow Leanne to move in temporarily. Bella is attacked again but isn't as lucky this time.

Episode 53

Monica is questioned about Bella's murder while Bea is given an alibi from Greg. Melinda is released on a good behaviour bond and goes straight to Greg to arrange an abortion. Noeline smuggles Bella's ring out to Leanne during her visit.

Episode 54

Greg leaves Wentworth to work at his own surgery. Noeline lags on Martha when questioned about Bella's ring, who later confesses to the murder. She is sent to solitary but attacks Vera and takes her hostage resulting in a rooftop rescue by Jim.

Episode 55

Karen's parole is granted and she is finally released from the prison. Doreen returns to Wentworth but appears to be even worse than she was before she went to hospital – she has an accident with a garden fork. Leanne's 'hold-up' job gets underway.

Episode 56

The women decide to start a hunger strike, in protest at having no prison doctor since Greg left. Bea is sent to solitary for her involvement in the strike when it's called off by Monica and Noeline. Melinda visits Greg and is shocked to find out she could be sent back to prison.

Episode 57

Karen moves in with Melinda. Gangster wife Toni McNally is brought to Wentworth for murdering Jackie Coulson in a bar. Karen doesn't have much luck when trying to find a job. Toni's witness is moved to a safe house but not for long.

Episode 58

Toni arranges a delivery of drugs to be sent to Wentworth and convinces some of the women to help her. Jim and Vera go out for a drink but Vera's hopes of starting a personal relationship with him are ruined. Erica investigates Toni's involvement with the Department.

Episode 59

Contraband is smuggled into the prison but the officers have no luck in finding it. Bea finds out about Toni's drug smuggling. Erica confesses to writing a letter of resignation. Karen is offered a job from Angela Jeffries as her secretary.

Episode 60

Angela convinces Karen to try and persuade Greg to return to Wentworth. Monica is hurt when Martha pours soup over her. Meg realises that she's being set up to retaliate and Monica's ordered to stay in her cell. Greg finds out that Angela is a lesbian.

Episode 61
Greg visits Wentworth and agrees to return twice a week. Bea appears to step down as Top Dog when she's released from solitary. Head of the Department, Mr Douglas, arrives to discuss Erica's resignation. Glenys is caught by two hit men and driven to an open grave…

Episode 62
Glenys manages to escape and flags down a passing motorist. Thinking she is safe in a guarded hotel room she receives a threatening note with her meal. Greg visits Mum and tells her to rest as she has low blood pressure. When Mum arrives home she collapses.

Episode 63
Greg suspects that Mum has pleurisy. Erica leaves the prison following her resignation and plans to get involved with the Halfway House. The women react angrily to Jim's new rules. Toni is found not guilty but is shot by her victim's daughter, Ros as she leaves the court.

Episode 64
The women are told that Erica will not be coming back. Karen agrees to move in with Mum and Judith-Anne to help them cope with Mum's illness and Judith-Anne's pregnancy. Ros arrives at Wentworth and is told that Toni has died.

Episode 65
A familiar face returns to Wentworth along with new inmate Pat O'Connell. The officers decide to strike so the women are locked in their cells. Karen finds out that Doreen's mother is looking for her and Erica is persuaded to visit her.

Episode 66
Erica changes her mind about resigning when some strong words from Ted Douglas make her realise what she could be leaving behind, under the control of Vera. After a visit from Erica, Doreen's mother comes to the prison to see her daughter.

Episode 67
Alice meets Doreen but keeps her real identity a secret. Chrissie causes trouble between the other prisoners and Meg, resulting in the women agreeing to ignore her completely. A mystery inmate steals some medicine from the prison hospital.

Episode 68
Chrissie becomes ill and Bea is sent to solitary when the suggestion is made that she poisoned her. Karen moves into the Halfway House. When the real thief of the medicine is discovered, she reveals a surprising reason for stealing it.

Episode 69
Chrissie tells Greg that she wants an abortion, but Greg tries to make her change her mind by suggesting she work in the maternity block. Pat's son visits Wentworth in the work party but Vera catches them talking, putting Pat's release in jeopardy.

Episode 70
Chrissie changes her mind and decides to keep the baby after all. Erica decides not to punish Pat. Doreen is released to the care of the Halfway House and spends an afternoon with Alice. Karen finds out the real reason why Alice is not being straight with Doreen.

Episode 71
Ros receives a life sentence and is returned to Wentworth after her trial. Alice spends more time with Doreen buying her new clothes and even offering to pay for her to go to college, but Doreen immediately realises who she really is when she opens a present that Alice has given her.

Episode 72
Vera celebrates her birthday at work but the only present she gets is from Lizzie. Chrissie is punched in the stomach by a confused Rosie. Ros escapes during a fire alarm but ends up at the Halfway House, with nowhere else to go.

Episode 73
Karen allows Ros to stay for the night. Doreen receives some bad news about her mother – she is in a coma. Ros finds a new place to live and is forced to work as a prostitute to pay her way. On her way to catch a bus to leave she is spotted by a passer-by and arrested.

Episode 74
The women begin organising their annual Christmas play, with Lizzie writing the scripts. Ros is sent back to the prison. Greg is forced to lie to the police so they don't suspect Karen of hiding Ros. Pat's mother visits her, but it's not good news.

Episode 75
It's Christmas at Wentworth and the play goes ahead as planned, but the officers leave when they find out that they're the main subject of all the jokes. Pat is released and is welcomed home by her children but is shocked when the police tell her David has escaped.

Episode 76
Lizzie accuses Vera of taking her cake. David steals some toys and leaves them as presents for the kids at the back of Pat's house. The police are on to him and set a trap, where gunshots are fired. Karen hears on the radio that someone has been killed… is it Greg?

Episode 77
Ros takes some pills from the surgery but is caught out and ends up in solitary for 48 hours. Greg and Karen declare their love for each other at last and a story is featured about them in the newspaper – but David reads it and vows to kill Greg for having Pat sent back to prison.

Episode 78
Security is increased inside the prison. Bea blames Ros for the changes and tells the women she will bash her when she gets out of solitary. Jim's friend Geoff takes a fancy to Meg. David carries out his plan of attack on Greg and a shot is fired into his house…

Episode 79
Karen has been shot by David in mistake and lies seriously ill in hospital. New inmate Janet Dominguez arrives and Ros takes a keen interest in her. Meg and Geoff to go dinner at Jim and Leila's. Greg gives permission for the doctors to operate on Karen.

Episode 80
Ros and Janet form an alliance and Ros agrees to see one of Janet's associates visit her as a 'friend' so some drugs can be smuggled in to help with the escape plan. When Kath queries the drugs, Ros tests it to prove everything's ok – and is knocked out straight away.

Episode 81
Ros can't be woken up the following morning so the officers take her to the infirmary. Bea tries to find out what she's up to, without success. Geoff turns violent. That night, Ros sees the signal to start the escape plan but the pen full of the drugs has disappeared.

Episode 82
The pen is found in the Rec Room and the plan is put in motion. Terrorists enter the prison as planned and Ros escapes into the prison grounds with Janet. Erica gets in the way and is shot by one of the terrorists.

Episode 83

Ros manages to escape. Erica is wounded by the shot and agrees to go to hospital. Meg tells Geoff she doesn't want to see him anymore but he refuses to leave. Jim realises and calls in to Meg's house – only to be threatened with a broken bottle by Geoff.

Episode 84

Meg is shocked by Geoff and Jim's fight. Chrissie lags on Bea when the women plan to steal goods from the kitchen. When Bea finds out she arranges to set Chrissie up. Ros accuses Jim of attacking her when he catches her and Lizzie stealing food.

Episode 85

Ros is punished for stealing from the kitchen and lying about Jim. New social worker Paul Reid begins his first day at the prison. Pat's appeal cannot go ahead, but she is even more devastated when Erica tells her that David has hanged himself.

Episode 86

Pat attacks Chrissie when she suggests that David is better off dead. Greg has a farewell party at the prison. Lizzie is interviewed by the police and it turns out that she may be innocent of the crime she committed over 20 years ago!

Episode 87

The VJ sends Ros back to solitary for another week. Bea gets suspicious about the police interviewing Lizzie so manages to sneak the story out to a visiting journalist. Lizzie is told the truth about why the police have been talking to her.

Episode 88

Paul is suspected of being guilty of telling the journalist about Lizzie. The women arrange a party for Lizzie who is released and plans to live in the Halfway House with Doreen, but she is left stranded at the prison when Doreen doesn't turn up to collect her.

Episode 89

Doreen finds out she has an admirer at work and agrees to go out with him to a disco but stands him up when Lizzie cooks a surprise meal for everyone. Caroline Simpson stabs her violent father in the back with a bread knife after he threatens her mother with a gun.

Episode 90

Caroline and Vivienne make up a story about burglars attacking Mr Williams but they can't keep to it. Tony is in trouble after drugs dealer Sharon Gilmour makes a delivery to his lodgings, as the police have followed her and raid the house.

Episode 91

Caroline and Vivienne are brought on remand to Wentworth, while Paul pays Tony's bail money. Sharon also arrives in Wentworth, making an enemy of Bea following an accident with a hot bowl of soup. Sharon tries to blackmail Paul.

Episode 92

Doreen and Kevin go out on a date, but Lizzie causes problems when she drunkenly phones Doreen's work to tell them she's not coming in. Some of the other women attack Sharon but Chrissie gets in the way and starts having contractions when she's pushed during the scuffle.

Episode 93

Chrissie is rushed to hospital and gives birth to a baby girl whom she calls Elizabeth, after Lizzie. Sharon reveals she is a lesbian, and Judy is her lover. Elizabeth needs specialist attention for a long time so Chrissie is returned to Wentworth alone.

Episode 94

Rhonda catches Lizzie drinking alcohol inside the Halfway House. Jim reveals Doreen's past when he turns up at a meal which has been organised by Doreen's friends from work. Sharon is sentenced to 2 years in prison while Tony gets a good behaviour bond.

Episode 95

Sharon is brought back to Wentworth and teams up with Chrissie – between them they take over and supply the other women with drugs. Look out for a classic Lizzie moment as she has problems getting up from Kevin's bean bag! Kevin proposes to Doreen.

Episode 96

Chrissie is told she can make regular visits to the hospital to visit Elizabeth – Sharon uses this as a way of getting drugs into the prison to avoid the searches which have been introduced. Chrissie is grabbed from behind when she collects the drugs from the hospital toilets.

Episode 97

Chrissie tries to convince Judy that she and Sharon are just friends and the drugs transfer goes ahead. Margo tries to take over but Sharon threatens to plant drugs on her. Bea manages to get released from isolation just in time to save Sharon from a beating.

Episode 98

Judy is caught smuggling drugs into the prison, resulting in her becoming an inmate herself. Kevin's mother meets Doreen for the first time. Bea and Pat plan to set up Sharon by planting some drugs on her but Judy walks in as Pat's hiding them in Sharon's soap dish.

Episode 99

Judy doesn't stop Pat and the drugs are found so Sharon ends up in solitary. Jim offers to pay Caroline and Vivienne's bail as long as he doesn't have to appear in court. Louisa and Doreen go shopping for the wedding but Kevin later tells his mother all about Doreen's prison past.

Episode 100

Louisa threatens Doreen that she'll disown Kevin if they marry, but Lizzie takes matters into her own hands – armed with a pan! Judy punches Bea to get herself put in solitary so she can talk to Sharon. Lizzie and Doreen make the mistake of getting drunk and broke.

Episode 101

Doreen is remanded to Wentworth while Lizzie is allowed bail. Sharon and Judy fall out when they speak in solitary. Lizzie tries to help Doreen by visiting the shop where they stole the booze from but her plan doesn't work. Doreen tells Kevin she doesn't want to marry him.

Episode 102

Bea convinces Chrissie not to side with Sharon as it will show the wrong impression when the decision is made about getting Elizabeth back. Lizzie is fined and returns back to the half way house. Chrissie's chances are in jeopardy when she's involved in a fight.

Episode 103

Judy tells the truth about the fight after Sharon lies to Erica. Caroline is released to the half way house. Lizzie goes on a shoplifting mission, and manages to walk out of a shop in a mink coat. She's over the moon when she returns home to hear that the police have been called.

Episode 104

Lizzie ends up on the inside again but is let off with another fine. Bea tries to convince Lizzie to stop committing crimes just to get sent back to prison. The drama group arrives at Wentworth. Jim's in trouble when Erica finds out he's been seeing Caroline on the outside.

Episode 105

The women find out about Jim and Caroline which results in him being the subject of some smart remarks. Lizzie has yet another try at getting sent back to Wentworth and this time succeeds when she upsets the Magistrate. Jim's wife finds out about his relationship with Caroline.

Episode 106

Doreen finds a dog in the prison garden and smuggles it inside. Vera finds the dog and decides to look after it herself. Geoff's trial begins - Meg and Jim give evidence. He is given a good behaviour bond but is approached by Michael Simpson to suggest they work together against Jim.

Episode 107

Michael offers Geoff $2000 if he can arrange for Caroline to come back to him. Bea agrees to try and make the drama group at Wentworth continue. Judy collapses in the garden and Erica gets the doctor to encourage her to take some tests. Leila has a nasty shock at home.

Episode 108

Leila phones the police but Jim becomes the prime suspect. Lizzie fakes a heart attack to convince Judy to go for the medical tests. Geoff persuades Michael to take a package containing drugs to Jim's hotel - not realising that the package contains a bomb.

Episode 109

Caroline receives an anonymous letter. The package is delivered to Jim's hotel and left at reception. When Leila and the children come to visit Jim, they take the parcel up to his room but disaster strikes when it explodes as the boys are carrying it – blowing the room apart. . .

Episode 110

Jim is devastated when he loses his whole family following the explosion. Pat is released. Bea suggests to Ken that a day inside the prison will make his daughter change her ways. Geoff visits Jim and plans to kill him while he's sleeping.

Episode 111

Geoff is disturbed when reporters knock at Jim's door. Debbie agrees to spend a day at Wentworth. Vera agrees for Lizzie to go on a day release with the Salvation Army. Judy goes to hospital for her operation. The funerals are held for Jim's family, but Geoff is lurking close-by.

Episode 112

Caroline phones the police so Michael is arrested. New prisoner, artist Kerry Vincent, arrives but Doreen is concerned for Bea when Ken takes a special interest in her. Jim arrives home to find Geoff waiting for him. . . but a police marksman steps in at the right moment.

Episode 113

Doreen suggests to Bea that Ken has more than a professional interest in Kerry. Jim returns to work but Erica tells him to go home as it's too soon. Sharon misunderstands Kerry and is rejected when she makes a move on her. She hints to the others that Kerry is lagging to Vera.

Episode 114

Bea tells Kerry that she's going to be watching her, following her apparent association with Vera. Temporary officer Jock Stewart arrives. Kerry convinces Bea that she's not a lagger. Kerry's agent, David, suggests to the press that a prison officer has been using her.

Episode 115

Vera is furious with David and demands to know why Kerry told him that she was blackmailing her. Judy and Sharon split up for good. Kevin asks Doreen to marry him and she accepts the offer. Vera is suspended from duty following the blackmail story.

Episode 116

Jock helps Vera to get the painting back. Kevin and Doreen are married in the prison garden. Bea spends a few moments with Ken in the storeroom but Vera finds them and Ken is banned from the prison. Judy is found nursing a dead Sharon at the bottom of the stairs.

Episode 117

Judy accuses Bea of killing Sharon but becomes a suspect when the police find out about their argument. David arranges for the press to report on Sharon's death in favour of Kerry. Lizzie receives information about her daughter. Jock tells Doreen that he killed Sharon.

Episode 118

Doreen agrees to sell her house after some gentle persuasion from Jock. Helen Smart reveals that Jock is well known for violence against prostitutes. Doreen tells Judy that Jock killed Sharon. Lizzie meets her granddaughter for the first time.

Episode 119

Judy apologises to Bea and the two of them confront Jock about him killing Sharon. Vera overhears them and tells Erica. Jock warns Judy not to make any more accusations. Doreen agrees to let Marcia and Josie stay at her mother's house while it's empty.

Episode 120

Marcia and Josie move into their new home. Leanne Bourke is admitted to Wentworth for two months – she tells the other women that Noeline now has a job. When the inquiry into Sharon's death is decided as accidental, the women stage a protest.

Episode 121

The women are locked in the Rec Room and sit in overnight. The following morning they continue their demonstration on the roof after taking Erica and Vera hostage. It all ends in tragedy when Leanne falls from the roof to her death.

Episode 122

Noeline is told the bad news about Leanne. Stolen money is found in her pockets – she is sentenced to six months. Lizzie finds out that Josie needs an operation on her leg. Kerry attacks David and hits him with an ashtray.

Episode 123

Lizzie finds out that Marcia isn't really her daughter. Kerry takes a combination of pills and alcohol, resulting in her passing out. David finds her unconscious but steals some of her paintings rather than help her.

Episode 124

Helen anonymously calls Paul Reid, telling him to come to Kerry's flat immediately. Meg moves into a new apartment. Marcia tells Lizzie the truth – but Lizzie still agrees to give her money for Josie's operation. Noeline gets locked in the store room.

Episode 125

The women cover for Noeline. Meg suspects her neighbour's husband of mistreating their son. A work release scheme is arranged for the women in a local clothing factory. Judy is set up by Margo.

Episode 126

Noeline cleans Margo out by winning a bet. Judy takes an interest in Noeline's money, offering to help her get it out to her family. The noise from next door gets too much for Meg so she calls the police, but Gail reveals that she's been hitting Jason – not her husband.

Episode 127

Gail is remanded at Wentworth until her trial – she is warned not to tell the other prisoners about what she's done. Factory accountant Kay White places a bet with Margo. Judy pays Kay for a dress to use when she escapes.

Episode 128

The women find out about Gail and call her a 'baby basher'. Judy suggests to Doreen that Kevin could get the factory's delivery contract if he puts a low bid in. Erica and Andrew arrange a dinner date. Vince locks Doreen in the store room with him…

Episode 129

Doreen tries to get out of working at the factory but her efforts only make things worse but Judy soon realises that Doreen is scared of Vince. Andrew and Erica have another dinner date. Noeline is allowed to work at the factory.

Episode 130

Doreen agrees to meet Vince in the storeroom again and finds out what the lowest bid is for the delivery job. Judy ends up in hospital after standing next to the laundry driers for too long, but has an ulterior motive and manages to escape.

Episode 131

Dressed as a policewoman, Judy is on the run but finds somewhere to stay. Bea gets a place on the work scheme. Judy arranges to get a fake passport to be made so she can travel to the US. Kay reports to Andrew that material is missing from the factory.

Episode 132

Noeline is caught giving material to her brother so the work scheme is cancelled by Vera. Erica overrides her decision – Noeline is transferred and the scheme is reinstated. Judy's time on the outside is over when the police catch up with her.

Episode 133

Judy arrives back at the prison and is sent straight to solitary. Bea gives Vince the shock of his life when she sabotages her sewing machine. The other factory workers complain about the prisoners taking their work, for less pay.

Episode 134

Lizzie thinks everyone has forgotten about her birthday but the women have secretly organised a party for her – Lizzie even manages to get drunk on non-alcoholic wine! At the factory, Kay has stolen all of the money for the employees' wages.

Episode 135

Kay is caught and sent to Wentworth under charges of theft and embezzlement. The women find out and Margo decides to poison her food with detergent. New social worker Agnes Forster arrives but worries staff and prisoners with her unusual approach to work.

Episode 136

A barbecue is arranged for the women but Kay's burger is laced with glass. She tries to make peace with the women by persuading Vince to visit her – which he does, and the women attack him… Doreen is pregnant with his baby.

Episode 137

Lizzie is disappointed with Agnes. The women plot to get back at Kay for lagging on them by tempting her to make bets for games she can't afford to pay when she loses. Agnes causes more problems when she tells Kevin about Doreen's baby.

Episode 138

Doreen tells Kevin that he's not the father of her baby and Kevin insists that she reports the rape to the police. The staff agree that Agnes should be retired off and prompt Erica into arranging a replacement. Doreen reveals to Kevin the truth about Vince.

Episode 139

Kevin tells Doreen that he wants a divorce. Kay is set up by the other women. Agnes makes yet more mistakes. Doreen is devastated and makes the drastic decision to kill herself when the women are in the Rec Room.

Episode 140

Jim accuses Erica of forcing Agnes to resign. Lizzie says goodbye to Ellen and Josie who have to travel to Chicago for Josie's operation. Meg suggests to Doreen that she keeps the baby. Kay is sentenced to five years.

Episode 141

Linda passes money to her son Danny during a visit. Kay provokes Bea and ends up with porridge being spilt onto her in the dining room. Drug smuggler Tracey Morris arrives at Wentworth. When drugs are found in the prison, Bea is ready to bash Kay.

Episode 142

Bea attacks Kay. When the fight is broken up, no drugs are found. Inspector Grace convinces Vera to put pressure onto Tracey to get her to confess to the drug smuggling charges. Doreen loses the baby. Danny runs away from Child Welfare.

Episode 143

Kay frightens Tracey into having some money brought into the prison. The other women search Kay's cell and steal her money. Jim finds Danny and offers that he stays with him. New inmate Kath is inducted but has a hidden agenda to 'protect' Tracey.

Episode 144

Vera ignores a threatening phone-call and continues to pressure Tracey. Danny finds Jim's gun when he moves into his house. Lizzie and Judy have an idea to set Kay up. Vera is attacked on her way back home.

Episode 145

Vera recovers in hospital but tells the Inspector that she's not helping the police anymore. Judy puts her plan into action but Lizzie is in danger when the plan backfires, and Kay ends up knocked out when Linda stops her from attacking Lizzie.

Episode 146

Lizzie takes the blame for Kay's death and is charged with manslaughter. Tracey is released and has a detective watching the house for her own safety. She manages to disappear unnoticed wearing a disguise but walks into even more trouble.

Episode 147

Tracey is rescued by the police and sent back to Wentworth for her protection when she reveals the names of Joe's friends. Vera and Meg have dinner together but Vera gets drunk. Kath is put in a difficult position but Bea comes to the rescue.

Episode 148

Bea warns Tracey that she's still in danger inside the prison. Vera goes to a disco with Jim and comes home with a stranger. Erica offers to look for a work release job for Doreen. A sniper fires into the prison garden. He is aiming at Tracey but hits Bob and Meg.

Episode 149

Meg and Bob recover. Judy suggests a group therapy session in order for the women to trust Tracey again but it doesn't go according to plan and all of the women argue. Jim meets Sarah Forrest at a party but lies about who he is. Doreen tells Erica the truth about Kay's death.

Episode 150

Lizzie sticks to her story and Linda also denies Doreen's accusations. Doreen is transferred to the maternity block and realises she needs to change. Bob and Meg become close. Lizzie is given an extra 5 years for Kay's murder.

Episode 151

Lizzie is persuaded by Judy and Erica to appeal against her conviction. Sarah starts questioning Jim's story about him being a builder. Doreen saves baby Elizabeth's life. Vera drops a hint to Tracey about Meg's involvement with Bob.

Episode 152

Doreen visits the local hospital making a good impression in the children's ward so is offered a job there. Meg tells Vera to mind her own business. Lizzie's appeal is a success and her sentence is reduced. Chrissie has a mystery visitor and Sarah finds out where Jim really works.

Episode 153

Jim realises why Sarah has left. Chrissie worries that Elizabeth will soon be taken from her as she's almost 1 year old. Erica allows a farewell party to be held for Doreen. On the way back from court Tracey's car is diverted and she's held at gunpoint by one of the 'policemen'.

Episode 154

Shots are fired but Tracey escapes with just a few scratches. Doreen has difficulty adjusting to life on the outside. Tracey is given a 2 year sentence. Bea celebrates her birthday. Erica is convinced that she has seen Sarah somewhere before.

Episode 155

Vera lets all of the hospital staff know that Doreen's been in prison. Erica recognises Sarah as Jacki Nolan, who had escaped from custody some time ago. Vera arrives at work drunk and the women take advantage and steal her keys. Doreen steals Elizabeth from the hospital.

Episode 156

Sarah makes a decision to turn herself in to the police – she is sent to Wentworth. Elizabeth isn't very well and Doreen has to bring her back to hospital. Bob tells Tracey that he wants to marry Meg, resulting in almost tragic consequences.

Episode 157

Doreen is sent back to prison for kidnapping Elizabeth. Chrissie changes her mind about getting back at Doreen when she realises why she stole the baby. Meg accepts Bob's proposal and Vera makes a new friend while she is drunk.

Episode 158

Tracey makes it up with Meg and congratulates her. Vera returns to Wentworth and confesses to Erica about her drink problem. She later takes action at home and pours all of her alcohol away. Tracey is transferred to Barnhurst.

Episode 159

Vera finds out about Jim and Jacki, who is later released – not before 'disappearing' when the women think she is being transferred. Mr Douglas advises Erica that the Department is not happy so a Government inspection has been arranged for the prison.

Episode 160

Lizzie finds out about Wentworth's history. New prisoner Anne Griffin arrives, charged with armed robbery. The women decide to investigate the old drainage tunnels underneath the prison. Mr Gillespie from the Department arrives. Bea is attacked by a mystery person…

Episode 161

The pantomime script arrives and the women begin casting for the star roles. Bea recovers from her attack but has no idea who bashed her. The officers go for rifle practice as an extra security measure. Money goes missing and Judy appears to be the culprit.

Episode 162

Judy tells Bea that the money was planted on her but the other women don't buy her story. The pantomime is cancelled and then re-instated when Erica goes above Gillespie's head to the Department. Vera begins to question Anne's story.

Episode 163

The women plan to escape during the pantomime and ask Helen to arrange to view copies of the underground drainage system where they will hide-out. Meg resigns. The women become suspicious of Anne and realise that she knows everything about their plans.

Episode 164

Rehearsals continue for the pantomime and the women try to convince Anne that the escape plans were just a joke but she doesn't believe them. Lizzie puts everything in jeopardy when she gives Meg a book containing plans of the drains as a leaving present.

Episode 165

The performance goes well and the women put their escape plan into action, with a surprise addition to their group – Lizzie. Disaster strikes when the tunnel roof caves in, crushing one of the women and trapping the others at either side of the rubble.

Episode 166

Mouse and Judy find a way out but Bea, Lizzie and Doreen are still trapped at the other side of the fallen rubble. The prison is in chaos and Colleen threatens to bring in the union. Bea realises she and her mates may never be found but vows not to let them die.

Episode 167

The trapped women are rescued and Bea finds out that it was Anne who covered over the manhole. Chrissie holds a party for Elizabeth's first birthday but the celebrations end when Child Welfare take her away. Judy finds somewhere to stay on the outside.

Episode 168

Wally agrees to post a letter from Judy which is published in the newspaper. The women also write their own letter to the Ombudsman but Gillespie finds out and opens it – he is immediately suspended. Lizzie collapses in the Rec Room.

Episode 169

Vera saves Lizzie's life. All of Gillespie's security measures are reversed by Erica. Lizzie makes headlines during her recovery and becomes hopeful that she may be released. Wally's daughter suggests Judy plans a TV appearance.

Episode 170

Lizzie returns to Wentworth. Judy's video recording is delivered by Micki but isn't shown on television as expected. The police arrive at Wally's and arrest him leaving Judy no option than to go back on the run again.

Episode 171
Judy ends up at Helen Smart's house where she finds out that Jock Stewart has been seen at the local massage parlour. New teacher David Andrews arrives but doesn't get off to a good start with the women. Judy attacks Jock in the massage parlour.

Episode 172
Jock forces Judy to work for him but the police catch up with him just in time. Judy is returned to the prison and Jock is refused bail. When Doreen volunteers to help David tidy up the library she kisses him, just as Jim walks into the room.

Episode 173
Erica reprimands David and orders him not to be alone with Doreen. Sid and Lizzie's friendship blossoms. New prisoner Sandra causes concern amongst the other women when she starts taking an interest in Judy and her escape.

Episode 174
Bea decides to send Sandra to Coventry so everyone ignores her. Vera taunts Doreen about her interest in David. Sandra is mysteriously attacked in the shower block but later reveals her true identity. Colleen finds Sid unconscious at home.

Episode 175
Sandra offers to pay the women for any information used by her newspaper. New inmates Georgie Baxter and Evelyn Randall are inducted. Doreen becomes ill after drinking some of Evelyn's home made medicine and the women find out why she was sent to prison.

Episode 176
Doreen recovers. Evelyn asks Lizzie to collect some pollen and weeds for her while she's on the outside visiting Sid. Georgie attacks Bea and ends up back in solitary. Some of the women become ill and it appears that Evelyn is not to blame this time.

Episode 177
The prisoners and officers are put into quarantine while an investigation is carried out. Georgie and Judy become friends. Evelyn creates a home-made remedy to give to Meg. Sandra tries to escape but is stopped by Jim, armed with a gun.

Episode 178
Bea's condition deteriorates but Meg comes out of the coma. Evelyn tries to convince everyone that her mixture made Meg's condition improve but the authorities disagree – they think she has poisoned everyone on purpose just so she can cure them.

Episode 179
Dr Granger's suspicions about Evelyn are correct. The women find out but are warned by Jim to leave her alone, however that doesn't stop some of them causing a nasty 'accident' for Evelyn. Margo decides she's 'going straight' when she gets released.

Episode 180
Margo is released but the living conditions at home with Wayne aren't exactly ideal. Georgie has some hospital tests and is found to have a hearing condition. David arranges a pottery class, which Erica attends with the women. Margo tries to visit Bea for some money.

Episode 181
Judy is upset when Vera taunts her about Georgie. Meg is offered the job of careers officer. Margo tries to earn some more cash by working as a stripper. Doreen taunts Georgie, resulting in a fight, but Bea sticks up for Georgie – lagging on Doreen.

Episode 182
As sides begin to take place the atmosphere in the prison turns very tense. Erica storms out of the pottery class when an argument breaks out between the women. Margo finds out that Wayne owes $6000 in gambling debts. Bea is knocked out during another scuffle.

Episode 183
Bea is taken to hospital. Margo and Wayne make their plans for the payroll job. Bea attempts to make peace with Judy but she collapses. The payroll job goes ahead but the gang end up in a police chase and have to take refuge in a shop, taking the workers hostage.

Episode 184
Margo asks for Meg to help in the siege as a messenger between her and the police. Trainee officer Sally Dean arrives and Vera takes delight in showing her how the prison should be run. The siege ends – Bazza and Wayne are both shot by the police.

Episode 185
Margo returns to Wentworth and is in shock when she finds out that Wayne has died. Bea tells Georgie she will teach her how to read. Sally is tricked into thinking that Georgie has hidden something in the newly made pots – she smashes them all in a rage.

Episode 186
Erica arranges a visitor for Lizzie, who steals her visitor's identity badge. Georgie is released on parole and moves in with her boyfriend Mike but they argue and she walks out. Lizzie manages to escape, leaving a note saying that she's having a day off!

Episode 187
Lizzie has fun on the outside but is disappointed when she tries to visit Sid. Meg and Bob argue when Meg's job is discussed during dinner with Bob's clients. Chrissie returns and starts to work in the laundry to earn money for Elizabeth. Bob gives Meg an ultimatum.

Episode 188
The women clean up the garden shed to use as a visiting suite. Meg decides to become a welfare officer and leave the prison. Chrissie gets a surprise visitor but is heartbroken when she finds out that she probably won't be seeing him again.

Episode 189
Erica is interviewed about the visiting scheme but Bea is disappointed when she reads it so plans to get the women to boycott it. Meg starts on her training course for the new job. Bea realises that she's beginning to lose support from the other women.

Episode 190
Bea is ignored by everyone in the Rec Room. Ken visits Bea in the visiting suite but the reporters outside run a story on it and it's featured in the newspaper. Mick proposes to Chrissie. Ken's daughter tells Bea that she wants her dad to try and make his marriage work.

Episode 191
Ken is shocked to find that his wife is waiting for him at home, who later comes to visit Bea. Chrissie's parole is granted and she's released. Ken tells Bea that he won't be coming back to the prison and is staying with his wife.

Episode 192
Chrissie tells Mick that she wants nothing from him and only cares about her daughter. David suggests a new project for Bea. Doreen reveals that she's got a pen friend, from a lonely hearts club. Chrissie finds it difficult to keep to the strict rules about visiting Elizabeth.

Episode 193

Doreen is forgiven for causing the women's mail to be censored. Meg provides a positive report for Child Welfare on Chrissie and Mick. Vera takes great delight in ridiculing Doreen over her new pen friend. Bea informs the women they are now on strike.

Episode 194

Colleen accuses David of causing the women to strike. Judy encourages Doreen not to hurt Peter's feelings. Vera and Colleen unite to bring the education centre down, calling it a security risk. Chrissie is devastated when Mick is arrested by the police.

Episode 195

Meg convinces the police that Chrissie knew nothing of Mick being an escapee. Mick is sentenced to three years imprisonment. Bea incites trouble for the officers by sabotaging machinery in the laundry and increasing their workload.

Episode 196

Chrissie refuses her brother's help, and is warned by Meg not to return to prostitution. The women's discontent continues by a protest in the dining room. Ted Douglas decides to relieve Erica of her duties. Bea's actions backfire when she is transferred to Barnhurst.

Episode 197

Bea is suspicious of the on-goings in Barnhurst, and more so of the prison top-dog Marie Winter. Chrissie is informed her father has died, but later gets approval to have custody of her daughter. Bea suspects Tracey Morris of being involved with the drugs in Barnhurst . Ted tries to persuade Erica to return to Wentworth.

Episode 198

The women create more unrest to persuade the authorities to return Bea. Bea attacks Marie for arranging for her to be drugged. Vera selfishly encourages Jim to look for another job. Erica arranges for Bea to return to Wentworth, but the prison van crashes knocking Bea unconscious.

Episode 199

Bea emerges from the van, confused and disorientated. She struggles to remember where she is, and goes in search of an old friend…. Officer Terry Harrison arrives in Wentworth. Worried about Bea, Mum turns to Meg for help.

Episode 200

Mum persuades Meg not to phone the police, but Bea is caught and taken back to Wentworth. Terry takes Vera out on a date!   The women become increasingly worried about Bea, but Vera relishes the opportunity to bring her down.

Episode 201

Margo vows revenge on Bea for attacking her. The officers cannot decide if Bea is telling the truth, and bring in Doctor Weissman to examine her. Mum discovers her pills are missing, and later collapses in her cell.

Episode 202

Bea finds Mum unconscious and seeks help. Terry continues to romance Vera, despite it being a bet with Jim. When Bea is attacked, her memory returns but threatens to kill Margo if she tells anyone.

Episode 203

Bea confesses to Mum that her memory has returned, but is hiding it from the authorities in a hope of being released. Margo testifies against Bea, but requests a transfer to Barnhurst for her safety. When Mum's freedom comes under jeopardy, Bea questions her own motives.

Episode 204

Mum is acquitted, while Bea is returned to Wentworth. Erica refuses Margo's transfer. Vera allows Terry to move in with her, while Nick causes some problems for Meg.

Episode 205

Meg is instructed to throw Nick out of her home, but Bob comes to his defence. Lizzie opens a new book, but later gets into trouble when she doesn't have enough money to pay the women. Margo steals Judy's recorder to set a trap for Terry.

Episode 206

Margo passes information to Terry in return for a bottle of Scotch. Nick's interest in Meg's private life begins to cause concern. Margo's plans backfire when she is found in a pool of blood.

Episode 207

Bea gives her backing to the Prisoners Needs Committee. Following her bashing and becoming an enemy to both inmates and officers, Margo is placed in isolation, vowing revenge on Terry. Meg sets the record straight with Nick.

Episode 208

Jim confiscates all of the women's recorders. Erica tries to rebuild her relationship with her mother, and asks her brother for help. Terry begins to worry when Bea reveals she has several copies of tape that incriminates him.

Episode 209

Erica's Mother reveals some secrets of her past before she passes away. Terry continues his quest to find Bea's tape. Judy is shocked when a visitor claims to be her daughter Lori.

Episode 210

Judy is overwhelmed at being reunited with Lori. Jim tries to help new prisoner Michelle Parkes. Lori gets herself arrested to be with her mother, but Judy hides her identity from the other women.

Episode 211

Lori tries to prolong her stay in Wentworth to be with Judy. Lizzie returns to share a cell with Bea and Doreen, and receives a letter from Sid. Judy confides in Bea about her past.

Episode 212

Judy tells Lori the truth about her sexuality. Colleen prepares Lizzie for the shock of seeing Sid. Michelle fears the worst when her trial goes against her.

Episode 213

Jim manages to get Michelle acquitted. Kathy Hall is inducted to Wentworth and is warned about Officer Terry Harrison, who is revealed as her ex-husband.

Episode 214

Terry tries to silence Kathy about their past. Erica visits Sid to discuss living with Lizzie when she is released. Sid proposes to Lizzie! Bea discovers that someone is out to harm Kathy.

Episode 215

Kathy is found unconscious after a bashing from one of the other prisoners. Alison Page is inducted to Wentworth. Lizzie accepts Sid's marriage proposal.

Episode 216
Erica takes Lizzie shopping for clothes for her wedding. Gordon threatens Lizzie over their marriage, believing she is only after Sid's house. Alison attempts suicide.

Episode 217
Bea saves Alison's life. Lizzie informs the other women about Gordon's visit, which angers Bea. Vera returns home to an unwelcome visitor – and a gun.

Episode 218
Kathy is warned to stay inside for her own safety. Doreen continues to threaten Alison. Bea seizes the opportunity of Alison working in reception.

Episode 219
Kathy's parole comes through, but she is terrified by what awaits her on the outside and tries to prolong her sentence. Vera considers applying for the Governorship of Barnhurst.

Episode 220
Judy is angered to find out Alison was able to read her file. Kathy's desperation forces her to threaten Vera. Bea persuades Alison to get hold of other prisoner's files. Kathy is released from Wentworth, but as she walks away from the prison is brutally murdered.

Episode 221
A gate guard sees what has happened and finds Kathy lying dead in the road. Erica is criticised for not reporting the numerous threats to Kathy's life. Bea suspects Terry of involvement in Kathy's death and accuses him of her murder.

Episode 222
Bea warns the other women that Terry is dangerous. A devastated Lizzie informs her friends of Sid's death. Vera is appointed the new Governor of Barnhurst prison.

Episode 223
Captain Barton comes to visit Lizzie. Vera becomes concerned about Terry's bizarre behaviour and asks Meg for advice. The prisoners celebrate the news that Vera is leaving Wentworth. Outside the prison, an argument between Terry and Vera is halted by a sudden gunshot.

Episode 224
News of Terry's death spreads through Wentworth. Erica and Jim plan a farewell party for Vera. Gordon is angry to find out Lizzie has inherited Sid's house. Fiona Spence's last appearance as Vera, the newly promoted Governor of Barnhurst.

Episode 225
Colleen receives a promotion to Acting Chief Prison Officer, much to the disappointment of Jim and the prisoners. Gordon threatens Lizzie during his visit but Bea hears and steps in. Lizzie finally comes to terms with Sid's death.

Episode 226
Don returns to work but doesn't last for very long when an accident stops him. Colleen charges Alison with assault. Gordon accepts Bea's idea of allowing Lizzie to stay in Sid's house until she dies. Jim surprises Erica with his resignation.

Episode 227
One of the neighbours at the day centre becomes suspicious about who the women are. Meg tells Alison that her children have been put into a home. Colleen backs down and withdraws Alison's report. Lizzie and Doreen find an unexpected guest at the centre.

Episode 228
Peter reveals all to the women and Doreen takes a fancy to him. Colleen is attacked outside the prison by some demonstrators. The main offender, Andrea Hennessey is brought to Wentworth as an inmate, but plans are quickly underway to break her out.

Episode 229
Colleen puts her foot in it by attending the day centre in her uniform. Bea and Judy disagree after Bea stops Andrea from escaping. Meg gives Peter an ultimatum: to give himself up, but when police arrive he runs for it – followed by Doreen.

Episode 230
Andrea has a letter smuggled out of the prison. Peter and Doreen are concerned about Martin's condition as he seems to be getting worse. Erica goes home after an exhausting day to find a window broken in her house… she is held at gunpoint by Linda and Ricky.

Episode 231
Erica is blindfolded and taken hostage by the women who drive her to a house at the coast. Lizzie tells Meg everything she knows about where Doreen and Peter might be. Judy and Bea hold Andrea inside a barricaded cell while Erica is in danger when she tries to escape.

Episode 232
Erica manages to get away but is caught again. Jim works out where Erica could be held so tells the police. New officer Janet Conway arrives. The police find the house and Erica is freed but Ricky dies following a shootout. Lizzie tries to get Doreen to tell Peter the truth.

Episode 233
Bea remembers Janet's past as an inmate. Doreen's time on the outside is over but Bea isn't too happy with her for ruining the day centre project. New arrival Linda and ex-friend Andrea end up in hospital after a fight, but their trouble has only just begun…

Episode 234
Jim is shot but manages to overpower Linda. Bea finds out that the Braille machine will arrive soon and she looks forward to doing something different. Bea tells Janet not to worry about the women's jokes. Lizzie makes an emotional farewell as she is released from Wentworth.

Episode 235
Lizzie settles in to Sid's house on the outside but some strange occurrences cause her to worry. Two new arrivals, Dr Kate Peterson and Sandy Edwards are inducted. Janet encourages Doreen to concentrate on her art work. Sandy challenges the top dog position.

Episode 236
Bea begins working on the Braille machine and is uninterested about the women's issues, and when she meets Sandy she has no problems in letting her take over the press. Lizzie receives more phone calls and knockings, and is sure that someone's trying to scare her.

Episode 237
Meg investigates Lizzie's problems and puts her mind at ease. Bea appears to be unwell, causing some of the other women to worry. A new television for the women arrives, courtesy of Janet's brother. Sandy vows to get even with the women after Kate is attacked.

Episode 238
Sandy begins to take over as top dog. Jim asks Meg to come back to work as an officer again. Lizzie and Gordon have another disagreement about Sid's house and Lizzie accuses him of trying to drive her out. Bea confides in Kate that she thinks she has cancer.

Episode 239
Meg returns to Wentworth as an officer. Kate and Sandy decide to try to help Bea, who refuses to see a doctor. Erica spills the beans to Jim about Janet's past. Lizzie decides the only way to solve her problem is to get rid of it – in tears she sets fire to Sid's house.

Episode 240
Sid's house burns down and Lizzie is nowhere to be seen. Bea tells Judy about her suspected illness and later has a dizzy spell in the rec room. Lizzie turns up at Meg's house. The doctor examines Bea and tells Erica that she may need a kidney transplant.

Episode 241
Doreen receives some good news about one of her drawings. Lizzie returns back to Wentworth and is charged with burning down Sid's house. Bea tells Lizzie that Sandy is now top dog. Kate's past is revealed and she almost loses control when Lizzie questions her.

Episode 242
The women decide to all get tested to see if any of them can donate a kidney to Bea. Colleen puts pressure on Lizzie by claiming to have seen her with the kerosene bottle. The letter from Colleen is published in the newspaper. Doreen gets some news from Dr Kennedy.

Episode 243
Jim is not amused when he returns to see Doreen's drawing. Doreen tells Judy about her news but is too scared to have the operation to help Bea. She later decides she will go ahead with it after all. Sandy lets on to Colleen that she has a copy of her letter.

Episode 244
Sandy gets a visit from a Mr Fitzwater who wants her to recruit young women to work as prostitutes when they are released. The prisoners get kitted out in new uniforms. Doreen tells Sandy she can't go through with the operation. Kate turns informer for the police…

Episode 245
Sandy asks Fitzwater to smuggle in some keys for her. The women create a new roster for the officers, causing nobody to turn up at work the next day! New officer Steve Fawkner arrives. Marie Winter also arrives from Barnhurst just as Bea is being taken to hospital.

Episode 246
Judy and Doreen are shocked to find that they are both being transferred to Barnhurst. Colleen is promoted to Chief Prison Officer while Meg becomes new Union Rep. Bea's transplant is a success but back at Wentworth a riot is brewing…

Episode 247
The riot is in full motion, with the officers forced to retreat outside, apart from Steve and Janet who are still trapped – hiding from the women. Bea hears about the riot on TV. Janet hides while Steve tries to find a way out, but he's caught by the women and stripped to his pants…

Episode 248
Steve is locked in an empty cell with only a pair of pyjamas to hide his modesty. Bea manages to phone Erica and offers to help stop the riot. The women throw Steve's uniform out of the building to signal that they've found him. Marie has a plan to escape.

Episode 249
Sandy is overpowered by Steve who locks her in the cell and runs for it. The riot squad enter the building following an attack of tear gas to disarm the women. Marie tries to escape as an officer but fails. Marie takes over from Sandy and arranges a drugs delivery from Fitzwater.

Episode 250
Lizzie is acquitted but immediately harassed by Gordon. Following the riot, the Department forces some new regulations to be put in place at Wentworth. Bea finds out from her doctor some interesting information about Kate. The officers consider strike action. Bea returns…

Episode 251
Marie tells Bea that she's taken over as leader of the women, but Bea is not well enough to fight her over it. The officers begin to strike against the new regulations. Lizzie gets drunk on the outside and makes friends with a con man. Jim arrives back at home to a shock.

Episode 252
Janet accuses Meg of having an affair with Jim. Security is returned to normal as the officer's strike ends. Lizzie gets herself into more trouble when she can't pay her taxi fare. Bea washes the latest drug delivery away and Marie is set up by the other women.

Episode 253
Marie is sent to solitary and Kate keeps her informed on what's going on, but takes over again when she comes back. Judy is disappointed when her hearing is delayed. Lizzie is, yet again, returned to Wentworth. Guard dogs arrive at the prison and Jim tells Janet it's over.

Episode 254
Lizzie tells Bea that she's concerned about Doreen. Sandy receives a worrying note from Fitzwater and later finds out that her husband in Pentridge has been killed. Kate lags to Colleen that Bea will be smuggling food from the kitchen. Judy is released.

Episode 255
Lori brings Judy to her new flat and they celebrate her release. Doreen tells Bea why she was bashed at Barnhurst. Colleen catches Bea in the act. Jim gets the job as Governor of Beachmount. Judy sees a face from the past when she's out at the races.

Episode 256
Jim learns that his new job starts in two days time. The other women give Doreen a hard time after finding out she has lagged. Jock Stewart traces Judy's new address. Sandy tells Marie that her drugs racket is now over as she has just killed Fitzwater.

Episode 257
Margo returns to H Block. Sandy explains to Bea how she killed Fitzwater and that Jim will back her up. The dog handler is concerned that the guard dogs are not eating their food and Bea finds out from Doreen why. Jock blackmails Judy, while Kate is tricked by the police.

Episode 258
Sandy sets Kate up to see if she is the lagger. Jock breaks into Judy's flat and attacks her – she is raped and beaten. Sandy agrees to protect Hazel but vows to get revenge on Marie. Jock is injured when he falls down a flight of stairs. Doreen makes an escape attempt.

Episode 259
Doreen saves Janet from the dogs but is in big trouble. Bea reveals to Sandy what her doctor told her about Kate. Marie starts selling drugs to the other prisoners and makes plans to get rid of Sandy. The dogs are removed from the prison and Kate steals some out-of-date drugs.

Episode 260
Wentworth's youngest prisoner, Susie Driscoll arrives. Meg is promoted to Deputy Governor but Bob isn't impressed. Sandy's meal is spiked with the drugs that Kate stole. When Sandy becomes ill she goes to the shower block to be sick, but Marie is waiting for her with a noose.

Episode 261

Doreen and Bea find Sandy just in the nick of time and give Marie and her cronies a beating. Meg declines her promotion so it goes to Colleen, although Meg's relationship with Bob has suffered beyond repair. Two of Judy's customers could get her in trouble.

Episode 262

Sandy is warned not to take revenge out on her attackers. A stunned Judy is returned back to Wentworth as a prisoner. Bea is told some secrets about Kate from the police. Susie steals Joyce's glasses. A plan by Kate to drug Sandy again backfires.

Episode 263

Kate runs to her cell to make herself sick after drinking the mixture. The women let on to Kate that they don't trust her anymore. Susie tries to escape in disguise but doesn't get past the front gates. Kate is left furious when the police reveal they have been setting her up.

Episode 264

Marie is questioned about the drugs racket and strikes up a surprising alliance with Sandy to get Kate, although a card game will decide who will do the deed. Colleen takes credit in showing Susie's injury to be a fake, after Kate lagged. Kate meanwhile has problems of her own.

Episode 265

In an unexpected twist, Sandy is the one to go missing and Kate appears unharmed. Hazel gets some bad news when George comes to visit. Marie attempts one final time to pay back Kate for all she's done and suggests that Kate murdered Sandy.

Episode 266

Susie plans another escape but Colleen finds her hiding in the garbage skip. Kate is moved in with Judy as an attempt to keep her safe from the other women, but Marie makes it clear that her number is up. Hazel loses control and attacks an officer.

Episode 267

Yet another escape is planned by Susie, this time through the air vents. Marie starts to throw her weight around but Bea returns and is quickly brought up-to-date on the news. When temperatures inside the prison begin to escalate, some drastic measures are brought in place to clear a 'blockage' from the air conditioning system…

Episode 268

A frantic effort is made to locate Susie and free her from the air vents before it's too late. Steve begins to question Kate's innocence and also believes that she had something to do with Sandy's disappearance. Bea tells Kate she's going 'on trial' with the other women.

Episode 269

Kate's mock trial is in full swing and only Judy can manage to defend her. Susie recovers in hospital with Colleen as her only visitor. Kate is surprised to find that she is being transferred but can't believe her eyes when she sees Marie in the truck as her travelling companion.

Episode 270

Kate refuses to get in the truck and the officers have no choice than to keep her in Wentworth. Susie finally makes a break for it whilst in hospital and manages to hitch a lift with a truck driver. Judy is devastated when her parole is revoked.

Episode 271

Susie runs away from the truck driver who is wanting more than just conversation during their journey. Judy tells Erica that she thinks Kate could be close to having a nervous breakdown. Susie's luck ends when she finds out who owns the house where she's been staying.

Episode 272

Susie returns to Wentworth, along with Helen Smart. Erica decides that Dr Weissman will have to be called to examine Kate, following her unusual behaviour. Judy's fears about Kate are confirmed: she is attacked from behind by Kate who tries to strangle her.

Episode 273

Bea and Steve manage to stop Kate who is later placed in solitary. When Colleen checks on Kate, she is found to be holding some kind of imaginary surgery in her cell. Bea takes an interest in the prison newspaper. Kate is transferred to a hospital for the criminally insane.

Episode 274

Susie believes that the new prisoner, Jo, is her mother. Helen arranges a surprise for Bea's birthday with Erica, but what Erica doesn't know is that Helen will change the plans without her knowing. Janet tells Ian she's pregnant.

Episode 275

The women's newspaper is published and Steve shows a journalist friend of his a copy – he likes it so much that Bea's article is printed in a real newspaper. Bea's surprise party is a huge success, much to the embarrassment of Erica. Colleen's daughter is kidnapped.

Episode 276

A worried Colleen and Patrick contact the police about Jenny's disappearance. Meanwhile, Jenny is taken to a hideout where she's locked in a room alone. Ted demands that the The Stir should not be taken outside of the prison. Susie learns the truth about her real mother.

Episode 277

Steve agrees to smuggle Bea's letter about censorship to The Dispatch. Doreen and Jo try to convince Susie to stop escaping. A mystery prisoner arrives at Wentworth and the women can't work out who it is. Doug plans to rape Jenny.

Episode 278

Carol finds out that Doug has attacked Jenny. Lizzie thinks that the mystery prisoner is Helen but the others don't believe her. Doreen sets fire to her bed so is sent to solitary but the other prisoner has been moved out. Jenny makes a run for it…

Episode 279

Jenny is caught and returned, to find that Carol has shot Doug. Jenny's later dumped in the middle of nowhere but found safe by the police. Lizzie's suspicions are right about Helen. Carol is apprehended and sent to Wentworth, inducted by Colleen.

Episode 280

Carol tells her side of the story to the other women, who agree to lay off her. Doreen, Lizzie and Judy make plans to concoct some alcohol in one of the old boilers. New prisoner Jackie arrives – Judy recognises her immediately as the woman responsible for her being in prison.

Episode 281

Jackie claims that she's never met Judy. The Dispatch get a copy of The Stir and offer Helen a substantial amount of money to back up the claims in Bea's article. Helen overhears Jackie confess to knowing Judy on the outside. Helen has a visitor but the meeting is cut short.

Episode 282

Judy is angry at Doreen for bashing Jackie and spoiling her chances of getting released. Carol gets a letter from Jenny, thanking her for making sure she was OK. The home brew is almost ready for consumption and Bea has to think of a plan to get a letter outside.

Episode 283

Helen is kept in solitary although her privileges can be restored. Colleen's treatment of Carole causes concern for Meg. The women arrange a diversion in the form of a loud noise – so Margo can try and bash the solitary lock open with a hammer to speak to Helen.

Episode 284

The plan doesn't work and Bea is questioned by Erica, along with Margo. Bea comes up with a new idea to contact Helen – it goes to plan and finally they are able to communicate. The home brew is shared amongst the inmates but when the officers find out there's disastrous consequences.

Episode 285

Steve recovers. Susie's parole is granted. Bea is questioned about the fire but Colleen notices Helen's note in her pocket and Bea's sent to solitary. The still is dismantled and cleaned. Erica sends Bea's article to The Dispatch and Helen refuses to plead guilty.

Episode 286

Chrissie plans to skip the State. Helen is relieved following a visit from the police who corroborate her story – she's later released. Chrissie steals some money from her boss and leaves to board a plane. Unfortunately the police are not far behind her.

Episode 287

Chrissie is brought back to Wentworth. New officer Joan Ferguson makes her presence immediately known and demonstrates her impressive experience during the cell search. Doreen is Joan's first victim in the form of a very close body search.

Episode 288

Joan keeps part of the money she's found in the laundry trolley but reports the rest of her find to Erica. Hannah Simpson is inducted and Joan takes an interest in her. Faye is bashed for not paying the women their winnings. Chrissie tries to blackmail Steve, but fails.

Episode 289

Colleen pushes Chrissie into accusing Steve of sexual harassment but Joan provides an alibi, putting him in the clear. When Meg and Joan accompany Hannah to her court hearing, the court room is invaded by gunmen and Meg is taken hostage.

Episode 290

Joan comes to the rescue and Hannah's escape attempt is a failure. Bea finds out from Chrissie that she lied, but wonders why Joan is covering for Steve. Chrissie and Hannah discuss escape plans, while Susie has problems on the outside.

Episode 291

Bea is furious when Chrissie tells the truth to Erica and threatens to kill Chrissie if it happens again. Lizzie has some money stolen so a plan is made to catch the thief in the act next time. Judy smuggles out a letter for Hannah when she's released.

Episode 292

Chrissie is found to be the thief so suffers a bashing from the other women. Duncan Campbell arranges Hannah's escape with Chrissie. Prostitute Donna introduces Susie to her pimp, Des – but he has plans of his own for Susie.

Episode 293

Bea attempts to set up Joan, using Hannah as bait. Des organises a double-date with Donna and Susie, but little does Susie realise that she's being used. Joan questions Chrissie about Hannah – Chrissie has no option than to lag about Bea's plan.

Episode 294

Susie wakes up and realises what has happened the night before. Distraught, she visits Judy who insists she stay at the half way house instead – unfortunately Susie ends up working the streets to help Donna. While Hannah is in solitary, Chrissie escapes in her place.

Episode 295

Chrissie tells Duncan she knows where the money is – but Hannah has not told Chrissie the full story. She's soon returned to the prison and ignored by the other women. Joan tricks Lizzie into spilling the beans about how they made the home brew.

Episode 296

Joan's left red faced when she shows Erica where the illegal still was kept. Donna is arrested and Des tells Susie she has to stay with him to keep out of trouble with the police. Joan pushes Chrissie too far and a fight is imminent…

Episode 297

Joan overpowers Chrissie and gives her a brutal bashing, leaving her in an appalling condition. New arrival Maxine Daniels joins H Block and realises she's seen a face from the past. When Susie refuses to work for Des anymore, he injects her with heroin.

Episode 298

Maxine tells Joan that she'll reveal all about her past if she makes life difficult for her. Chrissie agrees to sign the papers to give custody of Elizabeth to Derek and Brenda. Susie manages to escape from Des who is later arrested at the half way house.

Episode 299

Bea suspects that Maxine must have something on Joan. Donna steals money from Lizzie and gives it to Mouse in return for drugs. Joan keeps Doreen's release date from her. Maxine reveals Joan's secrets to Hannah, who uses these to make a complaint against Joan.

Episode 300

Erica decides to investigate Joan's past. Gloria Pitman arrives at the half way house and takes a keen interest in Donna. Doreen is released but isn't given the chance to say goodbye – she boards at the half way house but is shocked to find a gun with Gloria's clothes.

Episode 301

The women decide to boycott Joan so ignore all of her orders. Judy catches Donna injecting herself with more drugs. Doreen gets a new job and notices a very shady deal going on. The boycott continues and the women refuse to come inside when Joan orders them.

Episode 302

The women stay outside but Joan plays dirty and turns the fire hose on them, they have no choice but to come back inside – until the following day when they barricade themselves in the dining room. An attempt is made on Donna's life.

Episode 303

When Lizzie becomes ill, the women agree to end their protest. Doreen is interviewed about the fire at the factory. Donna injects herself once again, but this time it's her last… she dies in Bea's arms. Barbara's flat is searched and the missing money is found.

Episode 304

Barbara arrives at Wentworth with other new inmate Paddy Lawson who has to be restrained following her violent behaviour. Doreen finds a new job and moves out of the half way house, not before Judy returns to find Spud and his mates trashing the place.

Episode 305

Maxine apologises to Judy and promises to make up for the problems she's caused, only to cause more! Lizzie and Bea apply for parole. New prison nurse Neil Murray arrives. Faye taunts Paddy about her phobia of the dark.

Episode 306

Chrissie fakes a rash so she can visit Neil. Judy interviews for an assistant and chooses Tony Berman as her new partner. Maxine sells some of her stolen goods to customers who visit the house. Bea is upset when she realises how difficult getting her parole is becoming.

Episode 307

The parole board turns down Lizzie's parole application but Erica intends to produce medical evidence to support her request. Margo turns up at the half way house following an escape from Barnhurst. She's spotted by Meg who notices her breaking into her car.

Episode 308

Margo is arrested but Judy's also in trouble for assisting her. Margo vows to get revenge on Meg for phoning the police. Meg refuses to answer a question at Judy's trial so is imprisoned for contempt of court and ends up on the other side of the bars at Wentworth.

Episode 309

Meg demands that she's treated as a normal prisoner. Margo and her mates give Meg a beating but Chrissie scares them off before they do too much damage. Penny is released but on her first night on the outside she's murdered by someone wearing black leather gloves.

Episode 310

The women suspect Joan of being Penny's killer. Bea and Chrissie punish Margo for bashing Meg. Lizzie visits an old people's home but isn't impressed. Meg is released and she returns to work, with a plan on how to prove Joan is corrupt.

Episode 311

Erica doesn't agree to Meg's idea. Joan is angry with Neil for cancelling Chrissie's work punishment and suggests there's more to their relationship than nurse/patient. When another prostitute is killed, Colleen makes a shocking discovery about the owner of the gloves.

Episode 312

Joan pleads her innocence when the police question her. Bea starts offering the women the chance to buy contraband from her – but it's all part of a plan with Steve to catch Joan out. Is Tony now the prime suspect in the murder case?

Episode 313

Joan tries to clear her name and also points the finger at Tony. Maxine gets a new job as childminder but she finds that the Dempsters' marriage isn't exactly a happy one. Just as Paddy is making progress, Margo pulls a cruel trick and locks her in the store room.

Episode 314

Margo is sent to solitary. Maxine has to call the doctor when Michelle becomes sick, but the doctor is more concerned at the bruises on her body. The plan to set up Joan is revealed – Joan finds out and tells Erica that Steve and Meg are selling buyup goods to the women.

Episode 315

Bea has her first day on the outside with her work release. Neil's plan to abduct Chrissie from the hospital goes ahead. Steve is made a scapegoat and hands in his resignation to Erica. Chrissie's life is in danger as Neil turns nasty.

Episode 316

Chrissie manages to escape from Neil just in time – he's shot by the police. Cookie tells Bea about her daughter Kerry, who she is having a lot of problems with. Erica agrees for a joint concert between the inmates of Wentworth and Woodridge. Sally runs down Peter.

Episode 317

The half-way house is officially opened and Judy announces it is to be called Driscoll House, after Susie – their first success. Sally is sent to Wentworth and the women show her how much they hate child bashers. Rehearsals begin for the concert.

Episode 318

Margo shows off her talent at rehearsals with her rendition of 'Midnight Special'. Chrissie finds out that Neil has been sent to Woodridge. Joan pressurises Margo to ruin the concert by attempting to escape. Chrissie's life could be is in danger yet again.

Episode 319

Kerry tells Judy her real name and that she is pregnant. Sally opens her heart to Paddy and explains why she hurt her daughter. Joan forces Barbara into checking her staff file in Erica's office. Everything gets too much for Sally – she attempts to kill herself.

Episode 320

Sally is found just in time and is saved by Colleen and Phyllis. Neil is set up to kill Chrissie backstage but Andy and Paddy stop him, causing concern for Andy's partially clothed appearance. Joan finds her dog dead at home. Kerry reveals the baby's father is Errol.

Episode 321

Margo finds out that some of the Woodridge prisoners are planning an escape. Paddy and Andy are caught in a compromising situation behind the stage. Phillip gives Barbara some diaries belonging to Joan. Lizzie gets in the way when Margo attempts her escape.

Episode 322

The prison concert comes to a stop and Lizzie is led out on a stretcher. Barbara tells Joan that she's got her personal (and revealing) diaries. When Bea's latest work release is cancelled, she looks to try to return to hairdressing but Joan puts a stop to it.

Episode 323

Joan's wrists are slapped when Erica finds out she's stopped Bea's work release. Tony's girlfriend returns home to visit, but gets the wrong idea when she's greeted by Maxine. Joan performs an intimate body search on Paddy, but the women plan to retaliate.

Episode 324

Joan overpowers her attackers and manages to escape without any injuries. Bea has to keep her cool when Joan attempts to make her blow her parole chances. When she's sent to isolation a mystery person sends her a message advising that Lizzie has died.

Episode 325

When Joan suggests to Mouse that Lizzie has died, word gets around the prison – but fortunately it's untrue. Melissa and Tony fall out – so Tony drowns his sorrows and wakes up the next morning with Maxine in his bed. Alan and Sara take drastic action. Bea gets some bad news.

Episode 326 – Fire at Wentworth

Realising she's got nothing to lose, Bea plans to get Joan once and for all. A diversion is started so Joan is lured to the solitary block where Bea is waiting for her. A fight breaks out, but when an additional fire is lit by Margo – the whole prison goes up in flames, trapping Bea and Joan.

Episode 327
Bea tells Joan they're going to die together in the prison, but Paddy spots them and they're led up to the roof where they're rescued. Barbara and Mouse are not so lucky. Paddy is released. At hospital Joan reveals that Bea admitted to starting the fire.

Episode 328
The women settle in at Woodridge but the conditions are far from ideal. Following her recovery, Lizzie joins the other inmates. The male prisoners are unhappy at the Wentworth women using their facilities and taking over their work. Jeannie's baby comes early.

Episode 329
Bea and Chrissie deliver the baby and the women welcome Christopher Bea to the world. Colleen is relieved when she finds out that she's not responsible for the fire spreading so rapidly. Bea is charged with arson and murder.

Episode 330
Paddy returns to the prison plus newcomer Val Jacobs – an old friend of Colleen's. Bea and Chrissie are put back with the other women, both thinking that each of them has lagged. They soon realise that they're being used by the police to name the third person involved.

Episode 331
Lizzie finds out that the men have been making their own alcohol. Judy welcomes a new resident to Driscoll House: Jean Carter. Margo confesses that she lit the other fire but refuses to admit it to the police, so Chrissie and Bea are still no better off.

Episode 332
Bea's solicitor reveals some crucial evidence to her. Lizzie and Maxine set up the other women in a card game with some marked cards. Hazel steals Jean's money and disappears, but Jean is reluctant to contact the police. Bea and Chrissie's future looks brighter.

Episode 333
The women return to Wentworth but are disappointed that it looks no different. Jean goes on a stealing spree. Bea and Chrissie are only charged with minor offences, leaving Mouse and Barbara to take full blame for the fire. The women's party ends with the arrival of Joan.

Episode 334
Joan reports the illicit booze to Erica who suspends privileges and tells the women she's been far too soft with them in the past. Jean is sent to the prison as the latest inmate. Meg interrupts the VJ hearing and tells them everything she knows about Joan.

Episode 335
Erica introduces a 'points system' for the women – the more points they earn, the more benefits they will receive. Hazel is found with stolen money and signs a statement while she's still drunk – which the police later edit, to show that she has made a confession.

Episode 336
Hazel's sent to Wentworth under a charge of armed robbery… Jean quizzes her about the money. When Paddy finds out the truth, she lags on Jean without realising that she's using a hidden identity. Jean is revealed as Nola McKenzie, an escapee from W. A. on a double murder sentence, facing the death penalty.

Episode 337
Judy finds out the real reason behind her sister's visit and is upset when she's offered money to give up any claim on her father's estate. A points system is started by the women – for the officers. Judy attacks Frances but Erica arrives to break up the fight.

Episode 338
Frances leaves, threatening Judy with the police. Judy finds out that she's a grandmother. Bea warns Nola to stay away from Hazel. Paddy gets some good news about a job on the outside but tragedy strikes when she's caught by Nola in the wrong place at the wrong time.

Episode 339
The women mourn the loss of Paddy. Meg resigns, realising that she is about to be sacked soon anyway following her lapse of security checking. Frances drops her charges so Judy is in the clear. The women go on strike after hearing about Meg's resignation.

Episode 340
Meg's job is safe but the security measures have to stay. The women threaten to get Nola for murdering Paddy. Maxine arranges a bashing without Bea's permission. Faye is worried about spending the night in the cell with Nola.

Episode 341
Nola reveals that she doesn't want to be top dog as she's only interested in trading, but vows to get revenge on everyone who has bashed her. Lil and Jacko are badly beaten so Maxine gets worried about being the next victim. Joan sets up Bea and Nola for a fight…

Episode 342
The fight doesn't happen – Bea tells Nola that she'll fight when she's ready. Judy starts looking for a new location for Driscoll House. Bea sneaks to an empty cell close to where Nola is working and gives her an everlasting punishment for killing Paddy.

Episode 343
The women agree that Nola got what she deserved. Colleen confides in Meg that her marriage is breaking down. She moves into a hotel and spends the night alone. Hazel finds an abandoned baby on the doorstep of Driscoll House.

Episode 344
Hazel plans to look after the baby herself without telling the authorities. Nola breaks into the store room and steals some goods to sell on to the other women. Bea discovers that Nola's behind all of Faye's schemes. Judy finds out that Hazel's been hiding the baby.

Episode 345
Hazel's heartbroken when Judy calls the police and the baby is taken into care. Bea arranges with Erica that a television set be bought for the women but Nola offers to pay for it herself. Judy finds that the baby is actually her own grandson.

Episode 346
Lori is diagnosed with post natal depression but causes Judy to rethink her future when she refuses treatment. On her release, Faye has no option but to tell Joan about Nola's schemes. Joan decides to muscle in on Nola, demanding 50% of the takings.

Episode 347
Nola and Maxine arrange for some extra goods to be smuggled in from the outside, with Joan turning a blind eye – but Bea doubts their plans and is angry when the women appear to be happy to trade with Nola. Colleen visits Chris and stays for a meal with him and the kids.

Episode 348
Lizzie starts playing some practical jokes on the women in an attempt to cheer them up but it does anything than make them happy. New inmate Jill causes concern amongst the officers and prisoners with all of her questions and interest in the others.

Episode 349

The women decide to pay back Lizzie and make her think she's going deaf. Erica tells the women that some of them will be able to work at the new halfway house to help decorate it. Colleen goes to see Chris again – they kiss.

Episode 350

Meg tells Colleen that she doesn't approve of her relationship with Chris. Lizzie thinks that she has a brain tumour and decides to write her will but is reassured when she finds out she only needs some glasses. Faye tells Judy that Billy is her son.

Episode 351

Bea suggests to Maxine that another person is involved in their 'business'. Jill is sent to solitary after Colleen finds some smuggled goods in her bed. She reveals that Joan is behind everything and Nola lets on to Joan that her days are numbered.

Episode 352

Erica admits that Jill is a departmental spy. Lindy is upset when she spots Trevor watching her get undressed. Bea seizes the opportunity to escape and puts into action an elaborate plan… she walks out of the gates dressed as an officer!

Episode 353

News of Bea's escape spreads through the prison. Nola aims for the top-dog position. Ted Douglas questions Joan's efficiency prior to the escape, much to the delight of Meg and Colleen.

Episode 354

Lizzie vows to stand up to Joan in Bea's absence. Ted informs Erica of imminent changes at Wentworth following Jill's Report. Lainie Dobson and Ellen Farmer are inducted to Wentworth, but all is not as it seems….

Episode 355

Helen discovers Ellen's real identity. Lainie blames Maxine for the authorities finding out the truth. Alan is released from Wentworth.

Episode 356

Nola plans to bring booze and drugs into Wentworth. Helen is released. Erica informs Colleen a TV documentary will soon film life inside Wentworth. The women believe the new reforms are only in place because of the documentary.

Episode 357

Bea is enjoying her freedom in Sydney, but has to act fast when she is recognised from a newspaper. Joan refuses to let Alan visit Lainie. Nola smuggles drugs into Wentworth.

Episode 358

The police question Doreen about Bea's whereabouts, but she insists she hasn't tried to contact her. The smell of grass filters through the air conditioning ducts, into the staffroom! Lainie's interview is ruined when she accidentally reveals her tattoos. Bea arrives at Doreen's work.

Episode 359

Doreen is shocked to see Bea, but confirms she will do anything she can to help her. The women's predictions about the TV documentary are confirmed when it goes to air. Bea is thrilled to see Doreen doing so well for herself in Sydney.

Episode 360

Doreen arranges for Bea to hide in her flat. Judy persuades Ted Douglas to support the tattoo removal program. Doreen's flatmate Debbie arrives unexpectedly, leading to Bea's recapture. Doreen waves a final goodbye to her best friend.

Episode 361

Ted Douglas announces Erica's resignation as Governor of Wentworth. Lizzie tells the other women she has seen Bea in solitary. Nola vows revenge on Bea for stealing her money prior to her escape.

Episode 362

Bea is bashed by Nola's heavies. Zara Moonbeam is inducted to Wentworth, claiming to be a psychic. Lizzie finds Nola's stash of drugs and disposes of them at Bea's request.

Episode 363

Zara starts doing tarot and palm readings, with one of her predictions being Nola's death. Joan's father, Major Ferguson, is taken on a guided tour of Wentworth. When Bea humiliates Joan in front of her father, she conspires with Nola to dispose of her permanently.

Episode 364

Nola and Joan begin to plot Bea's demise. Colleen tells Meg she will leave Wentworth if Joan becomes Governor. Zara informs Bea that someone called Debbie is trying to contact her, but Bea warns her not to dare play mind games with her. Everyone is stunned when Ann Reynolds is introduced as the new Governor of Wentworth.

Episode 365

Joan visits a school friend of Debbie's in her quest to drive Bea mad. Bea becomes increasingly worried by mentions of her daughter trying to contact her, and unaware she is being drawn into Joan's web. Colleen patrols solitary and overhears Bea crying in her cell.

Episode 366

Joan brings Zara to solitary to imitate Debbie's voice. Bea begins to question her own sanity. Lainie is released from Wentworth and goes to find Alan. With their plans working so well, Joan and Nola attempt to drive Bea to suicide.

Episode 367

Joan invites Ann to socialise with her, and uses the opportunity to casually inform her of Meg's imprisonment and Colleen's affair. Nola gives Joan a list of items to purchase for her, to make a zip gun. Bea is pushed further to the edge.

Episode 368

The officers become concerned over Bea's behaviour. Tracey Belman arrives in Wentworth. Nola begins to make a home-made gun that will be used to make Bea commit suicide. The gun is hidden in Bea's dressing gown, but is found by Lizzie.

Episode 369

Nola informs Joan that Lizzie knows about their plot. Lizzie manages to visit Bea to tell her everything, and brings her the gun. Bea requests Nola visits her in the infirmary. As Nola leans forward to listen to her, Bea shoots her dead between the eyes.

Episode 370

Nola's body lies in the infirmary, revealing the branding on her chest. Joan warns Zara to keep quiet about their involvement leading up to Nola's murder. Tracey accuses Joan of trying to kiss her.

Episode 371

Joan is cleared of the accusations, but can no longer look after Tracey. Maggie May Kennedy arrives in Wentworth on a drug charge, with a twenty year sentence. When Maggie meets Lizzie, they realise they know each other.

Episode 372

Lizzie and Maggie enjoy talking about old times, but Lizzie warns her about Bea. Meg persuades Wally to start pottery classes in Wentworth. Pauline phones the police to blame Maxine for the robbery.

Episode 373

Pauline warns Maxine about the police, and she panics. Lizzie falls out with Maggie after overhearing a conversation with Ann. Maxine is captured and returned to Wentworth. Brandy Carter arrives at Wentworth.

Episode 374

Meg recognises Brandy, but cannot place her. Brandy begins to irritate some of the inmates, and is warned to stay away from Joan. Joan witnesses her neighbour stab her husband in the back with a knife.

Episode 375

Joan is kept as a hostage after the stabbing, until Meg becomes suspicious when she fails to arrive at work. Carol is brought to Wentworth, and the news spreads about her attempts to kill her daughter. Brandy's personality continues to change and causes concern, while Meg realises where she has seen her before.

Episode 376

Colleen warns Joan not to get involved in helping Carol's family. A heavily pregnant Roxanne Bradshaw is admitted to Wentworth. Brandy sabotages the driers so that maintenance men will have to visit to fix it. Roxanne tells Lizzie the real reason for her having a baby.

Episode 377

Carol tells Bea about Joan's involvement in her case. Brandy's alternating change in behaviour continues with two personalities emerging at different times. Sandy Gilham arrives at Driscoll House. Ann comes to talk to Carol but discovers her hanging in her cell.

Episode 378

Sandy's real name is revealed as Pixie, with various men visiting Driscoll house trying to find her. Judy finds a bank book belonging to Pixie and notices it is made out in another woman's name. The police visit Driscoll House, stating Pixie is to be charged with bigamy and fraud.

Episode 379

Pixie Mason arrives as Wentworth, with the possibility of having six husbands! Ann informs the police about Brandy's other name. Pixie is told she has no chance of an acquittal. Ann is shocked to see an undercover photo of criminal Lionel Fellowes together with Ted Douglas.

Episode 380

Meg is informed Laura will need psychiatric help. At Pixie's trial she blames her crimes on her twin sister! Paul refuses to hand over the photos to Ted Douglas. Bea has her own plans on how to deal with Ted, and bribes him.

Episode 381

Helen Smart visits Judy for advice over her sister, Sharon. Doctor Weissman believes Laura is suffering from Multiple Personality Syndrome. Meg's son Marty returns home, with a new friend Dennis.

Episode 382

Ann informs the police that Bea may have a copy of the photo that incriminates Ted. The police confront Ted minutes before boarding a plane. Meg continues to receive threatening phone calls.

Episode 383

Ted Douglas is charged with corruption. Helen's failed attempts to help her sister force her to take drastic action. Marty's friend Dennis visits Meg and is reveals himself as her anonymous caller. He pulls out a knife.

Episode 384

Meg persuades Dennis to drop the knife and he is arrested. Pixie continues her quest to find out who wrote her the letter, with her attentions turning to both Wally and Doctor Weissman. Helen's attempts to save Sharon end in disaster.

Episode 385

Helen, Sharon and Judy are taken in for questioning and charged. Helen and Sharon are taken to Wentworth. Pixie sees Scott kissing Petra. Peter tells Judy that Colin Burton has died.

Episode 386

Petra tells Lizzie that her father abused her when she was a child. Wentworth is thrown into chaos when a 'building inspector' turns up – he plants a number of bombs in the prison and everyone's lives are in danger.

Episode 387

The building is evacuated and most of the women are led out to their safety. Unfortunately for Bea, a bomb is wired up outside of her cell – it explodes with tragic consequences. Lucy is sent to prison and soon causes problems for Joan.

Episode 388

Lucy continues to blackmail Joan. Bea finds out that a much loved ex-inmate has died and left the women some money in her will. An escape plan is hatched for Lucy but Maxine finds out and decides to join her.

Episode 389

The escape is put into action and the two women vanish from the prison. Bea suspects that Joan had some involvement in the escape and Maxine has problems on the outside. Scott tells Petra some bad news – her sister is dead.

Episode 390

Maxine manages to find somewhere to stay and makes a new friend. Bea tries to get the women's ideas on how to use Mum's money. A highly infectious disease breaks out in Wentworth and the prison is placed into quarantine.

Episode 391

Scott is of little help in trying to control the disease. Ann tells the women that they are under quarantine. Scott tells Ann that there is no vaccine or cure for the illness. Belle escapes.

Episode 392

Meg tells Ann that Maxine is dead. Joan warns the PASSIVE visitors that Bea has killed three people. Colleen discovers the truth about Scott and Petra. Bea refuses to help Joan in any way.

Episode 393

Lizzie and Joan are still suffering from the fever. Judy and Wally give the money back to the factory. Officer Sharpe dies and Joan makes a full recovery.

Episode 394

Scott lifts the quarantine. Tony says his goodbyes to Bea. A new inmate, Sonia Stevens, arrives in Wentworth on drugs charges, the wife of a police officer who has arrested half the women in Wentworth.

Episode 395

Bea stops Phyllis from bashing Sonia. Hazel tells Judy that she has an inoperable brain tumour. Joan harasses Rosemary and Bea starts a war against Sonia.

Episode 396
Lizzie receives a telegram from Mick. Hazel sees her husband and children for the last time. Sonia tells Jerry that she wants to escape. Randi tells Meg that she is a prostitute.

Episode 397
Sonia tells Ann nothing about the escape attempt. Sonia sets up a numbers game with Phyllis. Hazel visits Wentworth and her illness worsens, resulting in losing her sight.

Episode 398
Scott prescribes morphine for Hazel. Bea announces that the numbers game is over. Colleen and Meg accompany Lizzie on her day release (another 'golden Lizzie moment'!). Petra receives a life sentence at her trial.

Episode 399
Sonia tells Bea that she intends to take over as Top Dog. Joan orders Lizzie to help her make some grog by stealing from the kitchen. Judy helps Hazel take an overdose.

Episode 400
Sonia suggests to Joan that Bea is transferred so that she can take over, which leads to Wentworth's first Top Dog, Bea Smith, being transferred to Barnhurst. The police come to Driscoll House to arrest Judy for the murder of Hazel Kent.

Episode 401
Colleen reprimands Joan over escorting Bea alone and explains that Lizzie has broken her wrist. Wally takes over the running of the half-way house. Meg is horrified to discover that Marty's new girlfriend is Randi Goodlove.

Episode 402
Meg tells Marty that his new girlfriend isn't right for him. Pixie and Lizzie's privileges are suspended. Cass refuses to take over as Top Dog. Petra tells the women she has been granted permission to marry Scott.

Episode 403
Judy is brought back to Wentworth. Joan tells Judy that Bea has been transferred. Lizzie refuses to accept Judy's reasons for killing Hazel. Joan visits Cass with Sonia telling her that her fight with Phyllis was a set up.

Episode 404
Sonia tells Joan their partnership is over. Judy refuses the position of Top Dog. Petra and Scott are married in the prison grounds. Arthur Charlton turns up at Wentworth claiming to be Lizzie's son.

Episode 405
Minnie Donovan and Bobbie Mitchell are brought to Wentworth on remand. Sonia asks Bobbie to tape Minnie's conversations as she is friendly with Ann. Joan bashes Cass in the shower block.

Episode 406
Alice and Wally find life difficult at Driscoll House. Randi threatens Meg that she'll get back at her for spoiling her chances with Marty. Lizzie visits her family but isn't impressed. Minnie forces Sonia to drink all of the home made brew.

Episode 407
A shooting at Driscoll House causes Alice to re-think her harsh stance on the residents. The women decide Minnie should be new top dog. Petra leaves Wentworth. Minnie has some alcohol smuggled in. Sonia blackmails Joan with a secret recording.

Episode 408
Joan hassles Bobbie over the tape and has her cell ransacked and all her tapes destroyed. Brenda, a new prisoner arrives in Wentworth with underworld connections. Cass attacks Minnie in her cell.

Episode 409
Cass is given the tape to look after. Lizzie is taken to the races by her family. Scott refuses to believe Joan's story about Bobbie's injuries. Gloria records a coded message about drugs that is discovered by Meg and when Ann finds out decides to use it against Joan to try and get rid of her once and for all.

Episode 410
Minnie tells Ann about the tape and that Sonia has another copy of it. Arthur asks Ann to arrange Lizzie's parole. A stranger offers to sell Joan a copy of the tape and David offers to help Mary.

Episode 411
Don Baxter blackmails Joan over the tape, telling her to pay $10,000 to get it back. Minnie tells the women that she plans to fix Joan. The women attack Joan and hang her from the shower block.

Episode 412
David cuts Joan down from the ceiling. Minnie rushes the women off to the Rec Room creating an alibi for them. Ann tells the women that Joan is still alive. Joan goes to visit her blackmailer but finds him dead.

Episode 413
Minnie suspects Bobbie of attacking Pixie. Joan tells Sonia she got the tape back. Ann makes an appointment to see a doctor. Two of Fellowes' henchmen break into Joan's house and force her to take LSD.

Episode 414
Wally is playing away with Sam. Ann is unable to discuss the fear she has surrounding her breast cancer. Joan pressures Sonia for details about the men who broke into her house. Randi mysteriously disappears.

Episode 415
Wally tells Sam that he and Ann are finished. Minnie forbids any other women from trying to escape and she tells David that they have to stop happening as a result of tightened security. Joan's life is in the hands of Lionel Fellowes.

Episode 416
Ann goes into hospital for a biopsy leaving Colleen as Acting Governor. Lizzie waits for the results of her parole hearing in the garden and discovers the hand belonging to a dead body under a pile of leaves…

Episode 417
Lizzie suffers a heart attack and collapses. David attempts to make Cass his latest victim, but instead unleashes her own inner demons as she brutally beheads him. News of David's death spreads through Wentworth, uncovering the full details of his past. Ann is unable to commit to a relationship with Wally, and Minnie continues her plans to undermine The Freak.

Episode 418
Joan clashes with Colleen over the women's attempts to make her look incompetent. Sonia attempts to find the person who put glass in her hand cream. Some of the women visit Lizzie in hospital, who appears frail and close to giving up, but pleased to see her friends. Sheila Florance's final appearance as Lizzie Birdsworth.

Episode 419
Minnie believes she was poisoned. News reporters gather at the gates, while Judy and Cass display a banner from the roof. Joan seizes the opportunity of Colleen's absence to visit the Minister in an attempt to enforce stricter security measures in Wentworth.

Episode 420
Minnie tries to persuade Judy to take over as Top Dog. Sonia is stabbed in the back by a piece of glass from the mirror in her cell. Ann agrees to patch things up with Wally. Joan witnesses Colleen run down a drunken man in the street, and drive off.

Episode 421
Pixie meets a man on the bus, but is embarrassed when he arrives at Wentworth and introduced as the new male officer Rick Manning. Cass is questioned about the attack on Sonia. Belinda steals a pair of scissors from the infirmary. Police arrive at Wentworth to question Colleen.

Episode 422
Cass remains terrified at the presence of another male officer. The Minister makes Joan Acting Governor, leading to tighter security measures! Reb returns to Wentworth, sentenced to seven years. Pixie is punished for smuggling goods into the prison. Paul Reynolds is shot outside his front door.

Episode 423
Judy stands up to Joan by arranging a protest in the Rec Room. Joan attempts to persuade Doctor Weissman to transfer Cass to Ingleside. Rod tries to bribe Colleen, but she later reports his whereabouts to the police.

Episode 424
Sonia attempts to undermine Judy's position as Top Dog. New cell allocations are given out to the women. Joan is stunned when Erica Davidson arrives to investigate goings-on in Wentworth. Rick heavies Rod into telling the truth.

Episode 425
Joan is furious at Erica's dissatisfaction with her short time as Acting Governor. Major Ferguson is kidnapped in an attempt to set Reb free. Belinda attempts to strangle Judy, but is stopped by Minnie. When the women find out about Reb's escape attempt, they hold her hostage in the prison.

Episode 426
Colleen returns to Wentworth and is informed of Joan's resignation. Kevin tells Reb about Gary's plan to kill her. The Major's kidnap ordeal ends in bloodshed.

Episode 427
Belinda attacks Sonia in her cell. The women are shocked when Joan returns to Wentworth, promising to change her ways. Belinda seizes the opportunity to lure Sonia to her death.

Episode 428
Belinda is unable to carry out her attack on Sonia. Cass becomes aware of Stan's heart problem, but promises she will keep it quiet. Erica announces her new position as Head of Department. Stan suffers another attack, he attempts to reach for his pills but Reb kicks them out of reach.

Episode 429
Sonia is concerned about the change in Joan's behaviour. Ann returns as Governor of Wentworth, informing the officers of Camilla Wells' arrival. Myra Desmond visits Driscoll House, and finds it in chaos. Stan is informed he must take on lighter duties in order to remain at Wentworth.

Episode 430
Camilla angers the other women with her views on life inside prison. Stan starts a Glee Club in the prison. Myra is concerned for Kay's welfare living with her father. Rick is knocked unconscious and faces almost certain death.

Episode 431
Eddie rescues Rick before his car is crushed. Myra explains to Judy she is unable to take over Driscoll House due to family problems. Myra's threats to kill her husband become a reality when she is pushed to breaking point.

Episode 432
Myra is brought to Wentworth, charged with murder. Cass unwittingly brings a deadly snake into the prison. Sonia finds a dummy hanging in her cell, with a note attached to frighten her.

Episode 433
Kay remains devastated over her father's death. Helen and Meg are bitten by the snake. The Fellowes gang plant a bomb under Rick's car, which Colleen's husband borrows to take the children to school. Rick receives a phone call to warn him of the bomb but is too late: the bomb explodes killing Colleen's entire family.

Episode 434
A devastated Colleen is unable to comprehend what has happened. Doctor Weissman visits Sonia, who reveals details of her past. The singing competition ends with a mass escape.

Episode 435
Doreen returns to visit her friends at Wentworth, but is saddened to find few of them are left. Meg eventually wakes up and informs Ann the women have escaped from the bus. Doreen attempts to get put back inside and Myra stands up for Sonia by challenging Joan.

Episode 436
Joan has a new nemesis in the form of Myra. Colleen turns to alcohol to forget about her problems. Judy and the other women return to Wentworth.

Episode 437
The police catch Reb at the airport. Judy tries to get Myra to take over as Top Dog. Minnie says goodbye to the women, and Eddie informs Rick that Lionel Fellowes wants him dead.

Episode 438
Detectives arrive at Meg's house to question Colleen. Doreen tries to prolong her stay in Wentworth. Gloria is brought to Wentworth, with Joan arranging a deadly confrontation with Myra.

Episode 439
Sonia stops Myra from choking Gloria. Myra discovers a weakness in Reb through Sarah and Joey. Gloria attempts to poison Rick.

Episode 440
Joan arranges for Phyllis to bash Reb. Colleen continues to sink deeper into depression. Bobbie accuses Rick of trying to rape her.

Episode 441
Rick is suspended following the accusations of rape. Meg takes over from Colleen as Deputy Governor of Wentworth. Sonia and Bobbie are informed they will be transferred to Barnhurst, but all is not as it seems.

Episode 442

Margo Gaffney returns to Wentworth, and immediately sets out to cause trouble. Sonia and Bobbie are taken to Sydney, unsure of what awaits them. Renner has plans for Sonia, but decides to dispose of Bobbie.

Episode 443

Myra tries to improve conditions in Wentworth, while Margo does the opposite by arranging for drugs to arrive. Myra is framed for a vicious attack on Gloria.

Episode 444

Bobbie is ordered to start work on the streets. Judy suspects Phyllis was to blame for the attack on Gloria. Margo discovers her drugs are missing, and attacks Myra in the laundry.

Episode 445

Reb tries to seize control Margo's supply of drugs in the prison. Colleen requests to be reinstated as Deputy Governor. Myra's trial gets off to a bad start as Kay gives evidence.

Episode 446

Doreen is released. The Major informs Joan he has leukemia. Myra is sentenced to eight years imprisonment. Bobbie is shocked when Joan finds her in Sydney.

Episode 447

Joan uses Bobbie to arrange a meeting with Sonia. Sonia escapes, but Bobbie is captured by police. The women decide to form a union in Wentworth. Sonia stands at the edge of a cliff and appears to contemplate suicide.

Episode 448

Meg's strange behaviour begins to cause concern. Doctor Edmunds is introduced as the new psychiatrist in Wentworth, and invites Ann to dinner. Margo is transferred to Blackmoor.

Episode 449

Cass receives a light punishment for attacking Frances. Rick's life is in danger when he's taken to the woods. Jonathan reveals his true plans for his case studies. Myra returns just in time to stop Reb taking over.

Episode 450

Myra tells Judy that another heavy blow to the head may kill her so she can't challenge Reb. Meg, Cass and Phyllis are hypnotised by Jonathan causing a complete personality change. Jonathan suggests that Cass kills Bobbie.

Episode 451

Myra gets back at Reb by forcing the dope down her throat. Erica Davidson arrives to negotiate with the women about the strike and a deal is suggested. Cass attempts to strangle Bobbie, but has she attacked the wrong person?

Episode 452

Pixie is OK and Cass is in the clear. Hannah is upset when Ann tells her she's to be deported. Cass and Bobbie make friends again but Cass is still determined to harm her. The women accept the Department's new offer.

Episode 453

Rick and Rachel become close. Colleen is surprised to find out that both Ann and Meg are dating Jonathan. Hannah takes extreme measures to ensure her stay in Australia is extended a little longer.

Episode 454

The women start a petition to try and help Hannah. Rachel's father is knocked down by a hit and run driver. Judy shows Ann a letter received from Scott advising of Jonathan's past so Ann confronts him.

Episode 455

Judy manages to save Bobbie's life. Colleen's house sale is completed and she announces she's leaving and plans to travel around the world with the money, inviting Meg along too. Bobbie finds out that she is pregnant.

Episode 456

The women prepare for the Wentworth fete. Myra discovers that Kay is in hospital but the chances of seeing her are slim. All isn't as it seems with Hannah's visitor. Colleen says goodbye to Wentworth for the last time – Judith McGrath's last appearance.

Episode 457

Judy agrees to help Myra plan her escape via the fete. Glamour model Leigh Templar is inducted as a new prisoner. New officer Dennis Cruickshank also arrives. Rachel takes action against her father's killer.

Episode 458

Leigh becomes the victim of a hate campaign. She also finds out that she's losing a lot of work due to her being in prison. The fete is put into jeopardy but Ann orders it still to go ahead. Rick leaves Wentworth.

Episode 459

Wentworth opens it's gates to the public as the fete begins. Cass tries to flirt with Charlie but it doesn't do a great deal of good. Myra's escape is a success and she manages to slip out of the prison grounds. . .

Episode 460

A fight in the garden leads to Bobbie being injured – she loses the baby. When Cass finds out she goes crazy and attacks Dennis. Reb seriously bashes Phyllis. Judy finds out that an old face from Barnhurst is due to join the women.

Episode 461

Cass is suspected of attacking Phyllis but Reb later confesses. 3 new additions join Wentworth – Marie Winter, Marlene Warren and officer Heather Rodgers. Myra finds Kay. Joan's house is broken into.

Episode 462

Joan's intruder is revealed as a young boy, Shane, who has run away from home. Heather shows off her karate skills when she breaks up a fight. Marlene finds a stash of drugs under Marie's bed.

Episode 463

Marlene escapes a bashing by Marie by offering some information on Heather which Marie uses this to blackmail her with. Tracey Morris makes a surprise visit to Meg. Joan arranges with Marie to cause trouble for Ann.

Episode 464

Marie begins to offer drugs to the women. Tracey and Mark hold Meg hostage as they plan their next move. Marie pressurises Heather to start bringing drugs into the prison. Marlene is bashed.

Episode 465

Heather has no option than to bring in the drugs when her brother is injured in an accident. Ann realises that Wally is helping Myra. Joan instructs Marie to start a huge riot in order to have Ann sacked.

Episode 466

Ann tells Wally that she knows he has helped Myra and would have to tell the truth if asked. The officers are drugged and Marie's riot begins. When Reb refuses to help Marie kill Myra, she's pushed down the stairs.

Episode 467
Bobbie is made the prime suspect for Reb's fall. Ann saves Leigh's life and rescues her from a burning cell. Joan promises Shane a birthday treat. Joan's plan is a success and Ann is forced to resign as prison Governor.

Episode 468
Joan is hopeful that she'll become the new Governor, but the women have other ideas. Joan suggests that Marie is transferred to Blackmoor. The women have a barbecue but Joan warns them that things will change when she takes over.

Episode 469
Reb explains to Bobbie that she can't lag on Marie so can't get her off the hook. Marie threatens to reveal all about Joan unless she helps her escape. Joan is surprised to learn that Ann is to be reinstated as Governor.

Episode 470
Reb tells Marie that she doesn't want to be involved in her drug schemes anymore. When Shane's dog gets stuck in a drain, Shane also finds himself stuck and in danger. Reb decides to lag on Marie after all.

Episode 471
Marie is sent to solitary. Shane narrowly escapes death but his rescuer isn't as lucky. New cook Ray Proctor arrives and Marlene notices that he's stealing food from the kitchen. Marie makes her move and escapes in dramatic fashion… cue the helicopter!

Episode 472
Reb is rushed to hospital and Joan's in the hot seat if she dies. New prisoner Bev Baker arrives and the women find out about her gory crimes. Joan is visited by the police who arrest her for abducting Shane.

Episode 473
Bev's behaviour alarms the women as she burns herself on purpose to see what it feels like. Reb names Joan when the police interview her. The women decide to attempt a world record. Bobbie escapes.

Episode 474
Bobbie's time on the outside doesn't last for too long, she's returned to the prison. Bev plans her next gruesome move. The Department ask Joan to resign, but the other officers decide to strike in support of her.

Episode 475
The women are all locked in their cells as the strike begins. Bev announces a raffle – Marlene wins $5 but it's not as lucky for Bobbie who wins the consolation prize: a very sick 'manicure' from Bev.

Episode 476
Heather is attacked by the demonstrators when she attempts to cross the picket line. Dot goes missing from hospital. Bev holds another lottery. Social worker Rob Summerton is stabbed with a knitting needle by Bev.

Episode 477
Bev injects air into her bloodstream causing a heart attack then death. Angela Adams is inducted to Wentworth. Phillip tells Bobbie that her mother has died. The women are surprised to see Joan back on duty.

Episode 478
Deidre drives Reb to their family holiday home but Reb's still not well. Angel stirs up trouble between Myra and Judy. Ann receives an anonymous death threat. Reb is arrested – she tells her mother that she'll kill her for calling the police.

Episode 479
Myra and Judy continue to argue. Angel causes problems for more of the women with her lies. Joan tells Reb that she'll pay for all the trouble she's caused in the past. Ann finds another death threat – this time inside her own house.

Episode 480
The dance marathon begins but Judy's health is in trouble when Angel purposely tries to make her pacemaker stop working. Heather finds out that Marie Winter has suggested she's smuggled drugs into Wentworth. Joan loses custody of Shane.

Episode 481
Ann's car is tampered with. Joan is accused of setting up Heather. Angel arranges for Meg to be raped by Peter Wright. Dot collapses during the dance marathon. An anonymous caller tells Ann that a bomb has been planted in the prison.

Episode 482
The prison is evacuated but the dance team refuse to leave until they complete their task. Heather tells Ann that she's seen Joan bashing prisoners regularly. She and Bobbie attempt to set Joan up. Meg has two intruders at home. . .

Episode 483
Meg is brutally attacked and raped by the two men. The women finally begin to realise that Angel is anything but an angel; this is confirmed to Ann when Mrs Adams visits and spills the beans. Judy and Myra attempt to stop Reb's mother being bashed.

Episode 484
Meg finally reports her rape to the police. Angel gets angry and reveals her true colours when the women continue to ignore her. Pixie Mason makes a surprise return to Wentworth. Joan is set up by the women but it doesn't work – Heather is sacked instead.

Episode 485
Reb finds Lou searching her cell for the knife. Ann is concerned when Stan's keys go missing. Myra makes Angel confess to setting up Meg's rape. When Reb is taken to solitary by Joan, an attempt on her life goes wrong and Joan is left hanging in the stairwell.

Episode 486
Joan is rescued when Reb tells Joyce that she might be dead. When Angel starts getting back at the other women, Myra and Judy agree to play tough with her – she's taken to the shower block and all her hair is cut off. Ann has an intruder at her flat.

Episode 487
Ann is horrified when she finds a policeman has been murdered at her flat. Angel vows to get back at the other women for what they have done to her. Neville forces Bobbie to have sex with her or he'll tell Ann about the dope plants in the garden.

Episode 488
Angel's plans to get back at Myra backfire, causing Angel to lose the plot. Kerryn tells Pixie she's going on a hunger strike until she can see Lyle. Bobbie takes action against Nev following another rape but she doesn't realise that Stan is in the way.

Episode 489
Bobbie is in trouble after the accident. Stan reveals to Edie that he'd like for Bobbie to be released on license. Marlene thinks of a new way of scamming the women. Kerryn is embarrassed by the other women during her visit. Lou finds out that Nev has lagged.

Episode 490

Lou plans to escape and tells Reb to help her. Kerryn refuses the women's apologies after Myra shows them how silly they were behaving. Pixie realises that Judy is in love with her. Lou puts her plan into action during a softball game.

Episode 491

Marlene stops Lou from escaping. Stan tells Edie the truth about his job. Ann tells Meg that Erica has resigned from the Department. Lou tricks Joyce and manages to escape – she turns up at Deidre's house but Lou ends up at the wrong end of a gun.

Episode 492

Lou is hurt when Deidre shoots her in the arm. Kerryn faints as a result of her hunger strike. Myra finds Bobbie's dope plants when she's working in the garden – she takes drastic action with her and Judy is not happy. Stan has a heart attack.

Episode 493

Joan finds Stan and saves his life. Replacement officer Len Murphy arrives but doesn't make a good impression on Joan or the other women. Department worker Sarah Higgins arrives as an inmate. Stan tells Bobbie to stay away from Len.

Episode 494

Bobbie tells Myra about Stan's warning. Pixie is upset when she finds out that her parents know about her prison stay. Len lets Judy know his opinions about her sexuality and later warns Joan that her days are numbered in Wentworth.

Episode 495

New inmate Samantha Greenway arrives, on the charge of drug possession. Joan tries to get some dirt on Len but has no luck. Pixie tries to cheer up Kerryn but it doesn't change anything; Joan and Joyce find her hanging in the visitor's suite.

Episode 496

Myra tells the women that they're going to have to try and get rid of Joan and Len. Lou confronts Sarah in her cell about her sentence but Sarah is armed with jug of boiling water. Ann receives a nasty shock in the post. Judy is attacked by Len.

Episode 497

Ann's worried about her safety so Meg offers to stay with her. Len slams the door on Marlene's face. Some new prisoners arrive but the Department order complete secrecy surrounding their identity. Armed Brian Lowe takes Ann and Meg hostage.

Episode 498

The Department receives a ransom note for Ann and Meg's release, who are tied up and held in a booby-trapped old building. In the meantime Joyce is to take over as Governor, much to the disappointment of Joan. Phillip is shot by Brian.

Episode 499

Myra decides to hold a 'trial' for Sarah. Meg and Ann try to find a way out of the building. Pixie finds Sarah dead in her bed – her throat cut. Brian tells Meg and Ann that he won't be coming back. . . but he does and falls to his death when he misjudges the weak staircase.

Episode 500

Marlene tells the women that she's seen a man in the prison hospital. Joyce announces that there are some male prisoners from Woodridge staying at Wentworth. Frances admits killing Sarah. Police find the hideout but don't know about the traps – the building explodes…

Episode 501

Ann is found at what's left of the building and Meg is later discovered underneath the rubble, injured but alive. Joan visits Shane and finds out he's to be fostered to a family – they later go skating together. Reb finds herself in trouble.

Episode 502

Reb manages to get out of the locked room just before she's missed. Geoff reminds Len of his past when he starts taunting the men in the garden. Ann has to tell Meg that Phillip is dead. Myra resigns as top dog, naming Reb as her replacement.

Episode 503

Reb gets Joan's backing as new top dog and they agree to try and get rid of Len. The doctor is concerned about Meg as she doesn't seem to be improving and has almost given up. Reb gives Marlene a drugged biscuit – she becomes seriously ill during the night.

Episode 504

Marlene is surprised when Ann tells her that the illness was due to an allergic reaction to a drug. A new prisoner arrives but refuses to speak. Frank attacks Matt in the garden. Myra confronts Reb about drugs found in her cell but Reb reminds her she's no longer top dog.

Episode 505

Frank tries it on with 'Jane' but she and Pixie manage to stop him. Marlene and Bobbie fall out over becoming friends with Matt. Myra tapes Reb dissing the other women and plays it back to everyone. 'Jane' speaks for the first time to try and save Pixie.

Episode 506

Myra and Judy come to Pixie's rescue. 'Jane' reveals that her real name is Yemil and she's in prison as she ran someone over when escaping from her violent husband. Myra takes over as top dog again. Reb is to be transferred to Blackmoor but warns Joan that she'll be back.

Episode 507

Len is made new acting Governor when Ann collapses and has to take time off. Len makes another visit to Lou but Joan is listening outside of the door. The two of them fight in the corridor. Judy finds Reb's key following her transfer. Frank tries to force himself on Bobbie.

Episode 508

Geoff saves Bobbie. Yemil tries to hang herself but Pixie stops her. Meg finds out that Frank is inside for rape and is surprised that the Department has sent him to a female prison. The men receive a death threat. One of Meg's attackers warns her off and punches her.

Episode 509

Meg reports her attack to the police. Lexie Patterson joins the women as the latest arrival to H Block. Yemil refuses a visit from her husband. 'Workmen' plant a gas canister underneath a bed in the men's cell – when they sleep it slowly begins to release the gas.

Episode 510

Meg smells the gas in the corridor and she and Joan manage to pull Geoff and Matt outside of their cell. Frank brutally rapes Pixie. She arrives in shock at the laundry. Myra decides to use Pixie's condition to help get rid of Len. Judy reluctantly agrees and the plan is put into action.

Episode 511

The staff and prisoners are interviewed by the police who charge Len with rape. Lexie and Marlene have a card game and Lexie wins all of Marl's money. Ann tells the women that Pixie has been moved to a psychiatric hospital. Matt attacks Frank.

Episode 512

Lou has LSD and cocaine smuggled into the prison. Sam and Geoff begin to work on the robot. Lexie finds Frank's beer in the garden, resulting in the pumpkins exploding all over the place. Peter Wright is found guilty at the trial. Shane turns up at Joan's house.

Episode 513

The Taylors struggle to cope with Shane. A new Witness in Yemil's case comes forward, giving her a chance of freedom. The women say goodbye to Bobbie.

Episode 514

Sam gives Joan a painting of her father and Shane. Lou notices Jan's hands trembling and offers to supply her with alcohol. Ettie Parslow arrives from Barnhurst. Joyce and Lexie are shot when a sniper opens fire on the inmates.

Episode 515

Geoff believes the attack was aimed at the men. Jan struggles to cope without access to alcohol. The skeleton key gives Geoff and Myra a chance to be together.

Episode 516

Myra warns Lou about selling alcohol to Jan. Sam wants to use the robot to escape, but Geoff attempts to dissuade her. Lou plots to kill Joan and frame Myra, but her plans go horribly wrong.

Episode 517

Lou is injured in the shooting. Sam escapes from Wentworth hidden inside the robot, but returns soon afterwards following her mother's rejection. Myra takes revenge on Frank for his attack on Pixie.

Episode 518

Myra brands the letter "R" for rapist on Frank's forehead. The men receive word that they are to be transferred. Lou hides Sam's palette knife in her sling, and Frank attempts to escape.

Episode 519

Sheila Brady arrives at Wentworth. Lou and Kath attempt to kill Myra, but the Top Dog overpowers them. Jan discovers some startling news about Ettie.

Episode 520

Myra asks Ann to be transferred to Barnhurst, unaware that the women are planning a surprise Birthday party. One of the women is electrocuted following another attempt on Myra's life. Judy discovers Sam hanging in her cell.

Episode 521

Judy is distraught over Sam's death, but is convinced it wasn't suicide. Inspector Grace arrives to question the women. Myra overhears Lou and Alice discussing their part in Sam's death.

Episode 522

Joan is informed of her father's critical condition. She visits him in hospital but as she reminisces with him he passes away. Geoff is charged with Sam's murder. Frank holds Dennis hostage in solitary.

Episode 523

Ettie is offered compensation, on the condition she doesn't speak to the media. Marlene and Matt plan their wedding, and where they will live following their release. Jan collapses in her cell.

Episode 524

Ann is informed that Jan was poisoned any may not survive. Lou uses one of Sheila's guitar strings to attack Myra. Ettie accepts the compensation and is released.

Episode 525

Geoff saves Myra's life. Joan uses Cynthia in Blackmoor to put pressure on Reb. Marlene is overjoyed to receive her parents blessing.

Episode 526

Sheila starts work on a song dedicated to Pixie. Ann refuses to take the blame for the Department's mistake over Ettie. Anita Selby arrives at Wentworth.

Episode 527

Joan warns the other officers about the need for heightened security the wedding. Anita tries to offer Joan her sympathy following the Major's death. Dennis is followed home by the police.

Episode 528

Marlene asks Anita for advice on how to get forgiveness over her crime. Lexie's temper backfires when Joan destroys her Boy George image by cutting her hair.

Episode 529

Inspector Grace tries to get Dennis to admit his guilt. Lexie steals Joyce's purse from the staffroom. Dennis' life starts to crumble around him.

Episode 530

Dennis is arrested for Murder. Myra forces Lexie to return Joyce's purse. Frank sets a trap for Joan in the library.

Episode 531

Meg and Dennis find Joan unconscious. Judy is surprised to see Sheila appear on television. The women witness Joan suffering blackouts.

Episode 532

Joan's behaviour begins to cause concern. Inspector Grace informs Dennis of a new suspect in the murders. Lou and Frank plot their revenge against Myra and Geoff.

Episode 533

Bobbie returns for Marlene's big day. Marlene is devastated to find out Matt will be transferred immediately after their wedding. Frank threatens to return and kill Dennis.

Episode 534

The wedding ends in tears as Matt is taken away. Marlene is comforted by her friends, and the news that she has been forgiven for her crime. Myra is devastated when both Judy and Geoff are released. Betty Bobbitt's final appearance as Judy Bryant and the only time that the closing theme tune is replaced with something else: "Pixie's Song".

Episode 535

Joan visits her doctor and is diagnosed with having a blood clot on the brain, requiring immediate treatment. Anita is sent to solitary for her own protection. Ann refuses to acknowledge Myra as Top Dog and threatens her with Blackmoor.

Episode 536

Myra returns to her cell feeling alone and is comforted by Lexie, prompting several flashback sequences of old friends and enemies throughout her time in Wentworth. Ann informs Meg of the imminent arrival of prisoners from Barnhurst.

Episode 537

Joan refuses to let Ann see her in hospital. Myra learns of Bea's death and is suspicious of the new inmates from Barnhurst. Ann imposes stricter security measures in light of the riot.

Episode 538
Ruth Ballinger arrives at Wentworth. Joan discharges herself from hospital. Ruth begins to make life difficult for the officers, demanding to be treated differently to the other inmates . A knife is planted in Myra's cell.

Episode 539
Ruth demands a private phone in her cell. Joyce informs Meg she has left her husband and asks to stay with her. Ettie decides to try and get back inside.

Episode 540
The women begin to find out more about the inmates from Barnhurst. Nora confides in Myra. The police grant Ruth's requests but make sure her phone is tapped. Terri and Joan plot their revenge on Myra.

Episode 541
A sinister side to Ruth emerges when she offers to bring drugs into the prison. Myra tries to regain Ann's trust by keeping the women in line. Joan and Terri try to weaken Myra.

Episode 542
Myra refuses to let Ruth bring drugs into Wentworth. Jenny Hartley struggles to cope with her overbearing grandmother. Meg arrives home to find Joyce unconscious.

Episode 543
Joyce confides in Meg about her failing marriage. Ruth ignores Myra's instructions by offering drugs to the inmates and spiking Myra's coffee with acid.

Episode 544
May and Nora confront Ruth. Ettie's bank raid goes horribly wrong when she shoots a policeman. Joan attacks Ruth following revelations of her involvement in child pornography.

Episode 545
Ann offers to help Joan. The police investigate the link between Ettie and the Fellowes gang, while Myra becomes increasingly more suspicious of Ruth.

Episode 546
May keeps Ruth occupied while Myra searches her cell for drugs. Pippa tempts Jenny to leave her grandmother and join her in Japan. Myra catches Daphne with cocaine.

Episode 547
Joan agrees to help Ruth escape, on the condition that she disposes of Myra. Myra suggests a new prison council to improve conditions for the inmates. Jenny makes a horrifying discovery.

Episode 548
Jenny is arrested for her grandmother's murder. Ruth informs Lou of the deadly plot to dispose of Myra. Daphne sinks deeper into depression. Myra faces certain death at the hands of Joan.

Episode 549
May comes to Myra's rescue. Ruth is taken to solitary but warns Joan of the consequences if she crosses her. Jenny struggles with life inside Wentworth. A terrorist squad break into the prison in search of Ruth.

Episode 550
The women's nightmare begins as the terrorists invade Wentworth. Ruth is released from solitary, but her escape is hindered by the police. Inspector Grace attempts to reason with the leader, Ram. The inmates are informed one of them will die every hour until the terrorists are able to free Ruth.

Episode 551
Joan informs the women of Ruth's evil past. The terrorists carry out their threat by murdering Tammy, with another inmate to be killed within the hour. Julie crawls through the air conditioning ducts to seek help. Ruth mercilessly uses Myra's Top Dog position to determine who will be the next to die.

Episode 552
Julie contacts the police, but is too late to stop the next death as Myra is brutally murdered in front of the inmates. Ruth realises Julie was missing and may have spoken to the police. Nora stands guard over Myra's body. The terrorists reach the airport but Joan ensures their escape is foiled.

Episode 553
Ruth is sent to Blackmoor. Daphne sinks further into depression, and is seen standing on the edge on the roof. Dennis is warned of Frank's escape. Joan wakens to find her house on fire.

Episode 554
Joan suspects the fire was an attempt on her life. Sister Hall discovers a possible cause for Daphne's behaviour. Dennis arrives home to find Frank pointing a gun at Meg.

Episode 555
Frank holds Dennis and Meg hostage. Daphne finds it hard to talk to Dr Weissman. Dennis is shot by Frank, and later overhears doctors informing Meg he may never walk again.

Episode 556
Nora attends Myra's funeral. Queenie Marshall arrives at Wentworth, and recognises Andrew Fry as one of her customers. Nora and May attempt to get their own back on Lou, but Nora is punched in the stomach during the fight.

Episode 557
Nora suffers a miscarriage and loses her baby. Lou attempts to take over as Top Dog. Mervin begs the women to keep his epilepsy a secret.

Episode 558
Lou heavies the women to join the insurance scheme. Jenny is warned not to make contact with her Aunt Harriet. When Nora is turned down for parole, she agrees to take over as Top Dog in Myra's memory.

Episode 559
Nora convinces Alice and Kath to avoid Lou. Lexie threatens to reveal Mervin's epilepsy if he doesn't agree to her demands. Julie receives bad news about her mother, while Jenny is stunned to hear a confession to her grandmother's murder.

Episode 560
Ann informs Jenny the confession cannot be proven. Dennis decides to call off his relationship with Meg. A gun is hidden in the prison, with its owner being kept a mystery.

Episode 561
Lou informs Daphne of her plan to kill Nora and escape. Lexie continues to pressurise Mervin. Pippa arrives home with a new Japanese boyfriend!

Episode 562
Pippa visits Jenny in Wentworth. Nora realises the authorities may be aiming to have Daphne released. Joan and Terri's dinner date ends in upset when Joan is mistaken for her mother. Willie is found unconscious in her cell.

Episode 563

Willie comes round, but appears to have lost her memory. Julie discovers more fraudulent invoices when working in reception. Joan is shocked when Terri's parents arrive to meet her.

Episode 564

Ann informs Pat she is to be suspended following the investigation. Lou and Lexie conspire to start a numbers racket to con the women. Ann discovers some contradictions in Chaucer's story.

Episode 565

A women's group demonstrates outside Wentworth following Daphne's case. Lou threatens to reveal Joan's relationship with Terri. Grace refuses to re-open the Hartley case.

Episode 566

Daphne becomes increasingly attracted to Ben. Pippa questions Ben's motives for taking on Daphne's case. Terri finds out about her mother's suicide attempt.

Episode 567

Terri informs Ann of her intention to resign. Lou turns Pippa's art class into a paint fight. Ann informs the officers that four juvenile offenders are to be brought to Wentworth.

Episode 568

Grace gives evidence at Jenny's trial. Ann is informed the juvenile offenders may benefit from their experience in Wentworth, but Nikki will pose more of a problem. Things go from bad to worse for Jenny, and Nora has a violent confrontation with Nikki.

Episode 569

The women create horror stories to get through to the young offenders. Nora starts a protest about the poor standard of food in the prison. Joan's attempts to discipline Nikki backfire.

Episode 570

Joyce and Mervin attempt to reach a truce. May suggests they use outside influences on Nikki to get her see sense. Ben tells Ann he intends to propose to Pippa.

Episode 571

Jenny finds out that Daphne has a crush on Ben so tells the other women. Chaucer is exposed in a newspaper story. Nikki gets cold feet and pleads with Willie to stop her involvement in the escape.

Episode 572

Joan's plans to surprise Terri with a meal do not go according to plan. Ben sets the record straight with Daphne. Joan finds Terri home in bed with her boss. Cindy attacks May. Daphne prepares to end it all.

Episode 573

The women find Daphne hanging in her cell. Joan tells Terri she will give her another chance as long as she doesn't know about what she gets up to with Barry. Daphne's condition worsens and she threatens the doctors.

Episode 574

Daphne is sent to solitary. Pippa tells Lexie that she's been commissioned to design some t-shirts. Eve Wilder arrives at Wentworth, pleading her innocence. Joan and Terri argue again.

Episode 575

Lou and Lexie are found guilty of conning the other women by the Council. Mervin finds out he's made it to the finals of the cookery competition. Joan comes home to discover that Terri has left her.

Episode 576

Daphne is told that she needs hormone treatment to stop her depression and outbursts. Terri tells Joan that it's over – Joan lets her guard down and Lou sees her crying in the corridor.

Episode 577

An old face from the past returns to Wentworth – Reb Kean, but something's not quite right with her. Myra Desmond makes a brief posthumous appearance. Eve's crime is revealed in a flashback. Lexie's t-shirts are ruined.

Episode 578

Lexie and the other women manage to fix her t-shirts. Nora tells Reb about some of the things she's done in the past but Reb can't remember anything. Mervin wins the contest and Meg finds a shocking discovery about Reb.

Episode 579

The women decide to hold a contest with Eve being the organiser and judge. Cynthia suggests to Joan that Reb's 'suicide' should be arranged. Lou reminds Reb that her brother is dead.

Episode 580

Joyce's husband has a heart attack and dies, causing Mervin to be confused about their own relationship. Meg finds out that Nora's mother is dead. Lexie recognises her own mother in a newspaper, but is it really her?

Episode 581

Rehearsals begin for the forthcoming contest. Ann tells Reb that she'll investigate what went on at Ingleside – she finds that Reb was given ECT without her permission. May and Willie are offered a ticket out of Wentworth.

Episode 582

The women perform in the contest with Julie being the overall winner. Reb begins to remember more of her past. May and Willie's undercover plan begins. Julie finds Reb in a bad state, assuming she is dead.

Episode 583

Pippa gives a journalist the report on Reb but it may have done more harm than good. Joyce becomes suspicious about Eve. David goes to Eve's house and finds the bullet still stuck in her mattress.

Episode 584

Joan tells Cynthia that she can't risk killing Reb. Jenny contacts Lexie's mother. Ann is concerned when the Inspector admits that he doesn't know where May and Willie are. Nora announces she's stepping down as TD.

Episode 585

Jenny tells Lexie's mother the truth about her. David is drawn into Eve's story and replaces her mattress with a new one, thus removing the evidence to find her guilty. A new prisoner arrives at Wentworth, with an audience of bikies. . .

Episode 586

Rita Connors is inducted by Joan, whom she makes an instant enemy of. Barbie Cox is also new to the prison but her crime is a bit of a mystery – rather like her! Joyce's suspicions of Eve are confirmed and she's brutally attacked by her. Rita appears to be no match for Lou and Alice.

Episode 587

The women think that Rita would be perfect for Top Dog but she's not interested. May is shot dead during the robbery. Willie accuses Ann of murdering May. David attempts to finish Joyce off in hospital.

Episode 588
David has second thoughts and returns back to Eve to stop their relationship. Lou pours paint on Rita's leather jacket. Nora is nowhere to be found. David ends everything and shoots himself while visiting Eve again.

Episode 589
James Dwyer threatens to sack Ann following all of the prison's recent disasters. Eve gets a new solicitor but unluckily for her it's a woman. Jessie is revealed as Lexie's real mother. Lou tells Joan she's in charge of the women now.

Episode 590
Lou arranges a hunger strike and a demonstration in the dining room. Ann resigns but is told to take a month's break instead. Jessie gets herself sent to Wentworth to see Lexie. Lou sets Rita up.

Episode 591
Joan is put into one of the driers by Lou and Alice but a mystery person cuts her free and leaves a note next to her, claiming that Lou is responsible. Nancy McCormack buries her dead husband in their garden. Wentworth has a 'Phantom Lagger' amongst the women.

Episode 592
Jessie is suspected as the Lagger. Joyce recovers in hospital – Meg visits her to keep her up-to-date on the news. Rita has a CB radio smuggled in so she can talk to her boyfriend. Lou tells Alice she's going to kill Lexie.

Episode 593
Lou makes plans to electrocute Lexie in the kitchen. Nancy is sent to Wentworth on remand, following her husband's murder. Joan destroys Rita's treasured leather jacket by slashing it with a scalpel.

Episode 594
Meg doesn't believe Joan's story about the jacket. Lou's plans to kill Lexie don't work, but she's still in danger. Joan gets a nasty surprise from Rita's bikie mates at her home.

Episode 595
Rita finds out about Joan's night with the Conquerors through her CB radio. Joan is forced to burn her damaged possessions. Steve Ryan gets the job as handyman at Wentworth. New Governor Bob Moran arrives.

Episode 596
Eve lags on Lou to Bob as she attempts to sweet talk him but it doesn't work and he can tell she's making it all up. A cell search is arranged and Rita's radio is found. Joan takes drastic action against the Conquerors.

Episode 597
Meg accuses Joan of starting the fire. Bob receives a note about Nora and later her dead body is found in the prison grounds. Nancy is bashed by Lou and Alice for answering Lou back.

Episode 598
Lexie manages to escape from Wentworth. Rita receives some bad news from Dan: Slasher has been killed in a gang brawl. Barbie sees Steve in a magazine as a naked centre-fold! Rita 'rides' on one of the driers in memory of her dead boyfriend.

Episode 599
Lexie makes friends on the outside with Pocco but her life could be in danger when the prison receives an anonymous phone call offering to track her down. Eve makes a confession but doesn't realise Alice listening in.

Episode 600
The identity of the Phantom Lagger is revealed. Lou takes control of the prison. Eve pays the ultimate price for lagging when she is hung by Lou. Joan and Rita are ordered to fight to the death.

Episode 601
Bob manages to seize control of the women. Eve is found hanging in her cell. Steve fears Julie may lose her fight for life. The women prepare for a new Top Dog.

Episode 602
Jessie is shocked to see Lexie's scars. Rita becomes the new Top Dog, and names her group the Conquerors. Bassinger goes in search of Lexie.

Episode 603
Bassinger attacks Lexie but she manages to escape. Lou realises she has lost control of the women. The women take revenge on Alice and Lou by preparing nooses in their cell.

Episode 604
Alice vows to stay clear of Lou. Pippa disapproves of Ann's relationship with Dan. Meg is demoted when Bob becomes Deputy Governor.

Episode 605
Julie becomes jealous when Steve mentions other women. Ann asks Rita to prepare a list of improvements to conditions at Wentworth. Lou plans her revenge on the women.

Episode 606
Steve stands up to Joan. Ann is concerned the women will find out about Dan. Lou is taken to hospital and Rita is placed in solitary.

Episode 607
The women prepare an alibi for Rita. Lou's injuries are confirmed as self-inflicted. Dan comes to Rita's defence, and Lou escapes from hospital.

Episode 608
Bassinger finds out about Lou's escape. Lou goes in search of Alice's family. Lexie believes she is pregnant.

Episode 609
Jessie tries to reveal her real identity to Lexie. Joan complains to Ann about Joyce's assault. Lou is raped by Sean when she rejects his advances.

Episode 610
Rita persuades Dan to become the new chaplain. Lexie remains furious with Jessie and refuses to accept she is her mother. The women smuggle Pocco inside Wentworth.

Episode 611
Jessie is rushed to hospital. The women find out about Kath's arrest. Lou takes revenge on Alice's family in a brutal shooting spree.

Episode 612
Alice is told Lou has murdered her mother and brother, and vows to kill her. Mabel persuades Lexie to forgive Jessie. New inmate Kath Maxwell arrives at Wentworth.

Episode 613
Janet Williams arrives from Blackmoor. The officers fear for Kath's safety, and Bob appeals to the women for their understanding. Joan tries to change her lifestyle.

Episode 614
Steve condemns Julie over her behaviour. Kath makes a bad first impression on the women. Janet finds out about Bob's friendship with Kath, and conspires with Lou.

Episode 615
The women prepare a wedding breakfast for Mervin and Joyce. Joan becomes suspicious of Kath and Bob. Lou is found dead in her cell.

Episode 616
The women are locked in their cells until the police arrive. News of Lou's death stuns everyone. Kath decides to stand up to the women. Bongo prepares to set Rira free.

Episode 617
Lexie is charged with Lou's murder, but the real culprit is later revealed as Janet. Mervin and Joyce get married. Bongo's attempt to free Rita ends in disaster.

Episode 618
Dan is rushed to hospital. Kath defends herself against the women, and Jessie plans to escape from hospital.

Episode 619
Ann is commanded to make Joan Deputy Governor, but protests about her inability to work with her. Meg is angry to be demoted and Julie is devastated when she is turned down for parole.

Episode 620
Steve appals his Mother by news of his relationship with a prisoner. Rita and Alice are sent to solitary for their attack on Kath. Bassinger pulls a knife on Jessie.

Episode 621
Janet wrecks Rita's cell. Joan embarks on a new hobby and makes a new friend. Kath attacks Rita with a knife.

Episode 622
Kath smuggles money into the prison for her protection. Roach and Ida are inducted to Wentworth. Amy conspires with Joan to increase Julie's sentence. Rita finds out about Joan's involvement in Slasher's death, and vows to kill her.

Episode 623
Amy continues her quest to keep Julie in prison. Joan recognises Lorelei Wilkinson while out with Andrew. Rita takes revenge on Joan by dragging her up to the roof and threatening to push her over the edge.

Episode 624
Joan sets out to destroy Rita and frame Julie. Lorelei is brought to Wentworth on remand. Kath attacks Julie and knocks her out.

Episode 625
Julie becomes high on LSD which almost leads to her death. Kath meets her new cellmate, Merle Jones. Joan informs the women of Merle's violent tendencies.

Episode 626
Joan threatens Amy when she discovers the money has not been transferred. The women realise Nancy's diary has been Joan's mystery informant. Lexie is injured when Merle attacks Rita.

Episode 627
Ann tells Julie she will be transferred after the wedding. Joan is bribed into bringing drugs into Wentworth. Janet attempts to ruin the wedding.

Episode 628
Julie marries Steve inside the prison. Ann persuades the Minister to appear on television. Merle mistakes cocaine for "plutonium" and the women say farewell to Julie.

Episode 629
Marty finds out that he has been posted to Wentworth and will work alongside his Mum. The women use Nancy's diary to set-up Joan. Lorelei is reluctant to join the women's plot against Joan.

Episode 630
Joan is furious at the women's prank and Ann sends her home. Rodney, Delia and Marty arrive as new trainee officers in Wentworth.

Episode 631
Rita is warned that Bongo will die if there is any more trouble for Joan. Nancy persuades Roach to make up with Rita. Marty clashes with Rodney.

Episode 632
Lorelei is granted permission to make a video message for Zoe. Merle knocks Rita unconscious. Joan halts Andrew's advances when he compares her to his wife.

Episode 633
Harry forces Joan to offer heroin to inmates who are due to be released. Lorelei worries that Zoe will have to go into care. Andrew finds out about Joan's involvement with Harry and phones the police.

Episode 634
Janet is sent to solitary. Joan is informed Andrew is dead. Ann and Meg question Joan's motives for bringing Merle to H Block.

Episode 635
Joan protects Andrew's daughter Jenny. Inspector Grace forces Joan to tell him all she knows about Parker's organisation. Kath refuses to help Janet get back at Rita.

Episode 636
Joan is informed of Parker's death. Delia proposes a new work release program for the women. Rita sets up a fight with Joan.

Episode 637
Joan bribes Kath by offering to testify for her. Lorelei begins to get closer to Kath by understanding her motives for killing her daughter. Roach and Ida are confident of release as their trial approaches.

Episode 638
Kath fears the worst when Bob is unable to attend court. Janet continues to taunt Merle. Kath is given a life sentence for murdering her daughter.

Episode 639
Janet is threatened with being sent to Blackmoor. Kath is released from solitary to help calm Merle. Marty lashes out at Rodney.

Episode 640
Roach and Rita attempt to escape. Mervin and Joyce contemplate being tenants of Joan's. Ann visits the boat and confirms the work release can go ahead, unaware the women are plotting another attack on Joan.

Episode 641
Kath sets up a casino in the Rec Room, using Merle as backup if the women act up. Nancy tries to convince Rita not to take revenge on The Freak but it's too late – the plan is already in motion.

Episode 642

With Marty and Delia off the ship, Rita bides her time to get Joan. Nancy stops Rita from attacking Joan but the ship drifts out further to sea and Mick admits that he's not sure where they are. . .

Episode 643

Joan decides to take the dinghy out to the shore in an attempt to get help. The women refuse to join her but she goes alone, not realising that Rita is swimming after her. In a surprise twist, Joan saves Rita's life when she slips down the cliff.

Episode 644

Kath starts collecting protection money from the other women. A surprise party for Merle ends in disaster when Vicki and Kath turn it into a food fight. Joan returns, via helicopter.

Episode 645

Kath decides to be Top Dog while Rita is in solitary. Lorelei is attacked by Kath's mates when she confronts her in the gym. Rita is released and immediately goes to see Kath to let her know she's back.

Episode 646

Rita attacks Kath but is saved by the bell when the fire alarm is sounded. Rodney appeals against the decision to send him to Smithton so ends up staying at Wentworth. Marty is given a chance to face his phobia.

Episode 647

Nancy becomes worried about Danielle. Kath flirts with Rodney and arranges for him to open a bank account for her on the outside. Dan tells Ann that he's been seeing someone else. Lexie's baby begins to arrive.

Episode 648

Lexie gives birth during the night, assisted by Alice. Meg tells Nancy that she could be right about Danielle after seeing her with a black eye. Meg gets some bad news about Marty – has he been killed in the fires?

Episode 649

Merle finds a package meant for Alice – a blow up male sex doll! Kath buys a new radio from Spider Simpson and offers to work with her. Marty is found safe and well. Danielle accuses Peter of murdering his father.

Episode 650

Nancy lies to the police about Peter. The women arrange a farewell party for Lexie who is about to be released. Nancy is also to be released when she decides to tell the police the truth.

Episode 651

The women are told that their telethon idea has been approved by the Department. Joan causes problems for Joyce as she decides to redecorate. Lisa Mullins and undercover cop Wendy Glover arrive. Kath is kidnapped from the prison.

Episode 652

Celebrity Greg Evans is a surprise guest in support of the telethon. Merle is upset when she hears that Kath has left without saying goodbye. Spider becomes suspicious about Wendy's background.

Episode 653

Alice becomes the new Top Dog. Lorelei demands that Zoe is returned back to her and takes drastic action. Alice and Rita have their clothes stolen during their shower and Rita catches Rodney red handed.

Episode 654

Wendy manages to tell Ann about the tape. The women decide to get back at Rodney during a tug of war match – he ends up covered in mud. Wendy offers to help Lisa to get a message outside. Rodney finds that Kath has given the police the slip.

Episode 655

Lorelei is heartbroken when she loses custody of Zoe. A visit by the dentist causes a rare moment of Joan in fits of laughter, along with Joyce – when they inhale laughing gas. Kath is returned and tells Rodney that she can't stand the sight of him.

Episode 656

Pamela's blind dates turn into a disaster. Kath threatens Rita and pulls out a gun on her. Merle makes Kath and Rita shake hands at a special party. Lorelei's in trouble on the outside when she can't find anywhere to stay.

Episode 657

Lisa sports a new hair colour (and a new head!), and tries to get a message out via Spider to Lester. Lorelei and Zoe manage to find somewhere to stay for the night. Merle causes panic as she finds Kath's gun.

Episode 658

Wendy's true identity is revealed to the women and Rita makes sure that she'll never forget that she's a cop. Sarah West is brought to the prison and makes herself known, destroying the whole of the Rec Room.

Episode 659

Sarah is brought under control and sent to solitary to cool down. Wendy tells Lisa that her boyfriend has been killed – distraught and upset, Lisa cuts her wrists. Sarah attacks Spider when she's released from the pound.

Episode 660

Sarah is painted white by Spider and Vicki. The women find out that they're to be treated to a fairly run shop in an attempt to stop all of the illegal trading. Rita shows Sarah that underneath their skin colour, everyone is the same.

Episode 661

Kath is chosen to run the shop, much to the disappointment of Spider – who later attempts to set fire to it but Merle comes to the rescue. Joan tells Rodney to bash Spider after lights-out, but the women find out what's going on. . .

Episode 662

The fight is stopped and Joan and Rodney stick to a story that clears both of them. The women fight back at the racist comments made by Vicki and Spider. Ann and Pamela find out that Sarah's mother has died.

Episode 663

Meg returns from holiday and brings some tacky presents home for everyone. Rodney smuggles drugs in during the shopping trip with Kath and Merle. When the shop prices are raised, Rita decides to boycott it.

Episode 664

Sarah finally starts to see reason and accepts her foster parents. The women decide to only boycott contraband goods when they are faced with losing the shop completely. Rita is set up and Joan orders she is transferred to Blackmoor.

Episode 665

Ann is furious with Joan's actions. Rita arrives at Blackmoor and is forced to undergo an unusual induction process. She finds that her brother Bongo, who is also there, has turned into a junkie.

Episode 666

Rita tries to talk to Bongo through a pipe but he doesn't understand what's going on as he's high on drugs. Rita takes revenge on Roo, starting a riot at Blackmoor and holding her new arch enemy hostage.

Episode 667

Shots are fired at Blackmoor as the riot continues. Kath arranges a roof top protest at Wentworth in support of Rita but tries to keep a low profile. Bongo is freed but shot down by one of Craven's officers. Rita decides to burn down the whole prison.

Episode 668

Following Blackmoor's demise, Craven and Joan arrive back at Wentworth with prisoners that have been transferred. The male and female prisoners are allowed to mix, so Lorelei uses this as a chance to get back at the men who have previously attacked Lisa.

Episode 669

Alice is locked in the freezer when an attempt to make friends with the men backfires – the women pay back Stud by stripping off his clothes. Lorelei is brutally attacked and raped by Stud and Billy, with Craven knowing exactly what's going on.

Episode 670

Joan threatens to expose Craven if he continues to cause havoc in the prison. Ann is sacked and Craven appointed Acting Governor only to have Joan step in his place when she makes more threats.

Episode 671

The women are horrified to see that Joan's their new Governor. Craven orders two of his officers to bash Rita in solitary. Rita warns the other women that her life's in danger and Craven makes an unannounced visit to her, vowing to kill her.

Episode 672

Craven reveals that he's brought a crossbow to Wentworth and plans to use it on Rita. Craven's attempts go horribly wrong. . . when he tries to set up Lorelei, she stabs him in the stomach and he dies in front of Rita.

Episode 673

The Minister demands that Lorelei is sent to a mental institution. Joan orders that the women stick to a new set of harsh rules. Nobody seems to want to be Deputy Governor with Joan in charge so Meg, Joyce and Marty are to be transferred out of Wentworth.

Episode 674

Spider makes an attempt to get Merle transferred by making her think that Craven's ghost has returned to haunt her. The women make a tape recording for Lorelei and Joan decides to deliver it herself.

Episode 675

Vicki and Spider scare Merle by holding a fake ouija board that tells Merle she has to kill Joan. Rita makes an escape attempt and visits Bongo's grave. Merle gets upset and tells Kath that she hates being dumb.

Episode 676

Rita returns but Brumby is set on escaping a second time. Meg agrees to go on a television documentary to reveal the truth about what's been going on at Wentworth. Lisa is asked to try to smuggle an incriminating video tape out.

Episode 677

The TV broadcast goes ahead and Meg names Craven as the person responsible for everything that has happened. The Minister has no choice but to reinstate Ann as Governor with Meg as Deputy. Joan has to take a leave of absence to decide on her future plans.

Episode 678

Joan tells Ann that she's going to look for a new job. Brumby makes her second escape attempt, but trying to leave the prison as "Joyce" doesn't work! Vicki and Spider make plans to set up Merle again, not realising that Kath has heard every word.

Episode 679

Ann makes plans to transform the prison. Alice meets Harry, who is working in another block of the prison. Lisa follows Rodney to try to get some dirt on him for the women inside.

Episode 680

Lisa and Marty land themselves in hot water when their investigations raise suspicion. Alice eats some poisoned chocolates meant for Rita, but Rita is the one who suddenly becomes ill – and collapes in front of the women.

Episode 681

Joan's attempts to find a new job do not go according to plan when she loses her temper. Lisa tries to get Spike to convince Marty to give up his investigations as he could end up dead. Kath proposes to frame Marty and Spike in return for money and passports.

Episode 682

Joan applies for a new job at a security firm. She thinks that her luck is changing but is taken by surprise when Willie Beecham is revealed as the boss. Kath receives a hypodermic needle to set Spike up with.

Episode 683

Stud and Billy make plans to get contact with the other women. Kath plants drugs in Marty's locker – he is later suspended when more 'evidence' is planted on him. Merle rescues Alice and Rita from the men.

Episode 684

Ann decides that the Blackmoor men will have to leave Wentworth as they've caused nothing but trouble. Lisa passes on to Rita all of the information she's found on Rodney. Kath escapes but Merle hurts herself and is left behind.

Episode 685

Lisa visits Rita and passes her the tape and photographs. Kath is taken to a hideout in the country, guarded by Matt Denson who is blind but has extra sharp hearing. The women play Rodney's tape through the PA. Joan is forced to come back to Wentworth.

Episode 686

Ann tells Joan that she doesn't want her back, but has no choice. Rita collapses again and tests are arranged to find out the cause. Kath finds out that her days are to be numbered. Joan pushes Ann too far.

Episode 687

Kath escapes from her captors. Marty visits Merle in Ingleside but she's so heavily sedated that she doesn't understand much. Kath makes it to the hospital to visit Merle but she rejects her. Dr Lunn tells Ann that Rita's tests are confirmed – she has cancer.

Episode 688

Rita is told of her illness and refuses any drugs. She tells Alice her news but makes her promise not to tell any of the other women. Tom arranges for Merle to be transferred from Ingleside back to Wentworth. Rita realises that Kath is about to kill herself in the punishment cell.

Episode 689

Kath is given some home truths from Rita. The women agree to boycott Joan together. Tom persuades Kath to work as his assistant in the hope that it will bring her and Merle on speaking terms again. Joan realises that she no longer has any power in Wentworth and is given an ultimate life changing opportunity when at the hospital with Rita.

Episode 690

Harry tells Ann that he wants to marry Alice. Rita reveals to Joan more about her planned robbery at a finance company. Joan's black gloves come out once more when she overhears Lisa threatening Rodney. After a particularly bad day at Wentworth, Joan agrees that she'll help Rita with the job.

Episode 691

Spike and her mother become friends again, as do Kath and Merle. Merle takes some drugs by mistake. Ida tells Rita that she's concerned about her new friendship with Joan. Lisa reveals to the women that Rita is dying so Rita admits the truth. The planned robbery begins – Joan helps Rita escape. . .

Episode 692 – The Final Episode

Rita goes through with the robbery, is swiftly caught and returned back to Wentworth. Her condition appears to worsen but she manages to make it to her birthday party where she steps down as Top Dog, naming Kath as her successor. When it's announced that Rita has died, Joan uses the opportunity to collect the money as agreed – but the police are waiting and Joan gets the shock of her life when she arrives back at Wentworth.

The authors with two of the series' legends. From left to right: Rob Cope, Maggie Kirkpatrick, Glenda Linscott, Scott Anderson, Barry Campbell.